The Scourge of Demons

Changing Perspectives on Early Modern Europe

James B. Collins, Professor of History, Georgetown University
Mack P. Holt, Professor of History, George Mason University

(ISSN 1542-3905)

Private Ambition and Political Alliances:
The Phélypeaux de Pontchartrain Family and Louis XIV's Government, 1650–1715
Sara E. Chapman

The Politics of Piety: Franciscan Preachers During the Wars of Religion, 1560–1600
Megan C. Armstrong

"By My Absolute Royal Authority": Justice and the Castilian Commonwealth
at the Beginning of the First Global Age
J. B. Owens

Meat Matters: Butchers, Politics, and Market Culture in Eighteenth-Century Paris
Sydney Watts

Civic Christianity in Renaissance Italy: The Hospital of Treviso, 1400–1530
David M. D'Andrea

Law, City, and King Legal Culture, Municipal Politics,
and State Formation in Early Modern Dijon
Michael P. Breen

Transforming the Republic of Letters:
Pierre-Daniel Huet and European Intellectual Life, 1650–1720
April G. Shelford

Reformation and the German Territorial State: Upper Franconia, 1300–1630
William Bradford Smith

Jenatsch's Axe:
Social Boundaries, Identity, and Myth in the Era of the Thirty Years' War
Randolph C. Head

Enlightened Feudalism:
Seigneurial Justice and Village Society in Eighteenth-Century Northern Burgundy
Jeremy Hayhoe

The King's Bench:
Bailiwick Magistrates and Local Governance in Normandy, 1670–1740
Zoë A. Schneider

The Scourge of Demons:
Possession, Lust, and Witchcraft in a Seventeenth-Century Italian Convent
Jeffrey R. Watt

The Scourge of Demons

Possession, Lust, and Witchcraft in a
Seventeenth-Century Italian Convent

Jeffrey R. Watt

UNIVERSITY OF ROCHESTER PRESS

Copyright © 2009 Jeffrey R. Watt

All Rights Reserved. Except as permitted under current legislation, no part of this work may be photocopied, stored in a retrieval system, published, performed in public, adapted, broadcast, transmitted, recorded, or reproduced in any form or by any means, without the prior permission of the copyright owner.

First published 2009
Transferred to digital printing and reprinted in paperback 2016

University of Rochester Press
668 Mt. Hope Avenue, Rochester, NY 14620, USA
www.urpress.com
and Boydell & Brewer Limited
PO Box 9, Woodbridge, Suffolk IP12 3DF, UK
www.boydellandbrewer.com

hardcover ISBN-13: 978-1-58046-298-3
paperback ISBN-13: 978-1-58046-564-9
ISSN: 1542-3905

Library of Congress Cataloging-in-Publication Data

Watt, Jeffrey R. (Jeffrey Rodgers), 1958–
  The scourge of demons : possession, lust, and witchcraft in a seventeenth-century Italian convent / Jeffrey R. Watt.
    p. cm. — (Changing perspectives on early modern Europe, ISSN 1542-3905 ; v. 12)
  Includes bibliographical references and index.
  ISBN-13: 978-1-58046-298-3 (hardcover : alk. paper)
  ISBN-10: 1-58046-298-7 (hardcover : alk. paper) 1. Monastero Santa Chiara (Carpi, Italy)—History—17th century. 2. Demoniac possession—Italy—Carpi—History—17th century. 3. Witchcraft—Italy—Carpi—History—17th century. 4. Carpi (Italy)—Church history—17th century. I. Title.
  BX4364.C37 W38 2009
  271'.97304542—dc22
                                                                2008041885

A catalogue record for this title is available from the British Library.

This publication is printed on acid-free paper.
Printed in the United States of America

For Julia and Erica

Contents

List of Illustrations	ix
Acknowledgments	xi
Introduction: Nuns, Witchcraft, and the Inquisition	1
Chapter 1 Female Religious, Claustration, and Santa Chiara of Carpi	21
Chapter 2 The Outbreak and *Maleficia*	37
Chapter 3 The Confessor and Love Magic	73
Chapter 4 The Exorcists and the Demons	104
Chapter 5 Sisters Dealta and Ippolita under Attack	141
Chapter 6 Bellacappa's Defense	157
Chapter 7 The Waning of the Possessions	181
Conclusion	197
Appendix A	215
Appendix B	216
List of Abbreviations	219
Notes	221
Selected Bibliography	279
Index	291

Illustrations

Figures

1	Map of Carpi (ca. 1670)	2
2	Floor plan of Santa Chiara, first floor (ca. 1615)	27
3	Floor plan of Santa Chiara, second floor (ca. 1615)	28
4	Floor plan of the apartments of Angela Caterina d'Este, first floor (ca. 1615)	29
5	Floor plan of the apartments of Angela Caterina d'Este, second floor (ca. 1615)	30

Acknowledgments

This book marks an important shift from my previous scholarship, which was based on archival research in French-speaking Switzerland. Over the past several years, numerous individuals have greatly facilitated my transition from Calvinist Geneva to Counter-Reformation Italy. I warmly thank John Tedeschi, the dean of American scholars on the history of the Roman Inquisition, who generously shared his insights to the fascinating material that can be found in the sources of the Holy Office. The Archivio di Stato di Modena has perhaps the richest extant registers of any Italian Inquisition, and its accommodating staff made my stints there from 1999 through 2002 most pleasant. I first became aware of the Santa Chiara witchcraft case, the subject of this book, while perusing the inventory–painstakingly compiled by Giuseppe Trenti, formerly associate archivist–of the voluminous registers of the Inquisition of Modena. Many kind thanks to Dr. Trenti for graciously permitting me to consult that handwritten index, which he has since published.

Most of the rare books that I consulted are housed in Modena's Biblioteca Estense, which has a splendid collection, a wonderful reading room, and a most obliging staff. Many thanks also to the staffs of both the library of the Archiginnasio of Bologna and the Archivio Storico of Carpi. I spent a few days in June 2002 in the Vatican City, where I was kindly given permission to consult documents in the Archives of the Congregation of the Doctrine of the Faith and in the Secret Archives. I also deeply appreciate the warm welcome that Ivan Rebernik gave me while I did research at the Vatican's Apostolic Library. In December 2006 I spent a pleasant afternoon in Bologna's Provincial Franciscan Archives, where Riccardo Pedrini and Father Bruno Monfardini helped me uncover some useful details concerning the fate of a key player in the witchcraft case. And I most definitely want to thank the Clarisses of Santa Chiara in Carpi. Although I did not conduct research at the convent, the sisters put me in touch with Anna Maria Ori, an expert in the history of Carpi and of Santa Chiara. I was overwhelmed by Dr. Ori's generosity in sharing with me her knowledge and resources. She most graciously allowed me to use her transcriptions of some very important documents concerning the monastery and patiently answered my countless queries about Emilian history. If this were not enough, she went the second mile by agreeing to read and comment on the entire manuscript. I also had some stimulating conversations with Grazia Biondi, who kindly shared with me an unpublished paper she wrote on Santa Chiara's witchcraft episode.

On this side of the Atlantic, I am most indebted to Anne Jacobson Schutte. Given her stature in the fields of the Inquisition and female religious, she has been an invaluable source of advice, which she has most generously provided at every stage of this project. She read an earlier version of the manuscript, and her very detailed constructive criticism has greatly improved this book. Many thanks also to Ray Mentzer, Merry Wiesner-Hanks, Jim Farr, Barbara Diefendorf, and Tom Safley for their guidance and encouragement. At the University of Mississippi, I thank Robert Haws, Kees Gispen, and Joe Ward, who have all expressed their interest in and support for this project over the past several years. I gratefully acknowledge the financial assistance I received from the university's Office of Research and College of Liberal Arts and offer special thanks to Crymes Pittman, who provided a very generous research grant that allowed me to dedicate the summer of 2003 to writing. Les Field and Paul Thayer very liberally shared with me both their expertise in Latin and their encyclopedic knowledge of all things Roman Catholic.

Working with the University of Rochester Press has been a distinct pleasure. Suzanne Guiod has been an exemplary editor, and I thank her and the series editors, Mack Holt and James Collins, for their unwavering support for this project.

More personally, my warmest thanks go, as always, to my wife, Isabella, who was a major inspiration behind the change of venue for my research. In addition to providing moral support and serving as my tutor in Italian, she made important contributions to this book; most notably, she spent several weeks in the archives comparing my transcriptions with the original documents. Our daughters, Julia and Erica, have grown up with this project and have cheerfully endured many conversations about nuns, witches, and demons.

Much of chapter 4 previously appeared in an article in the *Archive for Reformation History* 98 (2007): 107–33. I thank the editors for permission to reproduce that material here. All biblical quotations are taken from the Good News Bible.

Introduction

Nuns, Witchcraft, and the Inquisition

Today in the northern Italian city of Carpi, a small group of nuns pursue a quiet life of prayer and reflection in the Franciscan convent of Santa Chiara, located just a couple blocks to the northeast of the charming central plaza, site of the cathedral and the imposing Pio Castle (see fig. 1). In the seventeenth century, Santa Chiara was one of the most renowned nunneries in the duchy of Modena and the region of Emilia. A small town of about 3,600 inhabitants in the mid-1600s, Carpi had a very strong monastic presence with four monasteries and two convents, the most prestigious of which was Santa Chiara.[1] This convent belonged to the order founded in the thirteenth century by Clare of Assisi. Inspired by Saint Francis, Clare and her early followers sought to pursue a life of "perfect poverty" and refused to own any property either individually or collectively. Canonized in 1255, two years after her death, Clare inspired generations of women to join this Second Order of St. Francis, whose members came to be known as the Clarisses or the Poor Clares.[2]

The lifestyle of the Clarisses in seventeenth-century Carpi was far removed from that of Clare. The monastery of Santa Chiara was founded in 1490 by Camilla Pio (1440–1504), the grandniece of Pope Innocent VII (pontificate, 1404–06) and a member of the Pio family who ruled Carpi for generations until the 1520s. Admired for her saintliness, Camilla donated the land and the first buildings of the convent.[3] Although Clare and her earliest followers had supported themselves by begging, by the 1600s the Clarisses of Carpi, notwithstanding their monastic vows, experienced no poverty either before or after taking the veil. The daughters of many powerful, wealthy, noble families joined this religious community. For several years in the 1630s, Santa Chiara of Carpi was home to three members of the illustrious Este family, the preeminent Emilian dynasty that transferred its court to Modena in 1598 after being forced to relinquish the duchy of Ferrara to the papacy.[4]

In the 1630s Santa Chiara endured the most difficult ordeal in its history. Two residents of the convent began suffering from extraordinary ills in 1636, and later twelve other women endured similar afflictions in the nunnery. Reportedly, all these women frequently threw themselves on the floor,

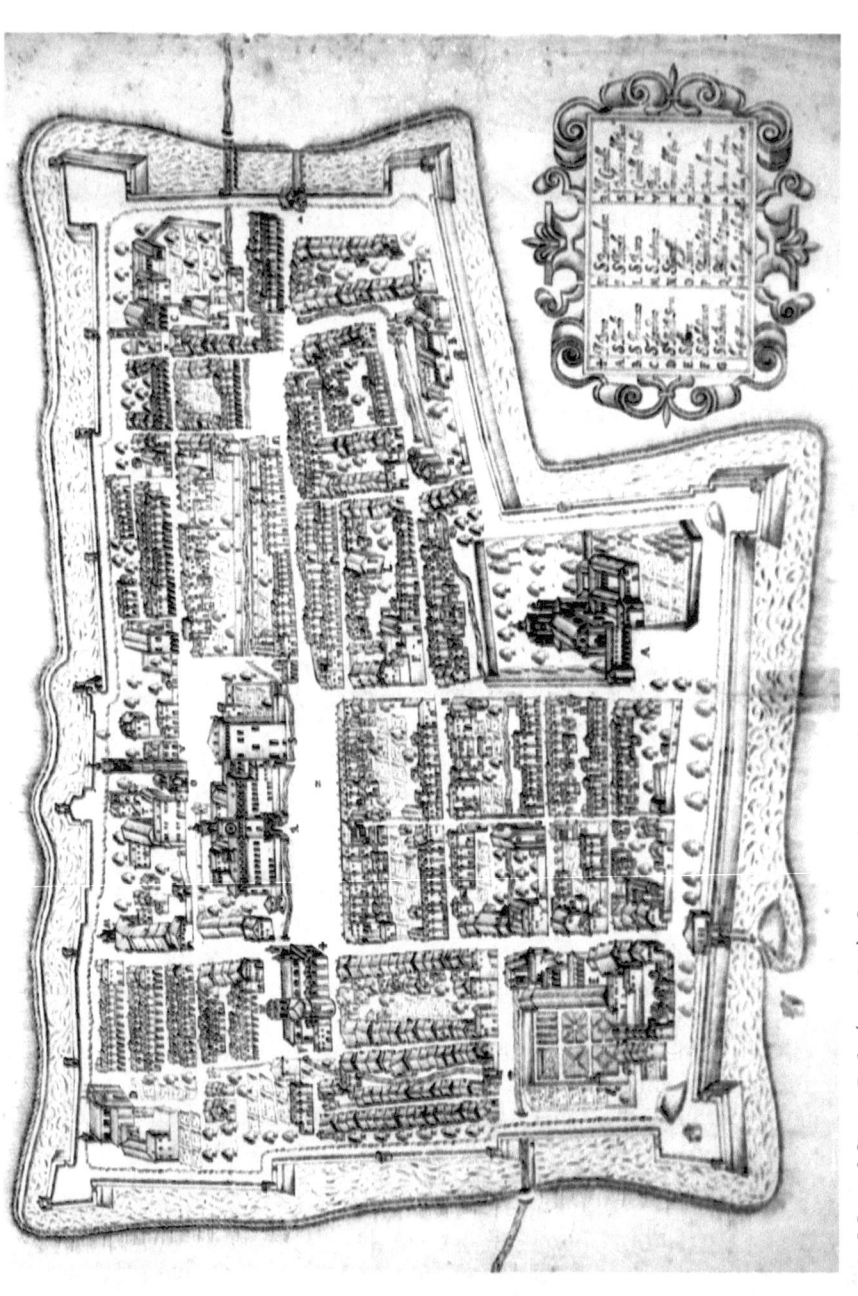

Figure 1. Map of Carpi, Italy (ca. 1670). Oriented toward the east, this map shows the city of Carpi surrounded by its fortified walls and highlighted by the central piazza (Z) and the Pio Castle (R). The convent of Santa Chiara is found in the lower left corner (E). ASM, Mappario Estense, Seria Generali, 336. Reproduced by permission of the ASM, Prot. n. 715/28.13.10/1.15 del 28.03.08.

screamed for no apparent reason, experienced abrupt drastic changes in body temperature, and fell suddenly into a deep sleep from which they could not be awakened. Everyone in Carpi, including the local priests and all the Clarisses, concluded that these troubles were diabolical in origin, that these nuns were possessed by demons. To make matters worse, the priests, magistrates, and nuns of Carpi all quickly deduced that human agents were responsible for having set these demons to work and that the witch or witches were actually in the convent. The ensuing turmoil relentlessly racked this religious community for over three years, and the Inquisition conducted a very lengthy investigation into alleged witchcraft.

The travails of Santa Chiara took place in an era when widespread fears of demons were at a peak in Europe. Beginning in the late Middle Ages, Europeans—first clerics and then laypeople—became increasingly alarmed at the apparent ability of demons to cause harm and lead people astray in this world. Belief in demons predated the birth of Christianity, and theologians continued to insist that Satan could do nothing without God's permission; but by the sixteenth century the devil seemed more powerful and menacing than ever before, capable of assuming an ever-increasing variety of forms. Experiencing a veritable "demonization" of the world, Europeans had never before perceived so many demons, which seemed far more numerous than the benevolent angels.[5] Although they could not control people's wills, the devil and demons could deceive people and could tempt them, among other things, to reject God and become servants of Satan. Demons could supposedly possess a person's body, and the second half of the sixteenth century witnessed an "epidemic rise" in cases of alleged demon possession.[6] Demons appeared, if anything, even more menacing at the time of Santa Chiara's tribulations; the seventeenth century has been aptly described as the "golden age of the demoniac," as contemporaries claimed to witness countless cases of people, especially women and children, whose bodies became possessed by demons, resulting in tremendous physical and psychological suffering.[7]

Not only were demon possessions increasing dramatically in the sixteenth and seventeenth centuries, but they were also perceived differently. For centuries Christians had thought that demons could possess a person's body, but the notion that demons might enter a human's body at the bidding of another person was quite new. The belief that witches were capable of inducing demon possession had been unknown prior to the 1400s. As the Santa Chiara case will illustrate, this change in attitudes had very important ramifications for the hunting of witches, as rumors of demonic possession could raise fears of witchcraft.[8] The new connection between possession and witchcraft resulted in the first significant numbers of trials of witches, which occurred in the fifteenth century in the regions of Switzerland and Savoy where French and Germanic peoples and cultures intersected.[9] It was surely not coincidental that the heightened fears of devils coincided roughly with the period of Europe's most intense witch-hunting, which peaked during the years 1560–1640.[10]

As it eventually was understood, witchcraft consisted of two elements: *maleficia,* magical spells cast to cause harm to people, animals, or crops; and diabolism, the belief that these supernatural powers came from the devil. Harmful spells had been associated with witchcraft well before the birth of Christianity, but the great emphasis on the role of Satan distinguished early modern from earlier attitudes toward witchcraft. True, already in the patristic era, Augustine had condemned all magic—that is, the manipulation of supernatural powers—as forms of superstition, idolatry, and diabolical deception.[11] In the late medieval era, however, theologians and other thinkers went beyond this notion and became increasingly convinced not only that magic was based on demonic power but also that people who indulged in magic received their power from a pact with Satan. The belief that witches were servants of the devil, though expressed as early as the ninth century, attained much greater prominence in the later Middle Ages. Thinkers elaborated that the diabolical pact could be made either explicitly or implicitly. An implicit pact with the devil might involve indulging in love magic, divining the future, or wearing a talisman to ward off evil, all of which apparently involved occult magical powers.[12] Although ideas of this nature originated among theologians, in the sixteenth and seventeenth centuries the conviction gradually took hold among larger segments of the population that all magic spells—even those cast for good ends, such as curing illnesses or protecting crops or livestock—invariably required the help of the devil.

From the fifteenth through the seventeenth centuries, theologians wrote unprecedented numbers of works on demonology, in which they described the nature and powers of Satan, demons, and witches. The most famous of these books was without a doubt Heinrich Kramer's the *Malleus Maleficarum* (*Hammer of Witches*). Appearing for the first time in 1486, the *Malleus Maleficarum* was reissued many times and was quite influential in northern Europe, though considerably less so in Italy.[13] A Dominican inquisitor, Kramer based his arguments on biblical passages and the works of church fathers, Scholastic theologians, and canon lawyers and repeatedly stressed that all witches were servants of Satan.[14] According to Kramer and other authors, witches supposedly not only made a pact with the devil but also formed an organized sect of devil-worshipers. This belief, which had never been expressed prior to the fifteenth century, played a key role in the great escalation of witch-hunting.[15] The growing belief that there was an occult network of devil-worshipers incited many theologians and legal scholars to call for the forceful extirpation of this supposed vicious anti-Christian conspiracy. Suspicions of *maleficia* could result not only in accusing likely suspects but also in aggressively eliciting from them the names of fellow devil-worshiping witches. Publications on demonology reached a peak in the late sixteenth and early seventeenth centuries, when theologians and jurists, often drawing on their own experiences as prosecutors or judges, wrote a plethora of treatises detailing the methods and mischief of demons and their human minions and giving instructions on how to crush witchcraft.[16]

To be sure, alleged demon possession did not always lead to accusations of witchcraft. Many, perhaps most, cases of supposed possession did not result in legal investigations of witchcraft. But by increasingly associating possession and other demonic mischief with witchcraft, Europeans greatly raised the likelihood that a case of possession or other misfortune would lead to charges of witchcraft.

Convents and Demonic Possessions

The "demonic" woes of Santa Chiara fit into a broader pattern, as the late sixteenth and seventeenth centuries witnessed a large number of reputed group possessions in convents in Germany,[17] France, and northern Italy, where there were demonic scares in nunneries in Reggio Emilia and Piacenza in addition to Carpi.[18] The most famous of these alleged diabolical attacks occurred at the Ursuline convent in Loudun in western France, where seventeen members of that community suffered the alleged torments of demons. Like Santa Chiara, the Ursuline convent of Loudun, catered to the aristocratic elite (it even included among its members a relative of Cardinal Richelieu). Attracting thousands of curious spectators, the cases of possession there led to a criminal investigation that resulted in August 1634 in the execution for witchcraft of a local parish priest, Urbain Grandier. The diabolical tribulations of Loudun have been the subject of a number of studies, including most notably Michel de Certeau's *Possession at Loudun*.[19] In Emilia itself several nuns were purportedly possessed in a Capuchin convent in Imola in the 1590s, and a number of nuns of Sant'Eufemia in Modena were suspected of being bewitched in 1635, though Alessandro Rangoni, bishop of Modena, was skeptical and claimed that they were "cured" of their ills when they were assigned a new confessor.[20]

Why were convents especially prone to demon possessions? At the time, theologians offered various explanations for the demons' penchant for attacking nunneries, the most common being the belief that the devils were committing a greater affront to God by tormenting pious female religious rather than people who were less devout. The *Malleus Maleficarum* also noted that the devil was more interested in tempting the holy than the evil; he already was sovereign over the wicked but desired to seduce "saintly virgins," who were not yet subject to him.[21] Various nuns themselves warned of the special dangers that Satan had in store for them. The famous mystic and Carmelite nun Teresa of Avila (1515–82) declared that the Evil One was especially eager to attack contemplative people who sought a spiritual union with God. In attacking would-be mystics, Satan purportedly hindered prayer, encouraged pride and self-righteousness, nurtured feelings of excessive guilt about sins, and sowed fears that the religious understanding acquired through contemplation was illusory. Teresa claimed that Satan frequently appeared to her visibly and even subjected her to physical abuse through invisible blows.[22] Contemporary physicians also warned that cloistered nuns faced a range of mental infirmities that allegedly made them more vulnerable to demon possession.[23]

Modern historians have offered a number of explanations for these cases of demonic abuse and possession. Living in a repressive environment and fearing damnation, nuns may have felt guilty about sexual impulses that they could neither satisfy nor squelch and about failures to measure up to the high spiritual standards expected of them. Sin was believed to be an important cause of demon possession; demons could possess a person's body only if God permitted them to do so, and possession could be viewed as divine punishment for the victim's sins. Aware of their own sinfulness, nuns might have interpreted their sins, including sexual urges, as demons that possessed their bodies. Possession could also have served as a channel through which an unhappy nun could express her rejection of strict religious discipline. Scholars base this interpretation in part on reports that many energumens became most agitated when they heard religious language or were in the presence of religious objects. Well documented were cases of nuns who, while supposedly agitated by demons, took part in very lewd and scandalous behavior, which included screaming, blaspheming, and unleashing overtly sexual language and gestures. Since female religious of the sixteenth and seventeenth centuries were exhorted more than ever before to suppress various instinctive desires, they may have felt terribly guilty when they failed to do so. When they could no longer control the pent-up tensions, which they interpreted as the torments of demons, they ran the risk of performing the very actions they were supposed to suppress. Though generally eschewing the idea that women could have merely been feigning these ills, some modern scholars use Freudian psychology to suggest that beliefs about demon possession actually provided a safety valve through which repressed sisters could vent their frustrations. Frequently they blamed males, especially clerics, for their "bewitchments" and thereby reversed the direction of repression by deflecting guilt away from themselves onto the clergy.[24] Applying modern theories from the social sciences to past phenomena can provide important insight, but to avoid being anachronistic or reductionistic, we must never dismiss the perceptions of these female religious regarding their troubling experiences.[25]

Some historians have also pointed out that the saintly and the demonically possessed seemed to exhibit similar unusual behavior that included trances, visions, and ecstasy. Although belief in demonic possession had existed for millennia—clearly depicted in the sufferings of the biblical King Saul, for example—the idea of *divine* possession did not truly take hold until about the twelfth century. Theologians detailed a number of reasons why they were convinced that females were more prone to both divine and demonic possession: women were weaker and more malleable than men, and their bodies more porous and more susceptible to penetration by spirits. The late Middle Ages witnessed some prominent female visionaries, such as Catherine of Siena (1347–80) and Bridget of Sweden (1303–73), who were eventually canonized even though some theologians initially believed their visions were demonic rather than divine. It has even been argued that the feminization of mysticism in the twelfth century helped lead to the "feminization of the demonic," which was very prevalent in the *Malleus Maleficarum* and other late medieval treatises.[26]

In the Counter-Reformation era, numerous Catholic women continued to have reputed visions, and Church authorities did not reject them a priori as demonic in origin. Spain had a long tradition of mysticism, and Stephen Haliczer has written a fascinating account, *Between Exaltation and Infamy: Female Mystics in the Golden Age of Spain,* in which he examines the biographies and autobiographies of thirty female mystics from the sixteenth and seventeenth centuries. The Church gave its official approval to all these treatises, though only five of these women were eventually canonized. In this age of confessional conflicts, religious leaders lent support to the supernatural visions of mystics, which they viewed as an effective means of showing that God favored Roman Catholicism. Various churchmen encouraged mysticism and viewed divine revelations to women as an especially good sign of God's benevolence precisely because they considered females intellectually inferior. To enjoy a reputation as a mystic, however, a woman had to come from a respectable (usually aristocratic) family, belong to a religious order, and enjoy the support of the powerful leaders in the Church and society. Obviously, her alleged visions also had to conform to orthodox Catholic beliefs. Although a number of Spanish women enjoyed a lofty reputation as pious visionaries, the Church was often skeptical when hearing reports of women's visions, particularly when the would-be mystics were lower class and had had only limited educational opportunities. In such cases, the Spanish Inquisition was apt to launch an investigation for pretense of sanctity; Haliczer examines fifteen such cases to complement the biographies of the "approved" mystics. In short, mystical experiences among women could be a source of both inspiration and suspicion among the Catholic clergy.[27]

Concentrating on the same period, Moshe Sluhovsky examines both mysticism and possession, which he believes were closely linked, and pays special attention to instances of group possessions in convents. Observing that these possessions of the late sixteenth and seventeenth centuries virtually always involved nuns rather than monks, he argues that these incidents were related both to the recent emphasis on female mysticism and to the post-Tridentine efforts to reform monasticism. Church leaders were uneasy with female mystics, since they were reportedly communicating directly with God without going through the medium of a priest. Sluhovsky claims that many of the female religious who were eventually diagnosed as possessed were first believed by their peers to be visionaries. Convinced that almost all these women were possessed by demonic rather than divine spirits, exorcists or other clerics ultimately persuaded the nuns themselves of the diabolical origins of their extraordinary experiences. Other cases of possession, he maintains, may have been reactions to the greater rigors that reformers imposed. The Ursulines were originally a group of uncloistered women who did not formally take orders, but they were obliged in the early seventeenth century to become cloistered nuns. Suggesting a reaction against greater discipline, Sluhovsky avows that it was not by chance that stricter claustration coincided with mass possessions at Ursuline houses in Aix-en-Provence and Loudun. Significantly, regardless if they involved resisters or proponents of reform, Sluhovsky asserts that the majority of these instances of spiritual turmoil in convents involved only demonic possession and did not include accusations of witchcraft.[28]

Although some possessions may have been reactions against monastic reforms, scholars have also suggested that demonic possessions could also be common among those nuns who eagerly embraced reform, purportedly because the devil could not tolerate such dedicated servants of God. In Madrid in the 1620s, members of a newly established Benedictine convent began showing signs of both mystical ecstasy and demonic possession. Through the mouths of the affected nuns, "demons" proclaimed that God had sent them on a mission and had specifically chosen eleven of the possessed to play a special role in the reform of the Church. They offered many prophecies, such as their confident (though premature) prediction of the death of Pope Urban VIII (pontificate, 1623–44), which would allow the great reform of the Church to begin.[29] Some of the most devout female religious, especially those with strong mystical inclinations, reputedly welcomed possession because they believed it gave them the opportunity to show greater devotion to God through the intense pains they suffered. Since they did not really want to be cured of these ills, these were considered among the most difficult possessed people to restore to health.[30] As we shall see, the Clarisses of Carpi appeared to be neither mystics nor the advocates or victims of unduly rigorous reform.

Although this is the first book-length study of the demonic travails of Santa Chiara, this case has already attracted the attention of other historians. Romano Canosa wrote a brief and rather superficial summary of the investigation.[31] Vincenzo Lavenia wrote a lengthy article that is very thoroughly researched (his citations have frankly been valuable guides to pertinent archival sources) but analytically problematic.[32] He argues that the possessions were essentially the by-product of a struggle for power between the Observant Franciscans and the local secular clergy over who had the right to govern the convent. Undeniably, there were conflicts between Franciscans and other clerics, but reducing the possessions to a by-product of these disagreements runs contrary to the facts that, as we shall see, the possessions began outside the convent and, more important, that the Clarisses actually preferred the Franciscans to the secular priests (as Lavenia himself acknowledges). In light of this latter fact, why would the sisters of Santa Chiara have played into the hands of Carpi's secular clergy by identifying—as we shall also see—a Franciscan as a key suspect of witchcraft? Moreover, like other scholars, Lavenia suggests that group possessions of female religious could stem from the increased discipline of the post-Tridentine era, especially in regard to the more coercive nature of frequent confession. On the other hand, he concedes that Santa Chiara was notoriously undisciplined until the outbreak of possessions, which could have served as a pretext for introducing stricter discipline. He is unable to explain satisfactorily this apparent contradiction. Most important of all, Lavenia pays little attention to the ways in which members of this community understood and experienced possession, witchcraft, and exorcism. His vision of this episode is entirely top-down: in his presentation, the nuns merely seem to be responding to the machinations of competing clerics.[33]

Relying entirely on the Lavenia article, Moshe Sluhovsky briefly discusses the Santa Chiara case and claims, misleadingly, that this was a mere case of possession, not of witchcraft.[34] Had there not been strong suspicions of witchcraft, the Inquisition would not have conducted an investigation. Although possession did not necessarily imply witchcraft, all parties in Carpi were convinced that a witch or witches were involved in these demonic woes. Moreover, I will argue that the women of Santa Chiara, both the healthy and the possessed, were not merely manipulated by male authority figures, be they exorcists, confessors, or functionaries of the Inquisition. Rather, the Clarisses played a very active role in this unhappy chapter in the convent's history.

The Roman Inquisition

Although in most areas of western Europe secular courts had jurisdiction over witchcraft cases during this era of the great hunts, in Italy the Roman Inquisition, or Holy Office, was generally successful in asserting exclusive jurisdiction over cases of witchcraft.[35] Borrowing legal traditions from Roman law, the Catholic Church created the inquisitorial system in the thirteenth century to combat heresy. Unlike the accusatorial system, which had heretofore prevailed throughout western Europe and continued to function in some regions thereafter, the inquisitorial system of justice did not require that an aggrieved private party serve as accuser and prosecutor of an alleged crime. Rather, inquisitorial officials themselves investigated and prosecuted the crime of heresy. They initiated procedures on the basis of either their own knowledge of the crime or that of an accuser whose identify was not revealed to the accused. By the later sixteenth century, both lay and ecclesiastical courts in almost all parts of central and western Europe had switched from the accusatorial to the inquisitorial system, and this transformation was a very important factor behind the growing intensity of witch-hunting.[36] A significant development took place in 1326 when Pope John XXII authorized inquisitors to prosecute cases of witchcraft, because he considered magic and witchcraft as the most vile form of heresy or apostasy and therefore under the purview of the Church. The earliest inquisitors, appointed by popes or bishops, had specific charges that were generally temporary. A typical task was to investigate an alleged heretical group in a diocese. No permanent ecclesiastical tribunal of this nature existed until the Spanish Inquisition was founded in 1478, primarily for the purpose of dealing with *conversos*, people (especially Jews) who had formally converted to Christianity but were suspected of being apostates who secretly practiced their former faith.[37]

Like its medieval predecessors, the Roman Inquisition was established in order to fight heresy. Founded in July 1542 by Pope Paul III, the Holy Office was to be an important weapon to combat Protestantism. Modeled to a considerable extent on the Spanish Inquisition, the Holy Office was championed by Cardinal Gian Pietro Carafa, who convinced the pope to create this institution and was in turn appointed inquisitor-general at its inception. Although in its first years the Roman Inquisition dealt strictly with heresy, Carafa expanded its jurisdiction considerably when he was elected pope in 1555 as Paul IV. During his four-year pontificate, the Roman Inquisition began hearing cases of blasphemy, simony, and the selling of sacraments, among others. Under Paul IV, the Holy Office took precedence over all other branches of the papal curia and became the principal organ for imposing the strict reform of the Roman Catholic Church that he promoted. Just as contemporary monarchs increased their authority by making their court systems more centralized, the pope could use the Inquisition as a means of scrutinizing more closely the religious beliefs and practices of Roman Catholics. In the century following its creation, the Inquisition played a central role in the administration of the Church, which is aptly seen in the fact that it served as a springboard to the papacy for several ambitious clergymen. In addition to Paul IV, Popes Marcellus II, Pius V, Sixtus V, Urban VII, Innocent IX, and Paul V all rose in the ecclesiastical ranks largely thanks to their service in the Holy Office.[38]

Though originally conceived as a temporary institution to deal with the emergency threat of Protestantism, the Roman Inquisition became a permanent tribunal with much broader powers. At the top of the structure of the Holy Office was a group of cardinals, who were appointed by the pope and originally numbered six and later became more numerous. These cardinals had direct jurisdiction over religious deviance in the Papal States and claimed to have ultimate authority on these matters throughout Christendom. In reality, their power rarely extended beyond Italy, where they oversaw a large number of regional inquisitions. A cardinal secretary oversaw this small group of cardinals, and a number of theologians comprised the *Consulta Teologica,* which was responsible for providing learned advice on theological issues. Already occupying a de facto privileged position in the hierarchy of the Vatican, Sixtus V officially established the Inquisition's preeminence in 1588 when he restructured the papal administration or curia into fifteen congregations. The Inquisition was reorganized into the "Congregation of the Holy Roman and Universal Inquisition," a committee of cardinals that served as the supreme tribunal over all local inquisitions, which in turn were responsible for investigating various sins, such as heresy, blasphemy, abuse of sacraments, and so on.[39] Throughout this book, the term "Holy Office" will be used generically to refer to the entire network of inquisitions or to designate specifically the Inquisition of Modena; the term "Congregation" of the Holy Office or Inquisition refers exclusively to the central command or supreme court of cardinals in Rome.[40]

Inquisitions were quickly put in place throughout most of sixteenth-century Italy. Their establishment depended on the permission of local political authorities, but Italian secular leaders almost always consented since they believed that heresy was a cancer that needed to be removed for the collective health of society. As Adriano Prosperi rightly notes, for at least two centuries the Holy Office was the only centralized institution that functioned throughout the Italian Peninsula.[41] For each local inquisition, the pope appointed an inquisitor who had to be a friar and at least forty years old. The inquisitor, who had authority over a bishop in his own diocese in matters of heresy, could also delegate responsibilities to vicars, who also had to be friars and at least thirty years old. An authoritative manual for the Inquisition excluded inquisitors from also serving as confessors. As a confessor, a priest or friar heard penitents confess their sins and prescribed various forms of penance to absolve them of those sins. Having heard confessions, clerics should not then conduct judicial inquiries and sit in judgment of sinners in this "tribunal of the conscience"; the struggle against heresy was believed compromised if the same clergymen were both confessors and inquisitors.[42] If, however, he concluded that a confessant had committed a sin serious enough to merit the attention of the Inquisition, a confessor could refuse to grant absolution until the guilty one "voluntarily" appeared before the local inquisitor to report the indiscretion.

From their creation into the 1580s, inquisitions in Italy remained concerned primarily with combating Protestantism. The most common cases heard by the Holy Office during its first four decades included criticizing Catholic beliefs and practices or praising aspects of Protestantism; possessing or discussing heretical books, especially those written by Protestant authors; and failing to observe certain rites, such as taking communion, fasting, or confessing, the latter two omissions possibly suggesting Protestant tendencies. By the 1580s, however, Protestantism had basically been squelched in Italy, and the Holy Office shifted its focus to other challenges facing Roman Catholicism. By 1600 the most common type of cases heard by the Inquisition pertained to "superstitions" and magic or sorcery, which probably comprised at least 40 percent of trials, inquests, and denunciations heard by Italian inquisitions. More numerous than actions against maleficent witches were investigations of alleged magic used to win another's love, discover buried treasure, heal illnesses, or protect oneself against harmful spells.[43] The Inquisition of Modena reflected this change in focus, concentrating on such various forms of "superstitious" activities beginning about 1580.[44] Throughout Italy, cases against superstitions continued to be the preponderant type of inquisitorial action during the course of the seventeenth century, and the percentage of defendants who were female increased dramatically compared with the earlier actions against Protestantism.[45] Adriano Prosperi has shown persuasively that with its network of tribunals set up throughout the peninsula, the Inquisition, not the bishops, was most responsible for eradicating a wide range of beliefs and practices and for imposing a form of social discipline throughout Italy.[46]

Among the most active inquisitions in Italy was that of Modena. The Inquisition actually had a presence in Modena already in the late thirteenth century, but scarcely any medieval records have survived and it may not have functioned much at all for most of the fifteenth century. By the late fifteenth or early sixteenth century, Modena was home to a vicar, a subordinate to the Inquisitor of Ferrara, the city that was then the capital of Estense lands. For the years 1490–1540, the vicar or ad hoc inquisitors in Modena heard about sixty cases concerning witchcraft, most of which ended with the defendants only having to abjure their errors publicly.[47] Prior to 1542, however, the Inquisition was the least structured and the least deeply rooted of all Church powers in Modena.[48]

Eventually, though, the Inquisition of Modena became a formidable and efficient tribunal. Immediately after 1542, the Holy Office's principal goal in Modena, as elsewhere, was to combat Protestantism. For a short time, the region surrounding Modena actually appeared to be a hotbed of Protestantism. In 1536 Calvin himself stayed briefly in nearby Ferrara, where he tried unsuccessfully to convert members of the Este family.[49] The aggressive actions of the Inquisition of Modena quickly succeeded in rooting out Protestantism in the area.⁵⁰ Modena's inquisitor was appointed directly by the pope, but with the approval of the duke of Modena; to wield power effectively, the inquisitor really needed the duke's support. By the post-Tridentine era, Modena's Inquisition was firmly entrenched throughout the duchy. At the top of the hierarchy of the Inquisition was of course the inquisitor himself, who was based in the city of Modena. Just below him were the vicars, all of whom were supposed to be friars (usually Franciscans) and who had jurisdiction over small towns and rural areas in the duchy.⁵¹ The extensive network of vicariates ensured that the Holy Office had a genuine presence throughout the extensive Estense landholdings. By the early eighteenth century, 204 people worked for the Inquisition of Modena in one way or another: 61 served the Holy Office in the city itself, and 143 assisted the various vicariates in the surrounding countryside.⁵² Fragments or complete records of 125 cases prior to 1630 show that the Inquisition of Modena had been very active in and around the town of Carpi. The majority involved accusations of superstitious or magical practices, such as curing ills, harming people or livestock, or winning the love of another through occult means.⁵³

The Inquisition of Modena has among the most voluminous and best-preserved records of any Italian inquisition, numbering over 300 volumes (*buste*) from its inception through its dissolution in 1785. The era of the Carpi witchcraft scare coincided with the Inquisition's most intense activity, as records of trials and investigations fill 113 volumes for the years 1601–50 alone, a figure that does not include volumes of correspondence, cases specifically involving Jews (*Causae hebreorum*), and other miscellaneous records of the Holy Office.⁵⁴ Consultation of these registers was greatly facilitated by the inventory of cases, now published, that was painstakingly drawn up by Giuseppe Trenti, formerly associate archivist at the Archivio di Stato di Modena.⁵⁵

Among the various sources I have consulted for this study, the registers of the Inquisition of Modena are by far the most important. The minutes from the investigation of the nunnery's possession and witchcraft scare fill about 500 handwritten folios. Less fruitful was my research in the Vatican's Archives of the Congregation of the Doctrine of the Faith, the direct descendant of the Holy Office. These archives have been open for consultation only since 1998, and most of its documents have been lost or dispersed over the centuries.⁵⁶ To my disappointment, my exhaustive research in those archives revealed no records pertaining directly to the Santa Chiara case. Fortunately, this obstacle is easily overcome as the correspondence between Modena and the Congregation of the Holy Office is fully extant among the vast sources of the Inquisition in the state archives of Modena. This correspondence reveals in minute detail the cardinals' reactions to the investigation in Carpi and their directives to the inquisitor of Modena.⁵⁷ Also quite important are the trials of some related cases in Carpi that predated the witchcraft outbreak in Santa Chiara. Numerous published sources, such as manuals for inquisitors or exorcists and theoretical works on witchcraft, are also essential to shedding light on contemporary learned opinion on the threat demons posed. Vitally important information about the convent itself is also found in the *Memoriale,* a volume in which a clergyman, usually the convent's confessor, recorded developments in Santa Chiara, most notably the election of officers, the admission of novices, the profession of vows by new nuns, and the deaths of members of the community. The extent of detail varied considerably depending on who was writing these records, but the entries are generally formulaic and shed virtually no light on the personalities of individual Clarisses. Preserved in the monastic archive of Santa Chiara, the *Memoriale* has been transcribed by Anna Maria Ori and is a valuable source for the convent's history for the period 1547–1683. There are, however, some very important and unfortunate lacunae. At some point in the convent's history, someone deleted a number of significant passages, including all but one reference to the demonic episode.[58]

With their very detailed testimony, Inquisition registers make for fascinating reading, but they are not without controversy.[59] On the one hand, they seemingly provide a window to popular piety. The testimony of defendants and witnesses, for example, could serve as a means through which illiterate peasants could describe beliefs and practices that would have been forever lost without the Inquisition's inquiry. On the other hand, how reliable are the records of the Holy Office in depicting what religion truly meant to common folk? Criminal records of any sort, it has been argued, cannot provide a simple window to popular culture, since they are closely shaped by contemporary laws, legal procedures, power structures, and the like. Among the most provocative publications based on Inquisition records are some works by Carlo Ginzburg: most important are his book about the *benandanti* (good walkers) of Friuli, who claimed to go out at night in spirit to fight witches in order to ensure abundant crops but eventually were convinced by inquisitors that they themselves were devil-worshiping witches; and his study of the miller Domenico Scandella, who, after freely discussing his unorthodox religious views before the Holy Office, was executed as a heretic in 1599. Ginzburg stresses that there was a huge cultural and even linguistic gulf separating the educated world of the inquisitors from that of the largely illiterate peasants who appeared before them: at times, judicial authorities actually needed translators for the testimony of peasants given in their local dialects. Even though the inquisitor's questions strongly shaped the testimony of defendants and witnesses, Ginzburg is convinced that one can nonetheless uncover some of their beliefs, especially in those instances when the inquisitor expressed surprise at the answers he received.[60] Ginzburg asserts that court records are the best sources for uncovering popular attitudes toward witchcraft and insists that there was often a real disparity between the questions and objectives of judges and the answers of defendants, a gap that provided a window to popular visions of the occult.[61] Ginzburg finds that the inquisitor was constantly engaged in a dialogue with witnesses and defendants and learned about the cultural differences that separated him from them. In this regard, the inquisitor had much in common with the modern anthropologist.[62]

An expert in the history of canon law, Andrea Del Col is far less sanguine about using the Inquisition's records to reveal the true beliefs of those appearing before it. He insists that these legal documents cannot be treated as the field notes of an anthropologist. As a rule, inquisitors carefully controlled the direction of the testimony and were usually successful in getting the statements they wanted. Rather than providing people with an open forum to express their religious convictions or worldviews, inquisitors often closely restricted interrogations to confirm or contradict the accusations that were the basis for the investigation.[63]

Although they should be used with caution, Inquisition records are far too important to ignore. As John Tedeschi points out, authorities of the Holy Office, in inquisitorial manuals as well as in correspondence with local inquisitions, repeatedly warned against both suggestive questioning and misrepresenting testimony to fit any preconceived "mental schema." Keeping very close tabs on provincial tribunals, the Congregation of the Holy Office required local inquisitors to send regular detailed reports of trials and investigations and to await instructions from the cardinals before passing sentences. The cardinals also circumscribed closely the use of torture in the interrogation of defendants, allowing it only when the evidence was already very compelling. This oversight helped provide considerable uniformity in practice in inquisitions throughout Italy. Moreover, in conducting trials and investigations, local scribes who served the Roman Inquisition, like their counterparts in Spain, scrupulously tried not only to write down in the vernacular every word that was spoken but even to record all gestures, facial expressions, and changes in tone of those who testified.[64]

In the case at hand, no one faced even the threat of torture, and the cultural gap between the sisters of Santa Chiara and the judicial authorities was not very great. Almost all nuns were at least of upper-middle-class background and most likely came from families that were more affluent than those of the inquisitors who questioned them. True, few Clarisses would have had a good knowledge of Latin, the language of scholars, and several could not (or chose not to) sign their names on transcripts of their interrogations. This could have reflected the fact that in early modern Europe it was not uncommon for some people, particularly females, to be taught the passive skill of reading but not the active skill of writing. Nuns were expected to be able to read in the vernacular, and all sisters of Carpi received a certain level of education in Italian. Some nuns of Santa Chiara demonstrated a very high level of literary culture and were composers of sonnets and songs.[65] The

Clarisses of Carpi also would not have been easily intimidated or silenced by anyone. Never did the inquisitor of Modena or his assistant appear to be browbeating the nuns, and, as we shall see, the sisters of Santa Chiara did not hesitate to express in writing their displeasure with some rulings passed by the Congregation of the Inquisition.

A host of scholars insist that much insight can be drawn from court records, including even the confessions of suspected witches made under duress. Lyndal Roper argues that the confessions of an alleged witch provide a window to contemporary understandings of magic and witchcraft: "The fantasies she wove, though often forced from her through torture, were her own condensations of shared cultural preoccupations."[66] Likewise, in his study of witchcraft in southern Germany, the site of large-scale trials in the late sixteenth and early seventeenth century, Jonathan Durrant concentrated on the narratives of confessions made by defendants during interrogations. For a confession to be convincing, prosecutors needed detailed answers, which, though made under duress, reveal, according to Durrant, the "fantasies" and knowledge that suspects had assimilated from sermons, public pronouncements of judicial sentences, neighborhood gossip, and pamphlets.[67]

If confessions made under torture can reveal much about the cultural understanding of witchcraft, the depositions of witnesses are even more reliable indicators of how *maleficia* and magic were popularly perceived. Significantly, the testimony of witnesses, freely given without even a remote possibility of torture, make up almost the entire dossier of the investigation in Carpi. Hardly any of the nuns who appeared before the Holy Office had anything to fear, since they themselves were not suspects. This study will also reveal that the inquisitor's fiscal or assistant, a lay attorney who oversaw much of the investigation, was wont to posit open-ended questions, such as asking witnesses whether they suspected anyone and why. He was thus giving them free rein to discuss at great length their suspicions against any individuals.

Similarly, Del Col's claim that inquisitors essentially got the testimony they desired is much more applicable to investigations of, say, Anabaptism than of witchcraft. Combating heresy was the Roman Inquisition's original reason for being, and inquisitors were ever vigilant to detect any beliefs or practices that smacked of Protestantism. Inquisitors in both Italy and Spain, however, apparently viewed supposed covens of devil-worshipers as much less threatening than Lutheranism or Calvinism. Spain and Italy both had low execution rates in witchcraft trials compared to those of various regions of northern and central Europe, largely because the Inquisition in both countries showed considerable skepticism concerning reputed diabolical pacts, even when suspects confessed to having made such a pact.[68] This standard played a very significant role in avoiding the domino effect seen in some of the most infamous mass trials of witches, especially in regions of Germany.

The Holy Office's mild treatment of witches also may have stemmed from the fact that it stressed the heretical aspects of witchcraft and was accordingly less interested in punishing witches than in effecting repentance in them and bringing them back, contrite, into the Roman Catholic fold.[69]

The assertion that inquisitors always got the testimony they wanted definitely did not seem to apply to the Santa Chiara case. Officials of the Inquisition of Modena became convinced that the nunnery was plagued by demons and witchcraft, but these fears were first born among the nuns themselves. We have every reason to believe that the ideas concerning demon possession and witchcraft expressed by these educated, aristocratic nuns were genuinely their own and not the result of the intimidating or manipulative questioning of inquisitors. In short, although the records of the Inquisition may not reveal exactly what happened in Santa Chiara—one need not accept at face value the Clarisses' claims that demons and witches were wreaking havoc in the convent—they clearly reveal how these female religious understood maleficent magic and how they reacted to the diabolical fears that took hold well before the Holy Office launched its investigation.

Trends in the History of Witchcraft and Possession

The literature on witchcraft is quite vast, and this is not the place to discuss in detail the historiography of early modern magic and witchcraft.[70] In very broad terms, scholars have offered a wide array of interpretations of witchcraft. In the past, some scholars concluded that witches actually existed, either as devil-worshipers, heretics, pagans, or social rebels.[71] In the 1960s historical works tended to stress the craziness of the hunts.[72] Beginning in the 1970s scholars shifted emphasis and sought to explain why the hunts occurred but still implicitly assumed that witchcraft was a form of superstition that had no basis in the real world.[73] Many historians have also inferred that the belief in witchcraft and the punishing of people as witches necessarily meant that something was wrong with early modern society. Some, for example, have attributed the hunts to social and economic changes.[74] Recent scholarship has eschewed monocausal explanations and has shied away from trying to explain why the hunts occurred in favor of seeking to understand witchcraft as a cultural phenomenon.

An issue that is quite pertinent to both witchcraft and possession is that of gender. It has long been known that women were much more likely than men to be suspected of being both witches and demoniacs. Be that as it may, historians of witchcraft and the occult paid little attention to the issue of gender prior to the 1970s. In the late medieval and early modern eras, authors on demonology and witchcraft, all of whom were male, had a ready supply of explanations as to why women were more likely than men to engage in witchcraft. Heinrich Kramer took an extreme stand in the *Malleus Maleficarum;* his use of the feminine plural word for "witches" in the title reflected his assumption that almost all witches were women. Lambasting females for their "slippery tongues," he described them as being mentally, physically, and morally inferior to males; deceitful and undisciplined by their very nature, women were more credulous than men, and the devil therefore pursued them because they were more easily corruptible. Kramer also insisted that females had an "insatiable" carnal lust, a theme he repeated so obsessively that one might suspect that he was projecting his own sexual desires onto women.[75] More than any theologian or demonologist before him, Kramer was adamant that women lacked the moral strength to resist demonic temptations. Although few other treatises came close to the level of misogyny found in the *Malleus Maleficarum,* all authors on witchcraft shared the assumption that women were especially prone to become witches. Many authors used the same reasoning to argue that demons had an easier time possessing the bodies of women than of men. One might wonder, therefore, whether the witch-hunts were simply the result of the mounting misogyny that was evident in the proliferation of treatises, most of them written by clergymen, that depicted women as likely minions of Satan.

It must be noted, however, that critics of the witch-hunts more often than not exhibited very similar sexist attitudes. Deploring the excesses of witch trials, the Jesuit Friedrich Spee observed in 1631 that accused witches were usually females, and such women were quite often "delirious, insane, fickle, babbling, changeable, cunning, lying, [and] perjurous."[76] Even outright skeptics exhibited the same negative attitudes toward women. The Lutheran physician Johann Weyer, perhaps the sixteenth century's most important skeptic about witchcraft, attributed the sabbat and diabolical pacts to the "self-imaginings" of women or to delusions that demons implanted in the minds of women because their uncontrolled passions, inconstancy, feebleness, and simplicity made them more likely to believe in the reality of these illusions. In short, writers on witchcraft and possession did not have a monopoly on sexism, which was endemic in sixteenth- and seventeenth-century Europe.[77]

Feminist scholars have effectively placed the issue of gender front and center in the analysis of the early modern witch-hunts, and today no serious treatment of early modern witchcraft would ignore gender analysis. Historians have offered various explanations as to why women were much more likely than men to be accused, tried, and executed for witchcraft. Some feminist historians have equated witch-hunting with women-hunting and have asserted that witches were women who were rebelling against the patriarchal norms established by men of the ruling classes.[78] The witch-hunts have also been described as a means of reinforcing the patriarchal status quo, of ensuring male dominance over females in a period of economic and social changes that threatened patriarchy.[79]

Feminist scholars must be credited for drawing attention to the importance of gender in early modern witchcraft, but critics warn that at least some have overstated their case. Although women undeniably were more prone to be accused of witchcraft than men, the reduction of the witch-hunts to a male conspiracy against females begs an explanation as to why men made up perhaps as much as a fifth of those executed for witchcraft throughout Europe and constituted a majority of executions for witchcraft in Finland, Iceland, Livonia, and Normandy.[80] It may also be argued that equating the hunts to women-hunting—inspired by clerical misogyny or the desire to reinforce patriarchy—runs the danger of reducing women who were tried for witchcraft to mere victims of Europe's male-dominated society.[81] Could it be, though, that some of the accused really were witches or at least wanted others to believe that they wielded supernatural power? Some historians have maintained that many women who were accused and condemned of witchcraft had in fact tried to compensate for their subordinate status in this world by acquiring supernatural powers.[82] Women were less likely than men to seek revenge against enemies by inflicting physical violence or by pressing charges in law courts but may have sought redress of grievances through witchcraft.[83] Feminist anthropological scholarship has also suggested that the more women are denied authority, the more willingly they resort to illicit means, such as witchcraft, in order to curb male power.[84] Various studies on witchcraft have been a very important part of one tendency in women's history since the 1970s: shifting from studying the oppression or victimization of women to examining ways in which females expressed themselves, sought self-fulfillment, and attained degrees of autonomy.[85] In this present study, the issue of gender is even more important for the examination of possession than of witchcraft; all those in Carpi who were deemed possessed were female religious, but, as we shall see, one of the principal suspects of witchcraft was a male.

In this study, I will be trying above all to understand possession and witchcraft as cultural phenomena. Witchcraft and possession involved deeply held communal beliefs that were every bit as real and are as worthy of study as the growth of the state, conflicts between different religious confessions, or men's subjugation of women. The ways in which people experienced witchcraft and the ideas and values associated with it can provide invaluable insight to the mentality of an age. From the fifteenth to the eighteenth centuries, perhaps 40,000 to 50,000 Europeans were executed as witches, but beliefs in witchcraft were deeper and much more widespread than even these numbers suggest.[86] In effect, virtually all sixteenth- and seventeenth-century Europeans believed in the reality of witchcraft and demon possession. They were convinced that certain individuals manipulated supernatural forces to cast harmful spells and that devils, either at their own initiative or at the bidding of witches, could possess the bodies of people. By studying witchcraft and possession as an integral part of early modern culture, we are afforded a window to a mentality that was radically different from those prevailing among us.

The following study attempts to examine not only how the Inquisition of Modena conducted this investigation but, more important, how nuns, priests, and some laypeople in Carpi experienced and understood possession and witchcraft. It will attempt to explain why a convent seemed a likely site for a group possession to occur. By uncovering attitudes toward demons and harmful magic, we can gain a window to the mentality of this age, especially to that of female religious in the era of the Catholic Reformation.

Chapter 1

FEMALE RELIGIOUS, CLAUSTRATION, AND SANTA CHIARA OF CARPI

For centuries Roman Catholic Church leaders had preached that the celibate life was superior to matrimony and believed that women had a stronger libido and were more easily led into temptation than men. Given women's supposed propensity to lust and commit other sins, the convent was viewed as the site where women could best pursue a life of virtue. A degree of enclosure had always been part of monasticism. The contemplative life, aspired to by both monks and nuns, required a considerable degree of peace, solitude, and separation from the world. Enclosure, however, was always viewed as more essential for female than male religious. When enclosure of nunneries was introduced in the early Middle Ages, it was primarily viewed as necessary for the physical protection of nuns in an era of invasions, endemic violence, and political instability. In the central Middle Ages, churchmen called for the enclosure of convents for another reason: the need to keep nuns entirely separate from males to preserve their sexual purity, based on the misogynous assumptions that women were by nature more prone to sin, less able to control their impulses, and unable to govern themselves. In 1298 Pope Boniface VIII published a decree, *Periculoso*, that mandated enclosure for all professed nuns, women who had taken the solemn or perpetual vows of poverty, chastity, and obedience. The degree of enclosure varied greatly, however, from convent to convent into the Counter-Reformation era.[1]

Sixteenth-century Catholic authorities emphasized more than ever before the need for enclosure to shield religious women from the temptations of the world. The Council of Trent (1545–63), which was called in response to the challenge of Protestantism, mandated strict enclosure of female religious within the walls of convents, and this reform was implemented more rapidly than any of the other Tridentine disciplinary changes. This insistence on claustration reflected not only the concern to shield female religious from sexual temptation but, more broadly, to avoid distraction from their spiritual vocation by mundane matters in general. Convent walls were erected, grates were installed, and windows facing the exterior were boarded up. In the parlors of many nunneries, nuns and their visitors were to be separated by a grille and a curtain so that the religious could be heard but not seen.[2]

In Italy and most other regions of Catholic Europe, it was no longer acceptable for a woman to pursue a "semireligious" life as a member of a third order or lay order, an example of which was the Ursulines, founded by Angela Merici in 1535, who took temporary vows of chastity but did not live in convents, preferring to serve in the world as nurses and teachers of girls. In 1566 Pope Pius V mandated that all women currently associated with religious orders through simple vows—that is, vows that could be either temporary or perpetual—had to take solemn vows, which were by definition permanent. Henceforth, the only religious life for a woman was that of a nun in an enclosed convent, considered a haven for these virtuous women.[3] By the later seventeenth century, Giovan Battista de Luca, a prominent cardinal, noted the need to enclose nuns to safeguard their chastity but also observed, "We must feel pity for these women imprisoned for life and deprived of all satisfactions which lay women of comparable rank enjoy."[4] That a cardinal who helped oversee the administration of convents should refer to all nuns as prisoners for life underscored the rigorous manner in which nuns' contacts with the outside world were supervised.[5]

Santa Chiara of Carpi was actually an enclosed convent from its foundation in 1490. Once they had taken vows, nuns were generally never allowed to go outside the convent, and nuns visited with guests only in the parlor on opposites sides of the grate. In this regard, Santa Chiara already conformed to post-Tridentine dictates concerning female religious. We shall see, however, that in other ways discipline in Santa Chiara fell well below the expectations of Church leaders until the conclusion of the demonic misadventures of the 1630s.

A key feature of daily life in all convents, including Santa Chiara, was the celebration of the liturgical hours or divine offices. Every day nuns rose well before dawn, probably about four o'clock, to celebrate matins and congregated six more times each day for the other divine offices: prime, terce, sext, nones, vespers, and compline, celebrated respectively at sunrise, midmorning, midday, midafternoon, sunset, and just before bedtime. For each of these liturgical hours, nuns came to the choir where they took their seats, sprinkled themselves with holy water, and then proceeded to worship God through readings, prayers, and hymns, much of which was experienced in the form of group singing or reading.[6]

In spite of the prominence of liturgical hours, Santa Chiara, like so many convents in Italy, in many ways resembled more a warehouse for upper-class women whose families forbade them to marry than a home for women who eagerly embraced the religious life.[7] There were cases of mature women freely choosing to take the veil, occasionally even against the wishes of their families, and Italian women who truly felt a religious calling and voluntarily chose the religious life were most likely to join Capuchin or Discalced Carmelite communities.[8] Far more numerous, however, were those who entered the convents as girls and committed themselves for life by taking vows in their teens. Convents themselves, including Santa Chiara, tended to prefer receiving girls in their teens in the belief they were more likely than older women to be able to adapt to life in the cloister.[9] Moreover, many families had strong financial reasons to push some daughters toward the convent rather than marriage. Marrying daughters off to men of comparable social status required very large dowries, and early modern Italians had a strong aversion to allowing their daughters to marry men beneath their station.[10] To avoid dissipating their wealth, families tended to limit the number of daughters who married. For many middle- and upper-class families, those daughters who were not to marry were destined to a life in a convent. Attracting the very upper crust of Emilian society, Santa Chiara in the early 1600s was home most notably to Angela Caterina d'Este (1597–1661), the daughter, sister, and aunt of three successive dukes of Modena, who served as abbess for almost ten years. Virtually all nuns of Santa Chiara were from wealthy families, and many were of noble stock. Alsuinda Malaspina was the daughter of the "Most Illustrious" Marquis Alfonso Malaspina, and Sister Camilla Violante Pio, the grandniece of the founder of Santa Chiara, was a member of the Pio family, who still enjoyed considerable prestige even though Carpi was now subject to the Este dynasty.[11]

Entering a convent generally required donation of a type of dowry to the institution, the amount of which varied considerably according to the wealth and prestige of the institution. For much of the seventeenth century, the minimum dowry for admission to Santa Chiara was 300 *scudi* in cash and the same value in movable goods (linens, fabrics, and furniture) for residents of Carpi, whereas "foreigners"–those who were not *Carpigiane*–had to provide a dowry of at least 400 *scudi* and goods valued at 300 *scudi*. There was no maximum limit to the dowry, however, and some families contributed very large sums to secure entry into the religious house. In the seventeenth century, the community of Santa Chiara was generally limited to sixty professed nuns, though it sometimes exceeded this figure by accepting a few "supernumerary" nuns, for whom the minimum dowry was higher.[12] The arrival of Angela Caterina d'Este in 1608 definitely enhanced the reputation of the nunnery and intensified the competition, especially among "foreign" women, for the limited number of slots in Santa Chiara. This competition caused considerable inflation in the dowries, evident in the admission in 1629 of Clara Maria (born Isabella) Amoldoni of the town of Correggio, whose guardian agreed to a dowry of 1,500 *scudi,* payable in installments.[13] In spite of such substantial costs, a nun's dowry was still much less of a financial burden than a marriage dowry. In Tuscany, for example, the former was typically only a third or fourth the value of the latter.[14]

From the fifteenth into the seventeenth centuries there was a huge increase in the number of nuns in Italy. This trend reflected population growth and the contemporary increase in the cost of marriage dowries, which precluded matrimony for many aristocratic and patrician females. In Bologna, about sixty kilometers (under forty miles) to the southeast of Carpi, women residing in convents represented about 10–14 percent of the adult female population from 1574 into the 1630s. Peaks in admissions to convents coincided with economic crises, when forming marriages was a greater financial burden, but the overall trend clearly was toward ever growing numbers of women living within the walls of nunneries.[15] Nuns probably made up about 9 percent of Carpi's female population in the mid-seventeenth century.[16] Though nuns' percentage of the population as a whole was relatively small, convents tended to house a very large proportion of women from wealthy families in early modern Italy. In the first half of the seventeenth century, for example, 48 percent of females of Milan's patrician class and almost as high a proportion among their Florentine counterparts were nuns.[17]

Upon taking the veil, all women and girls went through a novitiate, a probationary period usually lasting at least a year, before becoming professed nuns. This was to ensure that both the would-be nun and the community agreed that she was well suited for the religious life before taking irrevocable vows. Novices participated in the daily divine offices, studied the rule of the order, and wore a habit and a white veil, but not the cord, scapular, and black veil of the professed nuns.[18] At Santa Chiara, the family of a novice had to pay the *dozzina,* a pension that covered her room and board. Though the family transferred the dowry to the convent when the girl entered the community, it remained untouchable throughout the novitiate. In the very unlikely event that the novice or the community decided that the religious life was not for her, the dowry would be returned to her family. When the novice took solemn vows, most often at the age of sixteen, the minimum age of profession established by Trent, the dowry became the permanent property of the convent.[19]

In most cases, the monastic life was not an option for the poor. Although the dowry needed to join a nunnery was considerably less than one to form a marriage, it was beyond the reach of people of modest means—ironically, one usually had to be at least of middle-class status to take the monastic vow of poverty! Women who did not come from upper-bourgeois or patrician families might still be able to join religious communities as lay sisters (*converse*). Although Santa Chiara originally had no lay sisters, it admitted its first *conversa,* Orsina Cipolla, in January 1632. Cipolla was still the sole lay sister in the convent at the time of the possessions, but by the mid-seventeenth century the community included nine *converse,* compared to sixty-four professed nuns.[20] Like novices, lay sisters wore white veils and, like the professed or choir nuns, took vows of poverty, chastity, and obedience, though these were sometimes simple (that is, not necessarily permanent) rather than solemn vows. Occasionally lay sisters rose to the ranks of the choir nuns, but for the most part the two played very different roles in the convent. Although participation in the daily devotions was, at least in theory, the most important duty of choir nuns, lay sisters were not obliged to recite these daily offices. Often illiterate, lay sisters worked as servants in the community and had no voice in its deliberations. Accordingly, they were from more humble backgrounds than the choir nuns, but they, too, had to have a dowry for admission. Though considerably smaller than those of professed nuns, this dowry requirement in effect precluded the indigent from working even as servants in female monasteries. At Santa Chiara, choir nuns had basically done all the mundane work themselves before they started admitting *converse*. With only one lay sister serving Santa Chiara in the late 1630s, professed nuns themselves continued to perform most of the convent's mundane tasks, such as cooking and doing laundry. Some choir nuns also carried out skilled manual tasks, such as embroidering altar-cloths and silk vestments for use in liturgical functions.[21]

Among the myriad issues that the Council of Trent addressed was the reform of male and female monasticism. Representatives at Trent mandated that religious vows be made freely and that, as noted above, vows not be taken before the age of sixteen.[22] These reforms, however, have rightly been called "timid, incomplete, and poorly enforced."[23] Although there were examples of women who pursued a religious vocation notwithstanding parental opposition, far more girls entered convents under strong pressure from their parents. Among the most famous of these was the Venetian Arcangela Tarabotti (1604–52), who was obliged by her parents to join a Benedictine convent because as a "lame" woman the prospects of securing a good marriage were quite dim. In impassioned treatises such as *Inferno monacale,* Tarabotti insisted that religious vocations must be made voluntarily. Describing forced monachization as sheer hell, she viewed the ceremony at which she took vows under duress as tantamount to a funeral.[24] Be that as it may, both before and after Trent very few nuns whose vocations were largely decided by their families rebelled in this manner. Most of these young women probably accepted the view that what was best for the family was best for them. There were also certain advantages to taking the veil. They would never be subject to a husband or suffer an unhappy marriage. Various nuns, especially those from powerful noble families, could aspire to hold certain offices and thereby wield a degree of power and self-mastery they could not possibly have enjoyed outside the walls of the nunnery.[25] In her work on Spain, Elizabeth Lehfeldt warns against equating enclosure, the implementation of which varied considerably from convent to convent, to powerlessness. Convents remained permeable to the outside world and provided many opportunities for nuns to pursue administrative, economic, and creative activities.[26] Similarly, Gabriella Zarri rightly asserts that female monasticism provided important avenues for female creativity and self-fulfillment in early modern Europe.[27]

Princess Angela Caterina d'Este, who had a profound impact on the nunnery of Santa Chiara, was a prime example of a woman who wielded a degree of power and independence that she could not possibly have had if she had married. From early childhood it was clear that the nunnery rather than marriage was the destiny for this younger daughter of Virginia de' Medici and Cesare d'Este, the last duke of Ferrara (1597–98) and the first duke of Modena (1598–1628). Born Eleonora d'Este, she entered Santa Chiara and took the veil as a novice amid great fanfare in December 1608 at the age of eleven, even though the minimum age for entry was twelve.[28] In June 1611 she became a nun and took vows at a ceremony full of pomp and beautiful music (*con un nobilissimo Accompagnamento di Musica*), which was attended by the entire Este court and a large number of other dignitaries. Angela Caterina was only fourteen at this time despite the minimum age for taking vows being then sixteen. She had in fact needed papal permission both to enter the convent and to take vows before the prescribed minimum ages.[29]

Although in theory nuns of all orders were not to take glory in the nobility, power, or wealth of their families,[30] in reality Angela Caterina was much more a princess than a nun even after taking vows. Although the Clarisses slept in a common dormitory and ate their meals together in the refectory, as a mere novice Angela Caterina had two rooms and a personal kitchen reserved for herself and the nuns who served her.[31] She and her family, however, clearly found these arrangements insufficient. Although nuns' contacts with family members were supposed to be limited and all correspondence subject to the abbess's approval, the Este princess enjoyed a carte blanche to write to anyone about anything she pleased. In her earliest years at Santa Chiara, Angela Caterina's numerous letters to her father were full of requests for a wide range of items for her pleasure and comfort. The duke proved to be quite generous with her and Santa Chiara, providing his daughter or the convent with many pieces of furniture, a tabernacle, a church bell, and, much to the delight of the princess, numerous paintings.[32] Although the monastic vow of poverty received heightened emphasis in the post-Tridentine era, the duke promised in writing to provide his daughter and her three servants, all of whom were professed nuns, with all their essentials: food, clothing, furniture, all other expenses, and an annual stipend of 200 *scudi* for as long as she lived.[33] He also financed some major renovations in 1615–20, which provided very spacious private apartments for the princess. Extending over both floors of the nunnery, the apartments comprised a sixth of the entire space in the convent and provided, among other things, living quarters, laundry facilities, a kitchen, henhouse, and small chapel just for the princess and those who served her. See figures 2 and 3 for the respective floor plans of the first and second floors prior to these renovations and figures 4 and 5 for the floor plans of the first and second floor, respectively, of Angela Caterina's apartments.[34]

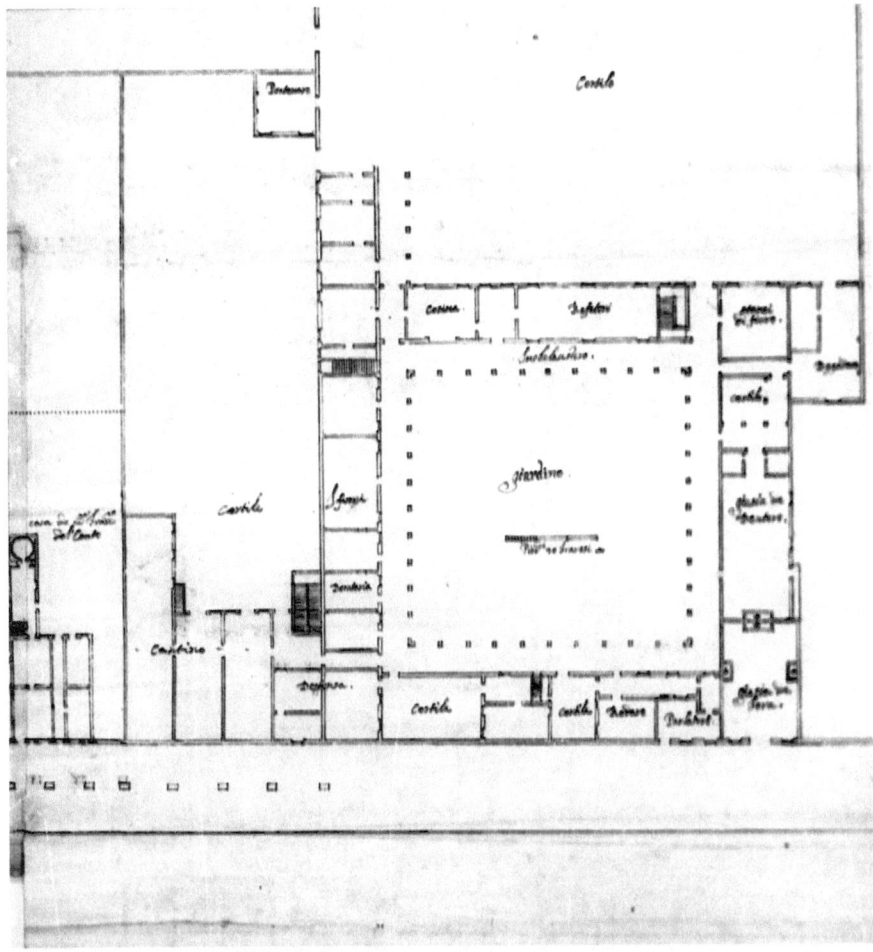

Figure 2. Floor plan of Santa Chiara, first floor (ca. 1615). Oriented toward the north, this undated floor plan shows to the south of the cloister (*giardino*); the turntable (*rodare*), or *ruota*, where objects could be passed into and out of the convent; the parlor (*parlatore*), where sisters and visitors could converse on opposite sides of a grille; and the exterior church (*giesia de fora*). Just to the north of the exterior church was the choir or interior church (*giesia de dentere*), where the Clarisses themselves worshiped. Located to the north of the cloister were the kitchen (*cosina*), refectory, and laundry (*bogadara*). The west wing had the ovens (*i forni*) and to the west of that wing was the area previously dedicated to storage (*cantino*) and a large courtyard (*cortile*), where Angela Caterina d'Este's apartments were later built. ASM, Mappario Estense, Fabbriche, 17 and 18. This and the other three floor plans are reproduced in *Clarisse in Carpi*, vol. 2, *Fonti*, ed. Ori, 163–67. Reproduced by permission of the ASM, Prot. n. 715/28.13.10/1.15 del 28.03.08.

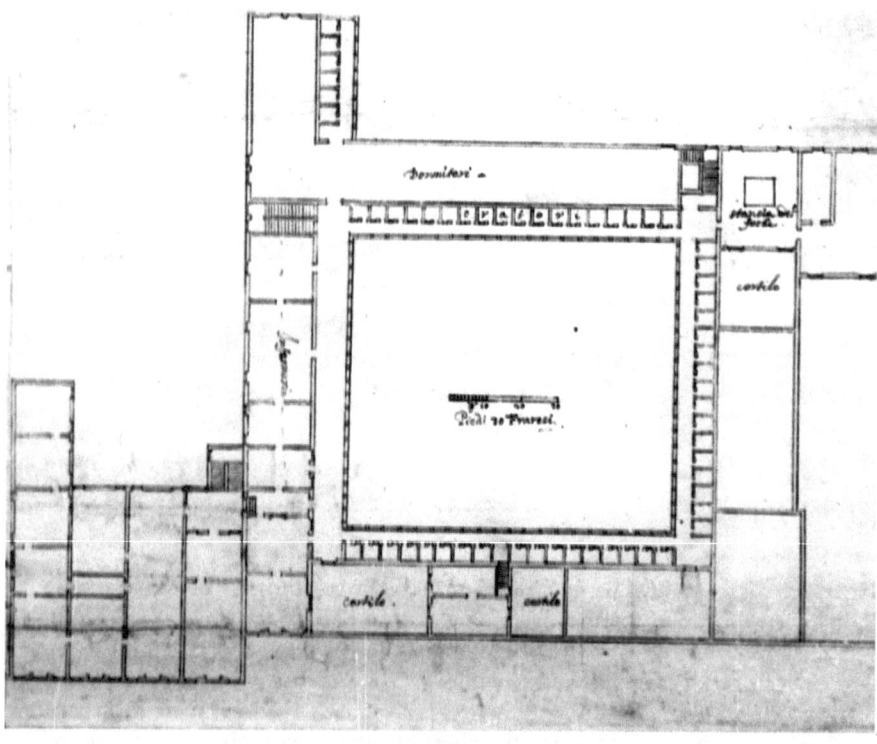

Figure 3. Floor plan of Santa Chiara, second floor (ca. 1615). The dormitory occupied the entire north wing of the second floor, and the infirmary comprised a good part of the west wing. Fifty-three cells or oratories were located on the north, east, and south sides of the balcony overlooking the cloister, and another seven cells were found in the extension to the northwest. The unmarked rooms to the southwest were later remodeled and expanded to become part of the apartments of Angela Caterina d'Este. ASM, Mappario Estense, Fabbriche, 17. Reproduced by permission of the ASM, Prot. n. 715/28.13.10/1.15 del 28.03.08.

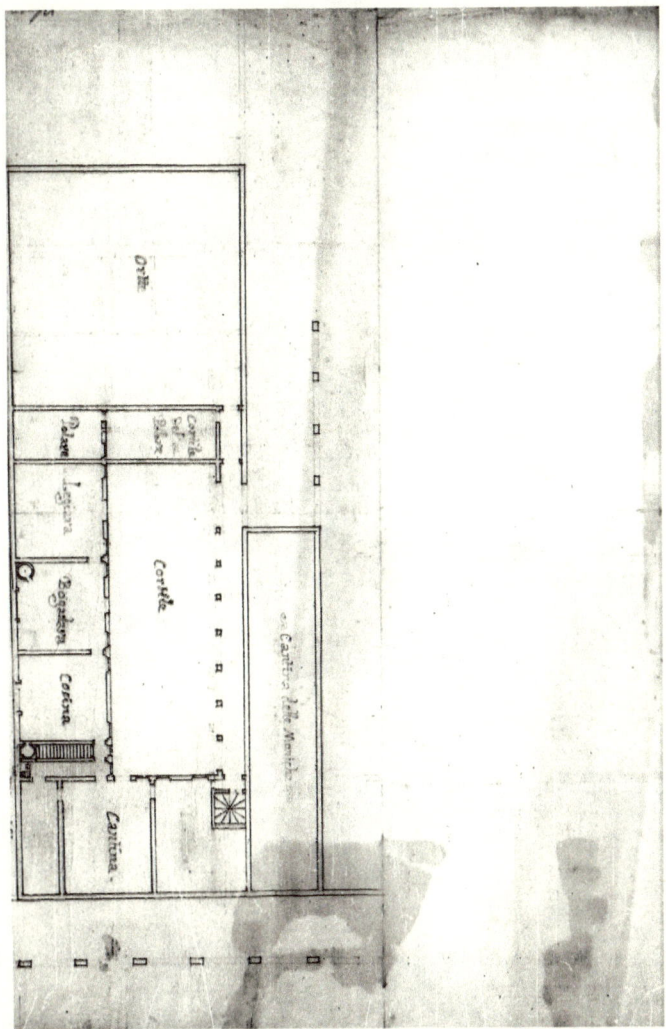

Figure 4. Floor plan of the apartments of Angela Caterina d'Este, first floor (ca. 1615). This floor plan, like those for the convent as a whole, is undated but was likely drawn up at the time these renovations began. To the right we see a long narrow cellar (*cantina*) that was available for storage for all the nuns of Santa Chiara. The remainder of this area was entirely for the use of the princess and her entourage. Going clockwise from the left of this cellar, we can identify another cellar, the pantry (*dispensa*), kitchen, laundry, woodshed (*legiara*), henhouse (*polare*), courtyard for the henhouse (*cortile del polare*), and a courtyard through which one had access to the rest of the convent. ASM, Mappario Estense, Fabbriche, 18. Reproduced by permission of the ASM, Prot. n. 715/28.13.10/1.15 del 28.03.08.

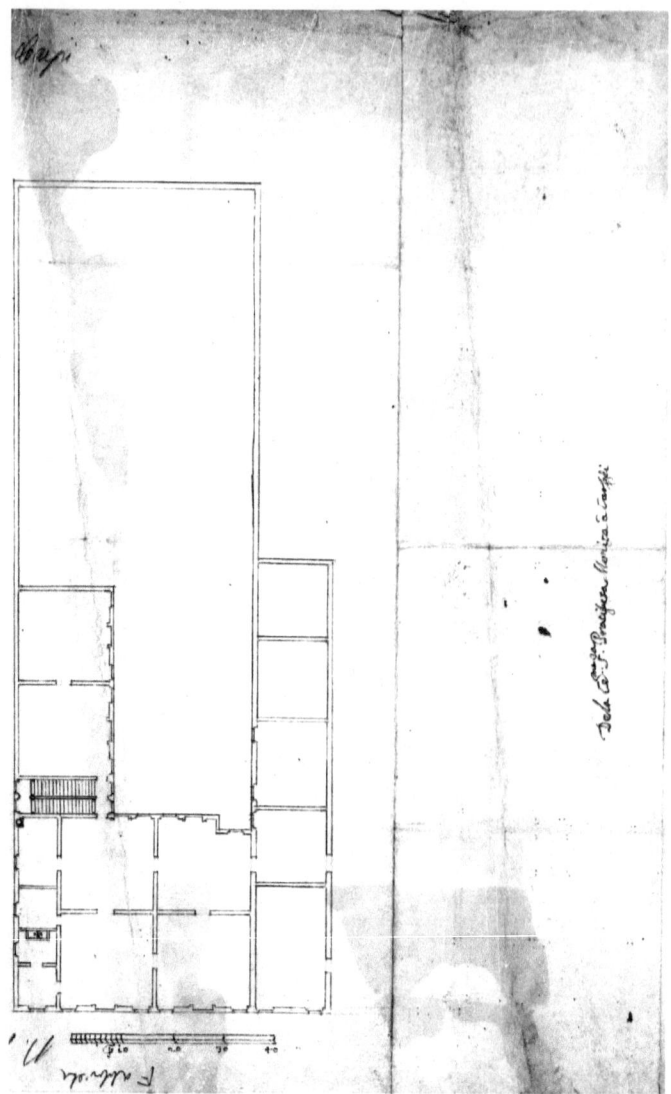

Figure 5. Floor plan of the apartments of Angela Caterina d'Este, second floor (ca. 1615). This floor plan, unlike that for the ground floor, did not identify the function of any of the rooms, though the small room in the lower left corner was clearly a chapel, as evidenced by the altar placed along the north wall. One assumes the princess and her retinue used all the other rooms for sleeping, dining, and visiting. To the lower right, we see the only two doorways that connected Angela Caterina's apartments to the rest of the convent. ASM, Mappario Estense, Fabbriche, 18. Reproduced by permission of the ASM, Prot. n. 715/28.13.10/1.15 del 28.03.08.

In February 1624, as she lay on her deathbed, Abbess Caterina Codebò summoned all the Clarisses to her. After asking forgiveness for her sins, she placed the keys of her office and the seal of the monastery in the hands of the confessor and asked Angela Caterina, in the presence of all sisters, to deign to take over the leadership of the convent. With encouragement from the confessor the princess accepted this charge, and upon receiving the news, the provincial head of the Observant Franciscans named her *commissaria* (acting abbess) after the death of Codebò until elections could be held. As recorded by her confessor, on 22 May the nuns gathered in the choir for the election, and a huge throng of people assembled in the exterior church on the other side of the choir screen. One by one the nuns approached the small opening in the screen and handed a ballot to the friars who were overseeing the vote. Having collected them all, the clerics read each one aloud. Their announcement that Angela Caterina had been unanimously elected abbess was met by enthusiastic applause, followed by the ringing of all the church bells in Carpi, an artillery salute, and fireworks. Although Trent had set the minimum age for abbesses at forty, Angela Caterina was only twenty-seven when she first became abbess of Santa Chiara.[35]

The position of abbess was ordinarily a term appointment, confirmed each year for up to three years. When the Clarisses unanimously renewed her appointment for another year in May 1625, they participated in a ceremony in which several of them, dressed as angels and saints, gave speeches advising the abbess on governing the monastery and sang a madrigal in praise of Angela Caterina and the entire Este dynasty.[36] She was renamed abbess numerous times, with the permission of the Congregation of Bishops and Regulars, an organ of the papal curia founded in 1588, which, as its name implies, oversaw the administration of both monastic communities and bishops.[37] True, the Church leadership clearly was uneasy with Angela Caterina's long tenure. Already in 1627, the Bishops and Regulars manifested impatience with her extended rule as abbess but nonetheless agreed to let her serve two more years. They did insist that the vote be made by secret ballot and that the princess give a report of her administration for the past three years.[38] Within Santa Chiara, Angela Caterina supposedly protested in 1627 that she wished to relinquish her charge and dedicate herself to the contemplative life but was ordered by her Observant Franciscan Superior to remain abbess.[39] When the two years expired in July 1629, she was appointed *commissaria* for another year,[40] and only in June 1630 did Angela Caterina finally step down after serving continuously as abbess (or *commissaria*) for six and a half years. She later served another three-year term starting in 1633 and abdicated definitively in June 1636.[41] By comparison, for the remainder of the seventeenth century, all other abbesses of Santa Chiara, when elected, were over fifty years old and had been professed nuns for well over thirty years. Moreover, since no other abbess served for more than three consecutive years, Santa Chiara was never again treated as anyone's de facto personal fiefdom.[42]

To a degree, the elections of Angela Caterina reflected the opinion, pervasive in most of seventeenth-century Europe, that members of the upper nobility were the "natural" leaders of society. The Clarisses no doubt shared this belief as almost all of them were from the very upper crust of Emilian society. In 1626 her personal confessor, Fra Angelo Lazzarino–admittedly not an unbiased witness–praised her incredible skills in governing the convent and declared that she had demonstrated, through her gentle and pious leadership, that princes "by nature" had the ability to "rule and govern people and kingdoms."[43] Her long tenure as abbess of course also reflected her family's deep pockets, and as abbess she was more likely to be successful in asking for money for the monastery from the duke, be he her father, brother, or nephew. In fact, Lazzarino, who had previously served as the convent's official confessor, also praised her for paying off the considerable debts that the convent had accrued under previous leadership. Angela Caterina undertook an ambitious renovation and expansion of the convent, increasing its size to accommodate, she hoped, up to a hundred nuns (though the number of nuns actually remained about sixty). Santa Chiara's major facelift began in 1626, involving the construction of new laundry facilities and a new dormitory, a very large room where the nuns (not including Angela Caterina and her attendants) slept communally. Renovations were also made in the refectory and the choir, and work began on her most ambitious building project: the construction of the *capitolo* or chapter house, a large auditorium, two stories in height, where the community of nuns met to discuss and vote on matters pertaining to the convent. The noted architect and engineer Antonio Vacchi played a role in the design of these substantial changes. The floor plans reproduced here were drawn prior to the major renovations that were initiated in the 1620s, and regrettably there are no extant plans from the 1630s. These plans do not show, for example, the addition of the chapter house, which extended to the north from the northeast corner of the cloister. It is important to stress that all this construction, which was not completed until the 1640s, was made possible by the generous funds supplied by the father, brother, and above all nephew of Angela Caterina.[44]

The Este family's connection to Santa Chiara was reinforced when in 1629 Angela Caterina's nieces, Anna Beatrice and Margherita (twelve and three years old, respectively) entered Santa Chiara for educational purposes. It was quite common for girls from wealthy Italian families to enter convents as *educande,* who lived and were educated in a nunnery even though they might later return to secular life.[45] Duke Alfonso III (1591–1644), Angela Caterina's brother, decided to send his two daughters to Santa Chiara at roughly the same time that, full of grief over the death of his wife, he felt a strong religious calling. In 1629 he abdicated the ducal throne and, taking the name of Giovan Battista, joined the Capuchins, an offshoot of the Observant Franciscans that was formed in the early sixteenth century.[46] In September of the same year, the new duke of Modena, Francesco I, the son of Alfonso and the nephew of Angela Caterina, accompanied his younger sisters to Santa Chiara, where he transferred the custody of his two younger sisters to his aunt. The pope had granted the two princesses permission "to live in secular clothing with five women [servants] each in the aforementioned convent, giving them permission to go out [of the nunnery] in the company of these women, sent out for any reason by Her Highness [Angela Caterina], and to stay away day and night when, where, and as long as they wish, and then return to the convent if they wish."[47] Changes in personnel among the five female attendants could be made at any time. The princesses and their servants could live with the Clarisses "bodily and spiritually" day and night in the choir and refectory without obliging them to embrace the religious life or subjecting them to claustration. The princesses and their attendants were, however, to sleep in Angela Caterina's private apartment rather than in the dormitory with all the other sisters. The duke also arranged for the two princesses and their retinue to have their own confessor, a Jesuit.[48]

The young Este girls bore witness to the fact that since the second half of the sixteenth century, Santa Chiara was recognized as a place that was well suited for the education of females from distinguished families.[49] Although the rules of most monastic orders provided that only novices, who expected eventually to take vows, be admitted to convents, nunneries throughout Italy and elsewhere commonly accepted such lay boarding girls. These *educande* usually did not enter convents before the age of seven and might remain in the nunnery into their mid-twenties. Their families paid a *dozzina*, similar to that for novices, to cover room and board for the duration of their stays.[50] Many of these boarders eventually took vows and became nuns, but others left the convents to pursue secular lives. In this case, neither of the Este princesses took religious vows: Margherita eventually married Ferrante Gonzaga, duke of Guastalla, and Anna Beatrice became duchess of Mirandola through her marriage to Alessandro II of the Pico family.[51] In the stricter rules that permeated Catholic institutions after the Council of Trent, *educande*–like lay sisters, widows, and battered wives–were supposed to be subject to the same rules of enclosure that applied to nuns in general.[52] In practice, some religious leaders and observant nuns complained that the presence of these lay girls could thwart the imposition of discipline in religious communities.[53] There is no record of complaints from within the nunnery about the freedom enjoyed by the Este girls, but they certainly were not subject to the rules that governed the lives of the Clarisses. Neither Santa Chiara's *Memoriale* nor the Holy Office's investigation mentions any other *educande* at this time, which suggests that the Este princesses were the only lay girls receiving an education there in the 1630s.

Several women from prestigious families—we do not know exactly how many—became professed nuns and served the Princess Angela Caterina or her nieces as *dame di compagnia*, ladies-in-waiting whose main task was simply to keep the princesses company. An excellent example was that of the "Signora Cavaliera" Barbara Forni, one of the very few sisters who took vows as a mature woman. A widow of about fifty-five, she entered Santa Chiara in 1630 and took vows the next year to great fanfare. Three years after Barbara Forni entered the monastery, her granddaughter, Barbara Leonora, the daughter of Count Paolo Francesco Forni, took the veil and became a novice. Both Barbara, who passed away in June 1634, and Barbara Leonora, who took vows a month after her grandmother died, entered the convent in the service of Angela Caterina's niece Margherita.[54] Prominent among these *dame di compagnia* was Giulia Angelica Sertori, a member of a prominent Modenese noble family who had an exceptionally close friendship with Angela Caterina, who was two years her senior. Through Angela Caterina, Sertori enjoyed a number of privileges, such as permission to keep many personal effects, including a number of silver items, even after taking vows. Sertori also served as vicaress (assistant abbess) for three years starting in 1627, when she was only twenty-eight. When leaving Santa Chiara in 1639, Angela Caterina tried unsuccessfully to have Sertori transferred with her. Even after Angela Caterina's departure, her former ladies-in-waiting continued to enjoy remarkable privileges in Santa Chiara.[55]

Angela Caterina in effect developed her own monastic court in Santa Chiara. Ever since the construction of her very large private apartments, she and her impressive entourage—consisting of a cook, servants, and ladies-in-waiting, all of whom were professed nuns—slept, ate, and more often than not even worshiped apart from the rest of the community. Angela Caterina had her own confessor, who generally also heard the confessions of those who served her. To be sure, private apartments could be found in other convents in seventeenth-century Italy. In a Benedictine convent in Brescia, for example, nuns not only could have their own private cells constructed but could even bequeath these cells to specific members of the community to use as they saw fit.[56] But far from having a mere cell, the princess had a sixth of the convent for her own private space. The little fiefdom that Angela Caterina created in this cloister was really quite exceptional and flew in the face of Tridentine reforms, which stressed the communal nature of religious life in monasteries.[57]

A lover of music, the princess-abbess greatly enhanced the musical experience available at Santa Chiara, even though the post-Tridentine Church had tried to limit dramatically the types of music that could be performed in female monasteries. The Congregation of Bishops and Regulars had forbidden female religious to play wind instruments, to take music lessons from anyone outside the convent, or even to sing polyphonic music; nuns were supposed to sing only monophonic chants, commonly known as Gregorian chants. Angela Caterina was able to ignore these restrictions, and Santa Chiara, like some other Italian convents, became renowned for the high quality of its music, which was on a par with that of contemporary musical academies.[58] As abbess she tried to attract musically talented women to the convent, and performances were not limited to liturgical music. Some concerts took place in the parlor in the presence, on the opposite side of the grille, of invited lay guests.[59]

Evidence indicates that discipline was rather lax in Santa Chiara at least through the late 1630s. As we shall see in the next chapter, many of the first names that the Clarisses chose for themselves when they took vows—names such as Dealta, Ippolita, Dianira, Olimpia, and Bradamante—were quite secular in nature and not the names of saints that female religious habitually chose. To a considerable extent, the princess-abbess was herself responsible for the very permissive atmosphere that pervaded the convent. The degree to which Angela Caterina, thanks to her family ties, could disregard rules of monastic behavior was quite striking. Angela Caterina blatantly ignored some of the requirements of "The Rule of the Blessed Mother Santa Chiara," a new version of which was translated, at her request, into Italian by Fra Lazzarino. Embracing standards established in the central Middle Ages, the fourth chapter of the Rule specifically addressed the sleeping arrangements in the convents of Clarisses: "All the nuns, the abbess like the others, are to sleep dressed and with belts on in the communal dormitory." Each nun was to have her own bed, and "the bed of the abbess is to be arranged in a place so that she may oversee all the other beds of the dormitory."[60] Moreover, as noted above, the Este family had received papal permission to allow Angela Caterina's nieces to reside in Santa Chiara as *educande*, even though the Rule explicitly forbade anyone to reside in the convent who did not enter as a novice with the expectation of taking vows.[61]

The princess-abbess's patent disregard for some of the traditional regulations governing the monastic life of Clarisses was no doubt a factor behind a major conflict, alluded to in the introduction, that brewed for several years before the outbreak of witchcraft fears and was not definitively resolved until the suspicions of diabolical possessions had largely faded away. Just as Clare had drawn inspiration from Francis of Assisi, many monastic orders of nuns developed as female versions of male religious orders. Consequently, many nunneries had traditionally been under the supervision of their male monastic counterparts. In the case at hand, Santa Chiara had been governed since its establishment by the Observant Franciscans (also known as the *Zoccolanti*), one of three independent orders of Franciscans.[62] The reforms of Trent, however, initiated a movement to place all female monasteries under the direction of the *ordinario diocesano*, a term that usually referred to a bishop.[63] In Carpi, however, the *ordinario* was the archpriest, who essentially had the same powers and dignities as a bishop, being subject to no one in the Church other than the pope. The office of archpriest of Carpi was eventually elevated to the status of bishop in 1779.[64] There was a decades-long struggle for power over the control of Santa Chiara between the Observant Franciscans, on the one hand, and the archpriest of Carpi, on the other. Already in 1587, the archpriest had attempted to wrest power from the Franciscans, trying in vain to prohibit them from even approaching Santa Chiara.[65] But the dispute between the friars and the secular clergy over the convent really began in earnest in March 1627. The princess-abbess fought aggressively to keep the convent under the governance of the Franciscans and earnestly petitioned her brother, Duke Alfonso III, to oppose any change.[66] Alfonso, however, was a principal force in favor of change, and in March 1629 he instructed the bishop of Modena, Alessandro Rangoni, to ask the pope for permission to assign a secular priest rather than a friar as confessor to Santa Chiara.[67] In theory, the city of Carpi and the archpriest were not under the jurisdiction of the bishop of Modena, but the Este dynasty wielded secular power over both Modena and Carpi. Alfonso was also wont to meddle in ecclesiastical affairs and was simply too powerful for Rome to ignore. Originally from the city of Reggio, Ludovico Niccolini was named archpriest of Carpi in 1629 and held that position until 1643. The "very learned" and ambitious Niccolini had previously been an apostolic protonotary, serving the papal curia in the area of record-keeping.[68] In July 1629 the convent was briefly removed from the Franciscans and placed under the direction of the archpriest, but the struggle was far from over.[69] The *Zoccolanti* definitively lost control of Santa Chiara in July 1637,[70] but as we shall see, supervision of Santa Chiara was temporarily taken away from the archpriest starting in 1639.

To sum up, Santa Chiara of Carpi was the home to the daughters of some of Emilia's wealthiest and most powerful families. Led by the princess-abbess, Angela Caterina d'Este, the Clarisses enjoyed a comfortable and rather mundane lifestyle within the cloister. The lenient atmosphere indicates that, notwithstanding *clausura,* the convent most definitely had not been reformed according to the strict discipline mandated by Trent.

Chapter 2

THE OUTBREAK AND *MALEFICIA*

The 1630s began rather inauspiciously for Carpi and the surrounding region. In 1630 northern Italy suffered a serious bout of the plague, images of which were immortalized in novelist Alessandro Manzoni's descriptions of Milan in *I promessi sposi*. The plague arrived in Modena in June, and Carpi was ordered quarantined on the twenty-first of that month, as efforts were made to restrict as much as possible movements of people into and out of the town. Over the next few months, thousands succumbed to the plague in Modena, Carpi, and the neighboring countryside before it subsided in November.[1] Nuns in early modern Italy tended to enjoy remarkable longevity and even a certain invulnerability to the plague, both of which can be attributed, at least in part, to *clausura*, which shielded female religious from many contagions.[2] In Carpi, too, Santa Chiara seems to have been largely spared the wrath of the plague of 1630. One Clarisse died in June and another in July, but it is not clear if they were victims of the plague.[3]

Although witch-hunts have at times been associated with fears of the plague, pestilence does not seem to have been a significant factor in the witchcraft scare in Carpi. Carpi's demonic woes did not first appear until more than five years after the waning of the plague and reached a crescendo only in 1638. Given this delay, it seems unlikely that the plague itself played a significant role in witchcraft fears and accusations. This is quite unlike the experiences in Geneva, for example, where witchcraft accusations were most often directed against people accused of spreading the plague through maleficent magic.[4]

Carpi's first demonic possession and witchcraft trial of the 1630s involved lay residents of the town who had no direct ties to the convent. In 1636 three people were tried for indulging in inappropriate occult activities. Bernardino Bosellino was believed responsible for a number of *maleficia* that resulted in the illness and subsequent death of a prominent churchman in Carpi, the archpriest's vicar, and blindness in one eye of a woman who had quarreled with Bosellino. He also reputedly possessed some written spells to serve a variety of purposes, such as winning at games of chance, causing the death of another person, and enduring the pains of torture. Another man, Marsilio Losi, was investigated on a number of counts, including providing love magic to a couple to overcome the opposition of the woman's father to the match and giving a powder (which he claimed was dried breast milk from the Virgin Mary) to make new mothers lactate. And Ginevra Loia, a beggar woman of seventy, was accused of bewitching members of families who had refused to give her alms.[5] On the basis of reports he had received from Carpi, Father Giacomo Tinti, the inquisitor of Modena and a native of the city of Lodi, declared that the whole town and surrounding countryside were gripped with fear and agitation.[6]

The Demons in the Convent

We can speculate that the Clarisses heard rumors of these alleged bewitchments in conversations they had with family members and friends in the convent's parlors. Family ties remained strong even after nuns took vows, and in the lax atmosphere of Santa Chiara nuns were given considerable freedom to visit unimpeded with lay friends and relatives. Rumors of possessions surely incited fears in the cloister, and the demonic woes that were plaguing the city quickly gained a foothold within Santa Chiara, which eventually became the center of alleged diabolical activity in Carpi. Already on 26 January 1636, Paolina Forni, a young laywoman who served as a lady-in-waiting to the *educanda*, Princess Anna Beatrice d'Este, took ill. Shortly thereafter, Leonora Galli, a more humble lay servant (*donzella*) who also worked for Anna Beatrice, began showing symptoms of the same extraordinary malady. (For a chronological list of the women who became possessed at Santa Chiara, see appendix A.) Had they been in the service of Angela Caterina or of any other nun, these women would ordinarily have been obliged to become at the very least lay sisters in order to reside in the convent. Since *educande* might be just temporary residents of a convent, laywomen could be in their service. No witness mentioned the ages of Forni and Galli, and their names do not appear in the convent's *Memoriale* since they did not take the veil. Nonetheless, they were surely rather youthful, as one Clarisse referred to Galli as "young" and to Forni as a "little maiden" (*puttina*).[7]

In March 1636 the Princess-Abbess Angela Caterina d'Este wrote to her nephew Duke Francesco I about Paolina Forni's ills. She noted that the young lady-in-waiting had been infirm for the past fifty days and had been under the care of a physician, who had prescribed a number of medicines, all to no avail. Convinced that Forni was bewitched (*maleficiata*), Angela Caterina asked permission to have her removed from the convent to receive better care for her ills and to protect Princess Anna Beatrice and others from this malady.[8] At some point between early March and late May, both Forni and Galli were in fact permanently removed from Santa Chiara. Given the presence of his daughters there, Giovan Battista d'Este, the duke-turned-friar who now lived in Carpi, was understandably quite concerned when residents of Santa Chiara first began to show signs of possession. In a letter to his son Duke Francesco, Giovan Battista warned in April 1636 that the level of urgency had risen: "More than ever I hope to find who dared to infect the convent of Santa Chiara of Carpi with fatal *maleficia*."[9] By the spring of 1636, both Angela Caterina and Giovan Battista d'Este were thus convinced that two residents of Santa Chiara were the victims not only of demon possession but also of witchcraft. For the Estes and others, it appeared that demons were attacking the godly, at the instigation of witches, by going after the true prize: Carpi's most prestigious religious house, which catered to women from the region's wealthiest and most powerful families.[10]

Based on the reports he received from residents of Carpi, who asked him to intervene, Inquisitor Tinti, a few miles away in Modena, at first did not think the evidence was strong enough to merit the intervention of the Inquisition. Even if everyone was convinced that the nuns were diabolically possessed, the Holy Office need not investigate unless there were also allegations of witchcraft. As we have seen, however, alleged demon possession became much more closely associated with witchcraft in the sixteenth and seventeenth centuries, and there were some experts on demonology who claimed that they could determine, through a close examination of demoniacs, whether they were not only possessed but also bewitched, the victims of spells cast by a witch.[11] In this case, the archpriest of Carpi, almost certainly with the earnest support of Giovan Battista d'Este, pleaded with Tinti to come personally to Carpi to investigate allegedly "strong evidence" against certain individuals. But rather than going himself, Tinti remained in Modena and sent a vicar in his stead.[12]

The vicar's visit in April 1636 showed that certain high-profile individuals in Carpi were already acting as de facto witch-hunters, even though the Inquisition in theory had exclusive jurisdiction over witchcraft cases. Quite prominent was Giovan Battista d'Este, who claimed in a letter to his son the duke, that he himself had the authority "to deal freely with these witches." The inquisitor's vicar discovered in fact that Giovan Battista had already ordered the imprisonment of Marsilio Losi and another person (probably Ginevra Loia) on suspicion of witchcraft. Other arrests were expected to follow, and Giovan Battista predicted that as many as ten or twelve witches would be jailed. The duke-turned-friar made a direct appeal to Tinti, asking the inquisitor to come personally to Carpi to aid this beleaguered town before the evil increased and "more creatures perished." Tinti duly went to Carpi in May, and his vicar had already arrested Bosellino, described as a man of "bad reputation." Upon his arrival, Tinti initially concluded that the evidence did not suffice to incarcerate anyone other than Marsilio Losi and ordered the release of the others.[13]

At this early stage in Carpi's woes, the inquisitor was not overly concerned that Giovan Battista d'Este and others were basically encroaching on the Inquisition's turf. In a letter to the Congregation in Rome, Tinti stated matter-of-factly that Duke Francesco himself was gathering information about the alleged witchcraft in the city and lands of Carpi and in the convent of Santa Chiara. Tinti noted that witchcraft was considered a crime that was under the purview of a "mixed forum," which could involve both lay and ecclesiastical judicial authorities. So the inquisitor of Modena saw no problem in having lay officials, such as the duke, investigating the alleged demon possession and witchcraft.[14]

Duke Francesco I was quite interested in helping lead the investigation into the alleged witchcraft, especially because the demons had attacked Santa Chiara and reputedly possessed the bodies of close associates of his sisters. His concerns were only heightened when rumors briefly circulated that one of his younger sisters was also bewitched (although neither Anna Beatrice nor Margherita was ever among the residents of Santa Chiara who were commonly recognized as possessed).[15] Convinced that witchcraft was behind Santa Chiara's troubles, the duke wanted to publicize widely an announcement to ask for information leading to the arrest of suspects. Giovan Battista wrote this announcement but passed it on to Inquisitor Tinti, having decided that it was impolitic to disseminate it without the approval of the Holy Office. The friar first included in this announcement an offer of impunity, later removed, to accomplices who revealed their fellow witches.[16] In short, the duke and especially the former duke were taking the lead in the early stages of the investigation of witchcraft in Carpi.

In the spring of 1636, the Congregation of the Inquisition in Rome sounded the alarm about the involvement of secular authorities in the investigation of witchcraft in Carpi and Santa Chiara. Presiding over the Congregation was Francesco Barberini (1597–1679), named a cardinal in 1623 by his uncle, Pope Urban VIII (pontificate 1623–44). At the end of May 1636, Barberini instructed Inquisitor Tinti that under no circumstances should he allow laymen to gather information about the supposed *maleficia* in Carpi. Even though such matters had in the past been treated in a "mixed forum" of both lay and ecclesiastical authorities, "the constitutions of the Supreme Pontiffs have removed all authority from lay judges to interfere" in such matters. Accordingly, the cardinal asked Tinti to speak frankly about this with the prince-friar, Giovan Battista d'Este, who has shown "so much zeal that the delinquents be punished." With "similar ardor," Tinti was to ensure that the jurisdiction of the Holy Office remained uncompromised throughout the lands under the jurisdiction of the Inquisition of Modena.[17]

Inquisitor Tinti had a hard time convincing Giovan Battista to stay out of these matters. The Capuchin protested that he had already pursued similar cases, during both his and his father's reigns as duke. Tinti also spoke about the issue of jurisdiction with some ducal ministers, who generally shared the opinion that witchcraft, according to "ancient law," was subject to both lay and ecclesiastical courts. And lest he be perceived as blameless, Tinti admitted in a letter to Barberini that he, too, had been under that impression, noting that when he served the Holy Office in both Milan and Como, secular courts often heard various cases concerning witchcraft. He now realized he had erred, however, and pledged not to allow lay authorities to interfere in witchcraft cases.[18]

Eventually the Holy Office did take full charge of the case, and in November 1636 it banished indefinitely Bernardino Bosellino from the lands that were subject to the Inquisition of Modena under pain of the galleys. It also prescribed fairly standard "salutary" acts of penitence: for the next three years he was to recite the rosary weekly and confess his sins and take communion four times a year (at Easter, Christmas, Pentecost, and the Assumption). Marsilio Losi and Ginevra Loia were sentenced only to similar acts of penance for the next three years.[19]

With the conclusion of this trial, the Inquisition of Modena did not investigate any further alleged witchcraft in Carpi for about a year and a half. For the next few months, Carpi in fact apparently enjoyed something of a respite from diabolical harassment. But in the spring of 1637, Sister Ottavia Bendidio of Modena became the first choir nun to take ill, entering Santa Chiara's infirmary around Easter for treatment of apparent demon possession.[20] In the fall of the same year, the devils began to unleash their full fury, striking first one then another sister of Santa Chiara. Eventually twelve Clarisses were deemed demonically possessed in addition to the laywomen Forni and Galli.

Before the Inquisition of Modena even got involved, exorcists were offering their services to the ailing women and quickly concluded that they were the victims of witchcraft. The exorcists had easy access to the convent even though for several years prominent figures in the Holy Office had been urging caution in the use of exorcisms, especially in regard to female religious. A Dominican and native of Lombardy, Cardinal Desiderio Scaglia (1567–1639) served on the Congregation of the Inquisition in Rome after previously working as inquisitor in Pavia, Cremona, and Milan. In the early 1620s he authored the *Prattica,* a handbook of important guidelines for inquisitors that circulated widely in manuscript form in the decades that followed.[21] In the *Prattica,* an extant copy of which is found among the records of the Inquisition of Modena, Scaglia opined that religious superiors often made matters worse by sending priests to exorcize nuns who were deemed possessed. He believed that many of these afflicted women were not really possessed by demons and that the exorcisms only exacerbated the fears and turmoil that were plaguing the community of nuns.[22] Despite such warnings, Giovan Battista d'Este himself conducted at least one exorcism in Carpi, which convinced him that Ginevra Loia was indeed a witch.[23]

The fears of demons and witches in Santa Chiara were definitely heightened by the extraordinary fact that its first three residents who were discovered "possessed" all died of their ills. Within weeks or months after they left the convent, Barbara Forni and Leonora Galli passed away on 23 May and 13 December 1636, respectively.[24] After an illness of about nine months, Sister Ottavia Bendidio, the first nun to take ill, died in January 1638 at the age of thirty-three.[25] Bendidio's illness and death undoubtedly made more of an impression on her fellow Clarisses than did those of Forni and Galli. While the two young laywomen left the convent shortly after taking ill, they saw Bendidio languishing for months, and it was surely no coincidence that almost all subsequent possessions took hold during her illness. In any event, although alleged demonic possessions were very common in this era, these deaths were highly unusual. Unfortunately, the records are almost entirely silent on the specific ailments that these three women suffered, in part because they all perished before the investigation of Santa Chiara began. The *Memoriale,* for example, made no mention at all of the deaths of Forni and Galli, who, again, were not nuns and were no longer at the convent when they perished. As for Bendidio's death, the *Memoriale* merely recorded the date and the fact that the abbess and confessor were at her side when she passed away. The most detailed description of the ills of any of these women is found in the testimony of one nun who reported that Ottavia Bendidio suffered from wounds all over her body and was unable to move without assistance and that she was "also possessed . . . like the other nuns."[26] This testimony could be interpreted as meaning that she died from a natural malady that was unrelated to the possession. The physician, surgeon, and exorcists who testified either had nothing to say about the three deceased women's ailments or merely stated that they suffered from the same maladies as the others.

Regardless of the cause, the deaths of these three women did not immediately precipitate an investigation by the Holy Office. Only when the fears of the devils and witchcraft reached a crescendo within the cloister did the Inquisition finally take action in April 1638. The attorney Orazio Giudici, fiscal of the Inquisition of Modena, was serving as the inquisitor of Modena's acting vicar in Carpi, even though, as a layman, he was technically ineligible to do so. Fiscal Giudici, who would prove himself to be a very zealous witch-hunter, opened the investigation in April 1638 following reports of very erratic behavior by numerous nuns. For several months, as many as twelve Clarisses had reputedly been suffering terribly in body and spirit from diabolical possession. Although Giudici had not witnessed firsthand the tribulations of the nuns, he claimed to have heard from very reliable witnesses of their sufferings. They were described as frequently throwing themselves on the floor, screaming abruptly without provocation, suffering sudden drastic changes in body temperature, and falling precipitately into a deep sleep from which they could not be awakened. As fiscal, Giudici ordinarily would have assisted the inquisitor or his vicar in conducting investigations. Although he would have been actively involved in the prosecution of cases, the fiscal normally would not have undertaken investigations himself. In this case, as the inquisitor had not appointed a vicar in Carpi, Fiscal Giudici conducted the investigation himself for a few months, often assisted by the archpriest of Carpi, Ludovico Niccolini, while Inquisitor Tinti remained in Modena.[27]

The Holy Office's Investigation

With the consent of the inquisitor of Modena, Giudici went to the nunnery on 19 April to start questioning the residents of the convent. Lasting several months, this investigation uncovered one of the most spectacular witchcraft cases ever to plague a convent. In its efforts to uncover the mysteries behind the ailments that plagued the convent, the Holy Office eventually questioned everyone living in and associated with Santa Chiara—in addition to suspects, fifty-five nuns and a half dozen people from outside the convent—with the important exception of the demoniacs themselves.[28]

The inquisitor of Modena wrote out guidelines for the questioning of witnesses, and these procedures were followed, more or less, throughout the lengthy inquiry. Before taking an oath while placing a hand on a Bible, witnesses were first warned of the importance of swearing the oath and of not committing perjury, especially before the Holy Office. False testimony, they were told, included not only telling a lie but also failing to reveal the whole truth. People also must indicate if they witnessed something firsthand or if their knowledge was from hearsay. When appearing before the Inquisition for the first time, witnesses were asked their name, their father's name, their place of origin, and their profession. The interrogator was also supposed to ask—though registers indicate that he did not always do so—when the witnesses had last confessed to a priest and taken communion; whether they had ever been imprisoned, investigated, or tried by the Inquisition and, if so, for what reasons; and whether they had ever been excommunicated and, if so, why. They were also to be asked how and by whom they were approached to submit to this interrogation and what they were told about it.[29] These instructions conformed to the standard procedures of the Holy Office, and the scribe dutifully recorded the answers to these preliminary queries as well as to the more specific questions that followed. Witnesses were always interrogated in private, usually in the presence of only the inquisitor (or the fiscal in his stead) and the scribe. On occasion, the archpriest or other clerics might also be present, but certainly no other potential witness was ever within earshot of the questioning.

For every interrogation, the scribe recorded the question in Latin but always transcribed the answers in the vernacular, replete with local colloquialisms and references to facial expressions, pauses, and forms of nonverbal communication. The unavoidable impression from the registers is that the nuns and others testifying before the Inquisition of Modena were quite free to express their opinions; in no way was their testimony coerced by an overbearing interrogator. Upon completion of the questioning, the scribe read aloud the transcript of the testimony to the deponent, who could make corrections or additions and then confirmed its accuracy by signing her or his name or, if unable or choosing not to sign, by making the mark of a cross below the transcription.

The interrogation on 19 April of the first witness, Claudia Cabassi, twenty-eight years old and a native of Carpi, set the tone for the entire investigation. (For a time line of the Holy Office's investigation of this case, including the interrogation of all witnesses, see appendix B.) Asked how long she had been a nun, Cabassi replied for twelve years, having previously been a novice for two years. Following standard inquisitorial procedures, Giudici then asked two questions made of all witnesses appearing before the Inquisition: whether she had any idea as to why she had been called and whether she knew of any heretics, blasphemers, or witches.[30] Like many subsequent witnesses, she replied in the negative to both. Giudici then proceeded with questions pertaining specifically to the case at hand. When he inquired if she knew of any nuns who suffered from maladies, Cabassi replied that as far as "ordinary" illnesses, one sister was afflicted with ailments associated with old age. In addition, several nuns were suffering from extraordinary ills, which were commonly known to stem from demon possessions.[31]

Witnesses revealed that in addition to the three women who had died from their ills—Paolina Forni, Leonora Galli, and Sister Ottavia Bendidio—eleven choir nuns had been discovered possessed by demons, one of whom had been cured of her possession by the time the investigation opened in April 1638. On the basis of witnesses' testimony and of the convent's *Memoriale,* the demoniacs' names, hometowns, and ages can be established as follows (see also appendix A):[32]

1. Giulia Angelica Sertori, thirty-nine and the daughter of a count from Modena, served Angela Caterina as a lady-in-waiting and was her closest confidante ever since Sertori took the veil in 1614.[33]

2. Barbara Leonora Forni, twenty, was also from Modena and served as a *dama di compagnia* to Angela Caterina's nieces, having entered the convent, as mentioned briefly in the previous chapter, not long after her widowed grandmother had joined the community. She was also the sister of Paolina, the young laywoman who was the first resident of Santa Chiara to be discovered "possessed" and who died of her ills in May 1636.[34]

3. Maria Maddalena Colevati, fifty, from Modena, was a servant of Angela Caterina in a more traditional sense—when she passed away in 1668 at the age of eighty, she was described as the former "embroiderer" for the princess-abbess.[35]

4. Flerida (also known as Paola Francesca) Federici (also known as Cimadori), thirty-five, from Carpi.[36]

5. Cinzia Ciarlatina, twenty-nine, from Carpi.[37]

6. Clara Maria Amoldoni, twenty-four, from Correggio.[38]

7. Degnamerita Solieri, thirty-two, from Carpi.[39]

8. Veronica Maria Coccapani, twenty-four, from Carpi.[40]

9. Caterina Margherita Ronchi, twenty-one, from Carpi.[41]

10. Anna Maria Martinelli, seventeen, from Sestola.[42]

11. Margherita Felice Castagnini, about thirty-nine, from Modena, was now cured of her possession. A professed nun who served as personal cook to Angela Caterina and her substantial entourage, Castagnini was the only choir nun who was permitted to leave the convent temporarily to receive unspecified treatment for her ills. After an extended absence, Castagnini returned to Santa Chiara to resume the religious life, her health restored.[43]

Asked when the ills of the currently afflicted nuns began, the Clarisses' answers reveal that the liturgical calendar was central to their marking of time; they referred to saints' days much more often than to months and dates. They reported that first Sertori and Barbara Leonora Forni, both ladies-in-waiting to the princess or her nieces, were discovered possessed on the feast day of St. Jude and St. Simon (28 October) 1637. They were followed by Sisters Cimadori, Solieri, and Castagnini, who took ill on St. Charles's Day (4 November), followed four days later by Amoldoni. Since then, the others fell ill one by one until Lent, when Ronchi and Martinelli became afflicted on St. Matthias's Day (24 February). Three or four of these nuns (Sertori, Forni, Amoldoni, and perhaps Colevati) were discovered possessed when people were "reading"—that is, saying prayers, reciting creeds, and so on—over Sister Ottavia Bendidio when she lay deathly ill. Cimadori was discovered possessed when an exorcist brought a relic to the convent, at the request of the princess-abbess, to be used to cure Bendidio.[44]

A casual glance shows that these possessed nuns, with the exception of Colevati and, to a lesser extent, Castagnini and Sertori, tended to be younger members of the community, ranging from their late teens to early thirties. This is quite similar to the pattern found in the possessions of female religious at Loudun and, a few years later, at Auxonne.[45] Other studies on early modern Europe have shown an even greater imbalance toward younger women among demoniacs. Research on England, for example, has shown a preponderance of children and youth, especially girls, among the possessed, and some view possession as a means of rebelling, even if not consciously, against adult authority.[46]

Another striking feature is that those in the service of Princess Angela Caterina or her nieces were clearly overrepresented among the energumens. Six out of fourteen were specifically dedicated to serving the Este princesses, be they professed nuns who were *dame di compagnia* (two), choir nuns who were more humble servants (two), or laywomen who were either a companion or a servant to an *educanda* (one each). All of them would have resided in Angela Caterina's private apartments where they slept, ate, and usually worshiped apart from the remainder of the community of religious. The most plausible explanation for this trend—beyond that perhaps the demons were targeting the Este family!—is that the possessions were contagious. These women lived in close proximity to each other, and their fears could easily breed on each other. As we shall see, given her family history, Angela Caterina had good reason to be especially concerned about demon possession, and she herself was widely suspected of being bewitched. She was bedridden for some time and was obviously ailing, and there were reports that exorcists came to minister to her in her private apartment. Though she was not explicitly recognized as possessed, as we shall see in chapter 3, Angela Caterina herself definitely believed that she was the victim of witchcraft.[47]

As for how they knew these various women were possessed, many Clarisses said the nuns' erratic behavior itself sufficed to convince them that they suffered from demon possession. Claudia Cabassi, for example, explained that on the basis of what she saw and heard with her own eyes and ears, there was no doubt that the women were "bewitched" (*maleficiata*) and "possessed" (*inspiritata*); the former term reflected her conviction that a witch was involved in these possessions.[48] Pressed further, Cabassi acknowledged that beyond her own direct observations she had also heard from three priests who had exorcized the nuns—Girolamo Cabassi, Agostino Bertesi, and Domenico Verrini—that the various women were the victims of witchcraft.[49]

Asked who was suspected of being responsible for the witchcraft, Claudia Cabassi demurred and insisted that one could not know for sure who was responsible for *maleficia*. But she then acknowledged that, like many others, she suspected that a certain nun had a hand in the diabolical afflictions that plagued Santa Chiara: Sister Dealta Martinelli. As subsequent testimony revealed, literally dozens of nuns shared these suspicions of Dealta, who was one of two principal suspects in this case, the other being the convent's former confessor, Angelo Bellacappa, who will be discussed at length in the next chapter.[50]

The Maverick Nun

Who was Dealta Martinelli? The daughter of Giuliano Martinelli and Riccialda Brusati, she had been baptized with the name Ginevra and was from Carpi, though the Martinellis were originally from a neighboring town in the Apennines. With a dowry of 200 *scudi*, she was admitted to the convent as a novice on 26 April 1609 and took solemn vows exactly a year later, at which time she chose the name Dealta.[51] Since nuns typically took vows when they were about sixteen, Dealta was probably about forty-four when this investigation began in 1638. She had held a number of offices in the convent and was serving as *refettorale*, the nun in charge of administering the refectory, when the Holy Office began this inquiry.[52]

Abundant testimony showed that Dealta was never very happy as a nun. It was common knowledge that Dealta had not wanted to join a nunnery but was forced to take the veil by her father, with encouragement from her sister Ippolita, another Clarisse who, at sixty-two, was considerably older than Dealta.[53] True, before taking vows, Dealta, like all soon-to-be nuns, was examined by a cleric to ensure that she was becoming a choir nun of her own volition. To no one's surprise, he concluded that she was taking vows not because of any pressure from her mother or father or from any mundane fear but only out of the desire to serve God.[54] This nunnery was full of women from wealthy backgrounds who had been strongly pressured by their families to take religious vows. Most of them either internalized the aims of their families or at least accepted eventually the religious life as their destiny, but Dealta apparently never adapted well to life in a monastery. She was said to participate less in the daily liturgical services than any other nun in the convent, though she did become more diligent in her attendance after accusations of witchcraft started circulating against her.[55] Several nuns reported having heard Dealta say that she had not entered the convent willingly and would never remain there of her own volition. Though she for the most part kept her antipathy to monastic life to herself, on several occasions Dealta had said to a number of sisters that if given the chance, she would leave the nunnery and return to her family home.[56]

Apart from her distaste for the monastic life, a principal source of suspicions against Dealta was the fact that she maintained close ties with so many people outside the convent. When asked if Dealta had intimate friendships with anyone inside or outside the nunnery, one nun replied that Dealta had no close friendships in the monastery since no one could stand being around her very much.[57] By contrast, she seemingly had countless friends outside Santa Chiara. To the modern reader, having friends would not in itself seem to be any cause at all for suspecting misdeeds, but to nuns living in a cloistered community, Dealta was far too attached to many people outside the convent. Nuns of all orders were expected to detach themselves from inordinately strong ties to their families and friends, respecting the instructions of David: "Hear, O daughter, consider, and incline your ear; forget your people and your father's house" (Psalms 44 [45]: 10).[58]

In Counter-Reformation Europe, nuns were in fact warned about the dangers of having excessively close friendships (*amicizie*) with anyone in particular, either inside or outside the convent. A nun's only strong relationship was to be with God, and she was supposed to have the same ties with all her fellow nuns, avoiding special intimacy with any of them. Friendships with people outside the religious community were feared as a source of corruption, of worldly concerns and vices that would distract from the religious vocation. Even within nunneries, strong friendships between nuns were deemed dangerous because they might divert attention from the worship of God, spawn lustful relationships, and upset community stability by creating factions. Try though they may, religious leaders in Europe never succeeded in eliminating entirely the external influences on or the divisive factions within convents.[59]

In this case, Dealta's friendships with outsiders were a source of real concern. The Clarisses all agreed that for years there had been a steady parade of visitors—male and female alike, rich and poor, clerics, town dwellers, and peasants—who came to visit Dealta. They would come to the *ruota* (turntable), immediately adjacent to which there was a parlor with a window where nuns could meet with visitors who remained on the other side of a grate, forbidden from actually entering the convent. The *ruota* proper, a staple of convent architecture, was a type of rotating receptacle, built into the wall, which allowed one to send objects into or out of the convent without parties on either side touching or even seeing each other.[60] Everyone agreed that Dealta received far more visitors than any other nun, and her excessive socializing with outsiders scandalized the other residents of Santa Chiara.[61] Sister Alsuinda Malaspina, fifty-five, expressed to Fiscal Giudici her strong disapproval of these friendships, a view shared by many other nuns: "I know for sure that she is asked to come to the turntable several times every day, which all nuns find most disgusting. It seems to us that this is not appropriate behavior for a female religious."[62] Malaspina and other nuns of Santa Chiara had fully assimilated the Counter-Reformation belief that nuns really needed to be protected from the dangers of corruption of the world—for female religious, the cloister was the only safe place to live. The close relationships that Dealta maintained with people outside the convent showed that her heart just was not into monastic life.

Among those who frequently called on Dealta were some Franciscans, Augustinian friars, and parish priests. The continuous passage of male visitors, even if many of them were clerics, in itself seemed highly suspect to her fellow nuns. To make matters worse, some of the male clerics Dealta frequented had rather bad reputations. She reputedly had an intimate relationship with Fra Francesco Maria Morisi,[63] an Observant Franciscan who had been tried by the Inquisition of Modena beginning in March 1636 for soliciting women in the confessional. The perquisition of his cell revealed some obscene letters, and at least one love letter from an unidentified nun at Santa Chiara. Morisi, who turned forty-two in 1638, acknowledged that he formerly had a "close friendship" with that nun, who was almost certainly Dealta. Refusing to confess to solicitation even under torture, Morisi was released from prison in February 1638 but suspended from hearing confessions.[64] Another priest she frequented was Claudio Brusati, also a Franciscan, who was briefly imprisoned by the Inquisition of Modena on suspicion of practicing astrology.[65] And a third close Franciscan friend was Valerio Trionfanti, whom the Inquisition tried but acquitted in 1628 for allegedly using love magic with a laywoman named Laura Coccapani. Laura and Valerio reportedly sent letters to each other through Dealta, and everyone agreed that facilitating an affair between a clergyman and a woman was hardly an appropriate activity for a nun.[66] By the spring of 1638, Dealta's critics perhaps took pleasure that, as suspicions against her grew stronger, very few friends now called on her.[67]

Dealta's frequent visits amounted to a violation of the Clarisses' Rule. The Rule, many aspects of which admittedly were not strictly enforced in Santa Chiara, forbade sisters to speak at the grate of the parlor without the permission of the abbess or vicaress. Even then, a sister was not supposed to speak to visitors without the presence of two other sisters, but both these requirements had largely been ignored at Santa Chiara. A curtain was to cover the grille from the inside at all times, a practice that definitely was not enforced, as testimony often indicated that sisters could see their visitors.[68] The "Constitutions" of Clarisses, outlined after the Council of Trent, declared that when nuns spoke at the parlor, they were not to indulge in idle and mundane chatter. All words "that come out of their mouths are to be honest, useful, and edifying, appropriate for use by the servants and spouses of Christ." They were also to avoid long conversations and were not to become too intimate with either laymen or laywomen.[69] Although Santa Chiara was notoriously lax in enforcing monastic rules, Dealta Martinelli was really testing the limits with the sheer number of visitors she received.[70]

Rumors abounded that other members of the Martinelli family had a penchant for dabbling in magic. Dealta had two brothers, Arcangelo and Gasparo, and gossip suggested that they, especially Arcangelo, experimented with magic.[71] Arcangelo was suspected of having procured some baptismal water and oil for magical purposes. In and of themselves, such suspicions might imply that he was involved only in sorcery. Although both sorcery and witchcraft supposedly involved casting magical spells, conventional wisdom tended to distinguish them by claiming that the former could be either beneficial or maleficent whereas witchcraft was, by definition, harmful to others. Some Clarisses, however, also believed that he had played a role in the possessions of Santa Chiara, which implied that he was engaged in witchcraft and casting harmful spells.[72] Early modern Europeans commonly believed that witchcraft was hereditary, and the hints that Dealta's siblings were witches or sorcerers exacerbated suspicions against her.[73]

In short, even without any evidence directly pertaining to witchcraft, Dealta was apt to be a suspect if, as the exorcists had concluded, the witch resided in or near the convent. She was suspect because she associated with so many people in the outside world, including many males and, as more than one nun noted, some low-life females. The fact that she was unhappy in the convent and had close family members who were rumored to practice witchcraft further fueled suspicions. Moreover, for the past two years, she was described as more withdrawn than ever from her fellow nuns, most likely a response to the rumors circulating that she was a witch.[74]

Not least among her accusers was Princess Angela Caterina d'Este, the powerful former abbess. A theme repeated by many witnesses was that Dealta and, perhaps even more so, Ippolita Martinelli had strong ill will toward Angela Caterina. A nun asserted that every time Dealta saw the princess or heard her name mentioned, she was wont to say, "Is it possible that this monastery will ever be free of this nasty woman?"[75] A few nuns testified that shortly after the young bewitched Paolina Forni died, Angela Caterina came into the refectory one day, leading her young niece by the hand. Some reported hearing Ippolita say in a threatening, though vague, manner that the abbess had better watch out.[76] Ippolita was also heard saying that although the princess was now hale, hearty, and assertive, the time would come when Angela Caterina would be punished by "the hand of God."[77] The antipathy was mutual, as Angela Caterina was quite open about her aversion to and distrust of the Martinelli sisters.[78]

Some witnesses also avowed that Dealta actively pursued friendships in a suspicious way with some of the younger Clarisses. Sister Grazia Lupagnini, thirty-three, reported that some years ago Dealta had earnestly asked her to be "her maiden [*putta*] and her friend." On several occasions, Dealta promised that if she agreed to be her maiden, Lupagnini would be the happiest woman and would receive all the flowers in the world. Lupagnini, however, obeyed the command of Princess Angela Caterina, who forbade her to be friends with Dealta.[79] Since Lupagnini was reporting this as suspicious behavior, little imagination is needed to surmise that Dealta supposedly had romantic inclinations toward the younger nun, a fear that the princess-abbess obviously shared. Dealta allegedly made similar aggressive overtures for the friendship of another young nun, Claudia Cabassi, twenty-eight. Sister Maria Calefi, also twenty-eight, gave testimony that strongly implied that Dealta had been lusting after Cabassi several years ago. According to Calefi, Dealta was deeply attached to Cabassi and desired the latter as her "companion" and as her maiden. According to Calefi, Dealta had told Cabassi that if she wanted to spend time with her in her cell and be her companion, she would give Cabassi all the pleasures and joys imaginable and make her the happiest woman in the world.[80] Regardless of whether Dealta really showed sensual inclinations for Lupagnini or Cabassi, this testimony certainly could have reinforced the fears of many early modern clerics that erotic relationships might develop between female religious.[81] Moreover, these descriptions definitely played into the stereotype of the lustful and "perverted" witch, whose sexual proclivities violated conventions set by canon and civil law.[82]

This evidence also pointed to the important role that cells could play in cultivating close ties, or strong suspicions, among nuns in Santa Chiara. Unlike some other Italian convents, Santa Chiara did not shift from sleeping in a communal dormitory to individual cells.[83] They still slept in one big room, but each nun at Santa Chiara had a small cell or oratory where she could go for prayer and contemplation. Tinti described them as quite small, large enough to hold a trunk for some personal effects and a small kneeling stand for prayer but too small for a bed.[84] Although the cells were apparently intended as a place for solitary prayer, they also were the best sites in the convent for private conversations between nuns.

Claudia Cabassi, an alleged object of Dealta's affection, recounted a conversation that had taken place a dozen years earlier in Dealta's cell, which caused her and others to harbor strong suspicions about the maverick nun. She asserted that on that occasion Dealta invited the young Cabassi to go with her to a witches' sabbat:

> After becoming a professed nun, I was once in Dealta's cell, and we started talking about witches. She told me that if I wanted to go to a sabbat [*striazzo*], she would take me there. She knew how to do so, as did other people she knew. [Dealta] told me that I would experience great pleasures and satisfactions there. And she told me these things with great pleasure and joy, and all that day she talked about this subject, saying that if I were with her, I would experience all the pleasures I could imagine and all the satisfaction that one can desire and I would be entirely golden. . . . And to tell Your Honor the truth, she urged me so strongly that I promised I would go with her; her promises and words made me want [to go to the sabbat]. But I later repented of this wish and told her that I was afraid to remain stranded in those meadows—which supposedly exist out there—if I uttered the word "Jesus." [Dealta] then told me to keep quiet [about all this], telling me that she was just joking [about going to a sabbat]. . . . I remember

that she also told me that in a meadow, foods of every sort were laid out and that the demons there were well dressed and they provided every sort of pleasure. And what gave me the most cause to think . . . was the great enthusiasm with which she recounted these things, and this is why I became suspicious of her.[85]

A few other witnesses reported that Dealta had characterized participating in a sabbat as a "sweet thing," but Claudia Cabassi was the only Clarisse who claimed that Dealta seriously expressed the desire to attend a sabbat.[86]

Regardless of whether Dealta actually said these words, this vivid description shows that Sister Claudia Cabassi had assimilated the most important ideas concerning the witches' sabbat. The concept of the sabbat was understood as a complete inversion of the Christian Mass, at which witches supposedly gathered at night to worship the devil.[87] With considerable precision we can trace the origins of this belief to the first half of the fifteenth century in the Alpine regions of Switzerland, Italy, and Savoy, an area that witnessed the first large hunt and that, not insignificantly, was home to a considerable number of Waldensians, a group considered heretical by the Roman Catholic Church. Works written by a variety of fifteenth-century authors—a lay chronicler, the Dominican theologian Johannes Nider, a lay judge, and a secular priest—revealed the most fundamental elements of the sabbat. It was believed that witches might apply ointments or powders to their bodies in order to fly even considerable distances at night to gather at the sabbat, where they renounced their Christian faith and paid homage to the devil by kissing his anus. At these encounters, they allegedly also sacrificed babies and ate their flesh, participated in orgies with other witches and demons, and received unguents and powders to kill or harm other people through maleficent spells.[88] These purported actions, along with desecrating the cross or the communion host, remained the most important elements of the concept of the sabbat throughout the period of the great witch-hunts. The sabbat has been aptly described as the trait that most distinguished early modern witchcraft from medieval sorcery, the latter referring to individuals (not groups) who allegedly manipulated occult powers.[89] The belief in the sabbat was of paramount importance in the dramatic expansion of witch-hunting in the early modern period. As more and more authorities came to believe that witches congregated to worship the devil, they increasingly tried to force suspects to identify others who participated in the diabolical cult.

Cabassi's description of the sabbat bore a strong resemblance to those found in the writings of various Italian authorities on witchcraft. Many spoke of banquets with tables loaded with every sort of good food and drink available, and demons were often said to be handsome, well-dressed men. Although Cabassi did not explicitly refer to orgies, it took little imagination to include sexual pleasures among the possible delights that Cabassi could experience if she agreed to go with Dealta. The exorcism expert Girolamo Menghi, an Observant Franciscan who spent much of his adult life in nearby Bologna, wrote that at a certain point in the sabbat, the devil commanded the demons and witches to start lewdly dancing together, each witch paired with a demon. Then they wined and dined on the most exquisite cuisine imaginable, consuming as much as they desired. After the feast, the torches were dimmed and each demon assumed the form of a man and took a female witch—or, if male witches were present, the demon took the form of a female—and all the couples fornicated.[90] Similarly, Candido Brognolo and others described nocturnal meetings where demons and witches played games, sang, danced and jumped about, feasted, and took part in orgies.[91]

Cabassi's specific concern about uttering the word "Jesus" at the sabbat also reflected the ideas of demonologists and exorcists. Menghi indicated that appeals to God through words or gestures could abruptly end a sabbat. He recounted the story of some female peasants from southern Italy who had taken part in sabbats. Having learned of their night travels, the husband of one of the women expressed the desire to attend one of these meetings. One night he and others put unguent on their bodies, climbed atop what appeared to be very large sheep, and were transported very quickly to a place where a great number of people had congregated. They sat down to take part in a sumptuous banquet, and the peasant man asked for some salt to sprinkle on his food. He repeated this request two or three times, though it was often believed that salt was not found at the banquets of sabbats because it was used in the sacrament of baptism.[92] Finally, someone did give him some salt and the man said, "May God be blessed for this salt." With those words everything disappeared—the tables, the food and drink on them, the great torches that had illuminated the feast, the witches and the demons, all were gone. The man found himself alone, nude, terrified, and shivering in the dark beneath a tree where he spent the rest of the night. The next day he met some shepherds who informed him he was near the town of Benevento, more than a hundred miles from his own village. The shepherds gave him some clothes and he set out for home by foot. When he finally arrived home ten days later, he denounced his wife and three other women, all of whom eventually confessed and were burned as witches.[93] Witnesses at trials elsewhere in Europe also reported that sabbats suddenly disappeared upon uttering the word "Jesus" or making the sign of the cross.[94]

Certain historians argue that belief in the sabbat was essentially limited to the clerical and judicial elites and that for early modern common folk the concept of witchcraft consisted almost exclusively of *maleficia* with virtually no mention of the devil.[95] Others have warned against a sharp dichotomy between elite and popular attitudes toward witchcraft.[96] By the time of the Santa Chiara case, many common folk in fact had ideas concerning the sabbat that had much in common with those expounded by witchcraft experts. Even if the idea of the sabbat first appeared among the clergy, the descriptions of sabbats in many witch-trials suggest that by the early seventeenth century there was at the very least a fusion of elements from ecclesiastical and judicial authorities, on the one hand, and European folklore, on the other.[97]

In the Carpi case the Clarisses who accused Dealta were very much aware of the concept of the sabbat. Significantly, none of the references to the sabbat was elicited by leading questions on the part of the Holy Office. Claudia Cabassi, for example, mentioned the invitation to attend a sabbat in response to Giudici's very vague query as to why she suspected Dealta. She and other Clarisses needed no prodding from an inquisitor to suspect that their nonconformist sister was involved in devil-worship. To be sure, the residents of Santa Chiara were definitely not humble peasants; virtually all of them came from wealthy, prestigious families and had educational opportunities that would have been the envy of almost all. Perhaps it should not be surprising that female religious had an awareness of the sabbat that reflected the views of some of the "experts" on witchcraft, many of whom were Catholic priests.

Though allusions to diabolical meetings were present in the Santa Chiara case, the sabbat was not the greatest concern of the Clarisses. Their suspicions against Dealta were based far more on the conviction that she was conducting *maleficia* than the fear that she was worshiping Satan. Early on, for example, some nuns suspected Dealta because, unlike all the other nuns, she did not come to see Ottavia Bendidio when she fell ill.[98] Several Clarisses were also suspicious because Dealta showed relatively little sympathy for the plight of the ten nuns who were still sick. Testifying in early May 1638, Dorotea Serafini Cabassi, twenty-two, gave a secondhand account of an episode that allegedly resulted in Veronica Maria Coccapani's becoming possessed. Coccapani had related that early one morning after matins about a year ago, she was cooking some meat, when suddenly she saw a shadow passing through the kitchen. The startled Coccapani fell to the floor and started screaming loudly, whereupon Dealta immediately appeared, seemingly out of nowhere, telling her there was no reason to be alarmed and repeatedly saying, "I am Sister Dealta." That, however, did nothing to calm the hysterical Coccapani, who allegedly told Dorotea Serafini that her bewitchment started at that moment, for which she held Dealta responsible.[99]

Dealta also brought suspicion on herself because she acted as if she knew who was and who was not possessed. Claudia Cabassi said that one day during Lent 1638, she and Caterina Maria Poggi were in the kitchen getting warm by the fire when Dealta Martinelli entered. Dealta began complaining that the demons were blaming her and that many nuns, too, believed she was the witch. She then told the other two nuns that she was sure that Cabassi was not bewitched but that Poggi was. Cabassi expressed surprise at these words, in part because Poggi had not yet demonstrated any behavior that suggested possession. Cabassi gently rebuked Dealta, insisting that "none of us knows who among us is or is not possessed."[100] Until that moment, Poggi had been feeling fine, but shortly thereafter she began suffering abdominal pains and exhibiting bizarre behavior, such as eating plaster. Contemporaneously, the demons, purportedly speaking through the mouths of the possessed nuns, said that Poggi, too, would be discovered *indemoniata*. Although in the end Poggi was not included among the possessed, the fact that Dealta claimed to know who was and who was not diabolically afflicted—she reportedly told some sisters that she could tell by facial expressions if a person was possessed—caused Cabassi and others to suspect that she was herself the author of these *maleficia*.[101]

Others were equally shocked when they heard Dealta say she was sure that Princess Angela Caterina d'Este was bewitched. The princess suffered from some unidentified ills for a considerable length of time, and one sister heard Dealta confidently say that Angela Caterina was in the same state of diabolical possession as Duchess Laura della Mirandola, the elder sister of Angela Caterina who married Alessandro Pico and was reputedly possessed for several years in the early 1600s.[102] One day shortly before Easter Dealta also told a nun that she was convinced that the young Princess Margherita d'Este and her servant Virginia were also both possessed.[103] Toward the end of Carnival 1638, many thought that Veronica Maria Coccapani—one of six Clarisses who were members of Carpi's Coccapani family—had been freed of her diabolical possession, but Dealta told another nun that she was sure that the demon had merely faked a departure. About a month later, Veronica Maria was again mercilessly tormented by demons.[104] All such talk was cause for suspicion. In early modern Europe, the ability to cure a person of *maleficia* implied the ability to inflict harm through spells. In Modena this attitude was reflected in the fact that most denunciations to the Holy Office against *maleficia* were made by former clients, mostly peasants, against would-be healers.[105] In the same manner, Dealta's knowledge that a person was bewitched could imply that she had a hand in the spell.

Testimony raised further suspicions that Dealta and Ippolita Martinelli were attempting to misuse sacred powers, an issue of great concern to the Holy Office.[106] Most notable in this regard, the Martinelli sisters were suspected of abusing sacramentals: ceremonies, benedictions, exorcisms, or objects that resemble or are related to the sacraments. According to Roman Catholic theology, the seven sacraments are automatically efficacious (*ex opere operato*). When an ordained priest administers the Eucharist, for example, recipients are certain that in consuming the host they are receiving the body of Christ and the grace of God. Sacramentals are inferior to the sacraments in that, unlike the latter, they do not work automatically. The successful use of sacramentals is contingent upon God's consideration of each specific case (*ex opere operantis*). The advantage of sacramentals was that they were much more accessible to nonclerics, and their use was more flexible than the more powerful sacraments. Most sacraments were tied to the life cycle and were experienced only rarely. Most believers partook of the Eucharist, the most frequently celebrated sacrament, at most four times a year or so. In early modern Catholic Europe, popular opinion held that the physical sacramentals–items such as bread, water, oil, or salt, which had been blessed or exorcised by priests–wielded some supernatural power, especially in the form of protection from harm. Once consecrated, these items could be removed from church and used where believers saw fit. Various objects associated with the Eucharist, such as the altar cloth or the corporal on which the priest placed the consecrated host were believed to possess healing power, as did objects that were placed illicitly beneath the altar during Mass.[107] If they fell into the wrong hands, however, these same objects could be misused, as holy candles, oil, or wine could purportedly be employed in love magic or harmful spells. According to testimony, the demons, speaking through the mouths of the possessed nuns, proclaimed that *maleficia* had been cast with the use of holy oil, an Easter candle, incense, water and "blood" from the chalice, and a consecrated host. Since Ippolita had served as sacristan, in charge of vestments and sacred utensils, and Dealta as her unofficial assistant, the Martinelli sisters had easy access to most of these items.[108]

Several Clarisses of Carpi articulated suspicions of abuse of sacramentals. When she served as sacristan, Ippolita Martinelli had ready access to holy oil, an extremely important element in many Roman Catholic rituals that is used in four different sacraments: baptism, confirmation, ordination, and extreme unction. Ippolita seemed particularly interested in procuring some holy oil, which is ordinarily consecrated by a bishop, usually on Maundy Thursday. Having served with Ippolita in the sacristy, Sister Anna Caterina Zuccari, twenty-four, reported that one year, about two weeks after Easter, Ippolita took a receptacle containing recently consecrated oil. Rather than returning the oil to its usual place in the sacristy, Ippolita kept it in a cupboard where it was more readily accessible. Zuccari and other sisters were concerned that she could have misused it.[109] In a similar manner, one day in the summer of 1637, Dealta supposedly asked Sister Maria Calefi, then assistant to the sacristan who had succeeded Ippolita, for some wine that was left over from the purification of the nuns, indicating that she wanted to give some to Ippolita, who was feeling ill.[110] This wine, though unconsecrated, was regularly used in sacred rites, either to cleanse the chalice or to "purify" the nuns' mouths after the celebration of the Eucharist. Because of these holy uses, this wine was viewed as a potent weapon that witches might use for maleficent rather than sacred purposes. Dealta's request accordingly could arouse suspicion against her.

Other Clarisses believed that Dealta was also using mundane objects as instruments of *maleficia*. Experts on witchcraft, such as Girolamo Menghi, long recognized that when spells were cast, witches usually used an "exterior sign, which is called a maleficent instrument, which they then hide in some secret place.... And as long as the sign stays there, with the demon assisting [the curse] according to the pact made with the witch, the *maleficium* will last and will vex some creature. Once the sign is destroyed, the vexation will also cease."[111] The issue of the instrument of the spell arose concerning the bewitchment of Sister Barbara Leonora Forni, *dama di compagnia* to one of Angela Caterina's nieces. According to Sister Clara Vittoria Massi, twenty-two, upon Dealta's arrival in church one day, a demon, speaking through the mouth of Barbara Leonora, declared that his mistress had just arrived. Forni herself replied, however, that she did not believe this, to which the demon noted that Dealta had asked Forni for her hair for the Madonna of San Giovanni. Later, at a moment that Forni was not vexed by demons, she told Massi that Dealta really had asked her for her hair, which, as with all would-be nuns, was cut short when she went through the "clothing" ceremony upon becoming a novice.[112] Although Dealta ostensibly wanted to use the hair to adorn a statue, hair was also believed to be a potent instrument of witchcraft. The hair, skin, blood, perspiration, and other bodily fluids or materials were believed to contain a person's "vital spirits," which could be manipulated to cause harm to that person. Even articles of clothing worn by a person were believed to be effective instruments used by witches for maleficent spells or love magic.[113] Since Forni was apparently now bewitched, Dealta's request for her hair was grounds for suspicion.[114]

For the nuns of Santa Chiara, undoubtedly the most important source of suspicion against Dealta was the alleged demonic declarations, through the mouths of at least nine of the possessed sisters, that Dealta was a witch. The demons became quite generous in sharing their knowledge; without any prodding from the exorcists, they pointed out to the nuns that Dealta was not very conscientious about taking communion. During Lent, most nuns took communion every Sunday. Emerenziana Duosi, fifty-seven, the current sacristan, reported that a devil said to her, "Sacristan, don't you see that there is a nun who does not take communion."[115] Tipped off by the demons, Duosi and several other nuns then noticed that Dealta was indeed not taking part in the Eucharist and was habitually leaving church at the start of the confession of sins (*confiteor*). Catching wind of these rumors, Ippolita Martinelli told her sister of the suspicions that various nuns had and exhorted her to go to confession and take communion in order to disarm her critics. On the third Sunday of Lent, Dealta did take communion but, according to various witnesses, immediately left church after receiving the host. This ran contrary to the Clarisses' custom of remaining in the choir through the purification, when the nuns received an ablution of the mouth with unconsecrated wine right after taking communion. Witnesses reported that later that day, when the nuns were again gathered together in the choir, the demons of all the nuns started jumping up and down and yelling that someone had removed the host from her mouth that morning. A demon named Zarfarello, who possessed the body of Sister Giulia Angelica Sertori, approached the communion window (in Giulia Angelica's body) and told the officiating priest about this misdeed. Some demons went beyond tattling and berated the officiating priest, asking why he had given communion to a witch.[116] One of the possessed, Clara Maria Amoldoni, in a lucid moment when she was not tormented by demons supposedly told the abbess that, having left the church, Dealta placed the host under a step in front of a gate that led to the garden. Though Amoldoni did not witness this action, she claimed that her demon, generously sharing privileged information, told this "to her heart." Amoldoni added that ever since, she immediately experienced pains each time she passed by that gate.[117]

The desecration of the host was a practice long attributed to witches by Roman Catholic theologians and lawyers. According to Catholic doctrine, once consecrated, the host is transformed into the body of Jesus and is therefore sacred. According to the demonologist Candido Brognolo, just as the sun was the most brilliant of the heavenly bodies, so the Eucharist was the most holy of mysteries among the sacraments. Consuming the host not only signified grace but conferred it as well. Accordingly, in order to show their contempt for their archenemy, witches relished all opportunities to desecrate the body of Jesus. In early modern popular culture, the host itself was also believed to be endowed with supernatural powers, and experts on demonology affirmed that both consecrated and unconsecrated hosts could be used for magical purposes, especially in regard to love magic. According to Brognolo, an unconsecrated host could be a powerful weapon in love magic, a consecrated host even more potent, and burning a consecrated host rendered it a still more powerful tool for winning the love of another.[118]

Other suspicions voiced against Dealta centered on her apparent ability to foresee the arrival of certain friends and to alter magically her own appearance. Some could not help but wonder if Dealta, a pariah in the convent, did not use some form of magic to enchant people outside the convent to make them love her. A few different nuns testified that when he was stationed in Carpi about two years ago, the military officer Count Camillo Forni called on Dealta every day. When Count Camillo came one day, Cherubina Giudici, who was in charge of the *ruota*, muttered that she did not understand why Dealta had so many callers since she was old and ugly. When Dealta was brought to him, Count Camillo said to Dealta, somewhat surprised, "They say that you are so ugly, . . . [but] you seem to me to have the face of an angel." The devils later revealed that they always made Dealta appear quite beautiful whenever a person came to call on her. Sister

Cherubina noted that the devil of Barbara Leonora Forni, herself the cousin of Count Camillo, added that Dealta always managed to be at the turntable whenever the count arrived, perhaps because she had used love magic to make him come to her.[119] Foreseeing future events and using love magic both suggested demonic powers and witchcraft.[120]

After learning of Cherubina's insult, Dealta reportedly sought revenge, declaring, "If I have an ugly face, she won't have a beautiful one either."[121] In October 1636 Cherubina was climbing the stairs to the doorkeeper's room, adjacent to one of the principal entrances to the nunnery. Near the top, she suddenly fell down the stairs and was seriously injured. Her face was badly smashed, and her arms and legs were also seriously injured. For more than a month, she was unable to move her hands or feet, and she was confined to the infirmary for more than six months after the accident. Suspecting that the fall was the result of a maleficent spell cast by Dealta, Cherubina, sixty-four, claimed that she felt as if she were lifted up by an unseen force, which she was sure was the devil, and then thrown down the stairs.[122] According to some nuns, Dealta was the first person to arrive after the fall, again appearing seemingly out of nowhere, but never went to visit Cherubina during her half year in the infirmary. And if this were not enough to arouse suspicions, the demons supposedly declared that Dealta was responsible for this almost fatal fall.[123]

The tumult in Santa Chiara reached a crescendo around Easter of 1638 as more and more nuns became convinced, thanks in part to the claims of the demons themselves, that Dealta was the witch who had cast spells on the suffering nuns. One witness, the lay sister Orsina Cipolla, thirty-two, claimed that Dealta's face, which she described as temporarily "deformed" during Holy Week, caused her great suspicion[124]–probably because she assumed that the distorted visage reflected the pain that witches and demons endured when faced with the resurrection of Jesus. On Easter Sunday, 4 April 1638, the nuns gathered to celebrate matins. When Dealta arrived in the choir late, the demons that possessed Barbara Leonora Forni and Clara Maria Amoldoni began shouting, "Here is our Lady. She could not come on time because she has been at a sabbat."[125]

The next day, the second Feast of Easter, or Easter Monday, marked a major incident that shook the nunnery and was probably the immediate cause of the Inquisition initiating the investigation. As many witnesses testified, after vespers numerous nuns were in the choir reciting the rosary in front of the venerated image of the Blessed Virgin of San Luca.[126] Several of the bewitched nuns–Barbara Leonora Forni, Cinzia Ciarlatina, Clara Maria Amoldoni, and Anna Maria Martinelli–were among those present. As they recited the prayers of the rosary, Dealta entered the choir through the large central doorway. Having come ostensibly to receive forgiveness, she knelt in prayer. Then, according to Maria Calefi:

Having risen to her feet, [Dealta] was going out by way of the small doorway, passing in front of the maidens who were saying the rosary. And when she was at the exit, she acted as if she had been called.... The nun then came back inside [the choir] and looked at the [possessed] maidens one by one. It seemed that she was looking for one of them, as if to say, "Is such-and-such a sister here? Did a certain sister call me?" This done, the demons in [the nuns'] bodies began screaming that her glance had cost them dearly. No sooner was Dealta outside the exit that all [the possessed nuns] fell to the floor, thrashing against the pavement, tearing off the veils from their heads, and remaining for a considerable time as if dead. All screamed that by looking at them, she had poisoned them and renewed the malefice. And they were so badly tormented and abused by the demons that we had to call for Father Girolamo Cabassi. Upon his arrival, all the spirits began screaming that it was Sister Dealta who had given them strength by renewing the malefice.[127]

Evidence from witch-trials and from the writings of the demonologists and exorcists affirmed that witches could cast spells merely by looking at their victims. Noting the power that the eyes wielded, the *Malleus Maleficarum* asserted that a gaze alone could cause considerable evil.[128] Citing earlier authors, Girolamo Menghi declared that the souls of certain witches were so morally depraved and maleficent that merely looking at people, particularly children who were tender and impressionable, could suffice to poison and torment their bodies.[129]

At other times as well, some of the possessed nuns were allegedly prone to falling into swoons at the mere sight of Dealta or the mention of her name. Testifying on 21 April, Maria Calefi said that the previous week, she was leading the possessed Sister Caterina Margherita Ronchi back to the dormitory after a meal. When Calefi merely uttered Dealta's name, Ronchi fell to the floor as if dead. When she came to, she told Calefi, "Please don't mention that name, which I can't stand hearing. [Whenever someone says it], I feel such a great pain that it's unbelievable." Calefi managed to get Ronchi to her feet, but when they passed in front of Dealta's bed, Ronchi again fell into a trancelike state.[130] On 7 May a nun avowed that earlier that day, the bewitched Sister Clara Maria Amoldoni was passing through the courtyard when she happened to look through a window and saw Dealta, whereupon Amoldoni immediately remained utterly immobile.[131]

In an incident that occurred on a Saturday shortly after Easter, all of the possessed in fact became most disturbed by the mere presence of Dealta. A new entrance had been made specifically for the purpose of taking the demoniacs into the exterior church, so the exorcists could conduct their rites there without entering the convent. On that Saturday morning, Dealta asked for and received permission from the sacristan, Emerenziana Duosi, to go take a look at the new entranceway. Dealta went into the bell tower from which she could watch the possessed women pass in front of her. When two of the ailing nuns caught sight of her, a real ruckus ensued. Purportedly screaming through the mouths of the possessed women, the demons erupted and yelled out that Dealta was in the tower. Thereafter, each time they went through the doorway, several of the bewitched women—especially Amoldoni, Forni, and Ronchi—fell to the floor in fits and some tore at and tried to eat the plaster covering the stone threshold. The exorcists then ordered the removal of the threshold, and Father Girolamo Cabassi concluded that a spell had been cast on the threshold and the plaster. After these were removed, the sisters could again go through the doorway without a problem.[132]

Dealta under Attack

Several days after the initial doorway incident, the possessed nuns or the demons themselves took matters into their own hands and physically attacked Dealta in the choir. The entire community of nuns was gathering there to celebrate the festival of St. Mark the Evangelist on 25 April. Before Mass started, the possessed were running all over the nunnery as if they were looking for someone. Ippolita got wind of this and, fearing the worst, strongly advised Dealta not to attend because the demons posed a threat to her. Dealta, however, insisted that she should go since it was a double feast, being both a Sunday and an important saint's day.[133] According to some witnesses, the demoniacs were actually waiting in groups at all three entrances to the choir. As soon as Dealta arrived for the service, they pounced on her and screamed that she was a witch. Roughing her up, the nuns dragged her to the center of the church and screamed, "Out of spite you have put us in such a state that we are suffering a thousand times worse than we would in hell."[134] But after this, it was no longer the nuns who were talking but rather the devils who spoke through the mouths of these frenetic sisters. According to Alsuinda Malaspina, the demons proclaimed:

> "It is God who commands us to reveal that you [are a witch]. He does not want this crime to remain hidden." And the spirit of Sister Paola Francesca Cimadori said to Dealta, "Oh, you scoundrel, you know that the host even spewed out blood." Dealta then said, "I place hope in my Lord," and the spirit replied to her, "Yes, your lord is Satan," adding, "you know full well that you wrote that note in your own blood." When she asked with what blood, [the demon] answered, "You know full well, you scoundrel." . . . Pulled to the floor, [Dealta] made a gesture as if to make the sign of the cross. But those who saw this—Sisters Portia Muzzi, Claudia Cabassi, and Grazia Lupagnini—[said] that this was not really a sign of the cross but another gesture that they did not recognize. Since she showed the intention of kissing that sign, the spirit of Sister Paola

Francesca told her, "You are quite right to kiss it and you know what sign it is." In short, they tormented her in a way that cannot really be described. And [the demons] told her that God demanded . . . that she mend her ways with her companions. If she did so, the most beautiful seat in the world would be reserved for her in heaven. If she did not, they have prepared [a seat] in hell for her made entirely of fire.[135]

Another nun added that in screaming at Dealta about the host that emitted blood, the demons were explicitly referring to the host that Dealta did not swallow and purportedly used for *maleficia*. God allowed the host to excrete blood in order to convince Dealta to repent and forswear her evil ways.[136]

Sister Portia Muzzi, forty-six, who was an eyewitness to this attack, provided some further interesting details. She, too, observed that while the nuns dragged Dealta across the floor of the choir, the demons, allegedly forced by God, told her that there was still time to repent. But at a certain point, the demon of Sister Flerida Cimadori, who was named "Ambassador," screamed out, "Be firm, be firm! I will help you." Dealta then responded, "Of course, of course. I will stay with you."[137] According to Muzzi's account, the demon Ambassador, having been commanded to lead the charge against Dealta, suddenly changed sides in the middle of this scene. Though the testimony made it appear as if he was able to free himself from God's command momentarily, an exorcist would have said that God was merely permitting Ambassador to express himself in order to show Dealta's true colors.

There were some discrepancies in the nuns' testimony. Some said as many as eight demoniacs assaulted Dealta, whereas others said only four were involved. Regardless of how many nuns took part in the attack, clearly Dealta was roughed up and humiliated in the presence of large numbers of Clarisses, and no one, not even Ippolita, tried to intervene to free Dealta from the clutches of the bewitched. For most, this inaction surely reflected their own suspicions of Dealta. For the minority who believed she was innocent, the fear of the demons and the possessed prevented them from lifting a finger to rescue Dealta. And the fear of guilt by association could have deterred some from coming to her rescue: helping a suspected witch could bring suspicions onto themselves.

The St. Mark's Day incident increased considerably fears about Dealta. According to most reports, the bewitched themselves initiated this attack and blamed Dealta for all their torments. But then quickly it was the demons who purportedly spoke, ordered by God to do so, and proclaimed that Satan was her lord. The note that was supposedly written in blood referred to a formal pact made with the devil, which was often said to be written in the witch's own blood, a sign of her pledging her soul to Satan. The fact that this written note was never found did nothing to make people less wary of Dealta. Later the demons started saying that Dealta had swallowed the paper on which she had written the pact.[138] Making the sign of the cross would of course signify a call for divine help, but the unknown gesture that Dealta reportedly made was interpreted as signifying a call for diabolical assistance. In short, not only did the possessed nuns who assaulted Dealta identify her as the witch, but many bystanders also interpreted her reactions as those of a servant of Satan.

A number of nuns also expressed shock at the manner in which Dealta reacted to this attack. Some noted that she made no effort to contradict the accusation that she had made a pact with the devil written in her own blood. Even more shocking was that she seemed quite serene throughout this ordeal. On this and other occasions, the demons made direct, aggressive accusations against Dealta, who in the presence of so many other sisters seemed utterly unfazed by the verbal and physical abuse. Although any other nun would have started screaming, crying, and pleading for mercy, Dealta allegedly remained composed throughout and did not shed a tear and indeed made no gesture other than that resembling the sign of the cross.[139] To many, calm reactions were themselves a sign of witchcraft, since it was commonly believed that the devil gave witches the power to suffer pains and indignities with equanimity. According to Girolamo Menghi, an exorcist should place his hands on the head of a suspected witch and pronounce the words, "by the tears of Jesus shed on the cross and those of Mary shed on his wounds" and all other tears shed for the love of God; if that person were innocent, she could weep; if she were guilty, she could not shed a tear.[140]

The Isolation of Dealta

Although the evidence at times almost suggests a plot against Dealta, it would be inappropriate to reduce the accusations against her to nothing more than the desire to harass and expel a nonconformist nun. Dealta would not have won a popularity contest in Santa Chiara, but clearly everyone believed in the reality of the diabolical possessions. After all, three of the afflicted women had died of their ills. We cannot know what the real cause of their deaths was, but they were certainly not feigning sickness. We also cannot understand the dynamics behind the diabolical accusations. One need not of course believe that demons actually dwelled inside the nuns' bodies and periodically rose up and caused their victims all sorts of physical and mental pain. Possession has been described as learned behavior that gradually takes shape as the "illness" tightens its grip on the victim.[141] All Clarisses believed that the ten women were possessed by demons, and this conviction was reinforced by the exorcists who concluded they were the victims of both witches and demons. Not much imagination is needed to see how profound psychic or spiritual torments could provoke the afflicted nuns to shout out the names of likely suspects and to believe that it was really demons, not themselves, who spoke.

Having never fit in at Santa Chiara, Dealta was understandably the nun most likely to be labeled a witch. Suspicions against her were not based on any particular incident but on a long trend of nonconformity that made almost everyone distrust her. Rumors at times distorted the way events actually took place. Geltruda Francesca Contessini had witnessed firsthand the kitchen incident involving Dealta and Veronica Maria Coccapani and had mentioned it to many of her fellow nuns. For Contessini this was a frightening experience that took place five years ago.[142] As noted above, Sister Dorotea Serafini Cabassi testified, incorrectly, that this was the moment at which demons entered the body of Coccapani and that it had occurred just twelve months ago. Though knowing that Veronica Maria Coccapani did not actually take ill until about four years later, Contessini nonetheless was recounting that incident to her colleagues and to the Inquisition because it demonstrated suspicious behavior on the part of Dealta. Moreover, the attorney Giudici definitely took all this evidence quite seriously, and at no point did he suggest that hearsay evidence was inadmissible.

The testimony also suggests that if she did not actually enjoy her bad reputation, Dealta Martinelli at least did little to ameliorate it. In a provocative work, Robin Briggs has claimed that while beliefs in and fears of witchcraft were endemic in early modern Europe, actual trials for witchcraft were not. Briggs found that people were reluctant to press charges out of fear of reprisals and lack of proof. Moreover, those who were brought to trial usually had bad reputations that stretched back for many years, and many apparently were able to use their ill repute to their advantage. If a poor woman knew that others thought she was a witch, she might, for example, "negotiate" with her neighbors for money or goods, making veiled threats if she did not get what she wanted.[143] Although Dealta would not have been motivated by the desire for financial gain, it nonetheless could have been to her advantage to have her fellow nuns at least a bit intimidated by her. Certainly there is ample evidence that, given the chance, Dealta would have preferred abandoning monastic life. If she could not really hope to be freed of her monastic vows, Dealta surely did want, as far as possible, to do as she pleased. Obviously it was very important for her to maintain contacts with many men and women outside the convent. An element of fear might have dissuaded some nuns from criticizing or trying to hinder this socialization.[144]

We cannot know if Dealta consciously wanted her fellow nuns to fear her, but her jokes about attending a sabbat, her refraining from responding directly to the demons' accusations, and her purported claim that she knew who was possessed and how to heal them, all could be viewed as giving her some leverage with the frightened nuns of Santa Chiara in order to do as she pleased. Another piece of evidence that lends itself to this interpretation is found in the testimony of Clelia Coccapani, fifty-four, who recounted a suspicious incident from the past winter, well after many had begun to suspect that Dealta was a witch. While chatting in the refectory, Clelia told Dealta that another nun had claimed that "the magical art is a science that one learns, but it must be studied." Dealta responded that one just has to "go there, and the devil will teach everything one wants to do."[145] Although her use of the word "there" (*là*) is ambiguous, Dealta was implicitly saying that she knew how to become a witch, which certainly exacerbated Clelia's fears about her. Even if she was not actively seeking to be a pariah and feared as a witch, Dealta did at times seem uninterested in deflecting the negative impressions that fellow nuns had of her.[146]

The assault on St. Mark's Day was the immediate cause of Sister Dealta's incarceration or, technically speaking, her forced isolation from the rest of the nuns. On 25 April, the very day of the attack, Archpriest Ludovico Niccolini, having seen the marks on her body from the assault, ordered that Dealta be held in isolation in the convent to protect her from the violent aggression of the demons. In a letter to Fiscal Giudici dated 1 May, Inquisitor Tinti confirmed that she should be "withdrawn" and held entirely apart from the other Clarisses.[147] Although aiming in part to secure the physical safety of Dealta, this order also revealed that Tinti, Giudici, and Niccolini harbored strong suspicions toward the maverick nun. In the same letter in which Tinti enjoined the incarceration of Dealta, he also called for a search and inventory of all her personal effects, undoubtedly in order to see if there were any items that might suggest that she was indulging in magic.[148]

To fulfill Tinti's order, Giudici, Niccolini, and a notary went to Santa Chiara on 1 May accompanied by two clerics as witnesses: Cesare Leonio, a doctor of canon and civil law; and Girolamo Cabassi, one of the exorcists who ministered to the ailing nuns and, as provost, second only to the archpriest among Carpi's secular priests. They were met by the abbess, who let them into the convent and led them to the last cell of the infirmary where Dealta was being held. In the presence of Dealta and Ippolita, the visitors took note of all her possessions, which proved to be surprisingly numerous for someone who had taken a vow of poverty.[149] Most of these possessions were quite predictable for a nun. On or around the bed were found a breviary and a good number of other devotional books (though no Bible).[150] Also found were a little cross made of wax, a small earthenware bowl containing holy water, and many loose cards—some handwritten but mostly printed—which had prayers, lyrics of religious songs, or sacred images on them. The investigators also had three nuns take all the stuffing out of the mattress but found nothing but straw inside.[151] This interest in the material found in mattresses and pillows reflected the learned and popular belief that bedding was a most likely place to put objects, such as needles or pieces of bones, for maleficent purposes. Objects such as these found in the mattress of the suspect or of the ailing person could be considered evidence of witchcraft.[152]

Giudici and the others then proceeded to conduct a search of things found on the person of Dealta herself. Around her neck she wore a cord to which was fastened a silver cross with an image of the Madonna holding baby Jesus, which, according to Dealta, contained a relic. The same cord also held a silver ring and a copper medal in honor of St. Helen. On her person were also found a small booklet in Latin that began with the words "Blessed is the man who trusts in the Lord," and an *Agnus Dei,* a small medallion of consecrated wax depicting the lamb of God that symbolized Jesus's sacrificial nature. Dealta had three rosaries with her, to which were variously attached a silver and a brass crucifix and some brass medallions. The manner in which Dealta bore these objects could be interpreted as reflecting a blurring between religion and magic; perhaps they served as a type of amulet to protect her from harm.[153] Elsewhere in the cell were found other breviaries, crosses, a vial with holy water, and a few more printed devotional cards. Dealta also apparently had plenty of things to snack on, as her cell had little baskets full of chestnuts, pine nuts, and walnuts. Having completed the search, Giudici informed the Martinelli sisters that under pain of excommunication, they were not to speak to anyone about this inventory.[154] This examination of Dealta's temporary cell surely could not have heightened suspicions and, if anything, should have diminished them. Nothing found in the cell appeared in any way to be an inappropriate possession for a Clarisse, and inquisitorial guidelines advised that the discovery of devotional books and other religious paraphernalia in the abode of witchcraft defendants was to their advantage and could help exonerate them.[155]

When, however, Giudici and Niccolini inspected a storage room the following day, the results were somewhat different. The room contained a large number of trunks, including one belonging to Dealta. Opening it, the clerics again found a number of items of a religious nature—a reliquary, several more *Agni Dei,* some glass rosary beads. Somewhat surprising is the amount of jewelry contained in the trunk: there were bracelets, pendants, rings, necklaces, many of which of course may have belonged to her before she took vows in 1610.[156] Of special concern was the discovery of an old communion host, broken in two and partially eaten by worms. The notary recorded that Dealta appeared quite uneasy when this host was found, and the investigating authorities immediately thought of the incident in which she left the choir immediately after receiving the host in her mouth and wondered whether this might be the same wafer.[157] If it had been consecrated—and there was no way of knowing that it had been—then according to Roman Catholic theology, the host would have been the body of Christ and deserving of the utmost care and respect. Since, as noted above, witches reputedly coveted hosts to desecrate, this find could have increased suspicions against Dealta.

Quite surprising was the large number of love letters and some love poems addressed to Dealta that were found in the trunk. The notary did not reproduce the entire text of the letters, and the clerical authorities did not try to identify the authors of these missives, mentioning only that these pieces were written by both laymen and friars. The notary quoted the words at the beginning and ending of each letter, one of which ended with the proclamation that Dealta's soul was "the nourishment of a weak heart."[158] A love madrigal addressed to both Dealta and Ippolita ended with the words "You both have my heart in your hands."[159] There were a couple other printed cards containing love verses, and another "amorous letter" that ended with the following melodramatic line: "the aim of this [letter] will be the kiss of the delicate mouth. Farewell, I tell you, farewell, oh my sweet enemy, farewell, farewell." This was signed by "Gabriele, the most devoted servant of Dealta."[160] In another letter addressed to the "light of my eyes," a certain Paolo Antonio expressed his love for "Sister Dealta."[161] A little basket contained a card with some amorous verses written on it. The author, whose heart was "suffering," drew a heart surrounded by flames and arrows under which he wrote, "I am burning, as you see."[162]

Although we do not know the content of the whole letters or the identities of the men who wrote them, the snippets reproduced here definitely suggest a romantic or even erotic love rather than spiritual love. Since they were all addressed to "Sister Dealta," the letters were clearly written after she had taken orders. The love letters obviously meant a lot to Dealta; otherwise she would not have kept them. The possession of love letters of course was in no way proof of taking part in witchcraft. It is also true that in other convents in seventeenth-century Italy, nuns and priests often developed amorous relationships, which included flirtatious visits, the exchange of love letters, and in exceptional cases, even the exchange of rings and marriage vows, though the relationships remained unconsummated.[163] The Holy Office did not pay undue attention to such relationships, most likely because, barring evidence of heresy or abuse of sacraments, it did not have jurisdiction over sexual offenses per se. Still, the love letters, together with her many visitors, could—and no doubt did—strengthen suspicions on the part of Giudici and Niccolini that Dealta was a nun of questionable morals. Also of interest were three locks of hair found among Dealta's personal effects.[164] These of course could have been kept purely for sentimental reasons, but, as noted above, people's hair supposedly could also be used as an instrument to cast maleficent spells against them or to assist in winning their love.

Ippolita's personal effects were also inventoried, and they revealed an impressive number of reputed relics, including two small folders that supposedly contained, respectively, the dried blood of a martyr and the dried milk of the Virgin Mary, the latter given to her by her brother Girolamo. Like Dealta, Ippolita also had preserved some locks of hair, some of which she identified as belonging to a certain Father Bartolomeo.[165] Although the half-consumed host and Dealta's love letters were surprising, the close examination of the possessions of the Martinelli sisters produced no "smoking gun."

Inquisitorial Dynamics and Guilt by Association

For the trials of most crimes, the victims, if able to testify, often provide the most important evidence against the accused. Believing they could provide invaluable insight to the nature of their ills and the likely cause of them, Fiscal Giudici eagerly wanted to question the nuns who were considered possessed. The Congregation in Rome, however, categorically forbade the interrogation of the afflicted nuns. The cardinals reasoned that if the nuns really were possessed, then one could never be sure if it was the nun herself who spoke or a demon who was speaking through her mouth. Since devils were the fathers of lies, one could never trust anything they said or, for that matter, anything uttered by a person whose body they possessed. Moreover, Cardinal Barberini maintained that even if the nuns were merely melancholic rather than possessed, one still could not assume that their melancholic humors would allow them to tell the truth.[166] As a possible solution to this dilemma, the archpriest asked if it were possible first to have the ailing nuns exorcized and then, once in their senses, interrogated. In a letter to the Congregation in Rome, Inquisitor Tinti opined that the archpriest's proposal might be a viable option, provided that the exorcists were not present at the interrogations.[167] In Loudun, where the investigation was conducted by a royal magistrate and judgment passed by a criminal commission of secular judges, the afflicted Ursulines were in fact allowed to testify when they were deemed in their right senses.[168] In August 1638 the "possessed" Clarisses told Inquisitor Tinti–at a time when they appeared to be in their senses–that if allowed to testify, they had some very incriminating things to say about Angelo Bellacappa, the former confessor. Tinti again inquired if he could question them after they were exorcized by a dependable, experienced exorcist who could affirm that the demons were not tormenting them at the moment. Predictably, the Congregation denied this petition.[169]

Fiscal Giudici was able to interrogate all nuns who were not possessed, however, and he consistently ended the interrogations, following standard inquisitorial procedures, by asking the witnesses if they were motivated to testify out of love or hatred or for clearing their conscience and giving honor to God.[170] The witness's answer to this question understandably influenced how much weight the inquisitor would give her testimony.[171] The witnesses invariably swore that they were impelled to testify only by the desire to have a clear conscience and to give glory to God. Typical was the answer of Clara Vittoria Massi, who insisted that she had no hatred toward either Dealta or

Bellacappa. She did concede, however, that she did not like some of the things Dealta had said about her or some of the pranks (*tiri*) that the confessor had pulled on her.[172] To ensure that their testimony was given full weight, accusers of witches throughout Europe went to pains to show an absence of malice on their part.[173]

Notorious for her many friendships outside the nunnery, Dealta seemingly had no friends in the convent. At any rate, no one admitted to being close friends with her. Already by late April 1638, only a couple weeks after the opening of this investigation, just being associated with Dealta Martinelli was enough to arouse suspicions of witchcraft. Ippolita in particular was suspect, largely because she was Dealta's sister and always defended Dealta against accusations of witchcraft. Based on hearsay, Claudia Cabassi reported that Ippolita had said that she did not know if Dealta was guilty but even if she were, she preferred being torn to pieces to testifying against her sister. Having served as sacristan when Bellacappa was confessor, Ippolita was also accused of carelessly handling sacred objects, such as the chalice and the cloths used for cleansing the cup after each use.[174] As noted above, the power of sacred gestures, words, and objects could purportedly be misused as part of maleficent spells. Ippolita's easy access to sacramentals aroused suspicions among some that she was manipulating supernatural powers with evil intent. In early May Giudici actually ordered that Ippolita, like her sister, be held in isolation. Inquisitor Tinti, however, wrote that she should be released since there were no grounds for her incarceration. Giudici nonetheless did not get around to releasing her until mid-June.[175]

Anyone who was inclined to give Dealta the benefit of the doubt in regard to witchcraft charges ran the risk of becoming herself a suspect. Apart from the Martinelli sisters, Dianira Bergamaschi was the nun most often suspected of playing a role in the possessions at Santa Chiara. More than one sister noted disapprovingly that during the past winter, Bergamaschi and Dealta often visited in each other's cells. One Clarisse was concerned merely because Bergamaschi did not like to hear other nuns say bad things about Dealta. She also fueled suspicions simply because she was quite upset by the St. Mark's Day attack. Doubts about Bergamaschi increased in mid-May 1638 when some demons reportedly identified her, too, as a witch, causing her to fear that she, like Dealta, would end up imprisoned.[176] The mentality of guilt by association kept growing, as many Clarisses began to believe that several fellow nuns were complicit in casting *maleficia*.[177]

When she was convoked on 23 May, Sister Dianira Bergamaschi defended Dealta but also wanted to distance herself somewhat from her. Bergamaschi, forty-two, said that she did not at all believe the demons when they implicated Dealta and bemoaned that "those devils are the ruin of this monastery." But asked about whether her testimony was swayed by love or hatred, Bergamaschi, whom others described as Dealta's confidante, replied:

> I have never had any close friendship with Sister Dealta.... In a way, all [the nuns] are my friends. I spent considerable time with Dealta during the novitiate, but not thereafter, Sir. Nor do I know much about her. It has been years since I've been in her cell, except one time during this past Lent. Sister Ippolita was also present, and we were there for an hour and talked about spiritual things.... Similarly, only one time did Sister Dealta come to my cell for a favor she asked of me. I believe that was after Easter, and the favor concerned some scarf buttons. And since that time, I don't believe that I have ever spoken with her.[178]

Others may have exaggerated the amount of time the two nuns spent together, but Bergamaschi may have been protesting a bit too much that she was not a friend of Dealta. Since she had been named by the demons and was suspected by some of her fellow nuns, Bergamaschi's reluctance to be closely associated with Dealta was understandable. Only a handful of nuns were willing to defend Dealta in any way when questioned before the Holy Office.

Although the nuns were not supposed to talk among themselves about the testimony they gave before the Inquisition, they almost certainly discussed among themselves the questions they were asked and the answers they gave. They nonetheless did know that their testimony was given in strict confidence, ordinarily heard only by the inquisitor—or for much of this investigation, the fiscal in his stead—and the notary who recorded the proceedings. Those who showed some sympathy for Dealta before the inquisitor were probably more reluctant to express these opinions in the presence of their peers.

The Reaction from Rome

Although all authorities in Carpi and Modena were increasingly convinced of the gravity of the diabolical attacks in Santa Chiara, the Congregation of the Inquisition was not happy with the way the case was proceeding. The cardinals were upset with the actions of Giudici, who, they thought, was too quick to believe that the ten nuns were diabolically possessed. Already in late May, the Congregation began demanding that Inquisitor Tinti go to Carpi to conduct the investigation himself with the assistance of the archpriest of Carpi rather than delegating this to Giudici. Be that as it may, Tinti did not personally take charge of the case until 1 July 1638.[179]

Still waiting for Tinti to shoulder the responsibility of directing the investigation, Cardinal Barberini attacked more directly the power that Giudici wielded, declaring that it was quite unacceptable for the fiscal advocate, a married layman, to be working independently in this case. The cardinal accused him of menacing the nuns by almost forcing them to bear witness against Bellacappa and others. Since Giudici was not a minister of either the inquisitor or of the archpriest of Carpi, Barberini declared that it was most inappropriate for him to be doing anything beyond assisting the inquisitor, as fiscals were supposed to do.[180] Barberini's disappointment with Giudici's performance undoubtedly stemmed more from the fiscal's credulity with respect to witchcraft than from the fact that he was a layman interrogating witnesses. Treatises on the Holy Office, written by respected inquisitors, noted that the office of fiscal was to be occupied by someone learned in both canon and civil law, a qualification that Giudici from all reports met. Although in Italy the fiscal was initially created to oversee the Inquisition's treasury (*fiscus*), the office quickly took on other responsibilities. Cesare Carena wrote in 1631 that in Italy the fiscal could not interrogate witnesses, unless he had been asked to do so by the inquisitor, which was definitely the case in the Santa Chiara investigation.[181]

Although Tinti did finally comply, he also defended the actions of Giudici. In a letter to the cardinals in Rome, he claimed that it was not at all true that the fiscal had coerced anyone to testify against Bellacappa or anyone else. Giudici did, at Tinti's command, post in the nunnery a general edict in which he exhorted the nuns to purge their consciences. If they were aware of some sins that were under the purview of the Inquisition, it was their duty to come forward and speak to the Inquisition authorities.[182] Tinti also complained about having to work with the archpriest, asserting that Niccolini's travels were keeping him away from Carpi for many days and thus delaying the investigation.[183] When Tinti did begin presiding over hearings in Carpi in July, the dynamics of the case did not change appreciably, and Giudici continued to participate alongside the inquisitor.

All told, in the spring of 1638 the sisters of Santa Chiara of Carpi were living in a state of terror. Although suspicions were overwhelmingly directed against Dealta, Bellacappa, and to a lesser extent Ippolita, all nuns were hypersensitive to words or gestures that could in any way raise suspicions of harmful magic. Some undeniable misfortunes had occurred in the convent, such as the deaths of three residents and Sister Cherubina's fall down the stairs, and fears were directed primarily against the nonconformist nun and the former confessor. The accusations made against Dealta (but not against the absent Bellacappa) could be viewed as a means of ridding, either deliberately or unintentionally, the community of an undesirable element.[184] In any event, the Clarisses were living in a constant state of fear as to who was responsible for these *maleficia*, who would be the next to fall ill, and who would be the next to die. The turmoil was so great that Princess Anna Beatrice, Angela Caterina's twenty-one-year-old niece, an *educanda* who had not taken vows, petitioned successfully in April to be allowed to leave Santa Chiara for another convent in Modena, taking her various servants with her.[185]

Moreover, though a few expressed skepticism as to the accusations by the demons, no one questioned the reality of the diabolical possession itself. When Dianira Bergamaschi said the demons were the ruin of the nunnery, she was clearly affirming that at that moment ten nuns truly were possessed. Faustina Comi, another Clarisse, defended Dealta, ignored Bellacappa, and decried that falsehoods were being presented as facts, but she did not deny the reality of the possessions. Although the Holy Office had been holding hearings regularly since 19 April, Ippolita Martinelli was not interrogated until 1 July. When Tinti questioned her a second time on 30 July, Ippolita bemoaned the insults that the demons had hurled at Dealta, especially on St. Mark's Day. Although it was obviously in her interests to reject the very existence of diabolical possession at Santa Chiara, Ippolita was absolutely convinced that it was demons, not the nuns themselves, who had maliciously attacked her sister.[186] The trial proceedings reveal no one who thought that the afflicted were suffering from natural maladies or feigning possession. Some did not believe what the alleged demons were saying, but no one doubted the evil spirits were actually speaking through the mouths of the miserable nuns. The one thing that all agreed upon was that there were diabolical spirits wreaking havoc within the cloistered walls of Santa Chiara.[187]

Chapter 3

THE CONFESSOR AND LOVE MAGIC

In 1627 Cardinal Ludovisi of Bologna commissioned the publication of a manual specifically for the confessors of nuns. The guidebook provided the following instructions for those clerics who had this special responsibility:

> The priest will always go to the confessional and deal with the nuns there just as if it were the first time he met them. By doing so, he will be able to hear confessions of the same nun for many years in a holy and exemplary manner. All told, I want to imply that [the priest] not treat the nuns with too much familiarity, even under the pretext of spiritual matters. Rather, every time that he goes to the confessional, he should speak with them seriously, as if he were a new acquaintance, just as he was at the time he began [hearing their confessions]. This is because the devil waits many years in order to kill in just an hour. From this it is clear that he should abstain from laughing and chattering with them, especially if he does not [naturally lead] an austere life.... He must be very cautious and prudent not to become too close to any one of them in particular—either because of her spirit or devotion, or because she has a fine intellect or leads an exemplary life—since, as St. Thomas affirmed, spiritual love can be converted into sensual love, if one is not on guard. Beyond this, [such behavior] quite often causes a scandal among the other sisters.[1]

If he read these instructions, Father Angelo Bellacappa, one of two principal suspects in the Santa Chiara witchcraft case, definitely did not take them to heart.

At first glance, Bellacappa appeared an unlikely person to be accused of witchcraft. Born in Parma in 1594, Bellacappa came from a well-established family. His maternal grandfather was a court gentleman (*gentiluomo di corte*) in the service of the princes of San Secondo, a small town near Parma, and for a period his father served as manager (*commissario*) of property owned by Milan's illustrious Borromeo family. In October 1610, a week before his sixteenth birthday, Bellacappa took vows in an Observant Franciscan monastery near Rimini. He studied theology and philosophy in various locations in the Observant Franciscan province of Bologna and quickly developed a reputation among his fellow *Zoccolanti* as a very learned cleric.[2]

Prior to his charge as confessor at Santa Chiara, Bellacappa had enjoyed a very impressive career in his Franciscan order and was entrusted with a number of important positions. The Observant Franciscans of the province of Bologna emphasized preaching and theological studies, and Bellacappa excelled at both. In 1628 he was named *Lettore Generale di Teologia*, charged with teaching theology to his fellow *Zoccolanti*, a clear sign of his reputed expertise in theological matters. In 1632 he was elected one of only four *Definitori Provinciali*, who advised the provincial minister, the superior for the entire province of Bologna. At this time the province included throughout Emilia and Romagna thirty-three monasteries and about four hundred to five hundred Observant Franciscans, who all elected the *Definitori*. Bellacappa's election to this post bore witness to the high esteem he enjoyed in the order. The same year he was also named *Concionatore* (preacher) and *Esaminatore*, becoming thus responsible for "examining" everything written or said by his fellow provincial Franciscans to make sure there was nothing that appeared in any way unorthodox. In 1635 Bellacappa was again named *Esaminatore* and was also given the title of *Predicatore Provinciale* (provincial preacher), who ranked above any friar who was simply named a *Predicatore* or *Concionatore*. Only the finest preachers were given the title of *Predicatore Provinciale*, which bestowed on them the right to preach anywhere in the province. He authored at least two manuscripts on canon law, one of which may have been published.[3] Regardless of where he served within the province of Bologna, Bellacappa had been admired especially for his knowledge of Roman Catholic theology and for his preaching abilities. His fellow Franciscans also obviously thought he was a competent administrator, naming him guardian of the Observant monastery in Parma in 1632.[4]

For most of his clerical life, Bellacappa had thus principally been engaged in teaching theology to his fellow Observant Franciscans. As a cleric, Bellacappa had surely heard confessions on occasion, but his stint in Santa Chiara was apparently his only formal appointment as a confessor.[5] In 1633 Bellacappa served as the convent's interim confessor, and at Princess Angela Caterina's recommendation, the "very learned theologian" and "most eminent preacher" was named the official confessor to the nuns of Santa Chiara in February 1634 and remained in that capacity until November 1636.[6] During that period, Bellacappa resided in the Observant monastery of San Nicolò of Carpi, which until recently had been responsible for governing Santa Chiara. Bellacappa in fact was the last Observant Franciscan to serve as confessor to the Clarisses; subsequent confessors were all secular priests or Jesuits.[7]

As confessor to a nunnery, Bellacappa did not ordinarily have access to the interior of the cloister. Most often he met with nuns in one of Santa Chiara's two confessionals, one of which was on the ground floor, the other just above it on the upper floor.[8] (Unfortunately, the extant floor plans, reproduced in chapter 1, give no indication as to precisely where the confessionals were located.) The confessor had access to both confessionals from the exterior, while the nuns remained inside the convent, separated from the priest by a grille. The confessional was itself a creation of the Counter-Reformation. Archbishop of Milan Carlo Borromeo (1538–84), who aggressively promoted Tridentine reforms and was canonized in 1610, was responsible more than any other person for the introduction of the confessional, which eventually took hold throughout Europe. Although many have assumed that the confessional was a means of making confession more private,[9] it actually was intended to ensure that people could confess their sins publicly, in a church in plain view of other parishioners, but in the utmost secrecy. The confessional provided a physical separation between the priest and the penitent in the form of a panel, often including a grille. Out of earshot of everyone else, the priest and confessants could be very close to each other but, to avoid scandals, were incapable of touching or, in many cases, even seeing each other.[10] Testimony reveals that in Santa Chiara, nuns regularly went to the confessional not only to fulfill the sacrament of penance but also, either individually or in groups, merely to discuss spiritual concerns and even just to chat with Bellacappa.

The physical separation between priest and nuns was supposed to be maintained at all times. Accordingly, when Bellacappa or another priest was administering the Eucharist, the nuns were in the choir, separated by a screen from the exterior church, where the priest and the lay congregation gathered, and received the host through a small opening in the screen. The confessor regularly received meals that were prepared in the convent, but he always ate in an exterior room, as nuns passed the meals to him through a window. The priest, like other visitors, could also talk with nuns in the parlor, the visitor being on one side of a grille, the nun on the other. In short, other than the rare occasions when he had to administer extreme unction to a nun on her deathbed, the confessor never entered the convent and, in theory, was always physically separated by a screen or grate from the nuns under his spiritual charge. As we shall see, this did not prevent Bellacappa from getting into mischief.

The main reason that many suspected Bellacappa of witchcraft was that virtually all the nuns who were deemed possessed were those who went to see him most often. With the exception of the two oldest afflicted nuns—the cured Margherita Felice Castagnini, thirty-nine, and Maria Maddalena Colevati, fifty—Bellacappa was said to have been in love with all the currently bewitched nuns. Most of the evidence given to show that Bellacappa had strong affection for the now afflicted nuns was hearsay. But even his defenders acknowledged that it was undeniable that these nuns, almost all of whom were young, spent an undue amount of time with the confessor. Those whom he most loved and saw most often were Sisters Giulia Angelica Sertori (age thirty-nine), Barbara Leonora Forni (twenty), Caterina Margherita Ronchi (twenty-one), Veronica Maria Coccapani (twenty-four), Clara

Maria Amoldoni (twenty-four), Anna Maria Martinelli (seventeen), Paola Francesca Cimadori (thirty-five), Geltruda Francesca Contessini (twenty-two),[11] and Obizza Foschieri (thirty-eight).[12] Of these nine, all but the last two were supposedly bewitched, and Bellacappa reportedly saw all of them very often.[13] A day did not go by that he did not see at least some of these women, and many met with him once or twice daily. Sometimes they came to see Bellacappa in groups of two or more, but most often they visited the priest on a one-on-one basis.

These visits always took place in one of the two confessionals in the nunnery and were clearly in direct violation of the code of behavior recommended for confessors of nuns. Barring some urgent need, the priest was not even supposed to go to the convent except on days designated for hearing confessions. The guidelines advised that nuns were not supposed to confess more than once a week, and the confessor was to warn them that diabolical temptation was behind going to confess too often "at the feet of the confessor." The female religious were supposedly in greater danger than the priest of being tempted by demons, since each of them dealt with only one priest whereas he met with all the nuns.[14] The author of the guidelines was implying that the confessor was more used to encounters with members of the opposite sex than were the nuns and therefore enjoyed greater immunity to demonic temptation. In any event, if nuns were to avoid going to see the priest too often to confess their sins, obviously they should not spend undue amounts of time pursuing matters unrelated or, much worse, contrary to their spiritual health.

A number of witnesses reported that Bellacappa often sent for various young nuns when they did not go to him at their own initiative. By sending for them to come meet him individually and even by accepting their requests to meet him privately, Bellacappa was again disregarding the detailed guidelines for confessors of nuns.[15] Many witnesses added that some of the nuns indicated that they did not want to go see Bellacappa, but went anyway when called, as if compelled to do so by a spell. One sister, Anna Caterina Zuccari, twenty-five, was convinced that the young women had to be under a spell, insisting that their visits were so frequent they could not possibly be natural. In particular, Caterina Margherita Ronchi, Giulia Angelica Sertori, and Clara Maria Amoldoni really appeared not to want to see the confessor but could not stop themselves from going to him.[16] Sister Olimpia Corradi agreed that these various nuns seemed enchanted and observed that there was also strong jealousy among them, as they all competed with one another for the love of the confessor. According to Corradi, she and other older nuns were especially shocked that these young women were totally disregarding their vow of obedience by continuing to frequent Bellacappa. In light of this unfathomable socializing with Bellacappa, Corradi was absolutely convinced that Bellacappa was the "necromancer" responsible for bewitching these nuns.[17]

Although a clergyman might seem at first blush an unlikely suspect of witchcraft, Bellacappa was far from the only cleric to have to fight accusations of witchcraft and magic. In the previous century many priests and friars had been investigated for magic in Emilia and Romagna, in part because they had easy access to sacramentals that could be misused in spells. Clerics were purportedly known to supply holy oil for love magic, either for themselves or for others. Many were also accused of baptizing objects for magical purposes. Such baptisms, which were strictly forbidden, reflected the belief that even mundane objects acquired magical powers through this abuse of a sacrament.[18]

In the case at hand, many people thought that the Clarisses' woes stemmed from maleficent spells cast by Dealta, but a good number at Santa Chiara believed that Bellacappa was employing a type of love magic to oblige those he loved to come see him. Many sisters clearly had their doubts about both. Moreover, there could be a real convergence between love magic and *maleficia,* as the effects of the former were believed just as harmful as the latter. At least some Clarisses suspected collusion between the ex-confessor and the maverick nun. Several reported that Bellacappa quite often asked Dealta, and to a lesser extent her sister, Ippolita, to fetch the young nuns he wished to see. Bellacappa was the confessor for most of Ippolita's three-year term as sacristan, which had ended in 1636. As sacristan, Ippolita had reason to meet with the confessor fairly often, and when interrogated in late July 1638, she confirmed that she had often beckoned nuns to come see Bellacappa at his request. Ippolita added that she did not know Bellacappa very well since apart from preparing the liturgical vestments and such, she did not have a whole lot to do with him. True, she did notice that certain nuns spent a good bit of time with him and acknowledged that she often went to fetch them herself–she explained that the sacristan was to serve the confessor, and if he asked her to summon a nun, she did so without inquiring why.[19]

During his first year as confessor, Dealta Martinelli was the nun on whom he most relied for leading young nuns to the confessionals. For example, she reportedly always accompanied Caterina Margherita Ronchi to the confessional and even encouraged the then seventeen-year-old to love Bellacappa. Bellacappa and Dealta were said to have a very close friendship during his first year at Santa Chiara,[20] but the two of them subsequently had a falling out, perhaps because he did not want her associating with Fra Francesco Maria Morisi, a fellow Observant Franciscan who was tried for solicitation.[21]

Although the possessed women could not be interrogated, a large number of other nuns asserted that Bellacappa's behavior in the confessional left much to be desired. In their testimony, most of which was given in May 1638, many younger Clarisses accused Bellacappa of flirting with them or of trying to caress their hands or faces. Cassandra Felice Poggi, twenty-four, recalled the very first time she confessed to Bellacappa. She was on her knees, but before the confession started, Bellacappa asked her to lift the cloth that covered the grate. When the reluctant nun complied, the friar told her she was very attractive and had beautiful eyes. Returning the cloth to its original position, Cassandra Felice gave her confession and left, rather upset by these compliments, which, even if they fell short of solicitation, definitely seemed out of place in the confessional.[22] Already in the early fourteenth century, Church authorities in Tuscany had forbidden priests to look into the faces of women while they were confessing, and several post-Tridentine authors urged confessors to avoid eye contact with all penitents, male and female.[23] Anna Caterina Zuccari heard Bellacappa tell several other nuns he loved them and claimed he also used the same language with her, begging her on a number of occasions to love him. When she showed that she was not interested, he told her that sooner or later she would "fall into the net" and "love him like the others." Although Zuccari never was enamored of Bellacappa, she did become deeply suspicious of him, as did others who described similar amorous words.[24]

On any number of occasions, Bellacappa went further and tried to kiss many of the nuns in one or the other confessional. One of the sisters reported finding Caterina Maria Poggi crying one day. Asked why, Poggi referred to an incident when she and two other nuns, both of whom were now bewitched, went to see Bellacappa in the lower confessional. At his request, the other nuns allowed Bellacappa to kiss them through a hole in the screen; he wanted to do the same with Poggi, who resisted his advances. Poggi was now weeping because she had been too ashamed to mention this incident in confession and feared that the devils would now recount this incident to the whole community, having heard rumors that the demons openly announced, through the mouths of the possessed nuns, unconfessed sins.[25] Beatrice Bendidio, thirty, saw Bellacappa try to kiss several nuns in one or the other confessional and claimed that he attempted the same with her. Avowing to Bendidio that he had kissed many women, including a number of nuns, Bellacappa maintained that he had not committed any sin by doing so, adding that kissing itself was not very arousing. Despite his entreaties, Bendidio did not comply and avoided going to see the confessor as much as possible.[26]

A very pertinent question asked of Sister Marcella Alessandrini, forty-six, was whether there was any place, other than the two confessionals, where Bellacappa could have talked with nuns, either individually or in groups. She answered that he could have availed himself of the two parlors at the front and rear of the monastery. Alessandrini further indicated that many of the older nuns were in fact scandalized that Bellacappa continued to call women to the confessionals when there were other, more appropriate locations for discussions. She added that no other confessors had used the confessionals for socializing–a statement, however, that was contradicted by the testimony of several other nuns.[27]

According to some Clarisses, Bellacappa at times went well beyond kissing and flirting with nuns. In her second lengthy appearance before the inquisitor, Sister Maria Calefi confessed, "Several times he tried to get me to touch him, not only his hands but other parts that I am ashamed to say. *And one time, at his entreaty, I touched the parts which I am ashamed to mention, and at that time he had just said Mass.* And this was at the lower level where sometimes we confess."[28] This occurred in his first year as confessor, and Calefi knew that Bellacappa subjected other nuns to the same immodest actions and words. Anna Caterina Zuccari claimed that several of the possessed nuns told her that they, too, had taken part in lewd touching in the confessional with Bellacappa. She heard details of this activity especially from the now-possessed Sisters Amoldoni and Veronica Maria Coccapani, who were both touched many times in the confessional. Zuccari assumed that the others were subjected to the same illicit petting.[29]

Sister Grazia Lupagnini, thirty-three, gave the following graphic testimony:

> Several times [Bellacappa] sent for me to bring him water from the pantry to the upper confessional. There he tried to get me to kiss him and to let him kiss me. But I did not want to consent to this both out of fear of God and because I didn't want him telling his other girlfriends. Two or three times he showed me his shameful parts, and one time he placed it through the hole and wetted the grating, and another time he did the same on his side [of the grating]. And when he placed it on my side, it was because he wanted to make some liquid matter, which I did not want to see. And since he was begging me to watch, he put it [through the hole] for me to see, saying, "I would do well if only I could have you in my arms," and he said certain other words which Your Honor can understand what I mean. . . . And since I was not fond of him nor did he show that he loved me the way he loved some others, I imagine that he behaved in the same way with the others.[30]

Lupagnini added that on a number of occasions, Bellacappa touched her hands, face, and breasts and besought her to love him.[31]

Another time, Lupagnini and a colleague, Leonora Brusati, were in a small room above both the sacristy and the upper confessional. In that room there was a hole through which a bell-rope passed into the room below in which the confessional was located; the confessor could ring the bell to get the attention of the nuns and vice versa. According to Lupagnini, Brusati and she were investigating whether, as alleged, someone had enlarged the hole so that one could watch while nuns confessed. Lupagnini recounted:

> Having heard us, Bellacappa came running upstairs [above the confessional] and thrusting his arm through the hole for the bell-rope, he grabbed one of my hands and pulled it [through the hole] over to his side. He put

something in my hand, which I realized was something indecent. Then I felt him wet my hand with this thing. And try though I may, I could not pull my hand away before he wetted it since he held my hand tightly with one of his. Afterwards, he tried to get the hand of my companion [Brusati] who, seeing that he had not wanted to let go of mine, refused to put her hand there for him.[32]

Convoked in August, Leonora Brusati gave testimony that did not square entirely with Lupagnini's, which had been given in May. Asked if she ever saw Bellacappa touch the hand of a nun and hold it against her will, Brusati paused a moment and then described the same incident. Brusati said that because it was dark, she could not see Lupagnini put her hand through the hole, but that Lupagnini told her, after she was freed, that the priest had held her hand and did not let go even though she struggled to free herself. When asked for how long he held Lupagnini's hand, Brusati replied that it was a period equivalent to two *misereres,* that is, the amount of time it would take to recite or sing the Vulgate's fiftieth Psalm, a typical means of measuring time among early modern nuns.[33] Brusati could not remember if Lupagnini asked her for help in freeing her hand or if Bellacappa asked her for her hand after relinquishing Lupagnini's. When questioned whether she was motivated by love or hate or simply by the desire to reveal the truth, Brusati of course claimed she spoke only for the truth but added that she did not want to see any harm come to Bellacappa because she loved him too.[34]

Dealta was reputedly involved directly and indirectly in sexual activity around the confessionals. As noted above, Dealta regularly accompanied young nuns to the confessionals to see Bellacappa. More important, one of the possessed, Caterina Margherita Ronchi, told Anna Caterina Zuccari that one day Dealta led her to the place above the upper confessional where one could look into the confessional through the hole for the bell-rope. There Ronchi experienced some illicit touching and other acts which Zuccari was too ashamed to describe.[35] We are left to speculate whether Ronchi was an active or passive participant, and whether Dealta on this occasion merely led the nun there or remained to participate as well. The testimony of another nun strongly suggested a sexual liaison between Dealta and Ronchi, who in 1638 was just twenty-one years old, half the age of Dealta. Sister Prudenzia Federici, sixty, reported that Dealta had spoken about her equivocal relationship with Ronchi. Dealta talked about taking flowers to Ronchi and said that the girl had told her many times, "Sister Dealta, you are blessed that no one has yet heard from your mouth what has transpired between you and me."[36] Although these words are somewhat ambiguous, they strongly imply a romantic and probably a sexual liaison between the older and younger nun. In this case, the witness Federici was able to dissociate sexual nonconformity from witchcraft. Though she did not believe the demons when they identified Dealta as a witch, she strongly suspected that her fellow Clarisse was guilty of sexual sins. Anna Caterina Zuccari provided more explicit accusations against Dealta. Like so many other younger Clarisses, Zuccari claimed that she, too, had regularly met with Bellacappa in the confessional, where he made sexual overtures toward her. She avowed that she successfully resisted these advances but did acknowledge that on two occasions in the lower confessional, Dealta lewdly touched Zuccari on orders from the confessor, who was unable to do so himself because he was on the other side of the grate. Insisting that she was disgusted by these incidents, Zuccari was the only witness to claim explicitly that Dealta indulged in lesbian activity.[37]

Claims of lesbian activity, whether true or not, certainly would have been taken seriously, as ecclesiastical leaders had long shown concern for sexual relationships between nuns. The Councils of Paris (1212) and Rouen (1214) prohibited nuns from sleeping in the same bed and required a lamp to burn all night in the dormitory. Monastic rules dating from the thirteenth century also enjoined that nuns not spend time in each other's cells, which were supposed to remain unlocked at all times. The implicit aim of all such rules was to thwart any possible sexual activity between female religious, and the manual of 1627 specifically exhorted confessors of nuns to be on the lookout for sensual love between sisters.[38]

In a case made famous by Judith Brown's book *Immodest Acts: The Life of a Lesbian Nun in Renaissance Italy,* Benedetta Carlini, the abbess of a Theatine convent in Tuscany, claimed to have divine visions and direct contacts with Jesus Christ, who supposedly personally gave her the stigmata. Although this in itself was cause for an investigation of possible fraudulent sanctity, more alarming still was the discovery in 1623 that she had regularly indulged in sexual activity over a period of years with a much younger nun. In her defense, the younger sister claimed that when they had these sexual encounters, a male angel, Splenditello, in effect possessed the body of Carlini, and assured the young nun that she was making love with him, not with Carlini, and that these acts were not sins. Eventually Carlini was sentenced to permanent imprisonment within the convent, probably more for the dangers she seemed to pose as a charismatic leader and mystic than for her sexual transgressions.[39] Quite similar to Dealta's case was an episode in Auxonne in the early 1660s involving Barbe Buvée, an Ursuline in her mid-forties who allegedly indulged in illicit touching with some young nuns and cast spells to make them and other young religious burn with lust for two confessors.[40] Suffice it to say that ecclesiastical authorities in seventeenth-century Italy were more sensitive than ever about possible lesbian activity in convents.

A very important question asked of all those who either experienced directly or heard of inappropriate words or actions in the confessional was whether these incidents took place during confession, right after or before it, or on occasions entirely unrelated to the sacrament of penance. The Inquisition had jurisdiction over cases of solicitation during confession ever since Paul IV had issued the bull *Cum sicut super* in 1559. With his constitution *Universi Dominici Gregis,* issued in 1622, Pope Gregory XV widened the scope to include indecent talk and to comprise actions not just during confession itself but also just before or after it—heretofore a priest who propositioned a confessant immediately after he had granted her absolution for her sins was technically not subject to prosecution for abusing the sacrament of penance. According to this edict, also known as the Gregorian bull, soliciting during confession or immediately before or after it was considered an abuse of the sacrament of penance, and those guilty of solicitation were "vehemently suspected of heresy" and accordingly had to abjure their errors by oath. It was also an abuse of the sacrament if one merely acted as if one were hearing confessions, without doing so, and then solicited in the confessional.[41]

A cleric who solicited during confession could be subject to severe penalties. Not only did he formally have to abjure, he was to be suspended for life from hearing confessions and could, at the discretion of the inquisitor, be deprived of his benefices and dignities in the Church. He also had to perform appropriate forms of penances, which involved regular fasts and the recitation of prayers for a certain number of years. Priests guilty of solicitation could be subject to major mundane penalties, possibly even condemned to life in prison or the galleys.[42] The Gregorian bull further asserted that a priest might also be subject to prosecution if he solicited in the confessional on occasions that were entirely removed from confession.[43] In these latter circumstances there was no abuse of the sacrament of penance, however, and the priest was not suspected of heresy and consequently did not have to abjure. In theory, the Inquisition could still take action against such priests, who could be liable to fines at the discretion of the inquisitors.[44] In practice, however, the Holy Office, although strongly disapproving of priests who solicited under any circumstances, rarely prosecuted confessors who performed immodest acts or said illicit words when they did not take place close to confession.

For the most part, the testimony against Bellacappa indicated that he was usually careful not to mix business with pleasure. Though she experienced illicit words and deeds only in the confessional, Zuccari asserted that at no time did Bellacappa say or do anything inappropriate during confession or just before or after it.[45] With respect to her illicit sexual activity, Maria Calefi replied, "He did not say or do lurid things before, during, or at the end of confession, but several times he asked me to kiss him the same day that I had taken communion and said dirty things to me many times the same morning after communion."[46] Calefi did say that she regularly touched and kissed Bellacappa's hand both before and after confessing but felt there was nothing wrong with this, since she considered his hands sacred.[47] Likewise,

Grazia Lupagnini, an unwilling partner in alleged sexual activity with Bellacappa, acknowledged that she was never subjected to these actions when she confessed.[48] Admitting to acceding once to Bellacappa's sexual advances, Silveria Chechi, forty, also insisted that these overtures never took place on the same day that she confessed but only when he called her for a visit.[49]

Even nuns who aggressively criticized Bellacappa's conduct conceded that he generally behaved himself when hearing confession. Beatrice Bendidio reported that another sister—she did not recall whom—recounted that one day Bellacappa called her to come for confession. When she arrived, she indicated that she wanted to confess and suggested they could have a chat after the confession. Bellacappa replied, however, that he "did not want to chat with her in confession about such [mundane] things since he was not Fra Angelo at the time [of confession] but rather Jesus Christ."[50] Though that may sound somewhat blasphemous, it is in accord with Catholic teaching that when people confessed, they were in effect speaking to God through the priest. Although Bendidio had many disparaging words for Bellacappa, she in effect affirmed that he refrained from lewd language and behavior in the periods during which he was hearing confessions.

True, some testimony suggested that the priest's words or actions came close to abusing the sacrament of penance. Anna Caterina Zuccari, for example, claimed that Bellacappa often told her he loved her just after she completed her confession.[51] Although inappropriate language in such a setting could amount to an offense punishable by the Inquisition, in this case Bellacappa at least could argue that he was referring to a purely spiritual love. One nun revealed that the possessed Paola Francesca Cimadori had said that sometimes when she went to confess, Bellacappa told her to remove her cord, a symbol of chastity for both male and female religious, since he did not feel like hearing her confession at that moment. He then proceeded to talk about other things, most often telling her that he loved her.[52] But when she actually did confess, Cimadori indicated that Bellacappa did not say or do anything inappropriate. Interestingly, Cimadori, though surely believing that she suffered from diabolical possession and that Bellacappa was partly responsible, was quite ambivalent about seeing the former confessor prosecuted. She told a fellow nun that if interrogated, she would really feel bad to have to say anything against Bellacappa. Though adding that she would tell the whole truth if questioned, Cimadori obviously had a soft spot for Bellacappa in spite of his unconventional behavior in the confessional.[53]

Confession and the Counter-Reformation

The interrogations concerning Bellacappa's actions reflected the increased attention Roman Catholic leaders gave to the sacrament of penance during the Counter-Reformation. Ever since the Fourth Lateran Council of 1215, all Christians were supposed to confess their sins at least once a year. Although practice varied widely from place to place, evidence suggests that prior to Trent, many Catholics did confess just once a year, usually during Lent. The confessor in many ways resembled a physician for the soul and sought above all to reintegrate the sinner into the Christian community. Thomas Tentler in fact has argued that late medieval confession offered a comprehensive system of social control, which provided both discipline and consolation for sins.[54] Demonstrating a heightened awareness of sin and defending penance vis-à-vis Protestant attacks, Catholic leaders at Trent called for more frequent confession (and more frequent communion) in the belief that this would lead to spiritual edification by requiring believers to monitor their consciences more closely and more often.

Certain Catholic leaders sought to enhance the role of confessors in effecting change in lay piety to conform with the ideals of Trent, goals that were clearly seen in the work of the quintessential post-Tridentine bishop, Carlo Borromeo. During his tenure as archbishop of Milan (1564–84), Borromeo zealously tried to transform the confessional into a vitally important instrument of social discipline, a means of directly attacking sin and nonconformity. He wanted the confessors in his huge archdiocese not to hesitate to withhold the Eucharist from the unworthy and earnestly sought the cooperation of secular authorities in rooting out superstitions and a host of other sins. In a persuasive study, Wietse de Boer finds that into the early seventeenth century, the reality fell well short of the goals set by the ambitious Borromeo. Secular authorities feared that excluding too many people from communion was more apt to hinder than nurture social discipline, and the local clergy was often reluctant to be so heavy-handed in meting out public penances. Although Borromeo favored public penances for especially egregious sins, confessors were often wary of counterproductive effects. They feared, for example, that obliging a woman to do penance publicly for having committed incest could result in a permanent loss of honor for her and might compromise the confidential nature of confession itself. Such consequences could deter others from confessing similar sins. In the long run, the most obvious success in the archbishopric was the noticeable improvement in the quality of the lower clergy, who were better trained and more professional than ever before. Through the pulpit and the confessional, the local priests could gradually effect changes in lay piety and social discipline, but they had to compromise to a degree with the laity, and the results would have disappointed Borromeo. The lower clergy along with secular authorities viewed reconciliation as a virtue in and of itself and concluded that policing the private sphere of the confession of sins in a massive or heavy-handed way was not likely to result in reconciliation.[55]

The Holy Office played a central role in the implementation of religious uniformity and social discipline in Italy, and Adriano Prosperi has convincingly shown the important connection that developed between confession and the Roman Inquisition in post-Tridentine Italy. Confession and the Inquisition both ultimately sought to root out unacceptable beliefs and practices and, ideally, to return sinners and deviants to the straight and narrow path.[56] John Bossy has provocatively argued that the sacrament of penance underwent a "Copernican revolution" between the fifteenth and seventeenth centuries. According to Bossy, Church leaders started to view confession less as a channel for resolving social conflicts than as a means of examining one's own conscience, and the aim of confession was thus to reconcile the penitent much more with God than with the community.[57] Facing the challenge of the Lutheran doctrine of salvation by faith alone, after Trent the Roman Catholic Church stressed more than ever before the "consoling value" of confession.[58] The Church sought a certain interiorization of the sacrament of penance, and confession accordingly was supposed to be strictly confidential, based on the notion that the penitent was speaking to God through the confessor. The confessor, however, wielded considerable power in granting absolution. Upon hearing of a sin that demanded more than the usual penances, the confessor could refuse to absolve the confessants and thus deny them access to the Eucharist until they "voluntarily" went before the inquisitor to confess their sins and, if applicable, to denounce their accomplices in sin. The inquisitor in turn prescribed sentences that, depending on the gravity of the sins, might occasionally impose a term in prison or the galleys but always included "salutary" acts of penance, which might consist of the regular recitation of the rosary or other prayers and creeds and the periodic confession of sins to a priest. Inquisitorial practice held that those who appeared "spontaneously" in this way before the Holy Office to confess their transgressions were to be treated more leniently than those who were denounced by others.[59] According to Prosperi, by the end of the sixteenth century, the Inquisition was increasingly transforming itself from a court of aggressive external restraint that crushed heresy, to a paternalistic tribunal of internal restraint that in attacking superstitions, blasphemy, and abuse of sacraments, subjected one's conscience to close surveillance by employing many of the same methods used by the confessor. Ideally, the confessor and inquisitor worked together to ensure that the faithful were fully respecting Catholic mores in word, deed, and thought.[60] Ultimately, though, confessors clearly were subordinate to inquisitors, as the post-Tridentine Inquisition insisted on the right to pursue "heretics" even if they had received absolution for their sins from their confessor. Absolution from the "internal court" of confession, which was purely penitential in nature, did not exempt sinners from investigation by the "external court" of the Holy Office, which had judicial powers.[61]

Since the Church was insisting more than ever before on the need to confess regularly, it also strove to ensure that people went unimpeded to confession. Perhaps the greatest danger posed by the new emphasis on confession was sexual solicitation during the confession. By misusing his power, a soliciting priest was blatantly violating the very purpose of confession by inciting a person to commit further sins rather than do penance for those already committed. The evidence from Santa Chiara indicates that Bellacappa conformed to the letter but not the spirit of the law by keeping lewd talk and actions separate from the sacrament of penance.[62]

Love Magic

Even if Bellacappa did not misuse any sacrament, the Inquisition would still investigate him of course if witchcraft were believed to be involved in the alleged seductive behavior. The registers of the Holy Office in Modena and elsewhere are filled with investigations of love magic, which the *Malleus Maleficarum* described as the best known and most common form of witchcraft.[63] It has in fact been suggested that the Modenese had a special penchant for love magic, which was the most common type of case of witchcraft or magic heard by the Inquisition of Modena in the late sixteenth century.[64] Numerous examples can be found of people trying to win the heart of another by co-opting divine power–through holy water, modified Christian prayers, blessed candles, and so on–conjuring demons, or even mixing menstrual blood or semen in the wine of a person whose love they wanted to bind.[65]

Various nuns expressed fears that Bellacappa was indulging in love magic. Summoned to appear on 19 and 20 May 1638, Silveria Chechi acknowledged that several times in the confessional Bellacappa flirted with her, tried to get her to kiss him, told her that he loved her, and begged her to love him. She confessed to kissing him several times, and Chechi, at forty, was the oldest nun to claim that Bellacappa made such advances.[66] On 21 May Chechi voluntarily appeared, feeling guilty because she had not divulged the whole truth. Not counting confessions, she reported meeting privately with Bellacappa eight times while he was confessor. Apart from the first meeting, on each occasion he begged her to take part in obscene acts that, "out of shame, I did not recount to Your Honor the first time [I testified]." The second time she met with him, in November 1634, Bellacappa "made me go to the upper confessional, where there is a hole for the bell-rope that one can pass a hand through, so he could touch me and I him. And this occurred only that time and the [mutual touching] that took place was so inappropriate that I am ashamed to describe it." She added, "I tell you this with great shame and I am trembling. I wanted to disclose this to you for the relief of my conscience." Bringing this testimony to an end, Chechi declared, "If it is true that he has cast a spell and has taken part in this *maleficium* [of the convent], I would say that he enchanted me at that time, that I could not help but go there."[67]

In a way, this last sentence should be taken with a grain of salt, since the use of love magic would obviously deflect responsibility away from Chechi and place the blame entirely on Bellacappa. But it must be remembered that Chechi and other nuns faced a real dilemma when their confessor called for them. The disparity in power between the female religious and the confessor was enormous. The daily liturgical offices, replete with the recitation of prayers and incantations, was central to the life of the nun, but even more important was receiving the sacraments, for which a priest was necessary. The confessor, who regularly celebrated Mass in the convent, wielded the power, which no woman could have, to administer the transformation of bread and wine into the body and blood of Christ. Nuns were obliged to confess to the priest alone all sins that they had committed since their last confession, and the confessor had the power to grant or withhold absolution for those sins. Even if Bellacappa did not threaten to withhold absolution—a charge that no one made—the discrepancy in power could make any female religious feel very uncomfortable when pursued by her confessor. She almost surely feared spiritual consequences regardless if she accepted or rejected the advances of her spiritual father.[68]

Lust almost certainly played a role in the feeling that Silveria Chechi and others had of being impelled to go see Bellacappa. In this cloistered monastery, the confessor was the only male the nuns saw on a regular basis and absolutely the only man with whom they could converse without any supervision whatsoever. When they were actually confessing, nuns had to lay bare all their transgressions, be they sins of pride, greed, anger, lust, and so on, and the bond that might develop between confessor and confessant could be quite strong. Though not subject to *clausura*, Bellacappa had virtually no occasion to speak privately with women except in the confessional. The evidence is overwhelming that Bellacappa was taking advantage of the intimacy of the confessional—even if not during confessions—to make sexual advances toward many nuns. Having no other sexual outlets, some women may well have given way to their lusts with the man who had the power to grant absolution for their sins. In all likelihood, most residents of Santa Chiara had been pressured by their families to pursue the monastic life, for which many of them surely did not feel a strong vocation. In Carpi and elsewhere, sexually frustrated nuns might be prone to find their confessors attractive and desirable, and contemporary ecclesiastical courts struggled to suppress romantic liaisons between nuns and clerics.[69]

The accusations of sexual misconduct made against Dealta and especially Bellacappa also bore witness to the strong sexual repression that was imposed on Counter-Reformation religious. More than ever before the Roman Catholic Church sought to enforce clerical celibacy, and convents were subject to stricter claustration to "protect" female religious from worldly corruptions and temptations. If one were to make the highly unlikely assumption that all the accusations of sexual misconduct made against Bellacappa were fabrications, then the stories themselves would still suggest that the minds of so many nuns were haunted by wild sexual fantasies, possibly the products of repressed desires among unwilling nuns.[70]

Although lust itself was probably a factor behind the confessional visits, the Clarisses—at least when they were being questioned by the Holy Office—tended to interpret the force as love magic. The testimony of the sisters of Santa Chiara, even those who took no part in illicit deeds and sordid conversations, shows that they clearly believed in the reality of love magic. The Roman Catholic Church officially rejected as anathema the belief that one can force a person to love another against his or her own will. Girolamo Menghi and other experts on demonology declared that it is "false and impious" to say that demons can force people to commit a mortal sin against their will; demons did not have the power to take away the free will of humans unless they voluntarily made a pact with the devil. That said, Menghi affirmed that demons could nonetheless excite various thoughts and feelings in people that could stimulate lust. Love magic, therefore, could strongly increase one's sexual desires toward a person but ultimately could not make one give in to those impulses.[71] Similarly, Cardinal Desiderio Scaglia condemned as heretical the view that demons could force a human to love another but recognized that they could, through dreams or the movement of blood or other humors, stimulate passions and fantasies, which could increase the likelihood of being attracted to a particular person.[72] The fear of the sexual impulse and of demonic powers engendered a strong belief that love magic could incite even in the faithful powerful libidinous passions that one had to resist most tenaciously.

Love Magic and the Pain of Love

If we try to assume the mind-set of Santa Chiara's witnesses, we might ask why Bellacappa would be suspected of casting a spell that caused such intense suffering for the women whose love he reputedly sought. Lust itself of course could suffice as an explanation. Throughout history, seducers or sexual predators have not been known to show much concern for the physical and mental well-being of their victims. For that matter, as modern behavioral scientists know, romances that go sour can result in extremely violent behavior. Many seventeenth-century Europeans viewed the connection between love interests and intense suffering through the lens of magic.

Incredible torments supposedly could result from love magic gone awry: though the spell was intended to cause a person to love another, the unintended consequence could have been physical and mental suffering. Moreover, a man suspected of having won the affection of a woman through magic and now lost it could easily be transformed into a witch who cast maleficent spells to render the life of his erstwhile lover miserable.

Love magic and *maleficia* in fact could be very closely intertwined. There was a certain logic behind the belief that a person in love with another might, if rejected, cast a spell on the erstwhile beloved. In his influential instructions for inquisitors, Cardinal Desiderio Scaglia wrote that the techniques employed in love magic and in *maleficia* were often quite similar. To win another's love, one might throw salt or "blessed beans" into a fire. Or one might recite or write down holy words, a reflection of the widespread belief in the magical power of certain words, especially those of a religious nature.[73] One might also make powders out of certain herbs and mix them with food that the victim ate. Desiring another's love, a witch might also use, in combination with an explicit or tacit invocation of the devil, a consecrated host or a magnet, noteworthy for its ability to attract, that had been illicitly baptized.[74] Quite often, Scaglia wrote, people seeking love wrote down unknown words or characters, which supposedly contained hidden powers, or created wax statues of the victims, which they pierced with pins or held over a fire while they uttered incantations to "light the fire" of love in the other person. Other objects that were deemed useful instruments for love magic were locks of hair or nail clippings over which the witch recited invocations to demons and then buried, preferably under a threshold through which the beloved often passed. Significantly, it was commonly believed that practically all these objects could also be used as instruments of *maleficia*.[75]

If rejected, an irate Bellacappa might have been suspected of taking vengeance because of unrequited love. This does not seem like the most plausible line of reasoning since the feelings appeared mutual for several of the nuns. Or, perhaps most likely, the suffering of the nuns could be viewed as the effect of being separated from the person who cast the spell *ad amorem*. If applied correctly, many love spells were supposed to allow the victims no rest as long as they were separated from the person to be loved. Suffice it to say that there was definitely a gray area between love magic and *maleficia*. Inquisition officials could pursue them both aggressively, and certainly the nuns of Santa Chiara viewed love spells as a grave danger that could lead them into temptation and mortal sin.[76]

As "evidence" against the former confessor, many Clarisses mentioned his penchant for giving presents to certain nuns, which, they feared, might be instruments of spells, either for love magic or *maleficia*. Many of those who had received gifts and things to eat from him now suffered from possession. He gave flowers and embroidered ornamentations to many, especially those whom he "loved," and several witnesses noted in particular that he gave numerous things, including a pair of gloves, to the now-bewitched Barbara Leonora Forni.[77] Just before he left, Bellacappa gave two live doves, raised for food, to Sister Clara Maria Amoldoni. One of the doves died, but Amoldoni got the chance to eat the other. Later, her demons informed her that the doves were bewitched, and ever since Amoldoni became most agitated every time she saw a dove. Doves in fact had a reputation for being particularly affectionate animals and were purportedly a common staple in love magic.[78] Moreover, both the exorcists and the demons declared that the items given to Barbara Leonora Forni and to Caterina Margherita Ronchi—books and notebooks to both, a breviary and a clavichord to the latter—were all bewitched.[79]

In Bellacappa's defense, one could point out that apart from the two laywomen who were the first to fall ill and later died, all the demonic possessions of Santa Chiara were discovered after his tenure as confessor had come to an end. He did return occasionally for visits, however, and more important, the memories of dubious words and actions remained and could sow seeds of suspicions in the nunnery. As with Dealta, several nuns claimed they long suspected that Bellacappa played a role in the possessions, but their suspicions greatly increased after the demons identified him as a witch.[80]

The demons proclaimed that the *maleficia* had been committed with abuse of all the sacraments, which cast considerable suspicion on the Martinelli sisters but even more on Bellacappa. Some experts on witchcraft asserted that almost all maleficent spells included a mixture of Christian sacraments or sacramentals and were often performed on the holiest days. By so doing, demons and witches could trick some people into believing these rituals were good rather than evil and increase the offense to God.[81] According to witnesses, Bellacappa had requested some holy oil from Ippolita, the sacristan, at a time when there was no apparent use for it. Using holy oil for purposes other than baptisms, ordinations, and the like would have been most inappropriate behavior for a priest. Confessors were to use this oil only for such special occasions, and no such sacred rites were on the horizon at the time he asked Ippolita for some.[82] Under questioning, Ippolita herself conceded that once Bellacappa did not return the oil to her as quickly as usual but nonetheless avowed that she had no suspicions toward him in that regard.[83] Still, rumors of the inappropriate use of holy oil raised the specter of magic, be it for harming or winning the love of someone.

There were also numerous reports that one year Bellacappa kept one of the Easter candles for several days. These are very big candles that are blessed on Holy Saturday and placed next to the altar, where they are lit for religious services until Ascension Day, forty days after Easter. When he finally returned the candle after Ascension Day, the candle was a fraction of its original size. Many Clarisses were concerned about this, and Abbess

Angela Caterina d'Este complained about the apparent misuse of the candle. Sister Ippolita Martinelli said that Bellacappa along with three other Franciscans had asked her for the candle, which he indicated would be used, at the request of the princess, to reduce the labor pains of a laywoman who was about to give birth. Adding that she understood that Easter candles could be effective in reducing such pains, Ippolita gave him the candle but did not know what he actually did with it. As it was commonly believed that such a holy candle could be used for *maleficia* or for love magic, his keeping the candle for many days, which apparently did not in fact have the approval of the princess-abbess, was another cause for suspicion.[84]

At times the testimony against Bellacappa did not amount to abusing sacraments or casting malefices but simply to improper behavior, over which the Inquisition did not have jurisdiction. Several sisters testified that Bellacappa often met with groups of nuns and led them in some activities that were deemed inappropriate for female religious. Several alleged that especially during Carnival, nuns frequently gathered around the confessional, on the other side of the grate, and Bellacappa led them in singing dirty songs or telling off-color jokes. A number of Clarisses revealed to the Inquisition their disapproval of Bellacappa's habit of teaching the sisters some risqué songs and even writing down the lyrics for them.[85]

Carnival was in fact the time of year when Bellacappa received the greatest number of social visits, and the Clarisses actually celebrated Carnival in the convent twice a year, before both Advent and Lent.[86] Early in her tenure as abbess, Angela Caterina herself had actively promoted the carefree celebrations of Carnival by providing musical entertainment and plenty of good food, thanks to the generous contributions of her father.[87] In taking part in the fun of Carnival, Bellacappa in a sense was merely following traditions that were already established at Santa Chiara. The small Carnival celebrations were even attended by nuns who did not regularly socialize with Bellacappa. Many Clarisses wore costumes at these festivities, which generally took place in the evenings, just before or after Vespers. The principal pastime was taking turns telling jokes, many of which, according to some, seemed inappropriate for nuns and priests to be saying.[88]

Although the festivities at Santa Chiara were quite mild when compared with celebrations in the outside world, they clearly show that the convent had not been reformed. Post-Tridentine Church authorities took a dim view of Carnival and sought to curb the hedonistic excesses associated with it. Moreover, starting in the later sixteenth century, reforming clerics, such as Archbishop Carlo Borromeo of Milan, tried to forbid all clergy and female religious to participate in Carnival, which they deemed as incompatible with the clerical mores they desired.[89] In the 1630s Fra Giovan Battista d'Este was among those who railed against the intemperance surrounding Carnival. In a sermon delivered in Milan in February 1633, the former duke warned that

God would unleash his wrath on all the sinners who overindulged during Carnival. When he returned to Modena, Giovan Battista delivered a Lenten sermon in which he berated the Modenese with warnings that fire and brimstone were the wages of their sinful customs. In this era, Modena was apparently notorious for its Carnival celebrations, and the masquerades, dances, and tournaments began already on the feast of St. Stephen (26 December).[90] Although there is no mention in the investigation of Giovan Battista's opinion of Santa Chiara's pre-Lenten festivities, he undoubtedly disapproved of them. Bellacappa's carnivalesque encounters with groups of nuns also violated the principles laid out for confessors of female religious. The guidelines explicitly stated that the confessor was to prohibit dancing and, even more so, dressing up in costumes, "including during Carnival," as such "profane games" were simply inappropriate for religious people. More broadly, the priest was to avoid meeting with several nuns at once for "spiritual conferences" or "spiritual exercises."[91] If the confessor was to avoid informal discussions of spiritual matters with groups of nuns, so much more should he shun group meetings where they danced, told jokes, sang profane songs, and wore costumes.

The Malady of Princess Angela Caterina

Like Sister Dealta, Bellacappa was also suspected in part because strong antipathy developed between him and Princess Angela Caterina d'Este. She was adamantly opposed to allowing Giulia Angelica Sertori and Barbara Leonora Forni, ladies-in-waiting to her and her nieces, to see Bellacappa frequently. Be that as it may, with the complicity of some other nuns, they went to see him without the princess's knowledge.[92] Several Clarisses strongly suspected that Bellacappa, perhaps with some help from the Martinelli sisters, cast a maleficent spell on the princess-abbess. To be sure, Bellacappa and the Martinellis were not the only ones who had trouble getting along with the princess. Indeed, although the sisters of Santa Chiara appreciated the material rewards they received through the Este connection, some clearly resented Angela Caterina's undue influence and heavy-handed ways. Sister Alsuinda Malaspina believed that the ills of the nunnery might be reduced entirely to animosity to Princess Angela Caterina, noting that a good number of the afflicted nuns were close associates of the former abbess.[93] In interrogating many nuns, Fiscal Giudici and later Inquisitor Tinti posited some questions that reflected a certain paranoia on the part of Angela Caterina. They asked a number of Clarisses if they ever had discussions among themselves about the health of the princess. When Tinti asked whether the princess was in good health or suffered from a "hidden infirmity" (*morbo secreto*), an oblique query about a possible diabolical possession, Colomba Ciarlini, fifty-six, recounted hearing the bedridden Angela Caterina bemoan, "I am here, my sisters, and I am reduced to this state; I have been mistreated to death."[94] Ciarlini conceded that she may have said to her confidante Teodora Pattoni, perhaps in the presence of others, that she believed Angela Caterina was also possessed by a demon. If so, this merely reflected the words that the princess herself had said.[95] Certainly, the words that Ciarlini attributed to the princess readily lent themselves to the belief that Angela Caterina was possessed.

At the time of the investigation, Angela Caterina had definitely been ill for a lengthy period, and rumors circulated that she, too, was possessed. Regardless of the cause of her malaise, Angela Caterina's condition was taking a turn for the worse in late July 1638. At that time, an unidentified clergyman, perhaps the bishop of Modena, wrote to Rome on behalf of Duke Francesco and of Fra Giovan Battista d'Este for permission to have Angela Caterina leave Santa Chiara to go either to the Este palace or to another nunnery, specifically the Benedictine convent of San Gemignano in Modena, in order to receive care for her ills. He noted that several physicians had examined her and concluded that she was in imminent danger of losing her life. According to this priest, the presence of many possessed nuns, including several in her service, had taken its toll on the princess's mental and physical health. This tense atmosphere had caused her "continuous fear with unspeakable spiritual unrest, resulting in the increase in melancholy and in pains in both the stomach and head, with continuous pains, tremors, and vomiting."[96] The princess in fact would remain at Santa Chiara only a few more months, transferring in April 1639 to the convent of San Gemignano, where she remained until her death in 1661.[97]

In the same period that Angela Caterina's health deteriorated badly, the inquisitor more aggressively pursued rumors about the former abbess and interrogated several nuns about conversations they may have had concerning her health. Although when she was first questioned in mid-May, Silvia Montalti, forty-three, claimed she had no suspicions of anyone whatsoever, on 23 July she was questioned closely about possible conversations about Angela Caterina's health. Montalti admitted that she, like several other Clarisses, had in fact said that the princess was possessed, a conclusion they reached by seeing Angela Caterina quickly alternate between doing fine and suffering horribly.[98] On 24 July Tinti questioned Teodora Pattoni, who affirmed that Angela Caterina's chronic ailments had engendered many rumors of bewitchment. Pattoni added that, while serving at the turntable one day, she overheard Angela Caterina say, "I believe that I too am touched," and assumed that this referred to the diabolical possessions that plagued the convent. Pattoni indicated that her suspicions of demon possession stemmed from seeing the exorcists come to the turntable several times to see the princess. On these occasions, the princess, wishing to speak to the priests in private, dismissed both Pattoni and the other nun overseeing the *ruota*.[99]

Apart from his desire to uncover the truth, Tinti surely pursued such questions in order to protect the integrity of Angela Caterina and the entire Este family. Although theoretically there was no shame in being possessed—one could rightly be viewed as the innocent victim of a demon and perhaps a maleficent witch—in practice there was ample reason to hush rumors of possession. Although in some cases female religious figures seemed almost to seek possession in order to show their spiritual strength vis-à-vis the temptations and torments of demons, having a devil in one's body could also be interpreted as revealing a lack of spiritual strength or a certain disfavor before God. Moreover, although in this investigation of Santa Chiara no one expressed suspicions of the ten bewitched nuns, there could be a gray area between being bewitched and being a witch. When a demon possessed not only the body but also the soul of a person, it was assumed that this individual had freely entered a pact with Satan.[100] Having served as abbess for nearly ten years and remaining the most high-profile resident of Santa Chiara, Angela Caterina was no doubt distraught that the worst epidemic of witchcraft in the history of this nunnery had broken out under her watch. Being possessed herself would only compound the scandal for the convent and the Este family.

Surely one of the most dramatic episodes of the entire investigation was the testimony given by Princess Angela Caterina d'Este herself. When the inquisitor questioned other nuns, he usually conducted proceedings near the unloading entrance, the place where carts brought goods into the convent, in a room that allowed for privacy without obliging the inquisitor actually to enter the cloistered convent. The bedridden princess, however, was deemed too sick to walk or even to be carried there. And so on the evening of 28 July and during the following day, the inquisitor took the extraordinary measure of entering the nunnery to question the ailing princess in her room. He was accompanied by Archpriest Niccolini, Fiscal Giudici, and the notary Ripalta, who served as scribe.[101]

Not only was the setting different, but the nature of Angela Caterina's testimony, apart from her initially touching the Bible and swearing to tell the truth, differed markedly from that of all the other nuns. The former abbess was scarcely interrogated at all but simply was given the opportunity to say anything she wished about the travails of Santa Chiara. Only at the end of her testimony, after she had volunteered all the information she could think of, did Tinti ask any questions. On the evening of the twenty-eighth, she immediately launched into a lengthy description of an incident in which she believed she was the victim of a maleficent spell cast by Bellacappa with some help from the Martinelli sisters. Thinking back to early in his tenure as confessor, Angela Caterina recalled that whenever she went to talk to

Bellacappa about affairs pertaining to her office, he always asked her how she was doing and gave her the impression that he was disappointed when she told him that she was doing fine.[102] Her good health, however, came abruptly to an end during Bellacappa's second year at Santa Chiara (1635). According to the princess, in that year on the feast of St. Bernardine of Siena (20 May) or its eve, she went to one of the confessionals in order to recite with him the prayer ordinarily spoken at matins—as was her custom, she said her offices separately from the community of nuns. Before starting, though, she told Bellacappa she was so thirsty she could hardly speak. Not wanting to leave her thirsty, Bellacappa summoned Ippolita Martinelli, who was downstairs in the lower sacristy with Dealta, to bring "Her Excellency" something to drink, even though the princess protested more than once that she did not want anything. It was too far to have Ippolita go to Angela Caterina's apartment to bring wine from her private supplies, so Bellacappa suggested that Ippolita just bring the carafe of wine that he had been drinking earlier. Angela Caterina related that she was becoming suspicious of Bellacappa's intentions and called out to Ippolita to bring some wine from the pantry instead. Shortly thereafter, Ippolita arrived with a carafe and was accompanied by Dealta, who was carrying a plate of sweets.[103]

The princess related that she became furious when they arrived, asking them imperiously, "Why did you bring me some sweets, since I asked only for some wine?" The abbess then exploded and unleashed the following tirade:

> I don't want this wine anymore since I see it has been altered, you traitors! Is this what I deserve for all the favors I have done for you! Am I not your Mother Superior? Do I deserve this from nuns? What error have I committed by which I have irritated the souls of nuns? Do you have the intention of offending God in this manner? I will never drink it! I will never drink it! Get out of my presence right now, and go back whence you came.[104]

According to the princess, the sisters Martinelli protested that she was greatly offending them. Ippolita said that she did not want to leave until Angela Caterina had drunk some wine, and both insisted that the wine came from the pantry. Ippolita even asked, "Did I not take the most holy sacrament this morning? Shouldn't you believe me?" The princess's ire did not subside, however, and she made as if she were going to smash the carafe. At this point, Bellacappa intervened, "My Lady, don't get angry. You must believe, as I am the confessor, and be assured that there are no such intentions toward you here. I have even heard the consciences of these nuns, and I have not found that they have any such [bad] intentions against you." After a moment's reflection, Angela Caterina said that these words could not pacify her since the confessor was forbidden to reveal what was said to him in confession. As Angela Caterina hesitated, Bellacappa finally ordered her "by

Holy Obedience" to drink some of the wine. Feeling herself thus compelled, even though she considered it unusual to give an order of Holy Obedience outside confession, Angela Caterina finally relented, saying, "Come now, God, I will go to my death through obedience." Ippolita gave her a glass, and the abbess went close to the grate so Bellacappa could see her and took a sip. But Bellacappa insisted, "When I ordered you by obedience to drink that wine, I meant that you must drink all or at least a good part of it." She dutifully returned to the grille and drank some more. To assure her that there was nothing wrong with the wine, he had Ippolita pass him wine through the turntable. He brought the wine to his lips, but, being on the other side, Angela Caterina could not see if he actually drank any. At Bellacappa's insistence, Angela Caterina also nibbled on one of the sweets.[105]

Angela Caterina told Tinti and colleagues that she began feeling ill immediately after drinking the wine. She experienced pains in her right side, as if a hand were grabbing her there. This discomfort eventually spread to her left side and was later combined with a certain discomfort in her stomach. First believing that the wine was poisoned, Angela Caterina consulted the physician. Many prayers were said for her, but these ills have plagued her almost constantly since she drank that wine three years ago. In addition to the abdominal pains, she complained of a chronic fever and extreme weakness, and her condition was so bad that her physician often feared for her life. She eventually asked the doctor if poisons could produce these painful symptoms, which lasted for months and years. He told her that such long-term ills were not possible from a poisoning, leading her to conclude that the wine had not been poisoned but that a maleficent spell had been cast upon it.[106]

Subsequent incidents exacerbated Angela Caterina's fears that Bellacappa was responsible for her ills. On St. Bartholomew's Day (24 August), three months after the wine incident, Bellacappa asked her if she, as abbess, were willing to pay the expenses for the fair that the nuns were going to celebrate. To this request, the princess expressed her amazement that he had the temerity even to speak to her, given what he had done to her on St. Bernardine's Day. According to the abbess, who could see through a hole in the grate, Bellacappa immediately threw himself on his knees, his hands folded on his chest as if in prayer, his cord around his neck, begging her to forgive him for what he had done. She further rebuked him by saying that he had offended not her but God, who was watching over her cause. Not wanting to hear another word out of him, the princess then rose and left.[107]

Concluding that she had nothing to lose, Angela Caterina decided at a certain point that she would confront Sister Ippolita Martinelli about the wine incident. In order to induce her to tell all, Angela Caterina informed Ippolita that thanks to all the prayers that had been said for her, she not only knew what had been done to her but also who was responsible for it. Though trembling at first, Ippolita was unable to tell the princess anything of substance. When Ippolita came to the princess's apartment for a second round of questioning, she was shaking and looked sickly and very pale, quite a contrast to her usual ruddy complexion. But Ippolita informed her that neither she nor Dealta knew anything more than what she had already told the princess.[108]

Having heard all the information that Angela Caterina volunteered, Tinti asked his first and, in effect, only question of the princess, inquiring of Bellacappa's socializing with the nuns who were believed possessed. The princess responded that the majority of them had asked her permission to go to him, as their confessor, in order to discuss matters of conscience. She gave them permission to do so one time but was upset when she saw that they were constantly going to see him. The princess reproached them for these contacts, but the nuns argued that they simply had not completed their discussions with their spiritual father. Angela Caterina told them they had ample opportunities to discuss spiritual matters when actually confessing and told the women who were in her service that they were to cease socializing with Bellacappa. Ultimately, though, she was most concerned because he had shown bad intentions toward her and feared he might also do harm to these young nuns.[109]

Angela Caterina's testimony is interesting for a number of reasons, not least of which is the fact that she clearly believed that she herself was possessed, the victim of an evil spell cast by Bellacappa, probably with a little help from Ippolita and perhaps Dealta Martinelli. Although Tinti and Giudici aggressively questioned any nun who reportedly said that the princess was possessed, Angela Caterina basically affirmed her demonic possession in her deposition. Though initially thinking she had been poisoned, the princess was convinced that the effects of poison would have worn off long ago rather than continuing to plague her three years later. True, she did not demonstrate any of the bizarre behavior of the other nuns. But the overall tenor of her testimony reveals that she, like her physician, was convinced that she was not suffering from natural ills. On a technical note, if Angela Caterina genuinely believed she had a demon in her body, her testimony should have been null according to inquisitorial procedures, since a demon could conceivably have been speaking (and lying) through her mouth. The inquisitor, however, made no mention of being circumspect in considering her deposition.[110]

Angela Caterina's family had actually had its share of reputed demonic possessions. Her mother, Virginia de' Medici, half-sister of Ferdinand I, grand duke of Tuscany, first started showing signs of a serious illness in 1607. Virginia was already upset after learning in autumn of 1605 of the alleged demonic possession, briefly alluded to in chapter 2, of her daughter, Laura, the duchess of Mirandola, wife of Alessandro Pico, and elder sister of Angela Caterina.[111] Laura evidently had not been very well ever since her marriage two years before and returned to Modena at her mother's request to receive spiritual comfort from her father's confessor and other clerics. Laura's health was eventually restored, apparently thanks to the ministrations of some exorcists, one of whom had been sent from Florence. Virginia's woes, however, lasted longer. Quite depressed during a pregnancy, Virginia was struck by a serious ailment shortly after giving birth to her last child in 1607. The modern observer of course immediately suspects postpartum depression, and some assumed she suffered from melancholic humors. Florentine physicians came to Modena to examine Virginia, who expressed a total aversion toward her husband, Cesare, and refused to have sex with him and to take any medicine out of fear that he would poison her. The first person to suggest that Virginia might be possessed was her brother, the grand duke, who knew all too well that Virginia's own mother had spent the last year of her life in a convent, allegedly also the victim of demon possession. Eventually all agreed that Virginia was in fact possessed by devils that were responsible for turning her against her husband. The documents that testified to Virginia's maladies, mainly the correspondence of the Tuscan ambassador to Modena, do not indicate when or if her health was restored.[112] All told, Angela Caterina's grandmother, mother, and sister all supposedly suffered from demon possession. Given this family history, it is not surprising if the princess-abbess may have been rather quick to attribute ills to demons. And it is conceivable that the princess's own fears could make her attendants exceedingly apprehensive of diabolical dangers, which might help explain why members of her entourage were vastly overrepresented among the possessed of Santa Chiara (six of fourteen).[113]

Angela Caterina's testimony was concerned overwhelmingly with the rapport between her and the former confessor. Only after she had talked at length of Bellacappa's supposed ill will toward her did she say anything about his frequenting the nuns who were believed possessed, and even these comments were only in response to a question from Tinti. Although she dissuaded nuns and prohibited her servants and attendants from seeing Bellacappa, the princess's doubts about his probity were based almost exclusively on her own dealings with him. Though surely aware of Dealta's numerous friendships with outsiders, she made no mention of them at all. Indeed, although the other nuns of Santa Chiara were particularly suspicious of Dealta, Angela Caterina scarcely mentioned this nonconformist nun and was far more worried about the actions of her sister, Ippolita, and especially Bellacappa.

From her testimony also emerges a portrait of the princess as a very high-strung, arrogant person who was used to bossing around everyone. In light of the condescending way in which she treated the Martinellis, one can easily understand why they and some other nuns were not overly fond of the abbess. But only to a degree can this explain the paranoia she displayed when offered the wine and sweets. Of course, she was testifying with the benefit of hindsight and was perhaps attributing to herself suspicions that she did not actually harbor until later. Regardless of when her fears arose, in the princess's mind Bellacappa was the culprit.[114]

It should also be noted that Angela Caterina's presence in Santa Chiara, combined with the meddling of her brother, Fra Giovan Battista, may have been a decisive factor behind the special attention that Tinti, Giudici, and even the Congregation of cardinals paid to this case. The Este family was one of northern Italy's most important dynasties, and the presence of Angela Caterina and her nieces surely heightened the interest in finding the source of the malaise that plagued the convent. The princess's own ills only augmented these concerns. Moreover, without the vigorous support of the princess and especially of her brother, the Holy Office almost surely would not have investigated this case so thoroughly. The Estes' conviction that Santa Chiara was plagued by demons and witches provided a very compelling incentive to conduct an exhaustive inquiry into these troubles. This dynasty and the former duke were far too powerful for the inquisitor of Modena or even the cardinal-inquisitors in Rome to ignore. As noted briefly in the introduction, in 1635, just a year before the outbreak of Santa Chiara's woes, several nuns at the convent of Sant'Eufemia in Modena were believed bewitched. In that case, various key figures, including Bishop Alessandro Rangoni, were skeptical, and the possession behavior quickly disappeared when the nuns received a new confessor.[115] Had Angela Caterina and Fra Giovan Battista exhibited a similar skeptical attitude, the Inquisition probably would not have even launched an investigation.

Defenders of Bellacappa

In spite of Angela Caterina's stinging indictment of the former confessor, there were some sisters of Santa Chiara who spoke in favor of Bellacappa, who was not himself interrogated until August 1638. One of the most important witnesses to defend Bellacappa was Sister Margherita Felice Castagnini, the only nun who had been cured of her demonic possession at the time of this investigation. Castagnini found that Bellacappa was always a "Father of good spirit." Personal cook to the princess and her retinue, she believed that the suspicions against him stemmed in part from the princess's antipathy toward him, which arose from her opposition to his seeing her ladies-in-waiting Sertori and Forni. Castagnini, however, did not understand this antagonism, since she was convinced the women saw him purely for spiritual reasons. It is important to remember, however, that Castagnini was also described as one of only two possessed nuns with whom Bellacappa was not in love.[116]

Like Castagnini, other Clarisses maintained that there were specific, justifiable reasons why the nuns went to see Bellacappa so often. Several witnesses claimed that the nuns were frequenting the confessor for spiritual concerns or for other acceptable reasons. According to some, Sertori and Forni were going to the confessional, at least in part, to receive lessons from Bellacappa in grammar and writing–the register does not indicate if these lessons were to teach them some Latin or, more likely, to improve their writing skills in Italian.[117] Sister Emerenziana Duosi, fifty-seven, admitted taking several letters to and from Bellacappa and Forni, since the princess did not want them seeing each other personally. Duosi defended her circumventing the princess's orders by claiming that the letters were pedagogical in nature. According to Duosi, Forni wrote letters or brief compositions to Bellacappa, who in turn corrected and returned them to Forni. Questioned further, Duosi admitted that the letters were sealed but did not know why. Both Bellacappa and Forni read some of these letters to Duosi, who found nothing at all inappropriate in them. In short, though Duosi acknowledged hearing Bellacappa say some very inappropriate jokes to some of the young nuns, she found his ties with Barbara Leonora Forni, one of those he was most suspected of being in love with, to be perfectly innocent.[118] Moreover, as the princess knew all too well, there were precedents of confessors serving as tutors to nuns at Santa Chiara. With some encouragement from the older nuns, in July 1609 the youthful Angela Caterina d'Este herself had written to her father to express her desire to learn the rudiments of Latin grammar. Duke Cesare concurred and arranged for Santa Chiara's confessor, Francesco Fognano, to serve as her tutor.[119] In short, the fact that many young nuns often visited the confessor did not convince all the sisters of Santa Chiara that he was guilty of moral turpitude, much less of witchcraft.

Even some who were quite critical of his flirting and sexual advances still had plenty of good to say about him. Beatrice Bendidio, who deplored his licentious conduct and his excessive socializing with many nuns, nonetheless was quick to point out that other than this vice, Bellacappa's service to the nunnery was exemplary–he satisfactorily heard the confessions of all the nuns and showed proper devotion in saying Mass.[120]

A number of older nuns, who may have been less likely to be the objects of his amorous inclinations, were less prone to have direct complaints against Bellacappa. Quite emphatic was Paola Coccapani's defense of the "poor, unfortunate" Bellacappa. Though she heard the demons implicate him, Coccapani, forty-three, said she would never believe it unless God himself told her so, because of the good deeds she always saw the confessor perform. During Bellacappa's third year as confessor, Paola was the assistant to the *abbacucca*–an officer in charge of preparing meals, doing laundry, and rendering other minor services for the confessor[121]–and had daily encounters with him, bringing meals to him at the turntable. She was also present when he met with some of those who later became possessed, and she testified that she saw no inappropriate actions.[122] Bellacappa also had an important defender in the person of Chiara Grillenzoni, fifty, who served as *abbacucca* for fourteen months while Bellacappa was confessor. Though admitting that there were nuns who spent an inordinate amount of time with him in the confessionals, Grillenzoni never saw him do anything improper with anyone.[123]

Giacinta Alessandrini, forty-four, also recounted the following incident to suggest a demonic plot to tarnish the reputation of Bellacappa:

> Maria Maddalena Colevati told my sister in confidence that two years ago one night, while she was awake, Father Bellacappa appeared to her with a laywoman . . . and told her, "If you don't do as I have done, I will maltreat you." Asked what he had done, he replied that he had renounced the faith. When [Colevati] responded that she did not want to do so, he started beating her. Then she had the idea of making the sign of the holy cross. As soon as she did so, he immediately disappeared. Since she was bewitched, one has reason to believe that the devil created this image to defame [Bellacappa]. I believe it was so, and we must not believe the devil.[124]

This story reflected the widespread belief, found in both popular and learned circles, that demons could appear in the form of a specific person.[125] Alessandrini interpreted this specter as exculpating Bellacappa, and Girolamo Menghi, the exorcist par excellence, would have agreed. Referring to demons' ability to dishonor a person, Menghi gave two examples of demons that purportedly assumed the physical appearance of upright clergymen, who were actually out of town at the time, and then made sexual advances toward women in order to defame the priests.[126] Simply put, Alessandrini and some other older nuns thought that the accusations against the former confessor were part of a diabolical plot to vilify a conscientious priest.[127]

Although the evidence appears overwhelming that Bellacappa made some unwanted advances toward many nuns, obviously many residents of Santa Chiara, including some of those who were now deemed possessed, were very fond of him. The bewitched Barbara Leonora Forni, an Este lady-in-waiting who regularly met with Bellacappa surreptitiously, was apparently upset enough about the suspicions against the former confessor to warn him about them. According to the vicaress, Aurelia Bendidio, nuns started expressing openly their doubts about Bellacappa already at the time of the early bewitchments of Paolina Forni, Barbara Leonora's sister, and of Leonora Galli in the spring of 1636. Distressed by these allegations, Barbara Leonora wrote to her former tutor and confessor to advise him of the rumors. When Bellacappa later returned to Santa Chiara for a feast day in the spring of 1637, Forni told Bellacappa personally about the suspicions against him, but Bellacappa curtly told her to mind her own business.[128] Barbara Leonora's warning showed at the very least that she cared about Bellacappa. If she had considered him nothing but a lecherous, opportunistic priest who took advantage of naive young nuns, she would not have bothered warning him. Attitudes toward Bellacappa were obviously much more ambivalent than those toward Dealta, who was generally disliked and distrusted by all but a minority of the sisters of Santa Chiara.

There are some interesting comparisons between the characters and experiences of Angelo Bellacappa, on the one hand, and Urbain Grandier, the priest burned in 1634 as a sorcerer in Loudun, on the other. Testimony from investigations indicates that both men were highly intelligent, well educated, charismatic, and articulate. Bellacappa was respected among the Observant Franciscans as a teacher of theology and wrote in very elegant prose—the obituaries he composed for the nuns who "passed on to a better life" were unmatched in eloquence, full of flowery praise of the sisters' piety.[129] For his part, Grandier was renowned for his very engaging sermons, and he wrote a most eloquent letter to Louis XIII in which he protested his innocence, excoriated his vicious accusers, and pleaded unsuccessfully for his life.[130] Both smooth-talkers seemed to enjoy considerable success in attracting women, which some people attributed to love magic. Grandier was from all appearances a feckless womanizer who blatantly flouted the vow of celibacy he had taken; he even wrote a treatise on celibacy, allegedly for his mistress, in which he insisted that marriage was ordained by the law of nature and that priests could marry. One woman claimed that merely a glance from Grandier sufficed to make her feel a "violent love" for him, and another reported that she encountered the priest in the street one day and shook his hand, whereupon she was immediately overwhelmed by a "strong passion" for him. But while the objects of Bellacappa's desires were nuns, Grandier seduced some laywomen from prominent families and was tried for immorality after apparently fathering a child with a young noblewoman. Unlike Bellacappa, he served a parish church rather than a convent. Although the Ursulines' demons identified him as the author of the spells, Grandier apparently had never actually met any of the "possessed" nuns, even though they claimed they burned with love for him and that he appeared as a specter to them at night in the convent and excited "impure thoughts" in them. Given his previous scandals, the priest's reputation as a sexual libertine could have easily penetrated the convent's walls without diabolical intervention. Bellacappa almost certainly participated in inappropriate conversations and actions in the confessional, whereas Grandier was never accused of abusing the sacrament of penance. Bellacappa was probably not as polarizing a figure as Grandier, who had a notoriously combative personality. Having been educated by the Jesuits, the ambitious Grandier coveted power, kept a very high profile, and came into conflict with some people of note, not least of whom was Cardinal Richelieu, who sought to reduce the power of the town of Loudun. These conflicts, along with the more lax standards of proof accepted by the French royal magistrates compared to the Congregation of the Inquisition, help explain the different fates that awaited these two clerics.[131]

All told, in 1638 many in Carpi harbored very strong suspicions that Santa Chiara's demonic woes were rooted in Bellacappa's use of love magic on many young nuns. Some probably believed he deserved a fate similar to Grandier's.

Chapter 4

THE EXORCISTS AND THE DEMONS

The women who were suffering at Santa Chiara received a variety of treatments for their ailments. When they first took ill, a physician and surgeon examined them and prescribed some cures. Once those proved ineffective, emphasis shifted to spiritual remedies. As the malaise of the ten nuns continued, in 1638 the entire community of Santa Chiara started holding special offices daily to beseech God to assuage the ills that plagued them, and the bewitched nuns went to Mass and received the Eucharist every day.[1] A half century earlier, Girolamo Menghi had listed a number of spiritual weapons to protect oneself against witchcraft: fasting, praying, making the sign of the cross, going to confession, attending Mass, invoking the saints, reciting litanies, sprinkling oneself with holy water, and putting exorcized salt in one's mouth. One could also carry with oneself either a candle that was blessed on Candlemas (2 February), oil or a palm that was blessed on Palm Sunday, or a card on which were written sacred words, such as "Iesus Nazarenus Rex Iudaeorum," the names of the evangelists or the Virgin Mary, or simply "In the beginning."[2] In other words, the most potent weapons against demon possession and witchcraft were the sacraments of penance and the Eucharist and a range of sacramentals, be they prayers, rituals, or objects. Menghi and other authorities on exorcism and witchcraft agreed, however, that it was totally unacceptable to fight witchcraft with witchcraft. That is, the Church strictly forbade invoking a demon to destroy a spell or putting an end to *maleficia* through any "superstitious" actions, since they necessarily involved, either explicitly or implicitly, diabolical assistance.[3]

Another traditional spiritual weapon that was repeatedly used in treating the afflicted nuns was exorcism. Exorcism was as old as Christianity itself, but the role of the exorcist became much better defined in the early modern era. In the Middle Ages exorcism was essentially unregulated, involving a wide range of rituals that were often administered by laypeople rather than clergymen. Moshe Sluhovsky has persuasively shown that although they had traditionally been viewed as mere "health practitioners," starting in the fifteenth century—an era that witnessed the appearance of the first lengthy exorcism manuals[4]—exorcists appeared more as decipherers of "interior truths" who had the ability to determine if a person were possessed by demonic or divine spirits. Since exorcists were dealing with maladies that supposedly were purely supernatural in origin, Church officials began in the sixteenth century to try to regulate exorcism closely and to prohibit all lay exorcisms.[5] Exorcisms were extremely common in early modern Europe, a reflection of the heightened fear of the devil and the increased number of cases of reputed possessions. Although Protestants, especially Calvinists, condemned exorcism as a "papist" superstition or even a form of magic that involved conjuring demons, many Catholic thinkers strongly reaffirmed the validity of exorcism, which they considered a sure sign of the truth of the Roman Catholic faith. Exorcism and possession have also been described as having important eschatological meaning. Specifically, an individual who was possessed and the travails he or she endured during exorcism might serve as a microcosm for all of humanity's struggles with the devil toward salvation.[6]

As this chapter will reveal, the interaction between the ailing Clarisses and exorcists shows that possession was a "culture-bound syndrome" that was strongly shaped by prevailing stereotypes.[7] If the various elements of demonic possession can be viewed as parts of a "text" or script, the ailing women and the exorcists were all reading from the same page and playing their respective roles in this real-life drama.[8] But the fact that possession behavior was predictable and even stereotyped did not make it any less real, traumatic, or painful.

Girolamo Menghi and the Art of Exorcism

The exorcists who served the nuns of Santa Chiara would have received training from other priests who were learned in the art of exorcism and would have studied various printed manuals that were recognized as authoritative for exorcists. Revered as the greatest exorcist of the sixteenth century, Girolamo Menghi (d. 1609) was probably the most influential and, as the author of several important manuals, certainly the most prolific writer on exorcism of the post-Tridentine era.[9] As noted in chapter 2, Menghi was an Observant Franciscan and spent most of his active life in Lombardy and in Bologna, a city not far from Carpi and Modena. Like Angelo Bellacappa after him, Menghi was a member of the Observant province of Bologna and was esteemed as a scholar and teacher.[10] Menghi's influence was strongest in his native northern Italy, where his books were commonly found among monastic libraries in the regions of Lombardy, Emilia, and Veneto. By far the most popular of his publications was his vernacular work, *Compendio dell'arte essorcistica*, published for the first time in 1572 and reissued in many other editions.[11]

The three books of the *Compendio* examined respectively demons and their capabilities; sorcery and witchcraft; and the remedies against demon possession and witchcraft, with special attention to exorcism. Throughout these works, Menghi based his conclusions on authoritative Christian texts, such as the Bible, works by Augustine and Aquinas, and more recent treatises such as the *Malleus Maleficarum*. In book 1, Menghi stressed the reality of demons, formerly heavenly angels who had fallen from grace because of their sins, and their ability to torment and lead astray humans. Throughout this book, Menghi emphasized the power of demons and the mischief that they alone, with God's permission, could inflict. In the second book of the *Compendio,* Menghi concentrated on witchcraft, looking at the evils that humans in conjunction with demons could perpetrate. Menghi was probably the most important champion of the idea, which eventually won wide acceptance, that demon possession was almost always caused by witchcraft, a conclusion that he arrived at following decades of working as an exorcist.[12] Describing different types of miscreants who took part in the occult, Menghi defined a "sorcerer" (*sortilego*) as someone who practiced a "false religion," who called on the saints or even recited the Lord's Prayer or the Ave Maria but really worked with diabolical aid. Some sorcerers sought to foretell the future or "to excite love in human bodies and hearts." Others undertook "vain" and "superstitious" remedies to heal people who were bewitched or otherwise infirm. The other important category of those engaged in occult practices was the witch (*malefica*), broadly defined as someone who endeavored "to do harm to one's neighbor," a rubric that included many different types of witches. Menghi stressed the central importance in witchcraft of the pact with demons, which enabled witches to call the demons to them at their pleasure by using certain words and gestures at designated times. The demons in turn taught witches various evil spells to help spread their diabolical intentions. The term that Menghi preferred for those who made pacts with the devil was *Strigimaghe,* roughly "witch-magicians," using the feminine form of the word because, he believed, more women than men take part in this "perversity." After renouncing Christianity, the witch made a profession of allegiance to the devil, placing her hands in his, either privately or in a group. Regardless of whether called a "witch" or "magician," she could not oblige an evil spirit to do anything unless she made a pact with a demon that was superior to the spirit that served the witch—superior spirits could constrain inferior ones to take certain actions.[13]

Witchcraft experts agreed that a witch could make a pact with the devil in a variety of ways. As Candido Brognolo noted in the 1660s, the pact could be explicit or implicit. With the former, the would-be witch explicitly accepted the devil either through words, which could be spoken or written, or gestures such as a nod of the head. In most cases, this was followed by the "profession," in which the person formally renounced all allegiance to God and agreed to serve Satan. An implicit pact occurred when a person used "superstitious" gestures and pursued goals that ran contrary to divine commands, the institution of the Church, and natural virtues. Combined, these actions indicated a tacit agreement between the person and the devil.[14]

Experts on exorcism and witchcraft went to pains to show that witchcraft, like demon possession, was a reality, not a figment of human imagination. Among other "proofs," Menghi referred to scripture, such as passages in Exodus 22 and Leviticus 20, that called for the death penalty for all sorceresses, wizards, and mediums. He claimed that the Bible would not prescribe capital punishment unless people really were inflicting diabolical harm. Menghi also cited the opinions of Augustine and other theologians, statutes in Roman Imperial Law, and even some stories of popular origin, all of which proved, to his satisfaction, that some people made pacts with the devil.[15]

Since demons were more powerful than humans and could, on their own, deceive people and even possess their bodies, one may wonder why they bothered with witches. Theologians acknowledged that demons did not need the assistance of human beings to cause trouble. Demons could do anything they wanted without the help of humans, provided God allowed them to perpetrate this harm. Be that as it may, a host of writers believed the devil preferred using witches. Kramer, for example, insisted that Satan favored using witches because this augmented the harm inflicted in three ways: it increased the offense to God by "usurping to himself a creature dedicated" to God; once offended, the angry God allowed the devil to do more harm to people; and Satan benefited from the perdition of the souls of witches. In return, demons, though metaphysically superior to humans, agreed to obey the commands of witches, respecting the pacts they had formed together. Consequently, Kramer was convinced that witches were almost invariably involved in diabolical mischief.[16] Menghi, too, believed that demons liked to involve witches since this magnified the insult to God—demons tempted people to fall into sin and renounce God and worship them instead, resulting in greater offense to God.[17] Writing in 1608, the Ambrosian priest Francesco Maria Guazzo further argued that God permitted witchcraft because doing battle with witches and Satan was a means by which humans could glorify God; God has given humans free will, and they are therefore free to sin; witchcraft itself reflected God's "benevolent government," as Satan, too, was granted free will and is allowed to exercise it through tempting humans; and the existence of witchcraft revealed God's mercy, wisdom, power, and justice—God has often denied Satan the power to do harm, allowing even the "foolish little creatures" of humans to overcome the devil though permitting demons to punish humans for their sins already in this life.[18] In short, by the early seventeenth century most writers on demonology were convinced that Satan preferred doing harm through witches than solely through demons.

Menghi and other experts recognized several different categories of diabolical torments endured by those whose bodies were possessed by demons. Some people who were possessed were tormented only in their bodies and suffered only physical pain. Others suffered not only physical ills but also harm to their goods and mundane stature, a prime example being the plight of the biblical Job. In addition to or in lieu of physical ills, others suffered major torments in their mental faculties. Of these, some were deprived of the use of their reason only at times, whereas others constantly behaved like "irrational beasts."[19]

Menghi insisted that medicine alone could not cure someone who was possessed by demons, but he also believed that there were certain physical and mundane remedies that could assuage the ills of a possessed person. Certain herbs could alter the disposition of the body, and Menghi placed special emphasis on St. John's wort, an herb also known as the *fuga daemonum* (flight of the demons), which unclean spirits absolutely abhorred. Like Kramer, Menghi observed that demons could more easily torment people who were prone to "melancholic passions"[20] and asserted that certain remedies, such as applying herbs, could make people more lighthearted and actually force demons to leave the bodies they possessed. So, Menghi concluded, it was perfectly correct for exorcisms to include the application of herbs and the like to people who were bewitched, provided these things were first blessed in the name of the Trinity.[21]

To rid a body of unclean spirits, Menghi insisted that exorcists ordinarily had to resort to conjurations to constrain the demons to obey by virtue of the invocation of God or of angels. According to Menghi, demons became most frightened every time the exorcist threatened to send them to hell. He declared that when the exorcist "calls and invokes the Holy Angels, who are ordered by God [to fulfill] this duty, . . . [the demons] fear [they will] be precipitated there. And they are so ignorant that even if some old woman . . . threatens them . . . , oftentimes they will leave [the body]."[22] All too aware of the pains of hell, the demons were enjoying a respite from those tortures while they possessed a person's body and became most frightened when threatened to be sent back to the infernal agonies.[23]

Some of Menghi's opinions on exorcism evolved over the course of his career. When he wrote the *Compendio* in 1572, Menghi noted with approval that there were rare examples of people who were not priests, including some women, who had successfully exorcized.[24] By the time he published the *Fuga Daemonum* in 1596, he had become much stricter in insisting that only priests could exorcize. By the late sixteenth century, Menghi and other exorcists were somewhat beleaguered in defending their office, whose utility was being questioned by a growing number of clerics.[25] In part to ensure greater uniformity in practice, Menghi gave several reasons in his *Fuga Daemonum* why only priests could exorcize. Before being exorcized, the afflicted were supposed to confess their sins sacramentally, but many demons did their best to impede these confessions. Menghi claimed he often had to spend an entire day adjuring demons until they finally relented and allowed the confession to be concluded. Since the exorcist in effect had to get involved already during confession and since only priests could hear confessions, only priests should exorcize. Likewise, the exorcist ought to be a priest because exorcisms should be preceded by taking the Eucharist. Only a priest could celebrate Mass, and the struggles with the demons could begin during the celebration of the Eucharist. Priests alone had the right to wear a stole or to bless objects to be used to liberate the demoniacs, and priests' hands–having been ritually consecrated upon ordination–regularly caused demons to "tremble" when placed upon the heads of the possessed.[26]

The exorcist had a most important responsibility, and Menghi asserted that the exorcism had a better chance of success if the exorcist was himself contrite and had sacramentally confessed his sins.[27] He must be "profoundly humble," realizing the power to expel demons came not from himself but from God alone. Since the success of exorcisms depended entirely on God, the priest must be careful that he not defile himself with "one scintilla of vainglory." According to Menghi, the exorcist must also have the knowledge–acquired from reading especially the *Malleus Maleficarum* and works by Silvestro Mazzolini and by Menghi himself–to recognize when it was truly necessary to exorcize. Exorcisms should be performed only when there was clear evidence that the ailing person suffered from demon possession, not from natural ills.[28]

The very nature of exorcism raised controversy. Some Catholics echoed the Protestant view that exorcists practiced magic or sorcery: exorcisms amounted to conjuring demons, not unlike the practices of magicians who allegedly manipulated occult powers.[29] Detractors, furthermore, accused some exorcists of ambitiously promoting themselves as enjoying a special status of holiness. Although, according to Roman Catholic theology, the sacraments worked automatically, when a priest performed an exorcism, there was no guarantee that the prayers and incantations he uttered and the holy objects he used would successfully expel demons. The success of these actions, like other sacramentals, depended on God's consideration of each particular case and "on the dispositions of those using them."[30] If one exorcism failed, the exorcist sought a formula that was "more pleasing" to God. Even though authorities like Menghi insisted that all credit for expelling demons went to God alone, those whose exorcisms succeeded more often than others' could develop the reputation of working miracles. After all, any priest could effect transubstantiation in celebrating the Mass, but apparently only a few people could expel demons. Moreover, trusting in the accuracy of the tests they conducted to verify the presence or absence of demons, exorcists viewed themselves as the sole arbiters of whether their actions had worked. By evaluating the words spoken through the mouth of an energumen, exorcists could determine, they claimed, where the demoniac's identity ended and that of the demon began.[31] In 1668, three decades after the episode at Carpi, Candido Brognolo provided ammunition for critics by writing that exorcists performed "superhuman" acts, ascended to the ranks of the angels, and in a way even attained divine status.[32]

Responding to criticism of exorcisms, Menghi pointed out in his *Fuga Daemonum* many abuses that must be avoided. Never should a priest pursue exorcisms for glory or money. The priest must never think that his exorcism could work automatically or even that his actions ultimately affected God's decision to free an energumen of demons. As for remuneration, a cleric, if poor, could at most accept some alms in return for his services. Exorcists also must not prescribe medicines or in any way act as physicians, a tenet that received official papal backing in 1614.[33] And they had no business touching certain parts of the bodies of the demoniacs, as some clerics were wont to do, during exorcisms. Menghi also insisted that they absolutely must never use "superstitious" methods in trying to free the energumens of their demons. He even opined that those who abused the office of exorcist in any of a number of ways deserved being sentenced to jail or the galleys.[34]

Menghi laid out the steps priests were to take in conducting exorcisms, an outline that the Carpi exorcists followed rather closely. Well before exorcisms were performed, the priest should exhort the victims of demon possession to show contrition for their sins and confess sacramentally. While confessing, they must indicate to the confessor if they were at that time under a ban of excommunication, and if they were not, then they were to take the Eucharist, which, Menghi reiterated, was a "fire that burns . . . against the malignant spirits."[35] Although one could exorcize at any time, Menghi avowed that it was best performed at "high morning" after Mass had been celebrated and was most effective on the holiest days, such as Easter, Marian feasts, and the like.[36] It was also best for the exorcism to take place in church both to instill greater fear in demons and to avoid the possible scandal if the priest performed it in a private dwelling. The exorcist should use special caution in dealing with women and, to avoid scandal, should never be alone with a female being exorcised.[37] Writing in 1501, Silvestro Mazzolini, who lived in Bologna and from whose work Menghi borrowed considerably, warned his fellow clerics to be especially cautious when exorcizing women, because some of them faked possession just so they could get priests to touch their bodies.[38] Always wearing a stole when he exorcized, the priest must "bless and exorcize" all things–be they food items, beverages, or other objects–that were to be applied to the possessed people and that might be employed to conjure demons.[39]

In his various publications, Menghi gave numerous formulas for exorcisms, which included many prayers and conjurations. The following is a typical command that the exorcist made of the demons, to be said after the priest entered the church with the afflicted and said a brief prayer before the altar:

On the part of the most Holy Trinity of the Father, Son, and Holy Ghost, I warn you demons, who have come in help of those demons that are vexing this creature of God, [name of possessed]. Under pain of being immersed in a pool of fire and sulfur by the hand of your enemies, under pain of being put under the control of your enemies and being condemned to the pool of fire and sulfur for a thousand years, insofar as you give any help or favor to those demons who are vexing the body of this creature of God, [name of possessed]. Go away at once and go to the places designated for you by God. Behold the Cross [exorcist makes the sign of the cross] of the Lord, flee, you adversaries. . . . I also order you demons who torment this creature of God, [name of possessed], that you exit from her immediately, that you go out and leave her free and healthy and [without] any lesion of the soul or the body so that she may serve God, her creator. I also command all your enemies, in the name of the most Holy Trinity of the Father, Son, and Holy Ghost, that they compel you to obey my mandates and orders. And under the same pains, I order that you say and do nothing that displeases those present or absent. . . . In the name of the Fa-[sign of cross]ther, and of the Son [sign of cross], and of the Holy [sign of cross] Ghost. Amen.[40]

After making this command, the exorcist encircled the neck of the possessed person with the stole, tying three knots in it; placing his hands on the bewitched person's head, the priest then uttered many names that referred to God ("Jehovah," "Yahweh," "Christus vincit," and so on) while repeatedly making the sign of the cross. Still placing his hands on the head of the vexed person, the exorcist then started reading the first verses of the gospel according to John: "In the beginning was the word, and the word was God," etc. As with most exorcisms, there followed many other prayers, readings, litanies, and conjurations made in the name of God the Father, the Virgin Mary, the angels, and many saints.[41]

Menghi advised that the exorcist must be extremely patient, as successful exorcisms could take hours and even many days.[42] When he gave commands to the demon in the body of the possessed, he must never let up on it, even if the demon seemed to scorn and mock the commands as if they had no effect. With patience, the exorcist was to continue and force the demon to obey the commands. Otherwise the demon would have in effect won the struggle with the exorcist, whose task of dominating the spirit would subsequently become much more difficult. Even if the exorcist pursued the same command for an entire day to no avail, he should not discard it in favor of another one unless inspired to do so by God.[43] Menghi offered a variety of reasons as to why some exorcisms might fail to free someone of demons. This could stem from a lack of faith among the people involved or from serious sins committed by those possessed. The exorcist himself could be responsible either because he demonstrated a lack of faith or because he did not select the appropriate remedies. Or God could allow the possession to continue in order to accumulate the merits of the afflicted person, as in the case of certain mystics.[44] Even so, the exorcist must not abandon hope of eventually succeeding.

In conducting exorcisms, the exorcist was to respect a number of rules. Citing some of the same rules outlined by Kramer, Menghi insisted the exorcist must never say anything that involved the invocation, either expressly or implicitly, of demons; that is, one dared not use the power of demons to expel other demons from the bodies of people. One must also never use unknown words or names, because they might have a superstitious meaning and therefore could involve the unintentional invocation of demons. The words that the exorcist uttered must not include any falsehoods, and he must not employ anything vain, including written characters. The exorcist was supposed to read passages and to say and write things only if they were pertinent to chasing away demons. Everything that he said and did was to be done with reverence, and the goal sought must be pleasing to God.[45] Under no circumstances should the exorcist joke with the demon. Menghi cited as a bad example a priest who ordered a demon to leave the body it possessed. When the demon asked where it should go, the exorcist replied to his outhouse. That night, the priest went to relieve himself in the outhouse and was almost "suffocated by the devil" and was barely able to escape.[46] For Menghi and other experts, the goal was to agitate the demon, and Silvestro Mazzolini advised exorcists to try to get the demon angry by hurling insults at it and by "pulling the hair, ears, and nose [of the possessed person]"![47]

When the spirits did speak, the exorcist must always doubt what they were saying and make sure that he not show too much familiarity with the demons—doing so allowed the demon to gather its strength and resist the adjurations. Unclean spirits were to speak only when the exorcist ordered them to do so and only about things germane to the possession. The one exception to this rule was when God coerced the demons to speak, a loophole that, as we shall see, was amply exploited in Carpi. There was a host of questions that the exorcist could and should ask of a demon: what is its name; how many demons are in the body; who is the head of these spirits; by what spell or spells is he detained in the body; by what means can the spells be destroyed; who are their enemies in heaven and in hell; what words torment the demons the most; by which saint must they exit the body; when will they leave the body, and what sign will they give that they are doing so; and why they are oppressing this particular person. All these questions served not to benefit the unclean spirits but to repel the harm they caused. If, for example, the demons indicated that the possession was a punishment for a sin and this seemed plausible, the exorcist would assign some penance to the energumen, which might lead to the expulsion of the demons. The priest must absolutely never ask demons for advice or for information about things unknown, such as future events. More broadly, an exorcist should never ask demons to do something for him. Doing so was a mortal sin because it involved an implicit diabolical pact.⁴⁸

On the basis of over thirty years' experience in battling demons, in the *Fuga Daemonum* of 1596 Menghi stressed more than ever before the role of witchcraft in cases of demon possession. Not only did he arrive at the conclusion that witches had incited demons to enter the bodies of most energumens; he also found that it was much more difficult to cast demons out of the bodies of the bewitched than of those whose possessions did not involve witches. Menghi also defended asking demons by what maleficent spells they were "detained" in the body of the energumen, only a short step from condoning the interrogation of demons to identify witches. Favoring more aggressive attacks against witches, Menghi thus helped strengthen the connection between diabolical possession and witchcraft, promoting exorcisms as an important tool in the hunting of witches.⁴⁹

The Exorcists of Carpi

The exorcists who ministered to the beleaguered Clarisses played a very important role in the development of this affair. These priests always conducted the exorcisms in the convent's exterior church, where they might be accompanied by other priests and perhaps a medical expert. At no time, however, were there any nuns present other than the energumens themselves. A key player behind the scenes was Fra Giovan Battista d'Este. Although he was never questioned by the Holy Office, the former duke firmly believed that the nuns were possessed and actively promoted the exorcisms in Santa Chiara. Although he had no formal authority over the convent of Santa Chiara, Giovan Battista had a vested interest in the safety of the convent, given the presence there of his daughters and sister. As we shall see, to avoid alienating members of the powerful Este family, even the cardinals in Rome refrained from being too brusque in trying to stop the duke-turned-friar from meddling in this matter.

Five priests performed exorcisms at Santa Chiara: Giovan Battista Zaretti, sixty-nine, an expert brought in from the outside to deal with this exceptional case of possession; Girolamo Cabassi, fifty-five, the provost of the college of Carpi and master of the art of exorcism; Gregorio Montaguti, seventy-two, a curate from Carpi who had been performing exorcisms in Modena, Bologna, and Carpi for the past twenty-four years; Agostino Bertesi of Carpi, thirty-five, a doctor of theology who had been practicing exorcism sixteen years; and Domenico Verrini, forty-three, also from Carpi, who had been an exorcist for a dozen years.⁵⁰ These priests were interrogated either in Fiscal Giudici's study or in the archpriest's home. Giudici questioned Montaguti on 19 May 1638,[51] but inexplicably, Inquisitor Tinti did not interrogate the four others until mid-July.

Zaretti, among others, reported that he was solicited by Giovan Battista d'Este, who, along with Archpriest Niccolini, urged him to come to Carpi to exorcize the demoniac Clarisses.[52] When Tinti asked him to describe his background, Zaretti took pains to show that he had broad experience in dealing not only with demon possession but also with a variety of mental illnesses:

> I have been a practicing exorcist for thirty years, and I have worked with a variety of brains: insane [*pazzi*], melancholic, infirm, and possessed ones. Most notably, I spent two years in Milan at the Hospital of the Insane, where I found similar sorts of diverse infirmities, especially those of melancholic humors and still other types. And I clearly saw the difference between those who are possessed by spirits and those who are dominated by other sorts of humors.[53]

Zaretti and the other exorcists were questioned as to why they were convinced the ailing women were possessed. Inquisitor Tinti or Fiscal Giudici repeatedly asked if the nuns could be suffering from natural ills, and the exorcists obliged with a long list of reasons why they clearly were not victims of a natural malady. One point they stressed was that the nuns (or the demons) responded to exorcisms. Had they been suffering from natural ills, the clergymen avowed, exorcisms would have had no effect on them. Montaguti explained that he was able to force the demons to obey his orders by making the sign of the cross and placing relics over the parts of the nuns' bodies in which the demons were found at a given moment.[54] Menghi and other experts in fact believed that a strong indication of possession was if a person became quite agitated in the presence of sacred objects and rituals, as demons invariably reacted violently to all things holy.[55]

Zaretti showed how the symptoms of the Clarisses differed considerably from various types of mental illness. He observed, for example, "those who have lost their brains and are crazy . . . are never in their right minds, nor do they ever make sense when they speak, talking about one thing one moment and another the next."[56] Describing something that resembles what today we would call paranoia, Zaretti further noted that those who were dominated by a melancholic humor were always timorous, fearing strange accidents for no reason at all. This would have a direct impact on one's spiritual life, as Zaretti had seen several people who were constantly afraid that they had not confessed all their sins and therefore repeatedly returned to the confessor, passing entire days confessing their transgressions to him. Other melancholics feared that they were going to be thrown in jail or killed, and they screamed desperately in response to the "bad humors" that tormented them. The difference between the insane and melancholic, on the one hand,

and the possessed, on the other, was that the former did not respond to exorcisms and did not make sense when questioned. By contrast, people who were possessed by spirits made perfectly good sense when interrogated, provided the demons had been rendered obedient by exorcisms. According to Zaretti, this was the case with "the poor nuns," who could be perfectly lucid when not tormented by demons. True, at times, it took long, persistent efforts on his part to make the demons obey, but eventually the evil spirits succumbed to the exorcisms.[57]

The demons were also wont to make the nuns throw themselves violently on the floor, causing injuries. The exorcists had personally witnessed such actions, but Zaretti made it a point to say that these acts were more common in the absence of the priests. According to Zaretti, the demons had less strength when the exorcists were present, and the afflicted nuns themselves told him that they were more prone to this and other abuse in their absence.[58] The Congregation in Rome had expressed strong reservations about the exorcisms already in May,[59] and so Zaretti and the others were by July 1638 somewhat on the defensive and tried to show the positive impact of their actions.

As evidence of possession, the exorcists mentioned a wide range of bizarre physical symptoms that seemed quite unlike any natural illnesses they were familiar with. According to Zaretti, often the spirits ascended to the nuns' heads quite suddenly, which caused them to close their eyes immediately and induced a sleep so profound that it was impossible to wake them. This deep sleep hit them when they were sitting upright in chairs, where they remained seated with their heads dangling backward or resting on their shoulders. Only through exorcisms could the nuns be awakened. According to Zaretti, when the devils stopped tormenting the nuns' heads, they started oppressing and wearing down their hearts, which subjected the sisters to such excruciating pain that they screamed and called out the names of Jesus and Mary. In other words, the nuns were in their right minds when the demons resided in their chests and, enduring terrible pain, called out to Jesus and the Virgin Mary, as they would ordinarily have done so. When, however, the demons occupied their heads, the nuns did not feel any pain in their chests but were utterly out of their senses, which enabled the demons to speak through the mouths of the nuns. For Zaretti, this dramatic difference in behavior was a clear sign of demon possession.[60]

Probably the most spectacular "proof" of demon possession that the exorcists reported was the extraordinary way in which some nuns contorted their bodies. Exorcisms were widely described as involving confrontations of ever-increasing intensity, and the demons put up their most violent resistance when they were on the verge of being expelled.[61] In exorcizing at Santa Chiara, Cabassi reported that when he and colleagues forced some demons out of the nuns' bodies, the demons' departures affected some of the nuns in a violent and most peculiar manner. Several sisters were forced to arch themselves, bending straight backward in a most unnatural way. Although this caused considerable pain, some of the nuns arched their backs so far that, while remaining standing, they could almost touch their heels with the backs of their heads, a position that was also witnessed by exorcists in Germany, France, and elsewhere.[62] According to the exorcists, this very unnatural position was hardly attainable by anyone, save perhaps a few acrobats who were born with phenomenal abilities. But even professional acrobats bent over backward very slowly, not abruptly and violently in the manner of these possessed Clarisses, nor could they remain in that position as long as the demoniac nuns, some of whom maintained the pose for half an hour. In short, the exorcists could not imagine anyone behaving thus who was not possessed by the devil.[63] This unusual manner of bending their bodies backward bore little resemblance, however, to the allegedly erotic gyrations that "possessed" nuns were said to demonstrate elsewhere, nor did any of the possessed of Santa Chiara (or their demons) proclaim that the devils inhabited their "shameful parts."[64]

Although not all the nuns bent over in this manner, they all demonstrated bizarre actions that seemed humanly impossible. According to Cabassi, when they forced some demons out through exorcisms, many nuns started hyperventilating and screaming constantly for up to two hours. But unlike a person who was not possessed, once they stopped screaming, the nuns did not show the fatigue, dryness of mouth, or loss of voice that one would expect after such an ordeal.[65] When afflicted by the demons, the Clarisses also demonstrated physical strength far beyond their natural capacity, a trait commonly witnessed by exorcists throughout early modern Europe.[66]

The exorcists also observed some unusual physical effects on the nuns when they succeeded in forcing some of the demons to leave their bodies. According to several of the priests, the spirits exited the bodies of the possessed in a most boisterous manner, causing the nuns to pass gas continuously for long stretches of time. This phenomenon dovetailed with the common belief that demons entered and exited the bodies of people through the openings of the body: the ears, nostrils, anus, vagina, or, most often, the mouth.[67] Although passing gas is of course generally associated with natural ailments, Bertesi noted that at times the agitated nuns passed gas constantly not just for two, three, or four hours but even for an entire day. Never had he seen anyone naturally subjected to such incredible flatulence. For Bertesi, the fact that all ten nuns were passing gas in the same manner at the same time showed beyond a shadow of a doubt that their ills were supernatural, and many treatises on exorcism recognized excessive flatulence as evidence of bewitchment.[68] The exorcists also related that when the demons left their bodies, the nuns' tongues became black and swollen, which they often bit until they bled.[69]

Not only did the possessed exhibit very peculiar physical symptoms; they also at times demonstrated knowledge that the exorcists were sure the nuns had not acquired by natural means. For example, Bertesi observed Sister Giulia Angelica Sertori, a native of Modena, speaking Florentine with a perfect Tuscan accent. The exorcist was sure that this was really the demon speaking through her mouth since Sertori, when not affected by demons, could not speak the Florentine dialect at all.[70] More important, at least some of them showed a level of learning that the priests thought women were utterly incapable of having. Bertesi discovered that some of the nuns understood or even spoke some Latin, even though they had never studied it.[71] Even more impressive was that on one occasion, a nun—or rather her demon—understood Hebrew. With Bertesi present, Cabassi held Sister Caterina Margherita Ronchi's hands and quoted from scripture in the original Hebrew: "Neither wisdom, nor prudence, nor advice, can stand in Yahweh's presence" (Prov. 21:30). The demon responded in Italian through Ronchi's mouth: "This is true. One can't do anything against him." Cabassi asked the demon why it had answered in the vernacular since it clearly understood what was said in Hebrew. The devil retorted that for this assignment of possessing the young Ronchi, it had been forbidden (one assumes by Satan) to do a variety of things, including speaking Hebrew, in order to trick people into thinking that these nuns were merely "crazy" and not diabolically possessed.[72] Santa Chiara of Carpi catered to the daughters of elite families and most likely all the nuns had a certain level of reading skills at least in Italian. True, a good number of the nuns who were called as witnesses did not sign their names. For Bertesi, it went without saying that the nuns themselves did not know Latin, and he was surely right that none of them had studied Hebrew. Consequently, the ability to speak Latin and to understand Hebrew was further proof that it was the demons, not the nuns, who were speaking.

Knowledge of events outside the cloister also showed the demons at work. The exorcist Verrini reported that one morning he was buying fruit and vegetables at a stand in Carpi's central plaza, when someone asked him to go perform an exorcism on a boy who was ailing. Verrini refused to do so and shortly thereafter went to Santa Chiara. At the convent he ordered a demon, "in virtue of charity" to depart from the body of Giulia Angelica Sertori. The demon responded that since Verrini had shown no charity to the boy he had declined to see, the exorcist had no grounds to order the demon to leave. Although we may wonder if news of this incident in the plaza could have reached the turntable and parlor of Santa Chiara, Verrini was convinced that Sertori could not have known about it. Persuaded that this knowledge was supernatural in origin, Verrini determined that this must have been a demon, not Sertori, who spoke.[73]

The amazing knowledge that these nuns demonstrated conformed to what experts expected to find in possessed people. In addition to Kramer,

Menghi, Bodin, and other authorities on demonology and exorcism, even theologians who were rather skeptical about demon possession found such evidence convincing. The Spanish theologian Domingo Soto (1495–1560), for example, expressed the following doubts about allegations of demon possession and the efficacy of exorcism:

> Most exorcists are mere impostors, as I myself along with many others am an eyewitness, for often they pretend to expel demons where there are none to begin with. What is more, many little women (*mulierculae*) fabricate an obsession by demons for monetary gain, saying they are the souls of the dead whom they thus put to shame. Therefore, barring some effective proof of these demons is available, one should not have faith in them, unless of course they speak foreign languages or remain immobile and cannot be moved by the strength of many men.[74]

Thus, even a skeptic like Soto found knowledge of "foreign" languages and superhuman strength to be valid proofs of diabolical presence. A quarter century before the Carpi case, the papacy as well recognized similar phenomena as true signs of demon possession. In 1614 Pope Paul V issued the *Rituale Romanum*, a book describing rituals performed by priests that proved to be a watershed in post-Tridentine reform. Though warning against mistaking a natural illness for possession, the *Rituale Romanum*'s chapter on exorcism accepted the inexplicable knowledge of distant events and the ability to speak or understand languages unknown to the one possessed as valid signs of demon possession.[75] A few years earlier in Loudun, exorcists were convinced of Urbain Grandier's guilt in part because the demons, speaking through the mouths of possessed Ursulines, uttered words in Latin (though some skeptical observers were bemused by the demons' weak knowledge of Latin grammar and their claim that God did not want them to respond in Greek, Hebrew, or other languages).[76] A few years later, one of the "proofs" of the possession of the Ursulines in Auxonne was that they all understood and some even spoke some Latin.[77]

Weighing all the evidence, the various exorcists had no doubts that the ten nuns were suffering terribly from demon possessions. All the priests would have agreed with Bertesi, who declared that if two hundred possessed people each showed a different symptom of possession, one could find all two hundred symptoms in every one of these ten Clarisses.[78] The testimony of the various clerics shows that they were very well versed in the learned treatises on exorcism and witchcraft, as they listed a wide range of symptoms—extraordinary physical strength, unnatural contortions, clairvoyance, and inexplicable knowledge of languages—that were commonly believed as proof positive of diabolical possession.

If Girolamo Menghi could have visited Santa Chiara, he surely would have agreed with the exorcists of Carpi that the ten nuns were possessed, but he would have rebuked them for committing a major error: although they always conducted their exorcisms in public and never had just one clergyman present, they regularly exorcized the nuns together as a group, which Menghi found very counterproductive. If demons in all the bodies were being adjured by exorcists at the same time, they could come to each other's aid—when one spirit was suffering, it might receive succor from another demon in someone else's body. Moreover, if several demoniacs were being exorcized at once, a demon might be forced out of one body but then go directly into the body of another person.[79] Apart from this one shortcoming—of which the exorcists in Loudun were also guilty a few years earlier—the exorcists of Santa Chiara were faithful disciples of Menghi and other experts.[80]

Physicians, Exorcists, and Inquisitors

An influential set of inquisitorial guidelines for handling witchcraft cases dealt explicitly with the role of exorcisms. Although not published until the mid-seventeenth century, the *Instructio* circulated widely in manuscript form among Italian inquisitors starting in the 1620s and became the Holy Office's most authoritative guide on witchcraft. These guidelines have convincingly been attributed to Cardinal Desiderio Scaglia, who (as mentioned in chapter 2) served on the Congregation of the Inquisition in Rome. Rather than enunciating new standards, his *Instructio* served to summarize the principles that the Holy Office was already employing in cases of witchcraft.[81]

In his *Prattica,* his more general guidelines for inquisitors from the early 1620s, Cardinal Scaglia addressed, among many issues, the subject of demon possession among female religious. Noting that nuns were especially prone to believe they were diabolically possessed, Scaglia expressed skepticism about the reality of many of the purported possessions in convents. Some nuns who had been forced to take the veil by their families might experience extreme feelings of despair that could lead them to doubt basic tenets of the Roman Catholic faith. When some nuns believed they were possessed or bewitched, he avowed, they all too quickly began to suspect fellow sisters they were not fond of. Revealing these suspicions to their superiors invariably caused much agitation in the convent, as other members of the community shunned a suspected witch and "every little infirmity" was attributed to maleficent spells. Soon rumors spread that the suspect had been seen "walking about at night," and other nuns began interpreting her "every action and word" as relating to witchcraft. According to Scaglia, the nuns then inevitably revealed their fears to family members and others outside the convent, so that rumors quickly spread throughout the city, causing great anxiety among the relatives and acquaintances of the female religious.

Scaglia believed that exorcisms tended to increase rather than assuage the agitation, and he further averred that some nuns even feigned possession in order to get attention or simply to continue receiving the frequent visits of the exorcist.[82] Cardinal Scaglia no doubt would have found his fears entirely vindicated by the unfolding of events in Santa Chiara.

Advising a degree of skepticism toward alleged cases of both demon possession and witchcraft, Scaglia bemoaned the fact that some judicial authorities were far too quick to conclude that demon possession or witchcraft were behind the ills or misfortunes that afflicted people. The *Instructio* proclaimed that if the woes could conceivably be the result of natural illness, before taking action against anyone, inquisitors were to seek the opinions of competent physicians to examine the afflicted individuals.[83]

Physicians in fact were widely recognized as playing a role in establishing whether a person was suffering from a natural malady or from possession or bewitchment. One must not think that physicians interpreted all ills as natural sicknesses or that exorcists always concluded that they were of supernatural origin. True, in Loudun various physicians expressed doubts about the possession of the Ursulines and suggested that their ills could have stemmed from melancholy, epilepsy, or hysteria. They opined that the afflictions even could have been mere fabrications on the part of the nuns.[84] Evidence from seventeenth-century Italy suggests, however, that the option of exorcism actually reinforced the status of physicians. When their cures proved ineffective, medical professionals could conclude that the ills were supernatural in origin and refer the patients to exorcists. By so doing, they effectively relieved themselves of any responsibility for the failure of their cures.[85] The testimony from the Carpi case clearly shows that the clergy and physicians were working in tandem, not at cross-purposes with each other. The exorcist Bertesi believed that, in addition to being bewitched, the nuns might also be infirm or tormented by some "humors."[86] As noted previously, it was commonly believed that melancholy could be either a cause or an effect of demon possession. While melancholy supposedly could be a symptom of demon possession, the melancholic were also generally believed more vulnerable to being possessed by spirits.[87]

The testimony of medical experts clearly showed that physicians and clergy viewed their tasks as complementary. On 17 July 1638 Inquisitor Tinti convoked Giovan Battista Abbati, thirty-eight, a physician who served the convent. Asked if he tried to cure any of the nuns who were reputed to be possessed, Abbati said that he had indeed examined them before they were discovered bewitched and later used his medical skills to assist the exorcists in their treatment of the nuns. Having seen that "natural remedies" did not work at all, Abbati concluded that the sisters' ills were supernatural in origin. When asked if he thought they were diabolically possessed, Abbati replied, "I'll leave that judgment to the experts in the art of exorcism, and

I, as a physician following the treatises of many of our authors, believe and judge that the poor nuns are very much possessed."[88] As for evidence of possession, Abbati pointed out that authors on both exorcism and medicine agreed that when medical remedies were applied and did not work—which happened not once but many times to these "poor nuns"—this was a good indicator that the afflicted people were possessed by spirits. Abbati noted, for example, that for two years he treated Sister Barbara Leonora Forni for "hysterical passions." Hysteria was understood as an illness unique to women, which was characterized by mood swings and whose roots were traced to the womb. Abbati recalled that at a certain point, the demon inside Barbara Leonora derisively asked what good medicine would do since he was in her body. Having seen no improvement in her condition, Abbati was now sure that he had misdiagnosed the ills of Barbara Leonora and that she was indeed the victim of bewitchment.[89] Like physicians elsewhere in the sixteenth and seventeenth centuries, Abbati concluded that his patients were possessed only after his medical cures proved entirely ineffective.[90]

Apart from the failure of medical cures, Abbati was convinced that the Clarisses were possessed for some of the same reasons cited by the exorcists. He mentioned the sudden contraction of nerves, which left them unable to move; the amazing ability of many to bend way over backward in a very unnatural way; the fact that some of the bewitched sisters—he was told by the exorcists—had spoken Latin and Hebrew, "a thing that is impossible in an idiotic person and a woman."[91] Abbati and the various exorcists shared the same mentality, sexism included, in dealing with the ills of Santa Chiara. Significantly, the physician Abbati examined the ailing nuns well before any exorcists and was the first person on record to conclude that the Clarisses were possessed.

The barber-surgeon Francesco Donelli, sixty, testified that he, too, collaborated with the exorcists to cure the sisters' ills. Donelli reported that at a certain point, the exorcists and the medical experts all agreed that the nuns should be given purges. The demons, however, foiled the application of purges by apparently closing off the canals and thus preventing anything from being expelled. In closing off the lower orifices, the demons also caused blood to flow from the nuns' mouths. Several times Abbati ordered that the nuns be bled, but Donelli, who was always called to perform these bleedings, declared that on more than one occasion he was unable to make them bleed at all from either the arms or feet. At first unaware of what malady afflicted the sisters, Donelli determined that they were possessed when the demon of Barbara Leonora Forni told the barber-surgeon that it would not allow blood to flow from the vein he was cutting. In fact, so long as no priests were present, Donelli was unable to draw any blood from the veins of any of the nuns. Upon their arrival, the priests touched the spots to be cut with their "sacred fingers," made the sign of the cross over those places, and started reading exorcisms over the nuns. Only then were Donelli's efforts to bleed the nuns successful. Convinced that there was no natural impediment to the flow of blood in the veins he was cutting, Donelli was sure that the devil had impeded the flow.[92] The exorcist Bertesi offered an explanation: the demons were congregating the blood around the heart and throat in order to choke the sisters, which also prevented the flow of blood from the veins.[93]

Put simply, the physician and surgeon were no less convinced than the exorcists that Satan was responsible for the travails of Santa Chiara. In a similar manner, a few years earlier, the treatment of the "possession" of Virginia de' Medici, mother of the princess-abbess Angela Caterina, demonstrated that medicine, religion, and magic were closely intertwined, reflecting deeply rooted religious and cultural convictions found throughout early-seventeenth-century Europe.[94] In analyzing the history of madness, Erik Midelfort has persuasively shown that in Germany the diagnoses of demon possession and of melancholy both became much more common in the late sixteenth and early seventeenth centuries, trends that showed that the roles of physicians and exorcists complemented rather than competed with each other.[95]

Exorcisms and Accusations of Witchcraft

The principal role of exorcists was of course to expel demons from the bodies of the people they possessed and not to hunt witches. That said, the exorcists in Carpi were providing plenty of ammunition to potential witch-hunters, such as the inquisitor and his fiscal. Tinti and Giudici asked the various exorcists if the nuns were possessed, bewitched, or both. Montaguti insisted that possession and bewitchment were distinct and independent of each other, a point of view no doubt shared by the other exorcists. Just as it was possible for a person to be possessed by a demon without witchcraft, so one could suffer the evil effects of witchcraft without having a demon in one's body. On the basis of the symptoms he had observed, Montaguti was convinced that at least six of the ten currently ill nuns were clearly the victims of witchcraft: Sisters Sertori, Forni, Ronchi, Cimadori, Amoldoni, and Anna Maria Martinelli. Zaretti was confident that all ten were both possessed and bewitched, though some were worse off than others. Having worked with the afflicted nuns for the past four months, Cabassi was also persuaded that all ten were bewitched as well as possessed, basing his conclusions on both his own experience and the learned writings on exorcism.[96]

As the interrogation continued, the exorcists shifted their focus from the demoniacs to the witches. Montaguti avowed that the number of motives for casting a maleficent spell was infinite; a witch could be hoping to inspire hate or love in the possessed person, or to drive him or her insane or to suicide. He further argued, however, that it was possible to ascertain the motives of the witch from the unusual effects of the *maleficium;* if demoniacs demonstrated inclinations directly contrary to those they ordinarily exhibited, this was almost surely the effect desired by the witch. For example, if a woman had constantly loved her husband and then suddenly found him repulsive for no apparent reason, she was probably the victim of a maleficent spell to make her loathe her spouse. According to Montaguti, love magic designed to attract someone was more difficult to discern. Since love is a perfectly natural form of affection, one suspects magic only if the love seems really out of place or exaggerated. In the particular case at hand, however, he said that he could not tell if any of the Clarisses had been bewitched for the purpose of loving or hating anyone.[97]

Of the five exorcists, Cabassi was by far the most active and confident in trying to discover who was responsible for the witchcraft. He and Verrini worked together in exorcising the nuns, but Cabassi's greater interest in witch-hunting is obvious in their different interpretations of a phenomenon they experienced together. During exorcisms involving all ten nuns, Cabassi and Bertesi heard the nuns say literally hundreds of "names," words that they spewed out when demons purportedly left their bodies. The exorcists carefully wrote down all the words they could, which numbered close to two thousand. Bertesi identified most of these words, many of which ended with the syllable "el," as belonging to the Semitic languages of Hebrew, Arabic, or Chaldean. Cabassi claimed that not even "the genius of Aristotle" could have come up with the multitude and variety of names that the demons had uttered. If a genius of Aristotle's stature could not invent so many names, then, as far as the exorcists were concerned, the fabrication of these words was obviously far beyond the ability of these ten nuns. In fact, Bertesi was quite shocked at how quickly and fluently the nuns pronounced so many names, concluding that "it is not possible nor is it believable that women were capable" of knowing all these words.[98] When the sisters were in their senses and not tormented by the demons, Bertesi asked them about all these words, but each claimed she knew nothing about them and did not understand them at all. In short, because these words were so unusual, Bertesi avowed that it really was impossible for women to say them, let alone to make them up.[99]

Although Bertesi portrayed these Semitic words only as evidence of diabolical possession, Cabassi was convinced that the words were actually part of maleficent spells. Bemoaning the "great impiety of these spirits," Cabassi asserted that with these words, the demons were misappropriating and abusing passages from both the Old and New Testaments, including the Gospels. Just as the host, holy water, and holy candles could be used for magical purposes, so it was believed that sacred words could be used–perhaps modified or rearranged—to cast evil spells. He gave the inquisitor a copy of the list they had compiled of all the words the demons had uttered.[100]

A close examination of these words might uncover the spells and, Cabassi hoped, even the identity of those who had cast the spells. Asked directly if he knew what instruments the witch or witches used in their spells, Cabassi replied that he knew only what the demons themselves had told him and was not sure how much faith one should put in that. Having paid lip-service to the need for caution in considering the words of demons, Cabassi proceeded to describe with confidence some of the means by which the spells were cast, relying exclusively on information he attributed to demons. Cabassi mentioned briefly that the devils said that the spells involved the abuse of all the sacraments, but he discussed at length the abuse of scripture and of sacred formulas. The demons told Cabassi that within the bodies of the possessed one could find the opening passage of the Gospel according to John ("In the beginning was the Word"), the sign on Jesus's cross ("Jesus, the Nazarene, King of the Jews"), the Song of Solomon, and the beginning of the Passion as found in John. The demons volunteered this information even before Cabassi had learned any of the words they were repeating. When he understood the words that the demons said, he realized that these sometimes unintelligible words actually signified different sacred passages or mottos: some, for example, represented the text of the Song of Solomon, others part of the Gospels, still others the sign on the cross, and so on. When Cabassi ordered a demon to give him the words with which they abused the Credo, the spirit said that they had devised words to misuse the creed only up until the passage "I believe in the Holy Ghost." The demon observed that diabolical spirits could not fittingly mingle with the Holy Ghost, and so they were unable to complete the abuse of the Credo. The demons further explained to Cabassi that if they gave him the words in the order in which they used them, he would immediately discover the spells they had cast. In order to make it more difficult for him to decipher the spell, they told Cabassi the words in an entirely random order.[101] In short, Cabassi was convinced that the inappropriate use of scripture was a very important instrument used in these evil spells.

Cabassi also recounted an unusual experience while exorcizing Giulia Angelica Sertori. According to the priest, one of her demons told him that the sign on the cross had been used in the spell and beckoned Cabassi to touch the navel of the possessed woman. He did so and felt something rigid inside her abdomen, about the length of the palm of his hand and the width of two fingers. The demon said that this object would eventually exit her body, but not yet. Cabassi was suggesting that the wooden sign on the cross was literally inside the body of Sertori, causing her a great deal of physical and spiritual woe.[102] Cabassi would have had no trouble finding experts on exorcism and demonology who affirmed that demons could surreptitiously, merely by means of a mental command, send physical objects into the bodies of victims to vex them.[103]

Though again saying that one should not believe what demons said, Cabassi proceeded to tell Tinti everything they were recounting about the instruments of spells. Several devils told him that somewhere in the convent were some buried statues, some of which included elements of the holy sacraments and even the consecrated wine and host. Such statues, if pierced with needles, were believed to serve as a means of causing great bodily harm and even death to the individuals the statues represented. The exorcist unsuccessfully ordered the demons to show him where these instruments were, but they steadfastly refused, telling him and his colleagues that they had to keep looking and that once the instruments were found, all the ills of Santa Chiara would disappear.[104]

All learned writings on witchcraft held that witches and demons could do no more than what God allowed them to do. True, if witchcraft depended on God's permission, it might seem odd that maleficent spells were more likely to work if they included the abuse of sacraments or sacramentals. Why should God be more apt to allow a spell to work if it involved the misuse of things associated with worshiping him? But, as noted repeatedly, objects such as the host, once consecrated, were perceived as having supernatural qualities, which could be badly misused if they fell into the wrong hands. Consequently, it was the responsibility of everyone to ensure the safety of the hosts, holy water, holy candles, and the like and to instill respect for them in all believers. Failure to do so could incite God's wrath, and he might therefore allow witches and demons to cause further woe.

An element of this attitude can be seen in Cabassi's reference to the Eucharist. He believed that Carpi's spells were cast with particular abuse of that sacrament, since the demons showed a special irreverence toward it. Cabassi castigated them for this lack of respect, but the demons replied, "If you priests don't show respect and reverence [toward the Eucharist], how do you expect us, a bunch of devils, to do so."[105] The spirit of Giulia Angelica Sertori then explained that they were not referring to the exorcists but to two other priests who maltreated the host; one of them was Bellacappa, but Cabassi did not learn the identity of the other.[106] When priests themselves misused the sacraments, divine wrath was a predictable result.

Provost Cabassi also related that Barbara Leonora Forni had an image of the Nativity, which turned out to be enchanted and an instrument of a spell. Every time she looked at or approached the picture, the demons threw her to the floor and tormented her for a good stretch of time. Significantly, Forni confided that a couple years ago, Bellacappa had kept this image for a few days, implying that he had had ample opportunity to use it in a spell. Cabassi decided to try an experiment with Forni. Hiding the small holy image under his vestments so that she could not see it, Cabassi came close to

Forni; the nun immediately began yelling and jumping up and down, which convinced the exorcist that there was indeed a spell on the image. The same thing happened with certain devotional books that Forni owned that had also been in the hands of Bellacappa; she could not return to her senses until the books were removed from her presence. Once Cabassi exorcized these objects, they were harmless.[107]

In the case of Caterina Margherita Ronchi, the exorcists Cabassi, Bertesi, and Verrini also identified a number of instruments of her bewitchment, all of which had been handled by Bellacappa. Ronchi had a breviary with some copper figures used as bookmarks. Almost all the copper figures contained passages from the Song of Songs, amorous phrases of the groom to his bride, such as "How beautiful you are, my love, how beautiful! Your eyes are doves" (1:16). Convinced that the spells included the abuse of words from the Song of Songs, Bertesi believed that the spells transformed passages about divine love into poems about human love. During exorcisms, whenever the priests quoted from the Song of Songs, the demons reacted in a most agitated manner. One day the archpriest of Carpi tried an experiment in the presence of Cabassi and Bertesi. The young Ronchi was lying on the floor, virtually unconscious, and Niccolini slowly brought the breviary toward her head, but in a way that she could not see it. When it was near her, though not in view, she immediately began shaking and shouting and did not stop until the breviary was removed. For the exorcists, the evidence was overwhelming that Bellacappa had used the breviary and copper figures as instruments of love magic.[108]

Bellacappa had also handled and, according to the demons, cast spells upon other objects belonging to Ronchi, including a clavichord, a book of litanies, and a book of music. Each time Ronchi placed her hands above the keyboard to play the clavichord, the nerves of her hands contracted in such a way that she could not play a note and her pains increased. Consequently, Cabassi ordered that the clavichord be removed to a corridor that led to the exterior church. On more than one occasion, he saw Ronchi walk near the musical instrument. When she got within two or three steps of it, she fell to the ground, her whole body agitated. When Cabassi subsequently had it removed from the nunnery, her vexations stopped.[109]

The possessed nuns or their demons also indicated that Bellacappa had used items such as an *Agnus Dei,* a fruit bowl, a handkerchief, a small prayer book, a rosary, a little wooden cross, and a reliquary as instruments of magic.[110] As we have seen, although sacred objects such as breviaries, crosses, and holy medallions were quite common, mundane objects could also supposedly serve as instruments for spells.[111]

Cabassi also expressed amazement—no doubt shared by many modern observers—at how the spirits seemed intent on identifying the spells and the witches. They told Cabassi that God did not want to provide miracles to reveal the culprits, but, they added, if the exorcists really applied themselves, God would help them. All the while the demons protested that they were not saying these things voluntarily but were being forced to do so by God. Demons in the bodies of all the nuns save two–Sertori and Veronica Maria Coccapani–declared that the witch was Sister Dealta Martinelli. Around the time of the feast day of St. Anthony of Padua (13 June), however, even these spirits fell in line, as the demons of Sertori and Coccapani claimed that St. Anthony himself obliged them against their will to identify Dealta as the witch. Offering to swear on the host that Dealta was the witch, these demons claimed that whenever they lied they faced the unmitigated ire of God and all the pains of hell.[112]

As for the purpose of the maleficent spells, Provost Cabassi again noted that he knew only what the demons told him but continued to show considerable confidence in what they recounted. The spirits told him that some spells had been cast for love and others for hatred. When the love spells did not produce the desired results, they were transformed into maleficent hexes. Cabassi mentioned only one specific case of a nun being subject to love magic. In a long conversation while she was in her senses, Caterina Margherita Ronchi revealed to Cabassi that Dealta had strongly urged her to love Bellacappa, but the young nun refused to do so. She also reported that Dealta once led her to the place above the upper confessional where there was a hole that was big enough for an arm to pass through it. Dealta encouraged her to put her arm through to the other side where Bellacappa was standing at the moment, but Ronchi said she did not comply. Cabassi told the Inquisition that the manner in which she told this story convinced him that Ronchi probably had taken part in some illicit touching, presumably with the former confessor. Later, one of her demons confirmed that Ronchi took part in immodest caresses, but God at that moment removed her cognitive faculties so she did not know what she was doing, thereby exculpating her.[113]

Cabassi referred briefly to the incident of Easter Monday, when Dealta supposedly "renewed" the evil spell with her glance at the possessed nuns who were in the choir saying the rosary. When several of them fell to the floor screaming, some healthy nuns sent immediately for Fathers Cabassi and Bertesi. When they arrived, the four unconscious sisters were carried to the exterior church where the two priests immediately began administering exorcisms; Cabassi recalled that when he first saw them on that occasion, the tongues of Sisters Ronchi and Forni were hanging outside their mouths. Only after long and exhausting exorcisms were the priests able to return the nuns to their normal state. During this session, the demons identified Dealta as the author of the spells. Bertesi further asserted that according to Martin del Rio, an authority on possession and witchcraft, bewitched people regularly faint at the sight of the witch who cast a spell on them. This of course could serve as a means of identifying the culprit. Subsequently, some of the possessed nuns, while in their senses, told Cabassi that whenever they saw Dealta or were seen by her, they felt increasing pain around their waists. They claimed they had noticed this discomfort even before they were discovered bewitched, and Cabassi, testifying in mid-July 1638, estimated that the spells had probably been cast as early as three or four years ago.[114]

The demons also seemed to know what was happening in the Inquisition's investigation, even though the possessed nuns themselves supposedly had no access to information concerning the case. One day, one of the demons of Giulia Angelica Sertori said to Cabassi that the "snake had fallen into the trap," and the demon seemed melancholic inside the body of the nun the entire day. When the exorcist asked what he meant by the "snake" in the trap, the demon replied quite clearly that his "lord" had been imprisoned. Cabassi observed that the demons referred to Bellacappa as their "principal lord" and Dealta as their "lady." The former confessor had in fact been put in prison in Bologna, but Cabassi argued that there was no way that Sertori could have known about this at that time. In fact, no one at Santa Chiara knew about Bellacappa's imprisonment until two or three days after this incident.[115] In short, through his work as exorcist, Cabassi had become convinced that both Bellacappa and Dealta were witches responsible for these possessions. At one point, he even told the archpriest that he would wager his own head that Dealta was a witch.[116]

The exorcists definitely had a supporter in Fiscal Giudici. Less than a month into her incarceration, on 19 May 1638, Dealta complained to Giudici that the damp cell in which she was being held in the convent was making her ill. Giudici in turn asked Abbati if the cell in its present condition could make her ill, and the physician replied that it certainly could. Giudici therefore intended to dry out the cell by sealing the window and burning coal in braziers in the cell for a couple days, during which Dealta would be removed from the cell. The exorcists, however, protested that Dealta dared not be moved, that this was just a ruse on the part of the demons so that she could do greater harm to the ailing nuns. There was no way, they argued, that the cell could be dried by fire since the demons themselves were causing the humidity as a pretext for moving Dealta. These concerns might cause one to wonder how powerful these demons really were. If they had the power to control the dampness in her cell, why did they need her services to do harm and how could incarceration prevent her from inciting diabolical mischief? Be that as it may, Giudici bought the exorcists' argument and left Dealta in her damp cell.[117]

The provost's own testimony also shows how he helped incite panic and suspicion among the Clarisses of Carpi. Upset that Dealta's incarceration had not put an end to the travails of Santa Chiara, an angry Father Cabassi one day proclaimed to a group of Clarisses—later admitting to Tinti that this was an exaggeration—that there had to be another traitor and wicked woman in the convent who was renewing the harmful spells. Later that evening, Sister Dianira Bergamaschi, having already been identified as a witch by the demons, made a hysterical scene and decried that the demons were going to be her ruin. Terribly upset that the demons were implicating her, she even went so far as to say that she was going to jump off the balcony and kill herself.[118] To be sure, the suspicions that Cabassi nurtured were able to take hold only because they fell on fertile ground. Everyone believed in the reality of the possessions, and many feared that there were still other witches wreaking havoc in Santa Chiara. It should be emphasized that even Bergamaschi blamed the demons, not the nuns themselves, for casting aspersions on her.

Not surprisingly, the exorcists all agreed that their ministrations were doing the nuns much good, even though they had not yet been freed of the demons. The nuns themselves avowed that they suffered less in their abdomens than before, and the exorcists observed that the sisters' faces had not for a long time looked as healthy as they did now.[119] When Tinti asked in mid-July if it might be better if the exorcisms ceased, Zaretti replied:

> Father, I think that it would make them worse. For one thing, this has been tried before, and these poor possessed nuns say that they were considerably worse off and ran much greater dangers [without exorcisms]. For another thing, every time that one has not used a remedy with exorcisms, the spirits have taken greater possession and have reduced the poor things to a worse state. Indeed, these exorcists in Carpi told me that when they suspended exorcisms, at least four of these possessed women (namely, Sister Caterina Margherita Ronchi, Sister Barbara Leonora Forni, Sister Anna Maria Martinelli, and Sister Clara Maria Amoldoni) appeared near death.[120]

For his part, Verrini pointed out that two women of Santa Chiara had already died from such spells and believed that the majority of the ten ailing sisters would perish without exorcisms.[121]

When asked what would happen if one ceased the exorcisms, Cabassi predictably said that things would go from bad to much worse. Along with Verrini, Cabassi noted that each time there was a gap of two or three days between exorcisms, the nuns' condition deteriorated considerably. The provost became convinced that the reason for this was there were not only evil spells but also witches in Santa Chiara itself. Since after each interval between exorcisms the nuns were faring noticeably worse, Cabassi concluded that the witch or witches were renewing the enchantments, which resulted in the continued suffering of the unfortunate nuns. He added emphatically that he was all but certain that exorcisms had saved the lives of three or four of the nuns and gave an interesting "scientific" explanation why. The demons, he claimed, accumulated menstrual blood in the hearts of the women, causing them to suffer "extreme passions." In the case of about four of these nuns, the demons collected so much menstrual blood that it not only filled their hearts but also ascended all the way to their throats and almost choked them. This finally caused them to regurgitate menstrual blood from their mouths, which Cabassi himself saw in the case of Anna Maria Martinelli–the only one of the "four" he identified–who exhibited very strange behavior and was clearly suffering excruciating pains. The exorcists finally relieved Anna Maria and the other three of the most acute pains by placing the host on their hearts. Only after performing this on Anna Maria for three or four days in a row did the demons finally give way and obey the commands of the priests. Without these exorcisms, Cabassi was sure that Anna Maria would have died.[122]

Cabassi's gynecological explanation for this diabolical turmoil was rather unusual. Although experts on witchcraft had long held that women were more apt to give in to diabolical temptation, Cabassi was implying that women were also more likely to be the victims of witchcraft. If a principal means of diabolical torture was congregating menstrual blood in one's heart, then males obviously could never be touched by that form of demonic suffering. Many authorities on witchcraft and possession, such as Girolamo Menghi, did indeed believe that women were more likely to be both witches and the victims of demon possession. Menghi believed that demons preyed more easily on women and "dim-witted" males (*huomini leggieri di cervello*) and that females were more susceptible to possession because their ills could be misconstrued as merely an imbalance of humors caused by the womb.[123]

Another author on exorcism, Candido Brognolo, observed that menstruation itself could cause some women to think they were possessed when they really were not. He asserted that there was a certain defect in the menstrual process for some women, in whom humors or toxic vapors ascended during menstruation to the stomach. There the humors were likely to taint food, resulting in indigestion and reduced appetite. The poisonous vapors then rose to the brain, which caused confusion, fantasies, frenetic disorders, and for some, the illusion of being possessed by demons. Similarly, when the humors or vapors descended from the brain and passed in all directions throughout the body, some women mistook them for unclean spirits and indeed acted much like energumens. Consequently, Brognolo warned, the prudent exorcist must not act impetuously in dealing with agitated women, whose woes could stem from menstrual humors.[124]

In this case, however, Cabassi was convinced that misplaced menstrual blood was a *symptom* of possession, not a cause of misdiagnosing bewitchment. He asserted that only the miraculous powers of the host could break this spell. He proclaimed that the body of Jesus, which along with his blood, had been sacrificed to save humanity from the tortures of hell, was needed here to disperse the bad blood that poisoned the hearts, bodies, and souls of these young nuns.[125]

On 24 July 1638 Tinti, assisted by Fiscal Giudici, interrogated Provost Cabassi about his exorcisms in search of more details that implicated Dealta or others who might have played a role in the possessions. When asked if the demons identified anyone as a witch, Cabassi replied:

> Father, the demons were made to swear above the sacrament so that one can believe what they say. . . . I ordered that, if what they were saying was true, they must expel three, four, or more key demons from the bodies [of the nuns], which they did so as a sign of the truth. Not one but several times they affirmed that Sister Dealta is the witch. . . . And they swore this even over the most holy sacrament. And this was done by threatening them with God's full anger and all the pains of hell for each time they did not tell the truth. The demons further said, "I know that we are devils, so that you should not have faith in us since we are the fathers of lies. But we protest to you that in this we are telling the truth, albeit unwillingly, since we are forced to do so by God."[126]

When witnesses referred to events surrounding exorcisms, they often were, in effect, enabling the possessed nuns to testify indirectly. Sister Clara Vittoria Massi, for example, told the inquisitor that the bewitched Caterina Margherita Ronchi was about to take communion one day but suddenly collapsed, as if she were dead. According to Massi, the exorcist Montaguti came to minister to Ronchi and began castigating the demons for blaming these ills on a nun in this convent. The demons, however, protested that they were willing to give any sign to show that what they said was true. Forcing the demon to speak by command of the Virgin Mary, Montaguti then ordered the demons to show that Dealta was in fact the witch by throwing themselves on the floor to worship the holy sacrament. The demons then dutifully prostrated themselves, through the body of Ronchi, in humble adoration of the consecrated host. Significantly, no one witnessed this occurrence other than the exorcist and the various possessed nuns. Exorcisms were always performed out of sight of the healthy nuns, and this incident occurred when the bewitched nuns were participating in the Eucharist separately in the external church. Apparently no healthy nuns were in the adjacent choir at the time, and Clara Vittoria Massi admitted that she had heard of this episode from Sister Cinzia Ciarlatina, one of the demoniacs.[127]

Similarly, another nun with an almost identical name, Clara Maria Massi, recounted a story that also originated with a demoniac sister. Referring to the Easter Monday incident, Massi reported that even before Dealta entered the church,

> The devil of Sister Barbara Leonora told her that its Lady was coming, and immediately thereafter Sister Dealta arrived. But Sister Barbara Leonora did not want to believe [that Dealta was its Lady]. The devil told her, "You

don't want to believe that Sister Dealta is the one who has put you in this state and has played a role in other things, but you have so many indications to the contrary that you really can't doubt it anymore. You also know that she asked for two things from you, and one she did not get but the other she did; [the thing that she got] was the hair that she asked to use for the Madonna of San Giovanni." And Sister Barbara Leonora in fact then told me that [Dealta] had indeed asked her for her hair when she started to wear the veil.[128]

This amounted to two accusations. Most obviously, the demon was purportedly telling Barbara Leonora Forni that he had entered her body at the order of Dealta. But the request to have Forni's hair was a transparent accusation that Dealta had misused Barbara Leonora's hair, which was cut short when she became a novice. Both Massi and another nun reported that Barbara Leonora, while in her senses, claimed that she gave Dealta her hair to adorn the statue of the Madonna of the Company of San Giovanni and that shortly thereafter the demon took control of her body.[129] Even if one assumes that Barbara Leonora Forni and Caterina Margherita Ronchi truly reported these incidents to the other sisters in good faith, according to inquisitorial practices, this testimony would have to be rejected as unreliable since demons, and consequently possessed people, cannot be trusted to tell the truth. Tinti, however, did not express any reservations about the depositions of the Massis, which both impugned the reputation of Dealta and amounted to secondhand accounts of demoniacs.

The unavoidable conclusion is that suspicions of witchcraft were based to a considerable extent on the words and actions attributed to demons, many of which were revealed through exorcisms. In this regard, the evidence against Dealta and Bellacappa was quite similar to the spectral evidence of the Salem witchcraft trials; the possessed reputedly were tormented by apparitions of demons in the form of the people who, it was assumed, had made a pact with the devil.[130]

The Skepticism of the Congregation of the Inquisition

Persuaded that the exorcists themselves were a major source of the problems at Santa Chiara, Cardinal Barberini and the other members of the Congregation on a number of occasions wanted to put an end to all exorcisms but faced considerable opposition from leading figures in Modena and Carpi. The cardinals anticipated by a century the views of the "enlightened" Modenese priest, scholar, and historian Ludovico Antonio Muratori (1672–1750), who observed that possessed and bewitched people were found only where there were exorcists.[131]

Pulling strings behind the scenes was Fra Giovan Battista d'Este, who actively supported the exorcisms in Carpi. As we have seen, he conducted some exorcisms himself early in the travails of Carpi and fully believed in their efficacy. The former duke also meddled in the investigation of witchcraft in the convent, especially concerning the use of exorcisms. The Congregation of the Holy Office, by contrast, had expressed concern about exorcisms already in October 1636, when, in recommending sentences against the three suspected witches (Bosellino, Losi, and Loia), it ordered:

> Those exorcists who are named in the proceedings, who exorcized the supposed bewitched people, must be declared by Your Reverence as unfit for such an office in the future. And to avoid the many inconveniences that are born from such exorcisms, the Holy Office orders that a general prohibition be made so that no one exorcizes without permission from the *ordinario* [the archpriest of Carpi], which must not be granted easily.[132]

Among those affected was Gregorio Montaguti, described as elderly, whom the bishop of Modena lauded as a man who led a saintly life and chased away demons with fasts and prayers. The bishop strongly hoped that Montaguti would be allowed to continue offering exorcisms to the faithful in Modenese lands. When, in December 1636, Tinti wrote to Barberini to bear witness to Montaguti's integrity and effective pastoral skills, he surely was also implicitly supporting the bishop's request for permission to exorcise.[133] In the following January Cardinal Barberini reluctantly acceded to this request but warned Montaguti to be prudent and to avoid causing "scandals" with his exorcisms.[134]

As Carpi's demonic woes intensified, Fra Giovan Battista d'Este managed at some point to bypass the Congregation of the Holy Office by petitioning and receiving permission to continue exorcisms from another committee of cardinals, the Congregation of Bishops and Regulars. On 21 May 1638 the Bishops and Regulars granted an extension to allow the exorcisms to continue at Santa Chiara for another four months. (We do not know when the Bishops and Regulars first granted permission to exorcise at Santa Chiara.)[135] Affronted by this challenge to its jurisdiction, the Congregation of the Inquisition overruled its sister congregation and issued the following instructions on 29 May to Inquisitor Tinti:

> Since it is not easy to judge if these nuns are really possessed by demons, or are oppressed by melancholic passions, or, worst of all, are made to feel [as if they are possessed] by the exorcists, the Holy Congregation is of the mind that you ensure that none of these [exorcists] comes near the monastery to exorcize the possessed nuns until [we issue] a new order, especially those [exorcists] whom the Holy Congregation has already suspended from exercising the office of exorcist.[136]

Two months later, Cardinal Barberini informed Tinti that he must convince Fra Giovan Battista that the only way to cure these "miserable women" was to keep them separated from one another and away from the exorcists, administer other spiritual remedies, and provide the convent with a "prudent and learned confessor."[137] Even though, as noted above, he had no formal role in Santa Chiara's governance and was never questioned during this investigation, Fra Giovan Battista had a considerable impact behind the scenes on the Carpi affair. Convinced that the nuns were possessed by demons, he furtively wielded his influence to promote exorcisms, which he believed were essential to restoring the women's physical and spiritual health.

In an obsequious letter to Barberini, Inquisitor Tinti claimed that he himself was not yet persuaded that the nuns were actually possessed and wished to defer to the wisdom of "Their Eminences" the cardinals. Referring to the desire of the Clarisses to continue the exorcisms, Tinti claimed he was moved simply by their "tears and prayers," not by a conviction that they were truly bewitched. Moreover, the inquisitor claimed that in these proceedings he never asserted that the nuns in question were possessed, always referring to them as "allegedly possessed." These protests notwithstanding, the tenor of his other letters and the questions that he asked of witnesses strongly indicated that Tinti was sure that the sisters were in fact possessed by demons.[138]

Writing in Modena in early August 1638, Tinti informed Fiscal Giudici of the need to respect the mandate of the Congregation and enjoined the exorcists to cease all their treatment of the afflicted nuns, who were to be kept separate from all others both in pursuit of their "spiritual exercises" and in their day-to-day living.[139] Spurred by Barberini's comment that exorcists merited punishment, Tinti forbade the clerics even to visit the convent, much less to exorcize the nuns. Aware that the nuns wished the exorcisms to continue, Tinti urged Giudici to console them and convince them that there is nothing more pleasing to God than obedience, emphasizing the need of all religious, male and female, to obey their superiors. Relaying the wishes of the cardinals, Tinti promised to assign to the convent a conscientious confessor—according to the wishes of the cardinals, specifically an older, experienced priest—to furnish the spiritual medicine needed to cure the nuns' infirmities.[140] Henceforth confession, prayer, and the daily offices—not exorcism—were the weapons to fight Santa Chiara's spiritual woes.

In his response, the fiscal assured the inquisitor that he was complying with the orders but reported that the condition of the afflicted nuns was worsening. In a letter dated 16 August 1638, Giudici wrote Tinti that the previous day, which was the feast of the Assumption of the Virgin Mary, the devils increased their torments apparently to show their disrespect for the Madonna. First the nuns all lay as if dead for two or three hours. Four of them contorted their bodies, bending over backward in the manner in which they had done on numerous occasions, for almost two hours. Giudici observed that Caterina Margherita Ronchi contorted her body in some other ways heretofore unseen at Santa Chiara. One of these was a modified lotus position: seated on the floor, Ronchi crossed her legs, her feet touching her knees and her head bent forward, resting between her feet. There seemed to be no remedy, although with great effort the princess finally provided relief with "the wood of the cross"—evidently a relic that was among the convent's most precious possessions. Giudici added that it was with great difficulty that he and others were able to restrain Cimadori, preventing her devil from throwing her into the well, the first mention that a possessed nun might try to kill herself.[141] Letters written within the next few days indicated that their condition was still deteriorating. Giudici was especially concerned about two sisters who had not eaten for two days.[142] He assured Tinti that he had dutifully followed orders and imposed the ban on exorcisms but added that both the ailing and healthy nuns were most upset by this ban.[143]

In early September Cardinal Barberini reissued the ban, more convinced than ever that the exorcists were the problem and that the solution was to be found in the spiritual remedies of a compassionate confessor and the natural remedies of a competent physician.[144] Barberini's convictions were strengthened when he received an initial report, later retracted, that three of the supposedly possessed nuns had been totally cured of their agitation. In response to a directive from Rome, Tinti convoked on 16 October the priests Cabassi, Verrini, and Bertesi, who all reluctantly signed a promise to obey the orders of the Congregation of the Inquisition not to exorcize the nuns or even to approach the nunnery for any reason, under pain of being sent to the galleys.[145]

On 19 October Provost Girolamo Cabassi voluntarily appeared before the Inquisition of Modena, showing a letter he received two days before from the abbess of Santa Chiara. He recounted that upon opening the missive he saw that it was actually written on behalf of the possessed "daughters and servants" of Santa Chiara, who begged for renewed relief from their troubles–that is, resumption of exorcisms. Cabassi protested that had he known about the letter's content, he would not even have accepted it. But Archpriest Niccolini was away from Carpi, leaving him in charge. Especially concerned about his responsibilities toward the convent, Cabassi felt obligated to read the letter. He insisted that he was obeying the Congregation's injunction to refrain from exorcizing but found himself in a bind. Because he had to fill in for the absent archpriest by hearing the nuns' confessions, celebrating Mass, and giving them communion, he could not help violating the Congregation's order to stay away from the convent. When he tried to administer the Eucharist, Cabassi reported that the demons rose up within the nuns and prevented them from partaking of the sacrament. At this point, Cabassi adjured the demons in order to allow the ailing nuns to take communion. This, he insisted, did not amount to an exorcism: he was acting as a priest, not an exorcist, and such a command could have been made by any cleric. Cabassi's attempt to justify his actions was not very convincing.[146] His defensive tone highlights the divergence of views on exorcism between clerics on the firing line in Modena and Carpi and their superiors, the cardinal-inquisitors in Rome.

Doubts about the efficacy of exorcisms were not new in the 1630s. Thanks especially to the aggressive efforts of Girolamo Menghi, exorcisms became more common in northern Italy and elsewhere about 1590, but this period also witnessed the first significant number of actions taken by the Roman Inquisition against exorcists for abusive practices.[147]

When Girolamo Menghi wrote the *Fuga Daemonum* in 1596, he felt compelled to defend his profession in a way that had not been necessary twenty years earlier. He complained that some people, themselves incited by demons, had urged the burning of books on exorcism. In certain cases, family members of energumens tried to claim that their relatives were suffering from natural dementia rather than demon possession. Upset with the methods of certain exorcists, some sought to discontinue all exorcisms. Insisting that adjuration was invented by Jesus, not by mortal men, Menghi defended the books and the profession of the exorcist though admitted there had been abuses. But just as one does not burn the Bible simply because heretics had misused it, so, Menghi asserted, exorcist manuals and the men who wrote them were not culpable merely because some miscreants had used them improperly. Such errors impugned the integrity of the specific exorcist, who should indeed be punished, but did not diminish the value of the books or of the profession of exorcist. Menghi referred briefly to a person from a very distinguished family in Lombardy whom he exorcized for about six months. This person manifested so many blatant symptoms, including superhuman strength, that virtually everyone was certain that the victim was demonically possessed. Be that as it may, "demons" planted the idea in the heads of some family members that this was a natural malady, not diabolism. The family referred the matter to a group of theologians, canon and civil lawyers, and physicians, who concluded that the person suffered from natural ills and had never been possessed. Referring to such resistance, Menghi avowed that one of the most devious tricks demons committed was to make people think that all the troubles they caused were simply the result of dementia or some other natural infirmity.[148] Forty years before the demons attacked the nuns of Santa Chiara, some residents of northern Italy thus already harbored serious doubts about the usefulness of performing exorcisms on people displaying very bizarre behavior and expressed a certain skepticism about some accusations of demon possession. Like Menghi before them, the exorcists of Carpi surely thought that their critics were prepared to leave Christians defenseless against dangerous demons. Significantly, in the early seventeenth century, the highest incidence of prosecutions of exorcists in all of Italy may have occurred in the inquisitorial district of Modena.[149]

Even when they believed that people were possessed, critics disapproved of some of the methods employed by exorcists. The inquisitorial guidelines for conducting witchcraft cases—as noted above, probably written by Cardinal Desiderio Scaglia—expressed considerable dismay about the manner in which exorcists were wont to implicate people allegedly named by demons during exorcisms. It explicitly took issue with Menghi, asserting that since demons could never be trusted, they must not be asked to identify witches.[150] In his *Prattica,* Scaglia further avowed that many inept or unscrupulous exorcists, interpreting every infirmity as a case of demon possession, often performed exorcisms on people who were not possessed at all. Such actions, he charged, could stimulate melancholic humors and cause other inconveniences and scandals.[151] Scaglia believed that problems such as witchcraft and the demonic possession of nuns were the result in part of excessively close relationships between female religious, on the one hand, and exorcists and confessors, on the other. Rather than enunciating new standards, however, Scaglia was in effect summarizing the principles that the Congregation of the Holy Office was already implementing in cases of witchcraft.[152] Many years prior to the turmoil in Carpi, the cardinals had demonstrated a strong distrust of exorcists, whose public conjurations were often tumultuous and painful, and held up as models confessors who nurtured penitence in and offered consolation to the confessants.[153]

The experiences in Carpi may in fact have been the cause of a strong word of caution issued by the Congregation of Bishops and Regulars in regard to the exorcisms of nuns. In 1639 this administrative body, which, as we have seen, had earlier permitted exorcisms at Santa Chiara, advised that if an allegedly possessed nun had been exorcised without success for "a considerable time," the exorcisms should cease, as the "visions" of demons could have been merely the products of imagination or mistaken opinion. The Congregation further averred that nuns could generally be liberated from such ills just by partaking of the sacraments and relying on the grace of God.[154]

Even some noted authorities on exorcism parted company with predecessors such as Menghi on what were acceptable practices when adjuring demons. Writing about a decade after the tribulations of Santa Chiara had died down, Candido Brognolo emphatically denied that exorcists had the right to ask demons how they entered the bodies of energumens. Most notably, it was absolutely forbidden to ask if the demons were bound by a maleficent pact with someone. According to Brognolo, demons entered pacts voluntarily, never by force, and such questions often resulted in accusations against entirely innocent people, since the fathers of lies preferred inculpating the morally upright. Even without the discovery of the "signs" of witchcraft, one can expel demons and destroy maleficent spells with spiritual remedies. Brognolo also pointed to King Saul as an example of a person who was demonically possessed but not the victim of witchcraft; God was permitting this possession as punishment for Saul's own sins. Brognolo also deemed it utterly ludicrous to ask a demon by what saint it could be expelled: "What is more foolish than the exorcist who wants to be told by the enemy which arms he should use to fatally wound it? Does one ask a fox with what traps it can be captured?"[155] For the same reason it was equally foolish to ask a demon what words made it suffer the most. Furthermore, asking a demon to name the saints who were its enemies was injurious to all the saints not named by the demon since, he implied, all saints were enemies of all demons. And since the timing of the demon's exit depended on God's will, not the devil's, it was futile to ask when and where it would leave the body. Brognolo explicitly rejected Menghi's claim that God forced demons to obey and answer exorcists' questions truthfully, insisting that one could never be sure that God was forcing the demons to tell the truth at a particular moment. He also took issue with Menghi who had deemed it legitimate to order a superior demon, such as Lucifer, to expel from someone's body a lesser unclean spirit and then subject it to infernal punishment. Characterizing this as "superstitious," Brognolo maintained that demons of all ranks wanted to harm, not help, humanity and that the exorcist had the power only to expel demons from bodies, not to send them to hell.[156]

Had Brognolo's standards guided the exorcists of Carpi, the Inquisition probably would not have even initiated an investigation. Though a staunch defender of exorcism, Brognolo in effect wanted to get exorcists out of the business of hunting witches because in his view under no circumstances could demons be trusted to tell the truth.[157] Faced with the evidence in Carpi, Brognolo without a doubt would have concluded that the ten nuns were possessed by demons and would have prescribed exorcisms. But he almost surely would not have tried to determine if they were also bewitched and most definitely would not have paid any heed to words attributed to the demons. His concerns were well founded. Although many witnesses protested that they long harbored suspicions against Dealta and Bellacappa, those misgivings were greatly augmented when the "demons" identified them as witches. In a number of seventeenth-century trials, people were sentenced to death on the basis of words spoken by demons through the mouths of demoniacs, notwithstanding the need to distrust the words of demons. The most famous such case involved Urbain Grandier, executed in 1634 for supposedly bewitching the Ursulines of Loudun. In his letter to Louis XIII in which he pleaded for his life, Grandier himself rightly pointed out that Jesus had declared that one should cast out demons in his name, not oblige them to tell the "truth." Moreover, if the devil was capable of lying in the presence of Jesus Christ, claiming that he was lord over all kingdoms on earth, then surely Satan and the demons could tell lies during exorcisms conducted by priests.[158] For his part, Brognolo showed that in the mid-seventeenth century some exorcists themselves disapproved of some of the tactics used by Cabassi and other witch-hunting clerics of Carpi. Criticism of exorcists only intensified in the eighteenth century, when the Inquisition of Modena took action against several who were found responsible for accusations of witchcraft.[159]

The Santa Chiara case highlights the issue of the connection between exorcism and witch-hunting. In his very influential book on religion and magic in England, Keith Thomas saw a certain inverse relationship between the availability of various orthodox remedies, including exorcism, and the hunting of witches. With England's conversion to Protestantism, the number of possible spiritual remedies to alleged evil spells was greatly restricted (limited to prayer, supplication, and fasting), thereby opening up the possibility of more trials of witches.[160] It has been suggested that retention of the remedy of exorcism in Italy (and other Catholic countries) may help explain the rather small number of witch trials in Italy: in cases of alleged *maleficia,* people may have resorted to exorcists rather than pursuing criminal charges.[161] Others have argued that far from serving as an alternative to witch-hunts, exorcisms could actually spark a local hunt.[162] Although Carpi did not experience a mass trial akin to those that occurred in parts of northern Europe, the evidence from Santa Chiara supports the latter view, as some of the exorcists were in effect acting as witch-hunters and contributing to the fears that necessitated the Inquisition's aggressive investigation.

Given that more exorcisms were performed on women than men, modern historians have rightly concluded that exorcists helped solidify the notion that females were more vulnerable to demonic invasion than males.[163] Just as women were deemed more likely to yield to diabolical temptation, so they were reputedly weaker vessels who were less able than males to prevent demons from entering their bodies. Within limits, however, the demoniac nuns of Carpi definitely exercised agency. Although they acted precisely as possessed people were expected to behave, these sisters were not mere puppets who were manipulated by the exorcists and other priests. Rather, they clearly collaborated, either consciously or unconsciously, with the exorcists. It must be remembered that the exorcists were called in only after the Clarisses exhibited very unusual behavior and did not respond favorably to medical treatment. The alleged demoniacs eagerly supported the exorcists' efforts and asserted that administration of the rite had proven to be the sole means of improving their sorry state. The nuns' fervent desire for continued exorcisms shows that they sided with the exorcists against directives from Rome. The ten nuns had a strong conviction, shared with the exorcists, that their woes were caused by demons and witchcraft.

All the behavior exhibited by the Clarisses conformed roughly to prevailing cultural codes and conventions governing possession behavior in seventeenth-century Europe. Being demonically possessed was a cultural reality in this era, and the nuns of Carpi exhibited a wide range of stereotypes—contortions, extraordinary strength, comprehension of unfamiliar languages, repulsion to sacred objects and prayers—that were associated with demonic possession. Referring to cases of early modern possession, Michael MacDonald has astutely argued, "Sickness roles are usually quite stylized and they are learned in complex cultural and social processes that are seldom consciously recognized by the participants."[164] He further suggests that possession was in effect learned behavior and that the nature of this affliction became fully apparent, often only gradually, as it developed.[165] As noted above, however, the mere fact that possession behavior was predictable did not make the suffering any less real. After all, three women died from their ills, and there is abundant reason to think that some early modern people who were convinced that they were bewitched may literally have been frightened to death.[166] Far from putting on an act, the Clarisses had assimilated the cultural understanding of possession to such an extent that they in fact suffered excruciating turmoil, and their bizarre behavior was simply the most obvious symptom of profound spiritual or psychological unrest. The exorcists' actions no doubt served to reinforce "possessed" behavior, but the malaise originated among the Clarisses themselves, and its development depended on the actions and collaboration, even if unconscious, of the afflicted women.

Many of the Clarisses collaborated not only with the exorcists but also, albeit in very different ways, with the former confessor, Angelo Bellacappa. Although they at times protested to the Holy Office that they felt compelled by unseen forces to go to rendezvous with him, these young nuns were not merely being manipulated by their confessor. They clearly developed very intense relationships with the Franciscan, just as they later had very close ties, though of a different nature, with the exorcists, unambiguously embracing the spiritual direction and consolation they provided notwithstanding opposition from Rome. To sum up, the ailing Clarisses of Carpi most definitely were not weak, ignorant women who were easily controlled by the male authority figures. They found solace in a form of religiosity that they felt provided the spiritual weapons appropriate for fighting the demons that appeared so threatening.

Chapter 5

SISTERS DEALTA AND IPPOLITA UNDER ATTACK

Suspicions against Sister Dealta Martinelli predated the Holy Office's investigation of Santa Chiara's possessions, and she was the first person witnesses named as a suspect (see chapter 2). In the wake of the attack of St. Mark's Day (25 April 1638), which occurred just six days after the opening of the hearings, Fiscal Giudici ordered that Dealta be held in isolation in the convent's infirmary. In one sense, this was a means of protecting her from possible further attacks by the demoniac nuns. But Giudici and Tinti clearly harbored strong suspicions about the nonconformist nun, since they forbade the other sisters to communicate with her in any way under ban of excommunication. This reflected the inquisitorial practice of keeping suspects incommunicado, based on the notion that they were to reflect on their own actions and, ideally, repent and confess their misdeeds.[1] Apart from one very brief release, described below, Dealta would spend the remainder of her stay at Santa Chiara in isolation. As we have seen, her sister, Ippolita, was briefly subjected to a similar form of incarceration in May 1638. Her release, which was ordered by the cardinal-inquisitors in Rome, did not put an end to suspicions against her. As we shall see, in the summer of 1638 Ippolita was increasingly ostracized within the convent until she, too, was again incarcerated within the nunnery.

The Clarisses' doubts about Ippolita were exacerbated by her apparent attempts to offer aid and comfort to her beleaguered sister. Already in May, the current abbess, Emilia Bellentani, and her vicaress, Aurelia Bendidio, designated two nuns, Angelica Rocchi and Anna Caterina Zuccari, to provide Dealta with her necessities—food, drink, bedding—but even they were not supposed to speak to Dealta about anything beyond these basic needs. Fiscal Giudici made a vigorous effort to enforce this order, which conformed to inquisitorial practice concerning the incarceration of suspected witches.[2]

In direct violation of Giudici's order, Ippolita Martinelli tried surreptitiously to communicate with her sister. On 1 June 1638 the abbess, the vicaress, and Angelica Rocchi all testified that a few days earlier Ippolita tried to send some things to Dealta, purportedly to lend her spiritual support. Ippolita gave Rocchi an envelope and asked her to give it to Dealta, which, she said, contained a card with a prayer written on it by their brother Gasparo.

Fearing that this was forbidden, Rocchi opened the envelope and handed it over to the abbess. The next day, Ippolita gave Rocchi another card to give to Dealta, which had on one side a printed prayer and on the other an image commemorating the birth of John the Baptist, of whom Dealta was a devoted follower, according to Ippolita. In response to Ippolita's later query that evening, Rocchi told a fib and assured her that Dealta had received everything. Thanking her, Ippolita asked Rocchi to remind Dealta that she must memorize the prayer and then burn the card. Appearing very nervous, Ippolita said that she would be ruined if anyone discovered that she had sent those items to her sister.[3]

Handing over the cards to Giudici, the abbess observed that Ippolita's actions were a direct violation of the orders of the Holy Office but also expressed the fear that Ippolita may have sought to go beyond providing spiritual comfort to her detained sister. Although the cards did indeed appear to be simple prayers, the abbess wondered if they actually might be charms, which, if worn on one's person, might enable an evildoer to avoid confessing to any crimes or sins.[4] As we have seen, contemporary popular beliefs did hold that keeping written prayers on one's body could allow one, among other things, to endure torture, which in turn could enable a person to avoid confessing to certain crimes. As it turned out, the card with the handwritten prayer also included some terse advice about the trial, and Giudici was furious at Ippolita's attempt to circumvent the ban on communicating with Dealta. On 15 June he expressed to Inquisitor Tinti his great displeasure at Ippolita's conduct. Not only did she try to communicate with her sister, she apparently also attempted to suborn witnesses. Although the nuns were not to discuss this case among themselves, according to Giudici, Ippolita was trying to play on "womanly sympathies" to dissuade her fellow nuns from testifying against Dealta.[5] A witness also saw Ippolita talking with Veronica Maria Coccapani, one of the afflicted women, even though Giudici had banned all communication with the possessed nuns a few days earlier. For her disobedience, Giudici ordered that Ippolita be held in seclusion from all the other nuns of Santa Chiara.[6]

On 1 July Inquisitor Tinti finally fulfilled Cardinal Barberini's order of 29 May and began presiding over the investigation himself. At this session–also attended by Giudici, Archpriest Niccolini, and a notary–Tinti convoked and interrogated Ippolita for the first time. Professing her ignorance about the possessions, Ippolita rapped the table in front of her saying, "I know as much about [them] as this wood does." Having recently been freed from her own isolation on the condition that she not talk to anyone about her sister's trial, Ippolita assured the inquisitor that she had discussed this matter with no one even before her own incarceration. Asked if she had ever tried to send Dealta anything, she at first said she had not but then admitted having sent a little card "for her needs," referring to the card commemorating John the Baptist's birth.[7] After considerable prodding by the inquisitor, Ippolita recalled she had also asked Angelica Rocchi to deliver a handwritten prayer to Dealta.[8]

Interestingly, though Tinti questioned her closely about her attempts to send messages to Dealta, he did not ask her anything about the possessions themselves. Unlike all the other nuns who appeared before the Holy Office, Ippolita was not asked who she suspected was behind the bewitchments. In spite of her service as sacristan, Ippolita was not asked at this time anything about Bellacappa's possible abuse of sacramentals. Because of her intimate ties with a principal suspect and considering the suspicions many had toward her, Tinti apparently had little faith in anything she would have said. Ippolita's attempt to circumvent the ban on messages to Dealta surely did little to inspire confidence in her as a witness.

Ippolita Martinelli's testimony on the following days probably did not diminish doubts about her. When Tinti asked her if she had ever shown or expressed hatred toward the princess, Ippolita insisted that she had not and that she loved, honored, and respected the former abbess. But when he inquired if she had ever said that someone should do the same thing to Angela Caterina that was done to Leonora d'Este of Ferrara, whose niece tried to poison her, Ippolita put her head on her knees and in a tearful voice said, "Father, I don't remember having said these words, but it could be that I said them."[9] She repeatedly denied having warned the princess, who was walking hand in hand with her young niece, that she had better watch out. Tinti advised Ippolita that witnesses had testified under oath that they had heard these words with their own ears, and he had every reason to believe that they were telling the truth. Fighting back tears, Ippolita insisted that whoever so testified was lying and was deliberately vilifying her.[10]

Tinti further questioned Ippolita closely about the reputed poisoning or bewitching of Princess Angela Caterina. Not surprisingly, Ippolita's account of the events of St. Bernardine's Day (20 May 1635) differed in some important ways from that of the former abbess. She reported that at Bellacappa's request she and Dealta brought some sweets and wine for him and the abbess. She remembered only that the confessor poured a glass of wine and that Angela Caterina said that she did not feel like drinking at the moment. Tinti had the princess's deposition of this event read aloud to Ippolita, who, the scribe recorded, first got pale and then blushed during the reading. Once it was completed, Ippolita proclaimed she was quite sure that the episode occurred as she had just described it, not as the princess portrayed it.[11] Although Ippolita's attempts to communicate with her sister understandably upset Tinti and the Holy Office, for the most part her answers to all queries did not give her accusers more ammunition concerning maleficent spells.

The "False" Visions of Dealta

Incarcerated since late April and forbidden to communicate with the other sisters, Dealta Martinelli sought consolation in prayers to God, the Virgin Mary, and various saints. During the long days, weeks, and months of isolation, she told the few nuns she had any contact with—those who brought her food and other necessities—that her prayers were answered with visions of Jesus and saints, who offered her comfort. Far from persuading her fellow nuns and judicial authorities that she was innocent, this was considered further proof that she was at least fooled by the devil if not actually in league with him.

Ever since the late Middle Ages, Church authorities had shown a certain ambivalence toward the growing number of people, many of whom were female, who claimed to have divine visions. The fourteenth century witnessed the growth in the number of mystical prophets, such as Bridget of Sweden (1303–73) and Catherine of Siena (1347–80), both of whom were canonized and whose visions inspired many others to imitate their form of saintliness. It was probably no coincidence that the waning Middle Ages also witnessed unprecedented fears of demons, and late-medieval clerics began to show great concern for demons' ability to deceive people with false visions.[12] In the early fifteenth century, concerned about false female visionaries, French theologian Jean Gerson expressed the belief that women, because of their mental inferiority and naive credulity, were more apt than men to mistake diabolical for divine visions. Worse still, Gerson suspected that because of their moral weakness, women were more likely to fabricate visions. Later experts such as Cardinal Desiderio Scaglia argued that nuns were especially prone to having false visions of saints—visions that were mere illusions, perhaps incited by demons—or even feigning such visions, most likely out of the vain desire for the reputation of saintliness themselves.[13] Francesco Maria Guazzo expressed similar concerns and added that because women are "lascivious, luxurious, and avaricious," one must be extra careful in considering their alleged visions, warning that they have dragged "even learned men to their destruction" for gullibly regarding them as prophetesses.[14]

Even some mystic nuns themselves, such as Teresa of Avila (1515–82), were wary of the devil's ability to deceive through illusory visions that could corrupt the credulous. Even when such visions actually came from God, Satan could still redirect them for evil purposes by tricking the recipients into becoming proud or cherishing the visions more than God himself.[15] Investigated by the Spanish Inquisition, Teresa herself showed that prospective saints and suspected witches, though at first glance polar opposites, endured similar treatment by the Church hierarchy. In effect, the Church put both on trial, closely investigating alleged saints to ensure that they were not feigning sanctity or deluded by demons.[16] Although Church leaders since the later Middle Ages had expressed concern about pretense of holiness and visions, Italian inquisitions began prosecuting people, mostly women, for this alleged sin only in the 1630s, contemporaneous to Dealta's reputed visions. By contrast, as early as the 1520s the Inquisition in Spain started taking action for false sanctity against so-called *beatas,* "semireligious" women who made informal vows of chastity and poverty without joining convents, many of whom claimed to have divine visions.[17]

According to some scholars, this fear of pretense of sanctity or false visions was part and parcel of declining opportunities for women as spiritual leaders in Counter-Reformation Europe. As noted in the introduction, post-Tridentine Church leaders looked approvingly on female mystics, whose visions were evidence of divine approval of Catholicism vis-à-vis Protestantism, provided these women were of lofty social status and belonged to a religious order.[18] Moreover, Ulrike Strasser found that though *clausura* in seventeenth-century Bavaria eliminated various mundane functions of female religious, it also enhanced the reputations of convents as centers of piety and mysticism, where zealous nuns experienced saintly visions and mortified the flesh.[19] Be that as it may, the post-Tridentine Church placed less emphasis on prophecy and mysticism, traits that were traditionally common among female saints, such as Bridget and Catherine. Weighing the experiences of female religious, including those regarded as saints, Gabriella Zarri finds that in the fifteenth century the number of female religious orders increased dramatically and that this growth was most pronounced in the third orders. In the following century, however, the reforms of Trent in effect dissolved the third orders, obliging their members to become nuns and reside in convents. Moreover, although female saints had reached their apogee in terms of power and prestige in the late fifteenth century, the number of women who were canonized declined considerably in the sixteenth and seventeenth centuries. Those few women who were canonized in the Counter-Reformation era were more likely to be reformers of religious orders than mystics—even Teresa of Avila's canonization was more a result of her reforms of her Discalced Carmelite order than her visions.[20]

In the case at hand, Dealta's visions reputedly began almost immediately upon her incarceration in the convent. On the first or second day of her internment, Dealta told the abbess, the vicaress, and Sisters Angelica Rocchi and Anna Caterina Zuccari that even if she had been abandoned by all the other nuns, the Lord had not forsaken her but always offered her solace. Testifying in July, Zuccari reported that when she asked what kind of consolation he provided, Dealta replied that one night St. Anthony of Padua appeared to her with a lily in his hand. Among the most popular saints in Italy, Anthony of Padua (1195–1231) was a Franciscan renowned as a miracle-worker who, beginning in the fifteenth century, was often depicted artistically holding a lily, a symbol of virginity.[21] Zuccari continued:

[A]nother time our crucified Lord appeared to [Dealta] and bowed his head to her, as if he were saying to her, "Come." And yet another time our Lord appeared to her again on the cross . . . and he also called to her, saying, "Obey." And one time Sister Beatrice [Bendidio], the mother vicaress, and I were with [the possessed] Sister Caterina Margherita [Ronchi] through whom the spirit was speaking. Sister Beatrice asked [the demon] if any saint ever appeared to Sister Dealta. It answered, "Don't say that, even if I do like to wear a lily." And we concluded that this was referring to the apparition that Dealta says she had of St. Anthony of Padua with the lily. The next day, Sister Caterina Margherita, in her senses, asked me if it were true that Sister Dealta had bragged that St. Anthony of Padua had appeared to her, and I told her, "Yes." And she said that she asked me this because her demon had sworn to [the exorcist] D. Agostino Bertesi that it [had] appeared to Sister Dealta in the form of St. Anthony. . . . Sister Dealta told not only me but also the Mother Abbess and Sister Angelica that in those apparitions of the crucified Christ, Saints Peter and Paul also appeared as two small saints at the feet of the crucified Christ.[22]

Thus although the incarcerated Dealta identified her woes with the sufferings of Jesus, her accusers were absolutely certain that the "saints" she saw were demons in disguise.[23]

Well aware of the belief that demons could supposedly cause illusions for the most rational of human beings,[24] the exorcist Cabassi claimed to have even more direct evidence that Dealta's visions were not only false but also diabolical. Knowing nothing of Dealta's descriptions of her visions to Zuccari and others the previous day, the provost was exorcizing the possessed nuns when several spirits suddenly started laughing heartily. When he asked what was so funny, one of the demons of Sister Caterina Margherita Ronchi proclaimed that it had appeared to Dealta in the form of St. Anthony and that some fellow evil spirits had played the parts of Paul, Peter, and the crucified Jesus.[25]

Ippolita Martinelli was also suspect because she, too, claimed to have had divine visions prior to the investigation. Testifying in late May 1638, Clelia Coccapani asserted that about a year ago Ippolita told her that she prayed for the welfare of the convent to Camilla Pio, the venerated founder of the convent of Santa Chiara. Ippolita heard a voice, which she claimed was Camilla's, that reassured her that the convent would be safe from its present travails but that the Este family would be eradicated. Ippolita also said she made the same prayer to Jesus and heard a voice give the same answer. When Clelia asked if she was dreaming or awake when she had these visions, Ippolita replied that she was dreaming when she prayed to Camilla and Jesus but awake when she heard their voices.[26] These visions, combined with the implicit ill will toward Princess Angela Caterina, increased rather than diminished suspicions against Ippolita.

When Fiscal Giudici questioned her about the vision, Ippolita affirmed that she had indeed prayed to the "Blessed Camilla" for the protection of the monastery but did not hear an answer from her. Camilla was not officially recognized as a saint–and indeed has still not been canonized[27]–but she was strongly revered in Carpi, and Angela Caterina d'Este played an important role in promoting devotions venerating the founder of Santa Chiara. Starting in 1632, confessors, Bellacappa included, had kept a record of the "graces" the devout had received through appeals for the intercession of "Beata" Camilla.[28] In interrogating Ippolita, Giudici was skeptical of her claims of having divinely inspired visions, believing they might actually have been diabolical in origin. When confronted by the fiscal, Ippolita emphatically denied hearing a voice say that the monastery would be safe but the Este family would die out. Although Giudici did not pursue this line of questioning further, he and Tinti were clearly concerned about her alleged voices and, even more so, about Dealta's purported visions, a reflection of the widespread belief that women were particularly prone to mistake diabolical for divine visions.[29]

In late July 1638 Inquisitor Tinti was concerned that Dealta, already incarcerated for about three months with no end in sight, might actually do away with herself. He ordered the removal of her Franciscan cord, belts, garters, and other objects, because he feared she might hang or stab herself. Explaining this order, Tinti described her reputed apparitions as "diabolical" visions that had no purpose other than pushing people who were "desperate" and incarcerated to take their own lives.[30] Tinti was also reflecting the views of various demonologists who averred that Satan, trying to prevent any repentance before a possible execution, often incited imprisoned witches to take their lives that he might thereby claim their souls for all eternity.[31]

Sister Angelica Zuccari reported an interesting conversation with the possessed Sister Clara Maria Amoldoni on the same day that Tinti ordered the removal of all objects from Dealta's cell. Or, more accurately, Zuccari claimed to have had a conversation with a demon that possessed Amoldoni's body. The demon asked Zuccari why she had gone to see its "Lady." When she did not deign to answer, the demon told her it knew she had removed the cord and other items and indicated it was quite upset by that action. The demon said it wanted to put Amoldoni to sleep, after which it would go console its Lady, Sister Dealta. To this, Zuccari expressed amazement that it should pay so much attention to Dealta since it seemed fully absorbed in "caring" for Amoldoni. The demon replied that its Lady took great pleasure in tormenting the body of the young nun, but it would nonetheless go visit its Lady and see what items had been taken from her. Later, while in her senses, Amoldoni told Zuccari that the demon had informed her that Dealta's cord had been removed, something no one else had told her.[32]

Zuccari further recounted that various demons addressed the same issue in subsequent days. The words attributed to Caterina Margherita Ronchi's demon, who claimed to be in charge of making visions of saints appear to Dealta, demonstrated the close connection in the seventeenth-century mindset between diabolical temptation and self-inflicted death. The demon allegedly pointed out that Dealta still had plenty of ways to kill herself: she could "bang her head so much against the wall that she could kill herself in a brutal way." And she still possessed other items that could be used for hanging, most obviously her bed sheets and scapular, a type of shawl that Clarisses wore.[33] This testimony reflected the belief, widespread in early modern Europe, that the desire to take one's life stemmed from diabolical possession or temptation.[34] The fear that Dealta might take her life stemmed from the conviction that Dealta's visions were diabolical, not divine. Truly divine visions were reserved for saints, and no one at Santa Chiara believed that Dealta's lifestyle in any way resembled that of a saint.

Although the Congregation of the Holy Office eventually forbade all residents of Santa Chiara to say anything, either among themselves or with others, about the alleged possessions, throughout the summer and fall of 1638 the residents of Santa Chiara apparently could openly discuss, unimpeded, the tribulations the convent was enduring. Details about the supposed bewitchments, the interrogations, and exorcisms obviously spread like wildfire throughout the convent. Facts surrounding various incidents or developments, such as the removal of Dealta's cord and other items, might reach the ears of the energumens, who might reinforce the belief that they were possessed by exhibiting knowledge of events of which they had no firsthand experience. Angelica Zuccari claimed to have been told by one of Clara Maria Amoldoni's demons that Dealta was bothered by the heat and needed to get her hair cut to stay cooler. The next time Zuccari took a meal to Dealta, the imprisoned nun in fact said she was quite hot and would like to have her hair cut. This knowledge could not have been received from any other sister of Santa Chiara, and certainly Amoldoni herself had no contact with Dealta whatsoever. For Zuccari, the demons' apparent knowledge of Dealta's needs was proof that they were serving her.[35]

The Release of Dealta and the Demoniacs' Attack

In the fall of 1638 the opinions of authorities of the Holy Office in Carpi and those in Rome increasingly diverged on how to proceed with this case. Tinti was very interested in interrogating Dealta,[36] whereas Cardinal Barberini became more and more convinced that there was no viable evidence against her. On 9 October 1638 Barberini and other members of the Congregation of the Inquisition revealed their reactions to the charges against Dealta and

Ippolita Martinelli, based on their perusal of the copy of Giudici and Tinti's investigation. "Amazed" that Giudici and company had arrested the Martinelli sisters, the cardinals declared that there were insufficient grounds even to call them to be questioned, much less to detain them. The cardinals further observed that the detailed perquisition of their cells yielded more evidence to exonerate than to implicate them. They accordingly ordered that Dealta and Ippolita Martinelli be released immediately from their de facto imprisonment to have the normal freedom of movement enjoyed by all nuns in this cloistered convent. They also enjoined that the archpriest provide the Clarisses with a "wise" confessor, whose first task was to persuade them all that the suspicions they had harbored stemmed from "feminine thoughtlessness" (*leggerezza feminile*), since there was not a shred of evidence to suggest that the Martinellis were in any way guilty. Although they allowed the investigation to continue, the cardinals determined that "the final and only remedy to this great evil is the removal of the exorcists and the appointment of new persons for the cure of souls of these unfortunate [nuns], deceived by too much credulity." Showing its disdain for Fiscal Giudici's role in this case, the Congregation also ordered that he cease meddling in the affairs of Santa Chiara because he had proven to be "most imprudent." Cardinal Barberini also chided Tinti, telling him he needed to be more cautious in dealing with such matters, especially since they concerned "women restricted to a cloister and dedicated to the service of God, to whom his divine majesty specifically aids with his holy grace, and so it is vanity to believe that they are bewitched and go to a place of pleasure [a sabbat]."[37] Although Barberini's confidence that nuns, often referred to as brides of Christ, could not be tempted by the sins of the flesh might strike us as naive, his claim that the exorcisms produced more angst than spiritual comfort was probably right on target.

As a result of this order, a chastened Inquisitor Tinti along with Archpriest Niccolini and the notary Ripalta went on 16 October to Santa Chiara, where they called the sisters Martinelli to the parlor and informed them of their liberty in the presence of Sister Alsuinda Malaspina and Abbess Emilia Bellentani.[38] Although this meant that, judicially speaking, the case was dismissed, this was far from the end of Dealta's troubles.

Just two days after her release, the possessed nuns again attacked Dealta in the choir, in a manner reminiscent of the St. Mark's Day assault but more frightening and more violent. On the morning of 18 October, St. Luke's Day, some of the possessed nuns discovered that Dealta was sitting in the choir with other Clarisses. Father Luigi Foresti, archdeacon of the collegial church of Carpi, was celebrating Mass in the church of Santa Chiara when the attack broke out. Foresti recounted:

> As soon as I had consecrated and elevated the most holy blood, I heard in the interior church of the nuns an incredible commotion and the banging

of doors. It turned out this came from some of the possessed nuns who came into the church, went to the place in the choir where Sister Dealta was found, pulled her away violently, and dragged her into the middle of the choir. I did not see this immediately because I was celebrating Mass, especially since at that moment I had just consecrated [the wine] and elevated [the chalice]. Because of the terror and confusion, I remained silent for a moment before uttering the appropriate words after the elevation, "unde et memores, Domine."[39]

Regaining his composure, Foresti told the few people who were in the exterior part of the church that they must immediately pray to God to prevent a terrible accident or scandal from occurring. Hearing this, one of the possessed nuns approached the grille at the altar that separated the nuns' choir from the nave and called out that everyone must earnestly pray to God for the conversion of this hardened soul. After she also told the priest that it was God's command that he say a prayer to that effect, the shocked worshipers and Foresti did in fact offer their own prayers in response to these entreaties. As soon as Mass was over, the sacristan called Foresti to the communion window, where he saw Dealta sitting on the floor in the middle of the choir, surrounded by five of the possessed nuns. Two of them were holding Dealta by the shoulders, screaming at her to confess to being a witch and threatening to strangle her if she did not. Swearing that they were acting on the command of God, the frenetic nuns told her she had twenty-four hours to confess, but Dealta replied she knew nothing about which they spoke. Upon learning of the attack, Alessandro Pezzoli, a noble notary serving the church in Carpi, hastened to Santa Chiara. There he spent long hours in the exterior part of the church in the morning, afternoon, and evening, surveying this very delicate situation.[40]

The bewitched nuns or their demons were, it seems, subjecting Dealta to some rough justice, which, so far as they were concerned, was an informal trial intended to prove her guilt.[41] After Dealta had been held for several hours, a number of healthy nuns feared the demoniacs might actually lynch her. The abbess accordingly ordered some of the younger, hardier nuns to try to rescue the beleaguered Dealta. Seeing these women entering the choir and sensing an imminent attack, the possessed nuns closed ranks and dared the others to go ahead and try to get their hands on Dealta. One of the healthy nuns approached them, but a possessed nun shoved her with one hand so violently that the would-be rescuer fell hard to the floor. Another healthy nun charged with a breviary raised in her hand, but one of the bewitched sisters disarmed her and sent the breviary flying through the choir. Seeing this attempt to rescue Dealta, the five possessed nuns started punching Dealta and another struck the would-be rescuer, sending her to the floor. Intimidated by the possessed nuns' seemingly superhuman strength, the healthy nuns quickly beat a hasty retreat and gave up trying to rescue Dealta themselves. The bewitched nuns defiantly proclaimed that they would not relent even if the pope himself came and asked for Dealta's release, because they were following the will of God.[42]

By the early evening of the eighteenth, many hours into the standoff, Dealta continued to refuse to confess but did try to deflect suspicion away from her onto Bellacappa, by telling the possessed nuns he had told her that he had a baptized magnet that he used for various purposes, especially to make women love him. Unimpressed with this revelation, four of the afflicted nuns told Dealta they would deal with Bellacappa at the appropriate time but right now they wanted her to confess to being a witch.[43] Still denying that she knew anything about witchcraft, Dealta expressed the desire to make a sacramental confession to Father Marc'Antonio Villani, chaplain of San Rocco. Villani was quite willing to oblige, but he needed a considerable amount of time to convince the possessed nuns or their demons to allow her to confess. Eventually they relented and allowed Dealta to confess her sins to Villani, with him on one side of the communion window and her on the other.[44] Lest she try to escape, the possessed nuns continued to surround Dealta closely and insisted that this sacramental confession would not satisfy their demand. After she had confessed to Villani, the demons said, "All right, you've confessed now. You've gotten your absolution. And you know that we still want you to confess to being the sorceress that we know you are and have always said that you are." Several times they punched her and made as if they were going to strangle her, which various onlookers, including the notary Pezzoli, seriously thought they might do. Pezzoli left at a certain time during the night, but Fathers Villani and Giovan Francesco Bosio remained to monitor developments, the latter (a young priest of twenty-four) spending the whole night at the communion window.[45]

For part of the night, there were no nuns in the church other than Dealta and her five assailants. According to Pezzoli, each time any other nuns entered the choir, the possessed women screamed at them to get out and accused them of being accomplices of Dealta. Pezzoli further noted that at one point Dealta made as if she wanted to say something but then refrained from doing so, as if she were almost at the point of confessing to being a witch. At that moment, Ippolita entered the choir, whereupon the possessed nuns immediately began screaming that Ippolita was bringing help to Dealta, whose heart, which had started to soften, had hardened again, thanks to the assistance received from her sister.[46]

As the standoff between the frenetic nuns and Dealta continued, Foresti and the other clerics present called for Inquisitor Tinti. Upon his arrival the morning of the nineteenth, he accepted the invitation to celebrate Mass, evidently in the hope that taking part in the Eucharist would have a calming effect on the nuns in the choir. From the small communion window through which the nuns received the host, Tinti saw Dealta surrounded by the angry sisters who were threatening to kill her. According to Foresti, as Tinti prepared to say Mass, the possessed nuns carried Dealta to the communion window with such ease that she appeared as light as a feather, another insinuation that they wielded the superhuman strength of demons. In a letter he wrote to Cardinal Barberini a few days after this incident, Tinti indicated that he was most anxious during this volatile showdown and still unsure if the nuns were possessed or insane. In either case, Tinti greatly feared they might strangle Dealta. The archpriest was presently out of town, and Tinti currently had no vicar. Feeling guilty because he had not yet found a remedy for Santa Chiara's woes, the inquisitor finally decided that regardless of whether they were suffering from demon possession or from melancholic passion, something had to be done immediately. Tinti rationalized to Barberini that he had to choose the lesser of two evils, and so he sent for Provost Girolamo Cabassi to conduct an exorcism, notwithstanding the Congregation's express ban against Cabassi and the other exorcists visiting the convent. Tinti immediately had second thoughts, however, and sent a second message to Cabassi telling him not to come to the nunnery. The Mass did nothing to assuage the anger of the demons or nuns, and Tinti departed for some time, leaving Foresti there, later joined again by the notary Alessandro Pezzoli, to try to calm the storm that was brewing in the convent's choir.[47]

Some of the healthy nuns who were witnessing these events asked Foresti to take action because they feared that the bewitched nuns were about to kill Dealta. Seeing that the possessed nuns were furious and fearing the worse, Foresti called through the little window to Dealta and exhorted her to tell the truth. If they killed her and she was innocent, he reasoned, she would be a martyr. But if she had done anything at the instigation of the devils, she should admit it so she could be free of this imminent danger, a clear indication that Foresti himself was strongly suspicious of Dealta. Several times she seemed on the verge of saying something, but in the end she always stopped herself. Still denying any guilt, Dealta did mention that some people suspected her because the princess took ill after drinking wine she had brought at Bellacappa's request. And she admitted that she had said some unflattering things about Angela Caterina. Further trying to deflect doubts away from herself onto Bellacappa, she noted that the former confessor asked her a number of times to bring young nuns to him and again mentioned his boast of having a baptized magnet, which, she implied, he was using for love magic.[48]

An interesting theme in the testimony of the clerics who witnessed this marathon standoff is that it strengthened their conviction that the afflicted nuns were really possessed. At one point during the standoff, one of the bewitched nuns, Paola Francesca Cimadori, was loudly giving a theological discourse on the mysteries of the Trinity. Pezzoli expressed amazement at this since he had never before heard "a simple woman" making an intelligent speech on such a sophisticated subject.[49] Father Foresti also spoke of Cimadori's speeches as evidence of bewitchment:

> I could never believe that a simple woman could discuss the mysteries of the most Holy Trinity as one of them [Cimadori] did. She said that Sister Dealta must tell the truth, that this was the will of the true living God, three persons in one sole essence, which cannot be known except by God himself. [She also said] that the eternal word descended into the womb of the blessed virgin and was there nourished by her most holy blood . . . and [made] other recondite discussions. . . . And she spoke about the human body that resulted from a mixture of the four elements of which we are all composed. And [the demon] added that he and all his colleagues knew more about medical care than any physician in the world.[50]

In this account, Foresti began talking about Cimadori but by the end was referring only to her demon. For him and the other clerics present, Cimadori was demonstrating far too much learning for a woman. Her intelligent speeches about theological and medical matters were incompatible with being a "simple" woman. Consequently, her speeches must have been the words of the demon, spoken through her mouth.[51]

The various witnesses were also impressed with the possessed nuns' endurance and strength, which again seemed supernatural in nature. The notary Pezzoli noted that they all remained in the same positions for hours, with one kneeling on one knee and the other four standing around Dealta. According to Foresti, the five nuns all went thirty-seven hours without eating or drinking anything–their last meal having been supper on 17 October–and four of them remained standing for 23 hours. Although apparently none of them got any sleep either, they all maintained their stamina throughout the ordeal.[52]

Dealta's reactions to the attack also heightened suspicions that she was a witch. As with the St. Mark's Day incident, Dealta seemed to take this violent attack in stride and remained unruffled for the most part. Foresti noted that she never came close to shedding a tear in all these travails, even though these actions would have sufficed to make "a courageous man" weep. The demons themselves pointed this out to him, saying "Luigi, take a look if her eyes have reddened at all."[53] Pezzoli, too, observed her "intrepid face" and asserted that few other women would have been able to endure such a traumatic attack without breaking down in tears. Even though the Congregation of the Holy Office had exonerated Dealta, local clergymen and authorities believed that her remarkable coolness under extreme pressure must have been diabolical in origin and amounted to palpable evidence of witchcraft.[54] The *Malleus Maleficarum* and other witchcraft treatises affirmed that witches were unable to weep, even under torture, because "the grace of tears is one of the chief gifts allowed to the penitent."[55] Indeed, some demonologists spoke of the "sorcery of silence," whereby demons supposedly could protect witches from the pains of torture, even enabling some to laugh while subjected to the rack or other forms of torture.[56]

Other incidents during the standoff also seemed to point to Dealta's guilt. At a certain point, a nun was allowed to give Dealta a pair of hard-boiled eggs, which she ate, much to the amazement of Pezzoli, Foresti, and other onlookers. They could not imagine anyone having the desire to eat anything under these difficult conditions. For these witnesses, the ability of the afflicted nuns to keep going without food or drink was evidence of demon possession, while Dealta's consumption of a couple eggs in dire circumstances suggested a diabolical pact.[57] Foresti recounted another interesting event that caused him to doubt her innocence. Many hours into this affair, the demons said to Dealta, "You keep saying that you're innocent. All right, if you're really innocent, get your clogs and put them on and go ahead and leave as a sign of your innocence. We'll let you go."[58] And the nuns all drew back to indicate that she was free to leave, if she truly were innocent. When Dealta refused to put on her clogs, the possessed nuns themselves put them on her feet and then told her to go ahead and leave. Dealta was able to get to her feet, but she was unable to take even one step. This could not be attributed to cramps from having sat on the floor for such a long time because the possessed nuns, at Foresti's request, had some time earlier conceded to let her sit on a chair. Furthermore, at other points during this ordeal she was able to walk; more than once, she had been allowed to get up and walk to the communion window to say something to the priest. But when the demons told her to leave as a sign of her innocence, try though she may, Dealta could not budge, a clear sign of her guilt in the eyes of Foresti.[59]

As one might expect, the possessed nuns wore down Dealta, who, fearing for her life, eventually gave in to their demands. Father Martino Barbieri, another priest of Carpi, spent a good part of the night at Santa Chiara, arriving just after Dealta had made her sacramental confession to Father Villani. Barbieri claimed that he heard one of the demons, "Ambassador," tell Dealta that it was useless to resist and that she would not get out of this alive without confessing. As Dealta slowly appeared to be getting close to giving in, Barbieri heard a voice coming from outside the choir. Speaking through the mouth of Veronica Maria Coccapani, a bewitched nun who was not taking part in the attack on Dealta, the voice said, "Sister Dealta, I am Astarot. I have helped you as long as I could. I would still help you now, but I can't. God does not want it, and he wants you to recognize your errors." The "demon" repeated these words two or three times, even though Veronica Maria had been described as the only demoniac whose demons had not implicated Dealta.[60] After Astarot's admonitions, Coccapani and other nuns approached Dealta and urged her to put an end to the standoff and tell the truth. As the twenty-four-hour deadline approached, Father Giovan Francesco Bosio also entreated Dealta to tell the truth, which, in his mind, was clearly that Dealta was a witch, pointing out to her that the demons were claiming to speak on divine command. The priests had gathered some "strong men," who were about to enter the convent to free Dealta by force, but their intervention proved unnecessary. Worn out, Dealta finally declared that it was true she had taken part in the witchcraft that was plaguing the convent. And since she had earlier told Ambassador that even if she confessed it would still not be true she was a witch, the same demon demanded that she confirm her confession to Father Bosio. The beleaguered Dealta complied and reaffirmed her confession two or three times to the priest. At the insistence of Ambassador, Dealta also formally renounced the devil and all the promises she had made to him.[61]

The demons also reassured Father Foresti that he could believe them because they were unable to continue telling lies for more than three hours continuously, even if they were not exorcized. They explained that the three hours corresponded to the length of time Jesus spent on the cross, the period it took him to subjugate hell. If they tormented someone for more than three hours, as they were doing now, then one must believe they were telling the truth in order to fulfill the will of God. Because Foresti expressed doubts when the demons said they would not hurt Dealta once she confessed to being a witch, they voluntarily took an oath that they would do her no harm. One at a time, all Dealta's assailants took Foresti's "sacred finger" in their hands, and through the mouths of the possessed nuns, each demon said, "I do swear on this sacred finger by the true and living God, Father, Son, and Holy Ghost, that if she confesses to having cast these evil spells or to be an accomplice to them, we will not do her harm. But, on the contrary, we also swear that if she does not confess to this, we have the authority from God to strangle her and we will do so."[62] As for the veracity of this oath, the demons assured Foresti that although they called Satan their god, they would never be allowed to call him "the true and living God," a title reserved to the God of heaven.[63]

Having made this oath, the demons released Dealta, bringing an end to the ordeal close to twenty-four hours after it had begun. Dealta had admitted her guilt; the demons had sworn they were speaking the truth; and the informal "trial" was now over. Although this extrajudicial confession and trial meant nothing insofar as the Inquisition was concerned, they did make quite an impression on the nuns and demons of Carpi. Quite amazing is the degree of trust that Foresti and the other priests placed in what the "demons" said.

According to Father Bosio, immediately after Dealta reaffirmed her confession to him, the demons that had orchestrated the attack were satisfied and "departed." In saying this, Bosio may have meant they merely went dormant, though he probably intended to mean that they actually left the bodies of the various nuns. Regardless of his intended meaning, these sisters were yet not free of their "diabolical" woes. After Dealta was released and allowed to leave the choir, other higher-ranked demons, who had not been badgering Dealta the past two days, were terribly upset at having lost this round in the battle. They accordingly rose up and caused a major disturbance, screaming, throwing the nuns on the floor and contorting their bodies, which the demons still possessed and tormented.[64]

As all the above evidence reveals, throughout this episode of rough justice the demons appeared to be the most effective witch-hunters imaginable rather than the minions of Satan. Rather than lauding Dealta as their mistress, they were doing everything, supposedly at the command of God, to make her repent and confess to being a witch. At a certain point, Dealta bemoaned that she was in this difficult situation as punishment for her sins. But the possessed nuns (or the demons) lectured her that she was enduring this tribulation for only one sin: that of being a witch. One of the bewitched sisters in fact said, "We'd be in big trouble if a person were molested in this way for every mortal sin she or he committed." They further noted that it was a very serious sin for a priest to have indecent relations with a woman and then celebrate Mass, but even heinous sins such as these did not suffice to give the demons the power they now had over Dealta. They declared she was not being punished for the terribly "dishonest" sins she had committed against her sacred vows but only for the sin of witchcraft. The demons hastened to affirm that they knew all too well about many unspecified carnal pleasures she had enjoyed with them. The demons protested that, though loath to mention this activity, they were forced to do so by divine command, adding that the demonic sexual activity never took place while Dealta wore her nun's habit, apparently because God would not permit such a desecration.[65] Although many had already accused Dealta of sexual improprieties, no one had suggested until now that she was having sexual relations with demons.

An immediate effect of this attack was that, in spite of the Congregation of the Holy Office's exoneration of them, Dealta and Ippolita Martinelli were again placed in isolation in Santa Chiara, no doubt mainly for their own safety. Before his return to Modena, Inquisitor Tinti met with the abbess, who lamented that if a solution could not be found for the woes of the convent, all the Clarisses might have to leave Santa Chiara and go to the homes of their relatives.[66] Dealta's coerced confession notwithstanding, two and a half years after the demons first reputedly started tormenting Santa Chiara, they showed no signs of letting up.

Chapter 6

BELLACAPPA'S DEFENSE

Santa Chiara's witchcraft case was, for the most part, merely an investigation and not a full-blown trial. Although Sister Dealta Martinelli was kept in isolation for several months during the investigation, the Holy Office never formally charged her and, though eventually given an opportunity to speak her mind, she did not have to prepare an actual defense. By contrast, Father Angelo Bellacappa did prepare a defense, supported by a talented canon lawyer. As we shall see, this was far more in response to the accusations of solicitation than of witchcraft.

In August 1638 Inquisitor Tinti ordered the arrest of Bellacappa, who was taken into custody by the Holy Office in Bologna, where he had been residing at the Annunziata monastery, and was then transferred to the Inquisition's prison in Modena. Tinti began interrogating Bellacappa on 9 August 1638, almost four months after the questioning of the sisters of Santa Chiara began.[1] For the first time since the beginning of this investigation, Tinti conducted hearings in the Inquisition's own building in Modena. Brought out of prison, the forty-seven-year-old Bellacappa, Observant Franciscan and professor of theology, in response to the formulaic questions asked of all suspects, claimed he had no clue as to why he had been imprisoned and why he was being questioned by the Holy Office. Asked about his current office, Bellacappa replied that until his arrest he had resided at the monastery in Bologna and that his profession within the order had always been to teach theology. Apart from his stint as confessor at the convent of Santa Chiara—almost surely the only time he ever officially served as a confessor—he had never exercised charges beyond preaching and teaching theology to his fellow Franciscans.[2]

Following the standard procedures of the Holy Office, the inquisitor asked Bellacappa if he had any enemies. If a defendant's accusers were among those he or she identified as enemies, inquisitors were to be more cautious in considering their testimony. Interestingly, Bellacappa's first thoughts about his enemies were directed not against any Clarisses of Carpi but rather against some fellow clergymen. He claimed that during his tenure in Carpi, he was vilified in two vicious pseudonymous letters addressed to his Franciscan superior, and some very negative memoranda were also sent to the Congregation of Bishops and Regulars in Rome.³ As for who was responsible for these alleged defamations, Bellacappa believed that a fellow Observant Franciscan and a secular priest wrote the letters and memoranda. Some colleagues told him that the shaky handwriting of one letter was that of Francesco Maria Morisi, an Observant Franciscan who was close friends with Dealta and who was tried and tortured by the Inquisition for soliciting in the confessional. Bellacappa believed that Morisi held him responsible for the latter's transfer from Carpi to Modena for immorality, even though Bellacappa insisted he had nothing to do with that. The former confessor of Santa Chiara added that Morisi had close ties with some of the Clarisses there, especially with Dealta and Ippolita Martinelli, both of whom now had an unfavorable opinion of Bellacappa. The ex-confessor also complained of two other Observant Franciscans in Carpi, as well as a layman, all of whom he suspected of speaking ill of him to the duke of Modena and his father, Fra Giovan Battista.⁴

Bellacappa also described a case of food poisoning he suffered in late October 1636, shortly before his departure from Santa Chiara. He believed it might have been deliberate, as Sisters Colomba Ciarlini and Teodora Pattoni, who had prepared his meal that evening, were not very fond of him. He had previously complained that they served meals not only to him but also to a certain Father Leoni, who was Pattoni's nephew. The two sisters were offended when Bellacappa told them they could not serve two masters at once.⁵ Bellacappa further stated that he distrusted Alsuinda Malaspina ever since his early days as confessor. At that time, the provincial head of Observant Franciscans conducted a visitation of the nunnery, which produced a letter, written in an unidentified hand, and undersigned by Malaspina. The letter contained many accusations–not specified in Bellacappa's testimony, but surely involving his close associations with many younger nuns–against many of the Clarisses and the confessor. Later he learned that the letter was written by Hercole Coccapani, then mayor of Carpi and the brother of two sisters at Santa Chiara. In spite of the presence of Malaspina's name, Bellacappa believed that the mayor actually wrote this at the behest of his sisters.⁶

Quite striking is that virtually all those Bellacappa initially named as bearing him ill will were males, mostly clerics. True, he made a fleeting remark about the Martinelli sisters and believed that Pattoni and Ciarlini poisoned his soup. But even in these cases, his real conflict seemed to be with fellow clerics–Morisi and Leoni–rather than the nuns. He made no mention at all of the supposed strong hostility between Dealta and him. Less surprising is his passing over in silence the poor rapport he had with Princess Angela Caterina. It definitely would have been impolitic for him to identify a member of Emilia's most powerful family as a personal enemy. But for a seventeenth-century cleric, it was perhaps normal to believe his enemies were to be found among his peers, rather than among female religious who were by definition subordinate to clergymen. And though there might be rivalry between different religious orders and between secular and regular clergy, Bellacappa nonetheless listed three fellow Observant Franciscans as quite prominent among his enemies.

Inquisitor Tinti then proceeded to question the former confessor about possible abuse of sacramentals, asking him about his use of holy oil and Easter candles. In regard to holy oil, Bellacappa insisted that the only time that he had possession of it was when it was "renewed" around Easter. On that occasion, he removed and burned the old oil and then sent the vessels to a church with the newly blessed oil. He insisted that the length of time that the vessels remained in his possession did not amount even to hours, let alone days. Once filled, the vessels were returned to the sacristan—Ippolita Martinelli for most of his tenure, Emerenziana Duosi toward the end of it—who kept the oil in the same place that the relics were held.[7]

Tinti then asked Bellacappa about Santa Chiara's use of blessed candles during Easter celebrations. The friar noted that at Santa Chiara, as in other nonparochial churches, three long candles were blessed and arranged in a triangle to the right of the major altar, where they remained from Holy Saturday until Ascension Day. When first brought to the convent, the candles were presented to the nuns in a small ceremony. Although he did not recall the details of the ceremony, Bellacappa believed that he would hand the lighted candles through the window to either the abbess or the sacristan, and the nuns then made a brief procession through the convent with the candles. From Easter to Ascension Day, the candles were lit for Mass every morning and for vespers. In response to the inquisitor's questions, the former confessor denied that in one year the candles were consumed more rapidly than in others or that the nuns complained or expressed surprise at how little of the candle or candles remained on Ascension Day. When Tinti directly told him that some had charged him with keeping and, presumably, misusing a candle, Bellacappa dismissed this as a vicious falsehood and swore that he had never shortened or taken with him any of the candles. In blatant contradiction to this statement, however, the friar conceded that once he did keep one of three candles, giving the other two to the sacristan. Asked why he did so, Bellacappa offered the explanation that laypeople often sought out these blessed candles because they were purportedly useful in helping women get through the birthing process. He added that he had maintained a special devotion for these candles ever since he was a lector in the Emilian village of Cortemaggiore, where "old folks" believed that the candles of Holy Saturday offered protection against lightning and storms. Bellacappa maintained, though, that he never used the candle for himself, nor did he ever lend it to anyone else.[8]

Tinti also showed a special interest in Bellacappa's rapport with Angela Caterina d'Este, whose tenure as abbess ended just a few months before his departure from Santa Chiara. Bellacappa confirmed that he regularly saw the princess and that they said matins together almost every day. Bellacappa also acknowledged that he often ate snacks and meals at the nunnery, prepared by the *abbacucca,* especially in the summertime. Desiring to know more about the alleged poisoning or bewitchment of Angela Caterina, Tinti asked if Bellacappa had ever given anything to drink to the princess. He replied that once, when she told him she was thirsty, he had a nun bring her some wine, although he could not remember who fetched it. At any rate, he did recall that both Angela Caterina and he drank some wine together on that occasion. After seeing that Bellacappa's recollections were quite vague, Tinti had the scribe read to him the princess's version of the St. Bernardine's Day incident. Apart from drinking some wine, however, Bellacappa remembered virtually nothing of that episode. He could not recall that Ippolita brought the wine and sweets, that Dealta was also present, that the princess became furious, or that he tried to calm her.[9]

Bellacappa very deftly dealt with the issue of whether he ordered her through "Holy Obedience" to drink some wine. If he did order her to do so—which he did not recall—he did so not as a confessor but simply as a prelate. If he ordered her to drink, it was purely to counteract Angela Caterina's penchant for self-mortification. He indicated that the princess, like many contemporary zealous Christian women, was wont to abstain excessively from eating and drinking. For the benefit of her own health, the Observant Franciscan conceded that he might indeed have ordered her to imbibe.[10] Of all the circumstances surrounding the incident with the wine, his allegedly ordering her to drink seemed the strangest and most suspicious. His explanation could make sense, especially since the princess apparently did not enjoy very good health, and might deflect suspicion away from him more than if he merely denied having ever given such an order.

Probing more deeply into the nature of his relationship with Angela Caterina d'Este, the inquisitor asked about two celebrations, each referred to as a "fair" (*fiera*), marked annually in the convent on St. Bernardine's Day (20 May) and St. Bartholomew's Day (24 August). Asked if he ever requested money for these fairs, Bellacappa said that once he jokingly said to the princess-abbess that he expected a tip and that a silver tabernacle for the holy sacrament would be nice. He did not recollect, however, ever asking the princess specifically about paying for the fair. Not getting the answer he sought, Tinti then directly asked if Bellacappa got on his knees and begged forgiveness of the princess when she claimed she had almost paid with her life for the fair of St. Bernardine. The former confessor bluntly replied that this was as true as "the devil is Christ."[11] On his third day of testimony, 12 August, Angelo Bellacappa said that he had thought long and hard about his many conversations with the princess-abbess but was still sure that their meetings on St. Bernardine's Day (when she drank the wine and fell sick) and St. Bartholomew's Day (when she confronted him about the poisoning or bewitchment) did not transpire as she described them. As Bellacappa proclaimed that his conscience accused him of no malice whatsoever, the scribe noted that the former confessor's eyes turned red and almost shed tears.[12]

The same day, Tinti got to the most important part of the interrogation of Bellacappa: the issue of his intimate relationships with the nuns who were possessed. Asked if he knew that some Clarisses were bewitched, he responded that almost everything he knew he had learned from hearsay since the first bewitched women, Paolina Forni and Leonora Galli, took ill only toward the end of his tenure at Santa Chiara, and all other possessions broke out well after his departure. As to whether he was a close acquaintance with any of those currently bewitched, Bellacappa replied that Giulia Angelica Sertori came to see him many times during Lent one year, sometimes praying for miracles and sometimes reciting matins. He added that since the princess, whom Sertori served, was not pleased with these frequent meetings, they came to an end and he never saw her again. Barbara Leonora Forni asked him for some lessons in writing so she could be more effective in her service to the princess-abbess. So every day, she wrote a letter to Bellacappa, which he corrected and sent back to her. The former confessor insisted that he was always "indifferent" toward all the other Clarisses of Carpi. Those who wanted to speak to him, came to see him; those who did not, stayed away. The nuns with whom he spoke most often were the *abbacucca,* the sacristan, and their assistants, whose duties often required them to meet with him.[13]

In an effort to deflect blame away from himself, Bellacappa pointed out that several of the possessed nuns did not actually confess to him, but rather to Father Angelo Lazzarino, who heard the confessions of Angela Caterina and all members of her entourage. These included Sisters Giulia Angelica Sertori, Barbara Leonora Forni, Maria Maddalena Colevati, and the now cured Margherita Felice Castagnini.[14] If this was a ploy intended to reduce suspicions, it did not succeed. Inquisitor Tinti observed that even if they did not confess to him, the evidence that the former two frequently met with him was overwhelming. When Tinti inquired about the other seven nuns who were currently possessed, Bellacappa affirmed that he knew them all and that they all came to see him at times, some more often than others. As for other nuns who came to speak with him often, the former confessor mentioned Leonora Brusati, Leonora Fontana, Obizza Foschieri, and others whose names he had forgotten.[15]

Tinti wanted to know what Bellacappa and all these nuns talked about during their many visits. Though first insisting that their conversations always pertained to religious matters, the Franciscan acknowledged, when pressed, that they also exchanged pleasantries or jokes (*facezia*). This was especially the case during Carnival when the sisters had the tradition of amusing themselves by wearing costumes. Bellacappa insisted that he never had immodest chats with them, though conceded that during Carnival he might have said some silly pleasantries.[16] As to the all-important question of whether he took part in such mundane activities or conversations when he was hearing confessions, Bellacappa said, "Heaven forbid that I ever mixed such actions and words with the sacrament of confession." He emphatically denied that he ever uttered amorous words to the nuns during or just before or after confession, pointing out that if he really wanted to talk about such things he had ample opportunity to do so outside the sacrament of penance.[17]

Pressuring Bellacappa to confess to wrongdoing, Tinti told him that "several" nuns did report that he made amorous solicitations or proffered words of love not only immediately before or after confession but even in the act of confession itself. Bellacappa attributed such accusations to the "ill will of those persons who were conspiring" to ruin him. Tinti then bluntly asked why one would assume that these nuns were lying: "The people making the accusations are religious, and in no way are they presumed to have antipathy toward you." Nor is it realistic that they wanted to testify against their own consciences, putting themselves in legal jeopardy and greatly offending God. All things considered, Tinti inquired, why should one not conclude that Bellacappa solicited for love during or around the act of confession?[18]

To this, Bellacappa turned the tables and portrayed himself as the conscientious priest who was the victim of these vicious nuns:

> From this I gather and conclude that they have abandoned God and his spirit, coming before such a judge to depose falsely against a priest who has served them with such affection. . . . And they must surely have been moved by a demon that instilled in their hearts this malignity, since much time passed after my departure before they alleged this deed. And yet they confessed to many good priests . . . who would have required them to reveal this. Nor should we presume ignorance on their part since even children and idiots now know that this would be a case for the Holy Office.[19]

From Bellacappa's point of view, the devil was making these nasty nuns say terrible things to smear the reputation of an impeccable priest. Thus far, all Tinti's questions pertaining to inappropriate language centered on whether he had made overtures or flirted with nuns around the act of confession. In defense of the former confessor, as we have seen, hardly any testimony from nuns contradicted Bellacappa's denials. With the exception of a handful of allegations, most nuns deposed that the inappropriate words and actions of Bellacappa did not take place on the same day that they confessed.

When Tinti shifted the questioning from words to deeds, Bellacappa unequivocally denied that he ever took part in acts that were illicit or unchaste with any nuns. He insisted, for example, that he never went beyond touching the hands of some of the nuns, made possible by a hole in the grating big enough for a finger to pass through.[20] Becoming more explicit, Tinti observed that various nuns reported obscene acts, alleging the priest exposed himself and masturbated in their presence, touched the private parts of some nuns and was touched by them in the same way. At this point, Bellacappa did not deny having ever committed such acts, nor did he argue that actions such as these, committed entirely outside the act of confession, were not under the purview of the Inquisition. Rather he tried to impugn further the reputation of the nuns and to dismiss the testimony as unreliable. Since the nuns were implicating themselves in these immoral acts, they could not be trusted, and the confessor was consequently presumed innocent.[21]

The inquisitor replied that this argument might hold some water if all the women who accused him of indecent words and actions during confession also confessed to committing immodest acts with him. But Tinti pointed out that some of the women who were allegedly solicited succumbed while others did not. And though some stated the illicit overtures occurred outside confession, others said they took place around the act of confession. Since both the "virtuous" and the "fallen" maidens were saying the same thing, one could surmise that they were telling the truth and that Bellacappa had in fact abused the sacrament of penance. According to Bellacappa, these extraordinarily malicious nuns fabricated these accounts of immoral actions outside of confession—which, he pointed out, would not be a concern of the Inquisition even if true—solely to tarnish his reputation. These fabrications, he contended, were part of a spiteful plan to vilify him and make the inquisitor more prone to believe the accusations of solicitation in the confessional (which was in fact under the jurisdiction of the Holy Office). Then Bellacappa for the first time avowed that he was not guilty of libidinous deeds with these nuns at any time or place and that his accusers would have to account for this calumny before the tribunal of God.[22]

Moving to even more explicit accusations, Tinti then read excerpts of testimony against Bellacappa, though, respecting a centuries-old inquisitorial practice, did not reveal the names of any of the accusers to protect them from possible recriminations. Both Dorotea Serafini Cabassi and Maria Calefi claimed that he tried to get them to touch and kiss his hand right before and after confession, accusations which Bellacappa denied. Anna Caterina Zuccari said that Bellacappa's efforts to touch and seduce her did not take place around the act of confession, but he told her several times right after confession that she must remember that he loved her, an allegation that Bellacappa described as an outright lie. Dismissing all accusations against him as part of a plot to ruin him, the friar denied having anything to do with the witchcraft spells in Carpi and asked for aid and protection from the Virgin Mary, St. Dominic of Sora (whom Bellacappa chose as his special protector), and St. Anthony of Padua, in all of whom he placed his soul and his life and the reputation of himself and his religious order.[23]

Tinti persisted and advised him to tell the truth—that is, to confess—since it seemed unlikely that these female religious would plot among themselves against him. More important, they were not alleging a single act but many different incidents. Rather than seeing collusion, the inquisitor found that, taken together, the testimony of different witnesses consistently painted a picture of a priest with a pattern of making overtures to nuns during or just before or after confession. There was no basis to believe that all the nuns who testified against him were motivated by ill will rather than the desire to clear their consciences.[24]

Tinti's persistent urging of Bellacappa to confess his errors shows that the inquisitor's role was closely related to that of confessor. Both the inquisitor and the confessor assumed that the person before them, like all humans, was guilty of many sins. For both clerical offices, the ultimate goal was the salvation of souls and the reconciliation of sinners with the Church. They accordingly urged all Christians to look deep inside themselves to reveal, confess, and show contrition for all their sins. Like secular judges, inquisitors tried to elicit confessions, which were widely regarded as the queen of proofs in early modern jurisprudence. Inquisitors, however, had a stronger desire than their secular counterparts to nurture penitence in the hearts of the miscreants.[25]

Though Tinti found the evidence overwhelming, Bellacappa ended the testimony of 12 August with a furious, misogynistic tirade:

> I know that these nuns were not directed or led by other persons who shrewdly knew how to attain the goal of making it appear that I solicited in confession. I will add, in fact, that in that particular monastery, there are women who are most shrewd, not to mention most malicious, which I have seen through my own experience. They steal letters from each other, going craftily and furtively into the cells of others to steal them, in order to bring harm to those who wrote them, and perform other similar actions of visceral hatred. [They did this] so much that Father Giovan Battista d'Este had to intervene [in the convent] to reconcile not just spiritual sisters but even blood sisters, who passed months and years without speaking to each other. And for this reason, it is not surprising that women, about whom Holy Scripture says, "there is no anger greater than that of a woman, nor malice greater than hers"—and, as far as I'm concerned, especially enclosed women, as the proverb says—would be [disposed] to form a conspiracy or to collude among themselves.[26]

In short, the former confessor reduced all accusations to a sinister plot to frame him hatched by a bunch of manipulative, backstabbing women whose anger and deceit knew no bounds.

Following this appearance, the inquisitor interrogated no one for over three weeks until Bellacappa was again brought from prison to the courtroom to face Tinti and his assistants on 4 September. When Tinti observed that more than one nun reported hearing him say that kissing was not arousing and that it was fine for him to kiss the nuns, Bellacappa replied that the Clarisses who said this either did not understand him or were lying.[27] In a later appearance, Bellacappa volunteered that those who claimed he had said it was no sin for him to kiss female religious may have misunderstood him. He told some nuns, in response to their queries, that it was not a sin for the female religious to kiss each other, unless the kiss was motivated by bad intentions, that is, by sexual attraction. But he dismissed the claim that it was not a sin for them to kiss him as being as far from the truth as "we are from heaven."[28]

Inquisitor Tinti observed that there was overwhelming evidence that he had socialized excessively with many nuns, especially the younger ones. Countless shocked and dismayed nuns had testified about the constant visits the confessor had with many different sisters, especially those who were now deemed possessed. There was also ample evidence that he kissed several nuns and tried to kiss still others. Most important, according to Tinti, so strong was the apparent attraction of the nuns to the confessor, one might well wonder if the nuns were compelled by magic to go to him.[29]

Although he did not try to deny that certain nuns came to see him often, Bellacappa aggressively rejected virtually all other charges. Claiming he never even tried to kiss any of the sisters, Bellacappa vehemently denounced as sacrilegious and heretical the belief that it is not a sin for a priest to be kissed by nuns. More important, he rejected absolutely that he had used any diabolical means to attract them, claiming he had never had any dealings with demons and knew nothing about magic and spells. Bellacappa also asserted that he never called a nun to come to confess unless she actually did give a confession. Complaining about the malice and conspiracy against him, the Observant Franciscan doubted that Jesus Christ had been watched so closely by his enemies![30]

Inquisitor Tinti then broached the subject of the antipathy between the ex-confessor and the Martinelli sisters. Bellacappa asserted that the ill will between them dated from when he advised the provincial father of the Observant Franciscans that Fra Francesco Maria Morisi be removed from the monastery in Carpi and transferred to Modena. (Interestingly, when he first testified, Bellacappa identified Morisi as an enemy but insisted he had nothing to do with Morisi's transfer from Carpi.) In any event, Dealta and Ippolita were furious about this and refused to speak to Bellacappa for quite some time. He knew that Dealta corresponded regularly with Morisi, and Bellacappa was sure she said many negative things about him in her letters.[31]

Tinti further asked whether Bellacappa had at first been good friends with the Martinelli sisters, noting that several nuns suggested that one or the other had willingly brought young nuns to see him. Dealta, for example, was described as not only accompanying Caterina Margherita Ronchi to see Bellacappa but also strongly urging her to love him. The Franciscan responded rather indignantly, saying that if the Martinellis ever did accompany anyone to see him, it would have been early in his tenure. Dealta may well have accompanied some nuns to see him, Bellacappa conceded, but he certainly never told her to encourage anyone to love him. If Dealta did so, she was acting on her own initiative. He added that Dealta would not be a likely person to choose to assist him since her reputation had already been tarnished by the trial of Fra Valerio Trionfanti, a friar who in 1628–29 was tried and acquitted for using love magic on Laura Coccapani, a laywoman and close friend of Dealta.[32]

Almost two weeks later (16 September), Bellacappa was again brought before Tinti. Apparently satisfied with the evidence gathered for and against Bellacappa, the inquisitor asked the former confessor if he was prepared to rest his case. Bellacappa answered that he was not and requested that the Holy Office provide him with a procurator who could advise him on how he could best resolve the case. Tinti acceded to this request and ordered that an attorney be sent to Bellacappa's cell to consult with him.[33] A few days later, the months of incarceration were taking their toll, and Bellacappa asked to be released from prison pending the completion of his trial, complaining about the physical conditions in prison and fearing he would fall ill if he remained there. Signing a promise not to flee, Bellacappa, described by Tinti as an exemplary prisoner, was released from prison on 21 September to a form of house arrest.[34]

Up until Bellacappa's request for legal counsel, Tinti was in effect conducting a *processo informativo,* whereby a defendant was confronted with the accusations of unnamed deponents and urged to confess his guilt. Research on the Roman Inquisition has in fact shown that it was rare for defendants to mount a full-fledged defense,[35] even though they had the right to do so. When defendants continued to profess their innocence, they could request the assistance of an attorney. If they could not afford to pay for the attorney themselves, they provided a list of possible lawyers, from which the Holy Office selected one. As seen in this case, for those unable to pay for an attorney—and Bellacappa, like all monks and friars, had taken a vow of poverty—the Inquisition was willing to provide at its expense an attorney for the defense.

Although the court-appointed attorney's main responsibility often seemed to be to convince the accused to admit his or her guilt, that would not be the case here. When a defendant and attorney met and agreed that a confession was not warranted, then the accused proceeded with a *processo difensivo.* In mounting a defense, the attorney received a copy of all the proceedings, although the names of witnesses were deleted. Ever since the central Middle Ages, inquisitors had insisted on secrecy, never revealing under pain of excommunication the names of witnesses and accusers, to shield them from reprisals on the part of the accused.[36] After perusing this transcription, the defendant and attorney could then submit questions in writing for those who had already testified and call for the interrogation of other witnesses. All interrogations, however, were conducted by the inquisitor, and neither defendants nor their lawyers were allowed to be present for this questioning.[37]

Three days after his release from prison, Bellacappa again appeared before the inquisitor, this time requesting that he have as legal counsel someone other than A. Bernardi, the attorney who was usually assigned to represent incarcerated defendants. On 24 September Tinti granted this request and appointed Francesco Barozzi to serve as Bellacappa's lawyer. The inquisitor then agreed to have a copy of the whole case written out for the defendant, with the names of witnesses deleted. The attorney had to swear upon the Bible that he would not show this document nor discuss the case with anyone and promise to return the copy to the Inquisition upon the completion of the case. Bellacappa received his copy of the proceedings in October.[38]

In order to prepare his defense of Bellacappa, Barozzi submitted on 1 November a series of "chapters" concerning the interrogation of witnesses and the gathering of other evidence. In the first chapter, he asked for letters to be sent to the inquisitors of Parma and Bologna for the purpose of interrogating people there.[39] These involved character witnesses, who, as was often the case for defendants in front of the Holy Office, were likely to give evidence of the accused's probity, orthodoxy, and genuine piety.[40] All the other chapters were directed toward the nuns of Santa Chiara. Convinced that Bellacappa was accused of many actions that he could not possibly have done, Barozzi asked that the inquisitor undertake a careful investigation of the upper and lower confessionals, providing a detailed description of their grilles and the holes in them to determine the feasibility of committing some of the alleged actions in those locations. The procurator also requested a similar examination of the communion window where other indiscretions were said to have occurred.[41]

After spending (no doubt) a few weeks preparing for the defense, Barozzi submitted a written statement–which unfortunately is not dated–that outlined the list of articles on which he based his claim that Bellacappa was innocent of all charges. Barozzi stressed four major points. First, he insisted his client was a devout, conscientious friar: "The truth was and is that Father Angelo Bellacappa from Parma, Observant Franciscan, theologian, and preacher, has always been a cleric of good life and reputation."[42] Heretofore, no one had ever heard of him being involved in any scandal, especially pertaining to confession. Barozzi's second point was that the upper and lower confessionals of Santa Chiara were places where matters other than confession regularly took place. A priest might meet the abbess there to discuss various matters concerning the convent; he might call a nun there for a rebuke, assigning her an act of penance; he could listen to the prayers and concerns of the "maidens and novices"; he could meet with nuns either as confessor or as friend, either privately or publicly, depending on the daily needs of the convent's residents. Third, an important distinction was made at Santa Chiara with respect to the use of the confessionals. When these locales were being used for hearing confessions, curtains were drawn over the grilles on both the priest's and the confessant's side. When the confessionals were used for anything other than confession, then the curtains were regularly kept open, a custom maintained at Santa Chiara before, during, and after Bellacappa's tenure as confessor. Finally, in an effort to reinforce the different uses of the confessional, Barozzi noted that the Clarisses of Carpi always wore a cord around their necks when they went to confess, and confessing without the cord was considered "scandalous." On 1 November 1638 Inquisitor Tinti accepted Barozzi's list of articles for Bellacappa's defense.[43]

The State of the Confessionals

In response to Bellacappa's request, the Inquisition undertook a careful investigation of the premises of the convent, examining closely the locations where Bellacappa supposedly took sexual liberties with the nuns. On 9 November 1638 Inquisitor Tinti along with Archpriest Niccolini, the notary Ripalta, and other witnesses went to the convent of Santa Chiara. First, they looked at the lower confessional from outside the cloistered area of the convent. They found that this confessional was covered with sheet metal that was perforated with many small holes, none of which was big enough to allow anything larger than a finger to pass through. This finding was none too startling, since none of the illicit touching was said to have taken place in the lower confessional. The group then proceeded to the small room overlooking the upper confessional. There they examined the infamous hole through which the bell-rope passed. First the notary and then the Inquisitor successfully stuck an arm through the hole. Each was able to extend the better part of his forearm into the cloister, and there was nothing to suggest that the opening in the wall had been altered recently in any way. The inquisitor and other investigators then entered the cloister, where they were met by the sacristan, Sister Emerenziana Duosi, who led them first to the lower confessional. The confessional was covered by a blue cloth suspended by a curtain rod on the nuns' side; unless it was pulled back, no one on the outside could see the nuns inside. When Tinti asked to see the upper confessional, the Clarisses told him that the room in question no longer served as a confessional and that the grating had been removed and its space in the wall filled in, undoubtedly a reaction to the notorious lewd actions that Bellacappa allegedly perpetrated there. Tinti asked to be taken to the granary where, according to the abbess, the grating had been taken after its removal. The notary reported that the iron grille resembled that of the lower confessional, and that it contained many holes, the largest of which was large enough to allow a thumb to pass through easily.[44]

With their detailed knowledge of the physical makeup of the confessionals, Inquisitor Tinti and the notary went to the convent the following day to interrogate some sisters concerning the charges against Bellacappa. In questioning nuns at Santa Chiara and later friars in Bologna, the inquisitor asked witnesses whether they had been shown the "articles," the questions Bellacappa had submitted and the charges involved in this case, and whether anyone tried to influence what they would say. The inquisitor questioned the nuns for Bellacappa's defense, but, as noted above, neither the defendant nor his attorney was allowed to be present at the questioning. Tinti asked detailed questions about habits associated with confession and the confessionals of several nuns, including Emilia Bellentani, seventy, the current abbess; Emerenziana Duosi, whose tenure as sacristan had begun while Bellacappa was still confessor; Chiara Grillenzoni, fifty-six, who served as *abbacucca* for most of Bellacappa's tenure as confessor; and Penelope Leonori, seventy-eight, who served briefly as abbess in the latter part of 1636, immediately after Angela Caterina's last term.[45] In response to Tinti's queries, all these nuns testified that they had not been particularly close to Bellacappa. Although Grillenzoni said that Bellacappa's current troubles stemmed from his excessive fraternizing with the young nuns, they all nonetheless expressed a high opinion of him and insisted he had been diligent in fulfilling his duties.[46]

When Tinti inquired about the confessionals themselves, the nuns indicated that the rooms containing the two confessionals were one above the other and that the grilles were mounted in the same sturdy stone wall on two different floors (until the upper one was removed). More important, they reported that in both confessionals, a curtain was nailed to the grating on the interior side. Although this curtain could not be removed, there were strips of it that were loose and could be lifted to allow the priest and nuns to see each other through the holes in the screen, some of which were fairly large. One nun estimated that the biggest hole in the upper confessional's screen was as large as the circle made by touching the tip of her index finger to the tip of her thumb. Moreover, there was another curtain on the confessor's side, which he could draw open or close. The witnesses indicated that the confessor closed this curtain whenever he heard confessions and left it open at most other times. Most important, all the nuns indicated that the confessionals were not used exclusively for fulfilling the sacrament of penance. Quite regularly nuns went there, even in groups, to discuss a wide range of matters with the confessor. This tradition dated from well before Bellacappa's time and was condoned by the rules of the convent. Several noted that these locales served as both confessionals and parlors. One reported that nuns used the confessionals to communicate not just with the confessor but with other priests as well, deeming the confessional a more convenient place than the parlor adjacent to the turntable to discuss spiritual and mundane matters. The *abbacucca* and her assistant reported that they quite often went to the confessionals to receive orders from and exchange information with the confessor and other clerics. Frequently they also fetched other nuns to come meet with the confessor, more often than not for matters unrelated to confession. In response to Tinti's queries, the sisters affirmed that the nuns always wore their cords around their necks when they went to confess as well as when they took the Eucharist, an "ancient" tradition that was always observed.[47]

Evidently not satisfied with what they had learned about the confessionals, Tinti and Ripalta returned to the convent several weeks later, on 28 December 1638, to reexamine the lower confessional. A closer examination showed that beneath the grating on the right-hand side there was indeed a hole that, if one removed a wooden board on the cloistered side, was big enough to stick one's hand through easily. In the corner of the same room in which the confessional was located was a turntable, through which the inquisitor and the notary also found that they could extend a hand into the cloister. The inquisitor and notary then entered the convent and examined the confessional and *ruota* on the cloistered side. They found that from the nuns' side, one could insert a hand through the turntable to touch that of someone on the outside, but only a small part of the hand could actually go through to the other side. Going to the confessional's grille, the investigators removed the curtain from the grating–which they found could be removed quite easily, contrary to the above testimony of several nuns. The removal of the curtain revealed a hole that was big enough to allow people on opposite sides of the grate to touch hands.[48] Although these findings applied only to the lower confessional and Bellacappa's hanky-panky all seemed to have taken place in the upper confessional and the small room overlooking it, one can assume that the physical makeup of the two confessionals was quite similar. In any event, a certain degree of manual touching was physically possible at the lower confessional–and if one were interested in kissing through a grille, that, too, would have been feasible.

Although the inquisitor did not make a note of this, the confessionals of Santa Chiara did not conform entirely to the guidelines for confessors of nuns. These rules prescribed that the priest was to hear the confessions of all nuns at a window that was to be covered constantly by a "thick curtain, not at all transparent and without holes, attached on all sides so that one cannot remove it or lift it at all."[49] These same guidelines also recommended that if a priest had to meet privately with a nun for something other than a confession, such encounters should take place in the confessional, "never in the parlor, especially with the grating open." This latter remark showed that it was understood that the priest and nun were not to see, let alone touch, each other. Moreover, such meetings were to be exceptional, and conversations were to be brief and to concern only the spiritual health of the sister.[50] Even according to the nuns who defended him, Bellacappa was not adhering to these procedures.

The Evidence from Bologna

The inquiry into Bellacappa's defense extended to Bologna, where he had lived for some time both before and after his charge in Carpi. In response to an inquiry from the Inquisition of Modena, the minister of the province of Bologna for the Observant Franciscans wrote a letter in which he stated that there was nothing in the order's provincial archives to suggest that Angelo Bellacappa, preacher and reader in theology, had ever been accused of any misdeed whatsoever. In the entire thirty years that he had been a Franciscan, Bellacappa had never been reprimanded or tried for misbehavior and had never shown insolence toward superiors or subordinates.[51] More important, six Observant Franciscans of the monastery of the Annunziata, where Bellacappa was living at the time of his arrest, gave very favorable testimony concerning his character. This testimony was made at the request of Bellacappa himself, who, with the approval of the inquisitor of Modena, wrote to the monastery's guardian (superior), asking that he summon several friars to serve as character witnesses. Since the letter is not extant, it is unclear whether the defense requested specific men as witnesses or the guardian selected friars who were close acquaintances of Bellacappa. Regardless of who chose the witnesses, Bellacappa was able to provide questions to be asked of the witnesses about his lifestyle, but no one at the monastery other than the guardian saw these questions before the interrogations.[52]

The Franciscans all gave their testimony before the vicar of the inquisitor of Bologna on 10 and 11 November. The first witness was the guardian himself, Giovanni dal Chierico, fifty, who claimed to have known Bellacappa ever since they were young men and to have spent five or six years with him in Bologna. Dal Chierico had no direct knowledge of why Bellacappa had been taken into custody by the Inquisition of Modena, but he and others in the monastery speculated that he may have been suspected of playing a part in Santa Chiara's possession or witchcraft woes. The guardian asserted that Bellacappa had always enjoyed a good reputation of leading a devout religious life. In Bologna Bellacappa was a teacher of theology and rarely heard confessions and, so far as dal Chierico knew, never had any "dishonest" relationships.[53]

Among the Observant Franciscans whom dal Chierico asked to testify was Tommaso Fabrizi, thirty-eight, who had equally positive things to say about Bellacappa, whom he had known for sixteen years. Although they were not close friends, Fabrizi affirmed that he had studied theology under Bellacappa and was now himself a professor of theology to his fellow *Zoccolanti*. Moreover, for two periods, including the six months before Bellacappa was taken away, Fabrizi had served as priest (*sacerdote*) to Bellacappa. Though aware that there were some possessed nuns at Santa Chiara, Fabrizi could not imagine that Bellacappa had anything to do with those travails. As a professor, Bellacappa, with his excellent judgment and good virtues, set a very positive example for the young Franciscans who studied under him. And in all the monasteries where Fabrizi had lived, Bellacappa was invariably praised as a fine clergyman. So far as he knew, his fellow friar had no scandalous relationships, nor had Fabrizi ever heard of anyone accusing Bellacappa of soliciting during confession or at any other time. Another friar, identified only as Fra Angelo of Bologna, sixty-five, asserted that Bellacappa had always led an exemplary life during the dozen years he had known him. Though he had heard rumors that Bellacappa had solicited some of the nuns of Carpi, Fra Angelo opined that carnal and venereal acts were quite alien to the former confessor's character.[54]

The most provocative defense of Bellacappa came from Salvatore Valotti, a thirty-eight-year-old friar from Bologna. Valotti had studied with Bellacappa for seventeen months at the monastery at Cortemaggiore and another four years in Bologna. Though the two were never close, Valotti claimed to be a "reverent disciple" of his teacher, adding:

> I have heard that Father Bellacappa is [held] in the Holy Office of Modena concerning certain nuns who, it is said, are possessed and that Father Bellacappa had a role in this. This, however, is against the common opinion of all of us who know the father. We are of the opinion that this has been a persecution on the part of Father Fra Giovan Battista of the house of Este against not only Father Bellacappa but also our religious order, and I have heard this said frequently.[55]

Valotti insisted that Bellacappa was a virtuous priest who enjoyed a good reputation and had no inappropriate relationships and was sure that he had never solicited anyone in the confessional in Carpi or elsewhere.[56] As we have seen, Giovan Battista d'Este promoted and facilitated the exorcizing of the ailing nuns, and he clearly actively interceded in the affairs of the convent, as witnessed by his alleged use of Easter candles and his supposed intervention to settle differences between feuding Clarisses. Be that as it may, Valotti was the first person to suggest that the former duke was in any way behind the attacks on Bellacappa. Fra Giovan Battista definitely played an important role in having Santa Chiara removed from the jurisdiction of the Observant Franciscans, and he and many fellow Capuchins tended to view the *Zoccolanti* as rivals who were lax in following the dictates of Francis of Assisi. To attribute all accusations against Bellacappa to a plot hatched by Giovan Battista implied, however, the complicity of a huge number of Clarisses who had testified under oath. And there was no evidence that the Clarisses themselves were plotting against the Observant Franciscans, as such a conspiracy would seem to require. Many of the sisters, most obviously Angela Caterina d'Este, preferred the *Zoccolanti* to the secular priests of Carpi. All told, though, Bellacappa could not have asked for better testimony from character witnesses.

Barozzi's Aggressive Defense

Much more so than his counterparts today, a defense attorney who worked before the Holy Office was in a very real sense an officer of the court. If convinced that his client really was a heretic, for example, the lawyer was to try to persuade him to admit his error and, if unsuccessful, was obliged to abandon the defense to avoid being suspected himself of heresy.[57] In this case, however, Bellacappa's attorney clearly was quite sure of his client's innocence and mounted an aggressive defense on his behalf. Barozzi wrote a lengthy statement in which he tried to discredit all accusations against the former confessor. Though undated, this brief was probably submitted in late November or December of 1638. Not doubting that the ill nuns were possessed, Barozzi claimed that the demons put into the mouths of those nuns vicious fabrications implicating the former confessor. Worse still, he claimed, many healthy nuns conspired with the demons to ruin Bellacappa, voluntarily coming forward to the Holy Office to reveal the flimsiest suspicions against him, accusations that had no more solid foundation than what "the devil contemptuously offered them." Suggesting collusion between the demons and the nuns who accused Bellacappa, the lawyer painted a picture of a sinister, diabolical plot to ruin the priest, which showed that "even the best of Christians" suffered from the lies of demons.[58]

Like any good defense lawyer, Barozzi tried to show that all accusations made against his client were bogus. He observed that the common thread running through these accusations was that Bellacappa reputedly had a strong lustful side and sought to lead the possessed nuns—and, he could have added, some other nuns as well—into moral turpitude by soliciting them in the confessional with illicit words and deeds. These suspicions led to the inquisitor's investigation, which uncovered two types of alleged crimes: those committed at the time of holy confession and others committed apart from confession. The attorney insisted that misdeeds performed outside the act of confession and the confessional were not under the jurisdiction of the Inquisition. Though he did not explain why, such acts would not have constituted an abuse of sacraments.[59]

The attorney then proceeded to try to discredit individually every accusation made against his client. In the copy of the investigation that Bellacappa and his lawyer had received, witnesses were identified by a code of letters, and a list that matched the codes with their names was preserved in the Inquisition's dossier. First he considered the accusation raised by a nun (Grazia Lupagnini) who alleged that Bellacappa grabbed her hand through a hole above the upper confessional (but not during confession) and committed a lewd act against her will. According to Barozzi, this amounted to isolated testimony that could not possibly be corroborated by a third party. He avowed that both canon and civil law rejected such unverifiable testimony, which amounted simply to her word against his.[60]

Barozzi's reasoning would seem to imply that one could never admit the testimony of a person who accused a priest of soliciting during confession; since only the priest and confessant were present during confession, ordinarily no third party could have witnessed the solicitation. In fact, Church law did recognize such isolated testimony as viable, and similar accusations by more than one person could suffice to convict a priest of solicitation, precisely because there were by definition no third-party witnesses to confession.[61] Thus, though affirming that women are "fickle, deceitful, fraudulent, mendacious, trifling, and corruptible," jurists nonetheless conceded that the testimony of two women against a priest might suffice to convict him of solicitation, provided they were of unquestionable virtue.[62] In this case, though, since Lupagnini was not alleging solicitation during confession, her testimony would not have carried such weight. Barozzi cast further doubt on her testimony by pointing out inconsistencies between it and Leonora Brusati's account of the same incident. Although the former claimed that Bellacappa asked for her colleague's hand after having ejaculated into her own, Brusati said that if her memory served her well, Bellacappa asked for her hand before he grabbed Lupagnini's.[63]

Another reservation that he had about Lupagnini's accusation was that her testimony was made voluntarily. Although most of the testimony in this case was made when nuns were convoked for interrogation, Lupagnini appeared "spontaneously" of her own volition to give this deposition. According to Barozzi, such voluntary testimony was permissible only for crimes of heresy or witchcraft, neither of which was being alleged in that incident. Otherwise, one could easily convict a person based on false testimony. In this case, the alleged indiscretion, even if true, was not a crime subject to the Holy Office but rather was merely a "trivial" matter.[64] Barozzi's suggestion that voluntary testimony could be offered only in cases of heresy or witchcraft did not square with inquisitorial traditions. Most obviously, denunciations for solicitation in the confessional were virtually always made in this manner. To clear their consciences, women regularly appeared before inquisitors to denounce priests who made sexual advances during confession, often pushed to make these denunciations by confessors who refused to grant them absolution until they did so.

Referring to the inquisitor's reports about the confessionals made at the request of the defense, Barozzi also argued that some of the accusations were physically impossible. Such was his assertion concerning the claim that Bellacappa took a nun's hand in his during confession while saying amorous words to her. According to Barozzi, the hole in question was large enough to accommodate only a thumb, not an entire hand. Even in cases where the alleged actions were not impossible but merely unlikely, Barozzi declared that such testimony must not be believed. He cited as authorities various jurists, such as Prospero Farinacci and Giuseppe Mascardi, both of whom wrote that testimony of actions that do not seem feasible must be suspected of being false and therefore rejected.[65] Further citing Mascardi, albeit selectively and deceptively, Barozzi also insisted that if some of a person's testimony were found to be false, then all of his or her testimony must be thrown out, not just the part that was disproved.[66] Mascardi did indeed avow that a person's entire testimony is presumed false, but only if the proven falsehoods were made out of fraud or malice.[67] In the very next entry, Mascardi actually contradicted what Barozzi was claiming. According to Mascardi, "If there are several headings [or allegations] separate from each other in a document, a falsehood committed in one does not render another heading false."[68]

Referring again to Lupagnini's testimony, Barozzi avowed that the most notorious actions she alleged were not physically possible. As for the captive-hand incident, Barozzi avowed that it was most unlikely if not impossible that Bellacappa could have pulled the hand of a nun through the hole over to his side. He observed that Inquisitor Tinti had shown that though he could put his hand through the hole, he could not pull another person's hand through it, given the narrowness of the hole.[69] In a letter to Barberini, Tinti in fact affirmed that he did not think it was possible to pull another person's hand through that hole against her will.[70] As for another lewd action that allegedly took place in the upper confessional with the same nun (Grazia Lupagnini), Barozzi asked rhetorically, "How could [the defendant] stick his virile member through the hole of the grating of the confessional to the side of the witness, if the hole is not even big enough for a finger?"[71] In short, Barozzi insisted that many of the reported incidents could not have taken place because the small size of the holes in the screens and grilles made the alleged physical contact impossible.

Another line of argument, which Barozzi stressed repeatedly, was that so many of the accusations of solicitation, even if true, were not germane because they did not occur around the act of confession and so did not involve an abuse of sacraments. He referred, for example, to a witness who reported overhearing illicit conversations between Bellacappa and various nuns in the confessional. Several nuns also told this sister that he incited them with amorous words, and she herself saw him touching their fingers and singing with them. To this, Barozzi noted that these supposed illicit conversations did not take place during or shortly before or after confession. There are no witnesses when one confesses sacramentally, and so when more than one woman were together at the confessional, clearly no one was there to confess. He cited the canon jurist Cesare Carena to argue that a priest who solicited in the confessional but not during or just before or after confession was not subject to any penalties of the Inquisition since there was no abuse of sacraments.[72]

There must be no confusion, Barozzi insisted, between the confessional and the sacrament of confession. The places known as the upper and lower confessionals at Santa Chiara were indeed the places where confessions were heard, but they also served many other functions. Nuns went there for discussions not just with the confessor but also with certain lay superiors, and the investigation for the defense clearly showed that the confessionals were regularly used as a type of parlor. Even evidence for the prosecution showed that many nuns gathered there at the same time, even though no one can be present except the confessor and the confessant for the sacrament of penance. Barozzi pointed out that "Sister C" (Dorothea Cabassi) acknowledged that she went to the confessional to have leisurely conversations with the confessor. The attorney noted, moreover, that when nuns went to confess, the curtains were drawn before the grating and, according to the rules of their order, Clarisses wore their cords around their necks when confessing. If, therefore, the grille was not covered by the curtain and the nuns were not wearing their cords, then they obviously were not there to confess. In such cases, the locale functioned as a parlor, not a confessional.[73]

Barozzi tried to discredit the testimony of "Sister B" (Maria Calefi) on two grounds. Calefi admitted taking part in illicit touching with Bellacappa in the confessional, "details of which, for modesty's sake, we have been requested to keep silent." As Barozzi noted, Sister B acknowledged that these actions never took place close to the time that she confessed. The only physical contact she mentioned that was associated with confession was her kissing the confessor's hand "out of devotion," just before or after confessing, a perfectly acceptable gesture.[74] Furthermore, since she confessed to taking part in venereal touching with the confessor, she was an accomplice in that sin. The attorney declared that a person guilty of a crime could not give valid testimony against an accomplice unless for purposes of unburdening one's conscience *under torture*. Since she herself admitted that she had brought dishonor to herself, Calefi's testimony was unreliable because it was not made under the pain of torture.[75]

Barozzi made the same arguments in considering the testimony of other nuns who accused Bellacappa of misconduct. When first convoked, "Sister CC" (Silveria Chechi) claimed that she and Bellacappa had kissed and that he had exposed himself to her. Later, she returned to the inquisitor and expressed the need to unburden her conscience and reveal that she had taken part in some illicit mutual touching with the priest, though not on a day she confessed. According to Barozzi, this testimony, too, was null because it did not involve the abuse of sacraments and because with this voluntary testimony the nun brought dishonor to herself and acknowledged that she was an accomplice to a crime. This deposition was rendered without torture and pertained to a sin over which, according to Barozzi, the Inquisition did not have jurisdiction and so must be thrown out.[76] For similar reasons, Barozzi discredited the deposition of "Sister M" (Anna Caterina Zuccari), a "lewd, trifling" woman who admitted that twice in the presence and at the instigation of Bellacappa she was touched "dishonestly" by another sister. The jurist argued that it would be most inappropriate to allow the deposition of this "unchaste" young woman to impugn the honesty of the confessor.[77]

The attorney repeatedly emphasized this argument that since these nuns admitted having committed serious sins themselves, with or without Bellacappa, they were untrustworthy and their testimony was therefore unacceptable. Ordinarily, Church law did indeed hold that the testimony of an accomplice alone did not suffice to convict a suspect. An exception was made, however, in cases where women accepted sexual propositions made by confessors during or just before or after confession. In such a case, the acceptance of the confessant was irrelevant, and the confessor was abusing the sacrament of penance. The priest was not liable to prosecution, however, if the confessant propositioned the cleric and he accepted.[78]

Barozzi further argued that other words or actions attributed to Bellacappa were not even inappropriate, let alone a sin over which the Inquisition had jurisdiction. Several nuns accused Bellacappa of encouraging them to love him. One nun claimed that, just before she departed after confessing, he told her that she must remember that he loved her, to which she responded that she loved him as her spiritual father. As Barozzi observed, the confessor could have been referring to a spiritual "love, of which we fully approve."[79] The attorney pursued a similar line of reasoning in considering the deposition of "Sister G" (Cassandra Felice Poggi), who claimed that when she confessed to Bellacappa for the first time, he asked her to lift the curtain over the grating so he could see her. When she did so, he told her that she was very pretty and had beautiful eyes. According to Barozzi, even if true, these were not "truly illicit" words that violated the rules on solicitation in confession as defined by the Gregorian bull of 1622.[80]

Yet another line of argument that Barozzi pursued was to point out that so much of the nuns' testimony was based on hearsay. Referring to a nun who heard other sisters say that Bellacappa used inappropriate language, the attorney cited various authorities who maintained, he claimed, that testimony from hearsay did not constitute proof. Among the jurists he cited was, again, Farinacci, who did indeed say, "A hearsay witness ordinarily does not prove" guilt.[81] Farinacci provided other arguments, however, that could have easily been used against Bellacappa. The jurist wrote that testimony from hearsay could be admitted for crimes that were hidden or difficult to prove, and misbehavior in the confessional was by definition committed in private and difficult to prove. Farinacci also asserted that hearsay testimony combined with some auxiliary evidence did constitute proof. Even without supporting evidence, testimony from hearsay combined with the reputation of the accused could lead to "violent presumption" of guilt.[82] Farinacci also asserted that the more witnesses who made similar accusations against a defendant, the stronger was the presumption of guilt.[83]

Weighing all the evidence, Barozzi concluded that all charges against Bellacappa should be dismissed.[84] Taken together, the nuns' testimony did not justify any charges against his client, Barozzi declared. All depositions were tainted because they came from nuns who were themselves accomplices in the sins they described; they were solitary accusations that could not be corroborated by any other witnesses; they charged the defendant with actions that were physically impossible to perform; they were based on hearsay rather than on firsthand observation; or they did not accuse the defendant of sins that were subject to prosecution by the Inquisition. In this last case, either the alleged words or deeds were not serious enough to merit the attention of the Inquisition—for example, complimenting a woman on her looks—or more often, the supposed actions, though inappropriate and sinful, did not justify an investigation by the Holy Office because they did not constitute an abuse of sacraments.

In all fairness, as noted repeatedly, the depositions of the nuns strongly supported the claim that Bellacappa was generally careful to separate his amorous words and sordid actions from sacramental confession. Several weeks before Barozzi had even been appointed to defend Bellacappa, Inquisitor Tinti confided in a letter to the Congregation of the Holy Office that Giovan Battista Bignardi, who succeeded Bellacappa as confessor at Santa Chiara, revealed on his deathbed that he regretted some of his actions that had helped spark the investigation of his predecessor. When many nuns told him about Bellacappa's "obscene" words and actions in the confessionals, the incensed Bignardi refused to grant them absolution unless they denounced the former confessor to the Inquisition. But since the inappropriate incidents mostly, if not exclusively, took place outside confession, the dying Bignardi feared he had been a bit harsh toward Bellacappa.[85]

That said, Barozzi's depiction of Bellacappa as a totally innocent victim who was ruthlessly framed by a bunch of wicked nuns stretches credulity beyond the limits. Dismissing all accusations as mere fabrications would require that dozens of nuns fabricated and recounted under oath accusations of illicit behavior on his part. Alluding to "evil women" who were "crafty, fraudulent, mendacious, corruptible, and trivial,"⁸⁶ Barozzi's statement amounted to a diatribe against spiteful female religious who were fabricating venomous charges against the former confessor. But for what purpose would the sisters of Carpi have hatched such a sinister plot? They did not need to get rid of him because, at the time of this investigation, two years had passed since Bellacappa had served as confessor at Santa Chiara. In fact, he had left Carpi about a year before the principal outbreak of possessions had occurred. Moreover, even some of the older nuns who had much positive to say about him expressed concern about the way he had socialized with so many young sisters. And the fact that Bellacappa had a fine reputation as a professor of theology in the all-male environment of the Franciscan order in no way precludes possible misbehavior when surrounded by cloistered female religious. Rather than a widespread conspiracy against the friar, the simplest explanation for the huge number of accusations is that Bellacappa was in fact taking sexual liberties, in deed and especially in word, with many younger Clarisses. Although he was usually careful not to mix sex with sacraments, priests were not supposed to be seducing nuns at any time. Even if he technically did not abuse the sacrament of penance, he almost surely was abusing his power over these female religious for whom he was entrusted the cure of souls.

Another point worth stressing is that Barozzi's defense was directed entirely against Bellacappa' alleged solicitation, never even mentioning witchcraft or magic. He did not try to defend the confessor against charges that the ailing nuns were the victims of love magic. He did not address the issue, raised by some nuns, of whether the confessor misused holy oil or an Easter candle. He did not refer to all the things Bellacappa had touched or given to nuns–books, food, even a clavichord–that many sisters believed were bewitched. Barozzi's decision to concentrate on the solicitation charges was nonetheless appropriate. Proving Bellacappa's innocence on the witchcraft counts would have been impossible. The seasoned attorney also surely realized that the solicitation charges against his client were much stronger than those alleging magic, be it to incite love or to cause harm. And he no doubt realized that the Holy Office itself, especially the Congregation in Rome, was more convinced that he was a seducer than a warlock. In a letter to Cardinal Barberini in September 1638, Inquisitor Tinti himself noted that the evidence of witchcraft was not nearly as strong as that of solicitation.⁸⁷ Quite significant is the fact that Dealta Martinelli, who was suspected solely of witchcraft, did not even have to mount a defense.

Taken as a whole, Bellacappa's defense consisted of two important elements. First, his fellow Observant Franciscans of Bologna provided important testimony as character witnesses, portraying Bellacappa as a devout cleric with a sterling reputation. Second, Barozzi asserted that all charges made against his client were groundless because accusations by individuals could not be verified by other witnesses; because the accusers, many of whom were implicated themselves in the sins they alleged, could not be trusted; and because the supposed misdeeds, even if true, were not under the purview of the Holy Office.

Barozzi's defense most importantly shows the Roman Inquisition's high standards concerning legal procedures. As Bellacappa's experience reflected, the Inquisition mandated that defendants had the right to legal counsel, often even at the expense of the Holy Office itself, in an era when most other tribunals paid little heed to the rights of the accused. Although many secular courts simply read aloud the evidence to defendants and demanded that they make their defense on the spot, the Inquisition provided defendants with a full transcript of the trial (minus the names of witnesses) and gave the accused's attorney ample time to prepare a defense.[88] It is now well established that the Holy Office set very high standards for proving the crime of witchcraft and for applying torture (which was never even requested in the Santa Chiara investigation). As we have seen, the Inquisition also denied the validity of extrajudicial confessions, reflected in the rejection of Dealta's coerced "confession." All told, the evidence from Carpi readily supports John Tedeschi's contention that in many respects "the Holy Office was a pioneer in judicial reform."[89]

Chapter 7

THE WANING OF THE POSSESSIONS

In the autumn of 1638, the Congregation of the Holy Office grew increasingly impatient with the convent's apparently never-ending unrest. In late October Cardinal Barberini wrote a letter to Archpriest Niccolini giving him detailed instructions on what to do with the afflicted nuns. He reiterated that the agitated sisters were supposed to be held in isolation from each other and forbidden to speak with or write to anyone inside or outside the convent. Fearing suicide attempts by the frenetic nuns, Barberini ordered that there be no objects in their cells with which they could do themselves harm.[1] Sharing these fears, Inquisitor Tinti expressed his concern that there were windows in almost all the rooms in which the ailing sisters could be kept at least somewhat isolated from the others. While in their senses, the demoniac nuns asked Tinti to have the windows nailed shut out of fear that, when agitated, they might jump to their deaths into the courtyard below. The inquisitor further related that one of the nuns actually tried to jump into a well, but was restrained by others.[2] Barberini instructed the archpriest to make sure that the ailing nuns be furnished with "holy images, holy water, and relics, which demons fear." But the cardinal also asked Niccolini and others involved not to be so quick to believe that the chaos and bizarre behavior observed was the work of the devil, because "among women, especially nuns," this could easily be the result of "melancholic passion" if not an outright fabrication.[3] In late October 1638 Barberini bluntly urged Tinti to cease all delays and aggressively seek an end to Santa Chiara's woes.[4]

Growing ever more anxious to see an end to the ills of the convent, the Congregation of the Inquisition decided to assume responsibility itself for governing Santa Chiara. Barberini and other cardinal-inquisitors accordingly removed the convent from the archpriest's direction and appointed Germanico Mantica, bishop of Adria, as temporary governor of the convent. Hoping to put an end to Carpi's travails, Mantica arrived in Modena in late November 1638, accompanied by a physician named Bonacorsi as well as an exorcist and a confessor, all of whom were from Bologna. But if Barberini hoped that Mantica would put an end to the rumors that these women were diabolically possessed, he was to be sadly disappointed. Accompanied by Tinti, this group went to Carpi to examine the agitated nuns. The first to evaluate them was the physician, who, though conceding that it was not impossible that their ills were of natural origin, strongly suspected that they were possessed by spirits. The next day the physician and the exorcist together examined the sisters. With the permission of Mantica, the unidentified priest conducted exorcisms on several nuns. He discovered, among various things, that the "seat" of Veronica Maria Coccapani's principal demon was in her heart. When the priest was trying to force the chief demon of Degnamerita Solieri to show itself, the nun became incredibly agitated—her face became swollen, tears flowed from her eyes, and her mouth emitted a very putrid smell. When administering the rite to Anna Maria Martinelli, the exorcist asked the demon if a handkerchief he found nearby was the instrument of the spell that afflicted her. He then exorcized the handkerchief, during which the demon inflicted incredible torments upon the nun, who returned to her senses when he finally burned the handkerchief.[5] Although the delegation led by Mantica had been sent to dissipate the fears that devils were running amok in Santa Chiara, the physician and exorcist both affirmed that the nuns manifested obvious signs of demon possession.

Beginning in early December, Mantica and Tinti entered the convent several days in a row. Mantica conducted a number of "experiments" that resembled the actions of exorcists, which confirmed fears that the nuns were indeed demonically possessed. On the first visit, Mantica entered the convent accompanied by his secretary, the notary, and Tinti. The bishop removed some relics from a silver reliquary, replaced them with a piece of coal, and then put the reliquary back in its purse. Mantica and company were led into a room where they found Sister Anna Maria Martinelli, who appeared very agitated. Invoking the power delegated to him by the Congregation of the Inquisition, Mantica demanded that the spirits obey him and stop tormenting Anna Maria. When he placed the coal-filled reliquary on Anna Maria's throat, she did not move and actually started to laugh. When Mantica asked what was so funny, she replied, "Oh, priest, do you think you are dealing with a buffoon?" The men then went into another room where they found Sister Barbara Leonora Forni, who was in a tormented state. The bishop repeated the same actions, and she, too, laughed when he placed the reliquary on her throat, telling him in a mocking manner, "You want me to say [what is in that purse], but I don't want to tell you." Later, he tried the same experiment with Sister Giulia Angelica Sertori. When he commanded the demons "in virtue of these relics" to descend and leave her head, the demon gave a long laugh through the sister's mouth. In short, the nuns seemed to know that the purse did not contain its usual relics, even though, as Mantica claimed, there was no way they could have known this.[6]

Mantica tried another ploy that could reveal whether the Clarisses were faking this possession. He took with him to the convent a bound copy of the

Annales by the Roman historian Tacitus, but the nuns could not see this tome and might presume that it was a book of exorcisms. Handing the book to the inquisitor, Mantica asked Tinti to start reading an "exorcism." Tinti dutifully started reading in Latin the words of Tacitus, which obviously had nothing to do with expelling demons, and the nuns started laughing derisively. Mantica reasoned that since the nuns had not studied Latin, their apparent realization that this was not an exorcism again suggested knowledge of diabolical origin.[7] Mantica added that for five or six consecutive days, Barbara Leonora Forni was tormented to the extreme, arching herself in the manner described by Carpi's exorcists. The physician told Bishop Mantica that this could not stem from natural causes but had to be the work of devils.[8]

On the second day of his visits inside the convent, Mantica repeated the experiment with the reliquary but this time with the relics inside, reputedly a piece of bone and "two or three" hairs of Mary Magdalene. When he approached Maria Maddalena Colevati with the relics, she instantly began hyperventilating and fell to the floor. When he placed the reliquary on her throat, Mantica asked the demon to identify what was inside the small receptacle. The demon said that it knew what was inside but did not want to answer until it finally exclaimed, "Cursed be the cross of Christ! Cursed be the death of Christ and those who were present at his death!" Mantica concluded that the relics provoked these words because Mary Magdalene was present at the death of Jesus and stood at the foot of the cross. This opinion was strengthened when the demon shortly thereafter cursed the male and female disciples of Christ (*Siano maladetti i discepoli, et le discepole di Xsto*). Mantica was convinced that the experiments with the relics and the book of Tacitus provided more evidence of diabolism, a conclusion that would have pleased the exorcists in Carpi but not the cardinals in Rome.[9]

The following day Bishop Mantica tried yet another experiment, hiding the little cross that he usually wore on his chest in a handkerchief. He found Caterina Margherita Ronchi very troubled, quaking in the abdominal area and then arching herself backward. When he succeeded in ordering the demons to stop torturing the sister, he took the handkerchief out of his pocket and acted as if he were going to blow his nose with it. Although the cross inside the handkerchief was not visible to anyone, several times the nun pointed at the handkerchief and said, "take that thing from there." Finally, as she suffered such terrible agitation around the waist that four people could barely hold her, Ronchi screamed, "Oh, that Virginity. It is my ruin! I can't stand it!"[10] Although for Mantica, this was another sure sign that the demon perceived the presence of something sacred, one might also postulate that the nun was bemoaning the life of chastity she was obliged to follow.[11] Similar experiments strengthened Mantica's conviction that the nuns were possessed.[12]

The Congregation of the Inquisition would not have received a stronger affirmation that the nuns were demonically possessed if Mantica's report had been written by Provost Cabassi. The suspicions of Tinti, Giudici, the exorcists, and everyone else in Carpi were apparently vindicated by the cardinals' would-be reformer. To put it mildly, Barberini and other cardinal-inquisitors were not pleased with Mantica's various "experiments," methods that had long been supported by experts on exorcism but that were now falling into disfavor, at least among some exorcists. A decade after these experiments, Candido Brognolo wrote that priests should not use fake relics in exorcisms in an effort to see the effects on the behavior of possessed people. He considered it inappropriate for priests to commit such fraudulent actions, and a very astute demon, knowing that the object used was not really a relic, could feign terrible torments so that the exorcist might conclude incorrectly that this was not a real case of possession.[13]

Disappointed with Mantica's performance, Barberini and the other cardinals sent another prelate to try to calm the waters: the commissioner Giovanni Lupi, who was to work in tandem with Mantica, Inquisitor Tinti, and Archpriest Niccolini. Arriving in early January 1639, Lupi bluntly told Tinti that the Congregation in Rome was disappointed with the way he had been handling this case. Almost immediately after Lupi's arrival, Mantica issued several orders, which almost certainly Cardinal Barberini had conveyed through Lupi. On 7 January 1639 Mantica forbade the Clarisses of Carpi to discuss with anyone the illnesses of the nuns:

> To avoid the many rumors and disturbances that could easily take place in this monastery of Santa Chiara . . . , I submit this order to all nuns of the aforementioned monastery, under pain of excommunication and other penalties at the discretion of the Holy Congregation, that no one in the future dares to say that such-and-such [a nun] is or has been possessed or insane, nor to speak of spirits in any way whatsoever or of the insanity of any nuns, neither outside the monastery, nor inside [the convent], not even with the infirm sisters themselves, still less among other nuns, neither at the grilles nor at the doors with anyone, nor in letters even if someone has permission to write. . . . Moreover, I add that if it pleases God that one or some of the infirm nuns be cured, . . . this same order will be made to them before anything else. And in the case that . . . these same nuns were first cured and then some or all of them returned to their prior [infirm] state, we want them again to be separated and restricted, not only as was done before but in a better way and [by a more effective form of] separation.[14]

Mantica similarly forbade anyone who came into contact with the Clarisses of Santa Chiara—their confessor, steward, gardener, barber-surgeon, servants—to discuss alleged demon possessions.[15] The same day Mantica also ordered the Clarisses to ensure that the infirm nuns were isolated both day and night both from healthy nuns and from each other so that they could not talk among themselves or with anyone else, apart from those charged with overseeing their care: the abbess, the vicaress, and Sisters Camilla Violante Pio, Alsuinda Malaspina, and Flavia Coccapani. The ailing nuns were not to receive any letters or messages from anyone, nor were they to meet visitors at the parlors or entrances or even leave their assigned rooms without special permission. The only interaction they were allowed, beyond receiving meals and other basic necessities, was to be consoled, when needed, by the five designated nuns.[16]

The measures taken at Santa Chiara were not unprecedented. Referring to events in the 1620s, Francesco Albizzi (1593–1684), a jurist and future cardinal-inquisitor, warned of the danger of illusions and fantasies concerning witchcraft among cloistered nuns. Seeking to avoid scandal and to restore calm, Albizzi recommended that when such rumors arose, silence must be imposed in an effort to stifle the belief that some of the nuns were bewitched. He referred to a letter written in 1625 that recommended a number of actions to prevent rumors of witchcraft from escalating into judicial proceedings—a letter that obviously neither Tinti nor Giudici had read! According to Albizzi, the letter suggested that the *ordinario* attempt to foster reconciliation among the nuns, which clearly implied that witchcraft accusations were more likely to appear in communities that were divided. Nuns were to be exhorted to seek divine help and to follow the rule of their order, and the convent was to have a "prudent confessor" who instructed the sisters about the "illusions" of demons and made sure that they regularly participated in the Eucharist. The nuns were absolutely forbidden to discuss witchcraft and demon possession among themselves, and the convent was to receive no visitors unless they were well known. Those visitors who were admitted were also forbidden to discuss these matters. All profane books, especially those that dealt with witchcraft and possession, were to be removed from the convent. And finally, since experience showed that exorcists were more likely than not to convince nuns that they were demonically possessed, no one was to exorcize without the express permission of the Congregation of the Inquisition.[17] Thus, a dozen years before the woes of Santa Chiara, a leader of the Holy Office had manifested a strong dose of skepticism toward reputedly possessed nuns and advocated aggressive measures to prevent their imaginations from running wild.

In this era of increasing claustration of female religious, Bishop Germano Mantica took more draconian measures to isolate the troubled convent of Santa Chiara. On the same day that he issued the ban on discussing the convent's troubles, Mantica, with the power of the Congregation of the Holy Office behind him, released a series of mandates pertaining to the movement of people and goods. Under ordinary circumstances, goods to be delivered to the convent were to be received through the turntable; if they were too big to pass through it, then they could be delivered through the parlor door, adjacent to the *ruota*. If the load was too big even for that door, then the supplies were to pass through the unloading entrance, which was to be opened only for such deliveries. This entrance for carts was to be locked with two chains, with the abbess having exclusive custody of the keys for the interior locks and the steward, overseer of the convent's grounds, keeping the keys for the exterior locks. The abbess was also to keep the keys to the parlor's two grilles, which were to be kept locked and were to be opened only to receive family visitors. No one was to be admitted into the parlor without written permission from the appropriate authority overseeing visitors, and the door of the parlor that enters into the cloister was to be kept locked and to be opened only for persons who had received special permission for entry. Those nuns who were assigned to supervise the turntable were forbidden to call anyone to the grilles unless "listeners" were present to monitor conversations. The nuns of Santa Chiara were also forbidden to write or receive any letters except those to or from their parents or siblings or, lacking these, their closest relatives. All letters sent or received first had to be seen by the abbess, who, upon detecting anything suspicious, was to submit the missives to the cleric governing the convent. Mass was to be said only by the convent's confessor, except on certain feast days when the male governor of the convent could authorize a chaplain to officiate. The turntable that opened into the church was to be kept locked and could be opened only for receiving vestments for the altar. The doors to the enclosed garden were to remain locked and the keys kept by the abbess, who was to open them only at appropriate times for recreation or work in the garden. As the convent had its own vineyards, Mantica also deemed it necessary to declare that when wine was being made, the sisters were forbidden to enter those places where male vintners were working.[18] In short, the bishop of Adria was mandating very strict enclosure for Santa Chiara, guidelines that were in line with Tridentine monastic reforms but diverged considerably from the rather lax environment that reigned when Angela Caterina d'Este was abbess.

In addition to issues pertaining to claustration, Mantica also expressed concern about differences in wealth and lifestyle among the sisters of Santa Chiara, all of whom, like nuns everywhere, had taken vows of poverty. Referring to four girls who had recently entered the convent as servants, Mantica proclaimed that for one year they must wear secular clothing. After that time, if they wished to pursue the religious life, they were to become lay sisters, wearing habits that they were to provide at their own expense. Clearly disapproving of the living arrangements of Angela Caterina d'Este and her circle, Mantica added that these young women were to be employed in the service of the convent in general, to be directed by the abbess and the vicaress; they were not to be the private servants of any particular nuns. Embracing the mandates of the Council of Trent, he affirmed that no one was to take religious vows before the age of sixteen. Once they had taken vows, nuns were no longer allowed to draw income from the dowries they had brought into the nunnery. Henceforth, once the vows had been made, their dowries were to be invested in the most advantageous manner, the fruits of which were to benefit the convent as a whole. Santa Chiara was to keep a safe with three keys, each held by three different nuns chosen by the entire community of Clarisses. All income was to be deposited into the safe, and no withdrawals could be made without the approval of the auditor, a priest who was to keep records of all deposits and expenditures with the help of his deputy, a nun in the cloister. At the end of each year, the governor of Santa Chiara was to make a reckoning of expenses and income. No nun could send away anything belonging to the monastery without the permission of the governor, nor could anything be sold without the approval of the auditor and the steward, who were to make sure to obtain the best price possible for the benefit of the nunnery. Upon the death of a nun, an inventory of all her personal effects was to be made immediately. Those not needed by the convent were to be sold, and the proceeds were to go to the monastery's treasury.[19] Santa Chiara had been cloistered ever since its creation, and the movement of people and goods into and out of the convent had always been circumscribed. But strict Tridentine reforms were introduced only now in 1639. Mantica's directives greatly restricted contacts with the outside world and, even more important, stressed more than ever before the communal aspects of monastic life. Wealth was to be held in common, and no sisters were to enjoy special advantages in the form of goods or services.

No doubt with some prodding from Giovanni Lupi and the Congregation, Mantica concluded this aggressive order with an urgent plea for the Clarisses to be more diligent in their religious vocations:

> In order to have divine protection and help in times of need, we must implore in a singular manner and prepare ourselves to receive [the Eucharist] with the appropriate disposition to obtain heavenly graces. In particular, one should do this if one has pledged oneself to the religious life and is obliged to endeavor as much as possible to pursue a life of perfection. Even though perhaps the rule of these nuns does not require them to partake very often of the most holy sacraments of penance and of the Holy Eucharist, at this time it is necessary to exhort them all, by the merits of the most precious blood of our Lord Jesus Christ, shed for the love of us in his very harsh passion, to partake more than usual and with that greater devotion that one strives for, of the aforementioned most holy sacraments, hoping that when they receive [them] worthily, [the nuns] may get from them great consolation, not just spiritual but also temporal.[20]

As witness to how important it was for Carpi's Clarisses to modify their behavior, Mantica's last order required the abbess to keep a copy of these rules and have them read aloud in the refectory to all the nuns once a month to remind them of their obligations. The carefree era that Santa Chiara had experienced under Angela Caterina d'Este, permeable to the outside world and opulent in its tastes, was officially over.[21]

In his guidelines for inquisitors, Cardinal Desiderio Scaglia had recommended similar spiritual remedies to assuage the troubles when nuns were believed to be diabolically possessed. Scaglia noted that younger nuns in particular could become terrified and believe that every shadow they saw was a demon. Theologians had long maintained that demons entered people's bodies more easily if they were frightened. According to Scaglia, rather than nurturing these fears by immediately conducting an investigation, religious superiors and inquisitors should exhort the nuns not to be so quick to believe that demons were involved. Afflicted nuns should not be left alone but rather surrounded by prudent sisters who should console them and try to disabuse them of the idea that their bodies were possessed. These healthy procedures should be followed, Scaglia declared, regardless if the nuns truly were possessed or if their "diabolical" woes were merely an illusion. He emphasized seeking consolation through taking communion and confessing to a conscientious priest.[22] Although Scaglia would have disapproved of Mantica's experiments or exorcisms, the bishop of Adria did embrace the cardinal's preferred spiritual weapons in battling demons and witchcraft.

About the same time that these tighter rules were being introduced in Santa Chiara, Mantica and Lupi, together with the archpriest and inquisitor, finally found a way to achieve a greater degree of separation between the agitated nuns and the healthy sisters. In January 1639 they ordered that the ill nuns spend their days in some workshops (*officine*) that were available in the convent. At night, however, they still had to sleep in the common dormitory with all the other nuns.[23] Santa Chiara did not have the facilities to keep the ailing nuns separated from each other, as Barberini and the Congregation had mandated.

The Testimony of Dealta

Clerical authorities were still grappling with what to do with Dealta and Ippolita Martinelli, who, unlike the demoniac nuns, had been kept in isolation ever since the violent attack on Dealta in October 1638. Apart from a very brief respite prior to that attack, Dealta had remained in isolation continuously since the previous April. Lupi certainly wanted to respect the mandate of Barberini, who, in a letter written New Year's Day 1639, demanded that the harassment of the Martinelli sisters cease immediately and that they be released to follow their normal lives in the convent.[24] There was good reason to fear, however, that their personal safety would be at risk if they were free to move about the convent. In late December Sister Clelia Coccapani declared to the Holy Office that the Martinellis must remain in separate rooms, isolated not only from the other Clarisses but also from each other. Coccapani insisted that the two could not stay with the other nuns because the "devils" of the possessed nuns protested they could not tolerate having the Martinellis around, and the healthy nuns continued to suspect them of *maleficia*. She added that her own suspicions grew when, by order of Tinti, Dealta was earlier released from prison, just prior to the October attack. According to Clelia, upon her release, Dealta defiantly menaced all nuns who had testified against her, especially Sisters Alsuinda Malaspina and Doralice Giudici.[25] The Clarisses' confessor even revealed that several nuns, including healthy ones, swore they would kill the Martinellis if released. Consequently, Tinti, with the approval of Mantica and Lupi, still refrained from executing the Congregation's order to set the two sisters free in Santa Chiara.[26]

Shortly after his arrival in Carpi, Lupi did finally give Dealta the chance to tell her side of the story.[27] The Congregation had found in the fall of 1638 that there were no valid grounds to suspect the Martinellis of witchcraft, but still asked Tinti to draw up a list of all the "evidence" against them, which he completed in early December.[28] On the basis of that report, neither Barberini in Rome nor Lupi in Carpi found that there was viable evidence to convict or even to suspect Dealta and Ippolita of witchcraft. On 8 January 1639, over eight months after Dealta was first incarcerated, Father Giovanni Lupi entered the convent of Santa Chiara accompanied by a scribe and went to the cubicle where Dealta was being held. This encounter was not an interrogation per se since Lupi, already convinced of her innocence, did not ask any questions. The record of this meeting, at which Lupi simply gave the beleaguered nun the chance to make a statement, is the only document we have of Dealta testifying directly to judicial authorities.[29]

Dealta began by informing Lupi that when Angelo Bellacappa was Santa Chiara's confessor, she often helped her sister Ippolita, who served as sacristan. Dealta affirmed that, at Bellacappa's request, she frequently looked for and brought to him Sisters Flerida Cimadori, Barbara Leonora Forni, Giulia Angelica Sertori, and especially Veronica Maria Coccapani and Caterina Margherita Ronchi. Although she did not know what they did together, Dealta observed that Bellacappa spent considerable time with each of these nuns at the grilles of the confessionals. Sertori and Forni were in the service of the princess, and Dealta claimed that the confessor began to suspect her of telling Angela Caterina about their frequent visits with him. Adding that the princess herself confessed to another priest, Dealta avowed that both Bellacappa and the nuns who frequented him were angry with both Dealta and Ippolita because they believed the two sisters were spying for the princess, a rather odd suspicion given the mutual distrust between the Martinellis and Angela Caterina. Once various nuns took ill, exorcists ministered to them, and Dealta seemed subtly to lay part of the blame on those clerics for the convent's woes. After the departure of Giovan Battista Zarreti of Reggio, the exorcisms were led by Provost Girolamo Cabassi, who claimed, on the basis of what the demons told him, that Dealta had played a role in the *maleficia* that plagued the young sisters.[30]

Dealta observed that her travails multiplied from the moment the "demons" accused her. She mentioned the attack she suffered the previous St. Mark's Day (25 April), when some of the possessed nuns roughed her up and called her a witch. Although she always protested her innocence, immediately after this incident the archpriest of Carpi ordered that she be kept apart from the rest of the community. Shortly thereafter, she went from merely being separated to being imprisoned, remaining incarcerated until she was released in October by order of the Congregation of the Inquisition. Dealta then described the brutal attack she suffered almost immediately upon her release:

> It was St Luke's Day and I was in the choir at Mass when Cimadori, Forni, Ronchi, Sister Clara Maria [Amoldoni] from Correggio, [Anna Maria Martinelli] from Sestola dragged me into the middle of the choir and held me there for twenty-four continuous hours until the following morning, striking me with punches, kicks, and other means, trying to get me to say that I had a hand in these *maleficia*. The other nuns didn't have the courage to say anything but prayed to God. And out of fear that they would strangle me, I said "yes," that is, that I did have a part in the *maleficium*, whereupon they let me go and the exorcist told me I had to go away. And the nuns put me in this room and locked it. I, however, did not have anything to do with any *maleficium* and told this to the archpriest who interrogated me about this fact, [telling him] that what I had said, I said out of fear, and I swore that to him.[31]

As for the nuns' infirmities, Dealta suspected that either they lost their heads over love or were ruined by jealousy. She further observed that some of the nuns went to see Bellacappa for instruction in writing, while others went there to sing. Before signing her name to the statement as recorded by the scribe, Dealta concluded this audience by beseeching Lupi to liberate her, pointing out that she had been held in isolation now for almost nine months.[32]

Though interesting, Dealta's testimony was hardly earth-shattering. That she protested her own innocence was entirely predictable, and her claim that, when attacked by the enraged nuns, she confessed to witchcraft solely out of fear for her life would seem obvious to any disinterested observer. More surprising was the fact that she did not aggressively try to deflect blame onto Bellacappa. Although the suggestion that the nuns' ills stemmed from love or jealousy implicitly incriminated the ex-confessor, she did not accuse Bellacappa of bad intent in sending for the nuns, and professed ignorance of what they actually did together. Dealta did not have firsthand knowledge of accusations made before the inquisitor against her, and she made no mention at all of her reputed discussions of sabbats or lewd touching of a nun in the presence of Bellacappa. By linking the ills of the nuns to love, Dealta left open the possibility that they were the victims of love magic, but of all the nuns of Santa Chiara, Dealta came closest to saying that the ailing nuns were not possessed or the victims of witchcraft. One can interpret this stand either as a means of exculpating herself—if they were not possessed, there was no reason to suspect she was a witch—or as a genuine conviction that the allegations were absurd: since she knew that she was innocent of all charges, she was convinced that their ills were of mundane origin.

The Verdicts

On 15 January 1639 the Congregation of the Holy Office came to a decision concerning Bellacappa, still under house arrest on accusations of both witchcraft and solicitation. Barberini and the other cardinals ordered that Bellacappa be released but declared that his case would remain open (*fermo*) indefinitely. Inquisitor Tinti was to inform Bellacappa's superiors in his order that he was banned for an indefinite period of time from hearing the confessions of nuns and from holding positions of authority in any monastery in the lands of the duke of Modena.[33] This amounted to a tacit exoneration on charges of witchcraft. Without saying as much, the cardinal-inquisitors apparently also determined that they did not have conclusive evidence to convict him of soliciting nuns during confession—inquisitorial manuals recommended lifelong bans on hearing all confessions and sentences of five to seven years in the galleys for the able-bodied, the same term in prison for the less physically fit.[34] In practice, suspicion of solicitation could suffice to suspend a priest from hearing confessions.[35] The ban on confessions showed that the cardinal-inquisitors were deeply suspicious of Bellacappa's behavior in the confessionals. By the end of January, Bellacappa had been released from house arrest, but the limitations placed on his ecclesiastical functions remained.[36]

Considering the fates of both Bellacappa and the Martinellis, Barberini wrote Tinti a week later still declaring that Dealta and Ippolita must be released. The cardinal reasoned that continuing to detain them gave every appearance that they were guilty. Dealta's recent deposition only reinforced the opinion of the Congregation that the Martinellis and Bellacappa were all entirely innocent of charges of witchcraft.[37] On 29 January 1639 Cardinal Barberini succinctly described in a letter to Lupi, still his representative in Carpi, why he and the other cardinals were convinced that the "evidence" of witchcraft was purely imaginary:

> With great satisfaction the Holy Congregation [sees] your accomplishments in the affair concerning the nuns of Carpi and desires that you continue, along with the Father Inquisitor [Tinti] of Reggio and under the direction of Monsignor Bishop of Adria [Germanico Mantica], in the diligent work through which we believe to have discovered the truth about the agitation (*spiritamento*) of the nuns believed to be possessed, who, when they are subject to the obedience of their spiritual father and leave aside their fears of having been bewitched by the Martinelli sisters and Father Bellacappa, return with the help of the Lord to their pristine health. The proceedings concerning the alleged *maleficia* have been examined with great care, and not the least evidence has been found against the Martinellis and Bellacappa, other than what the nuns themselves imagined. So the first concern of Monsignor the bishop, the confessor, and you is to persuade the mother abbess and all the nuns that there is no ground to suspect that an evil spell was introduced in the monastery, and from this one surely deduces that the aforementioned possessed women were actually agitated by a vehement passion caused by the strong fear of *maleficium*, rather than by demons. We gather from the letters from the abbess and from the discussion you had with Father Giovan Battista d'Este that for . . . [political reasons], they want to continue [calling this a] possession so that people will not consider the agitated nuns to be insane or malicious, which would result in discredit to their families. Do your best to disabuse [them] of this impression . . . , assuring them that the strong suspicion of evil is generally worse than the evil itself.[38]

Barberini added that the mere fact that strong fears could have profound effects on people's mental and physical well-being in no way implied insanity. In this case, the nuns unintentionally convinced themselves that they were actually afflicted by spirits, resulting in bizarre behavior. Eliminating the fears would cause the belief in the possessions to dissipate slowly but surely.[39]

In addition to proclaiming the suspects' innocence, Cardinal Barberini insisted in the same letter that Lupi tend to two other matters at Santa Chiara. Under no circumstances should the convent again be under the supervision of the Observant Franciscans. Without saying so, Barberini clearly believed that the poor leadership of the *Zoccolanti*, including Bellacappa, contributed in an important way to the disorder in the nunnery. Second, Lupi was to ensure that henceforth no exorcisms were permitted at the convent. The exorcists, Barberini claimed, were the source of this scandal; they had engendered "confusion" in the minds and lives of these "servants of God." Administering to "feminine weakness," the exorcists lit the fuse and started this terrible fire "that now burns in the monastery."[40]

Barberini was manifesting a remarkably skeptical attitude toward evidence of witchcraft, setting the bar quite high for convicting accused witches.

A half century earlier, the French political philosopher Jean Bodin (1530–96) avowed that three witnesses of unquestionable probity who testified to three unrelated instances of witchcraft sufficed to convict a suspect of witchcraft and to condemn her or him to death. For Bodin, the testimony of so many nuns and priests—whose integrity surely should have passed muster with judicial authorities—would have been enough to convict Dealta, Bellacappa, and Ippolita many times over, resulting in death sentences for them and probably for others as well.[41]

Although it is now well established that Italy along with Spain experienced very low execution rates of witches, until recently explanations for this phenomenon have not been very persuasive. Giovanni Romeo has offered the best hypothesis to date for the Roman Inquisition's mild record in handling witchcraft cases. Acknowledging that there were a number of significant witch-hunts in Italy in the sixteenth century, Romeo observes that there were differences of opinion among inquisitors and other Italian clerics as to whether witches' sabbats were real or merely diabolical illusions. He speculates that beginning in the 1580s, there must have been serious debates within the Congregation of the Holy Office, pitting believers in the sabbat against skeptics, which did not result in a clear victory for one side or the other. Even if the Congregation did not issue a definitive statement on the question of witchcraft and sabbats, a compromise position was evident in its rulings in dealing with local inquisitions. Without denying the possibility of the reality of the sabbat, in 1588 the Congregation of the Inquisition forbade using testimony about participation at a sabbat against anyone other than the person who confessed to being at the sabbat. Fearing that the nocturnal meeting could have been illusory, the Congregation refused to take actions against people named as accomplices at sabbats. This may have been the most important reason behind the Inquisition's very moderate record in handling witchcraft cases. Also significant was the Holy Office's eventual ban on torture for witchcraft confessions and its favoring sentences that treated witches as wayward souls that could be rehabilitated rather than apostates who merited the most severe punishment. In short, the Roman Inquisition's lenience was largely the result of the strong moderating influence of the cardinal-inquisitors in Rome.[42]

The cardinals' attitude reflected the standards laid out in the guidelines for inquisitors for prosecuting witches written in the early 1620s by Cardinal Desiderio Scaglia. Strongly skeptical toward many of the "proofs" of witchcraft, these instructions denied that love magic and other illicit activities necessarily implied a formal pact with the devil and rejected as evidence a "witch's" claim that another was present at a sabbat.[43] The evidence from the Carpi case shows unequivocally that, even though the sabbat was not very prominent in the accusations, Cardinal Barberini had strong doubts about the "evidence" of possession and witchcraft that had been presented. If the Congregation had indeed experienced conflicts in the late sixteenth century over the "proofs" of witchcraft, by the 1630s the skeptics had obviously won. Quite clearly, the Holy Office in Italy, along with the Inquisition in Spain, was in the vanguard in showing skepticism concerning evidence of witchcraft, including the reality of the sabbat.

The Fate of Santa Chiara

In spite of the Congregation's declaration of their innocence, Ippolita and Dealta Martinelli realistically could no longer stay in Santa Chiara after all they had been through. If they remained in that community, they would have faced hostility, ostracism, and continued risk to their personal safety. On 12 February 1639 an official document was signed for the transfer of the Martinelli sisters, drawn up by Bishop Germanico Mantica (who died after a brief illness just a few days after signing this transfer). By the authority of the Congregation, Mantica arranged to have the Martinellis transferred to the convent of Santa Maria Maddalena in Modena, claiming that the nuns there were "content" to accept them. The bishop of Modena agreed with this arrangement and gave leave to Inquisitor Tinti and Commissioner Giovanni Lupi to accompany the sisters with due "decency and safety" from Santa Chiara to their new convent. Mantica stressed, "We declare that this transfer is not being made because of any crime or guilt committed by these two nuns" but rather to protect them from any "harassment" and "unjust persecution" they might suffer at the hands of many other nuns.[44]

Contemporaneously, Cardinal Barberini was responsible for another change in the administration of Santa Chiara. With the departure of the Martinellis and Mantica's introduction of stricter discipline, Barberini was confident that normality would soon return and that the Holy Office could discontinue overseeing the governance of the convent. Following the advice of the Congregation of the Holy Office, Pope Urban VIII announced in a brief promulgated in February 1639 that the governor of Santa Chiara was henceforth the bishop of Modena, Alessandro Rangoni.[45] Although the pope offered no explanation as to why the convent was not returned to the archpriest–the town of Carpi was subject to the archpriest, not to the bishop of Modena–Barberini and his colleagues clearly were not happy with the archpriest's performance as governor since July 1637. And this change was definitely not made at the request of the Este family, as Fra Giovan Battista expressed his displeasure at this ruling, perhaps because he was better able to influence the archpriest than the bishop of Modena. In a letter to the duke, Cardinal Barberini asserted that the convent was independent of the local churches and, implicitly, of Giovan Battista.[46] Without explicitly saying so, Barberini also surely felt that the former duke's meddling in this affair had done far more harm than good.

Happily, the winter of 1639 marked the turning point in regard to the healing of the "bewitched" nuns of Santa Chiara. A report indicated that by midwinter only four nuns were still infirm, but the belief that all fourteen had been possessed was not "totally extinct." Following the dictates of Barberini, no one was to speak to the remaining ailing nuns unless they were calm and not exhibiting bizarre behavior. All were supposed to turn their shoulders to anyone who started discussing witchcraft and demon possession and to inform them that such conversations greatly inhibited the healing process by exacerbating the sisters' worst apprehensions. And the Clarisses quickly learned that those nuns, be they healthy or ailing, who spread rumors about witchcraft would be incarcerated for the well-being of the nunnery. When an ill nun appeared to be cured, she was not freed immediately but was only gradually reintegrated into the community, taking part again in communal life only for brief periods until she was deemed entirely restored to health. The Congregation issued a number of orders for Santa Chiara, not least of which was the installation of a new confessional and the walling up of the old one. Since the Clarisses had at their own initiative eliminated the former upper confessional, this meant that the convent was to be cleansed of all vestiges of the old confessionals, the sites of so many alleged illicit words and deeds.[47]

In the spring of 1639, three years after the first outbreak and a year after the Inquisition's work began in earnest, calm was finally restored at Santa Chiara. By the end of March, the new confessor, the Jesuit Giovan Battista Guadagni, was pleased to announce that all but one of the ailing nuns had been cured. Since his arrival in January, he had prescribed for them "spiritual exercises," numerous sermons, and frequent participation in the sacraments, all of which greatly consoled them.[48] Hearing this news, Barberini could not help but express his satisfaction to Tinti that the cardinal-inquisitors' skepticism had been vindicated.[49] A month later, in a letter dated 21 May, Cardinal Barberini praised the bishop of Modena, as governor of the convent, and the Jesuit confessor for their successes in restoring tranquility to the nunnery.[50] At that time Giulia Angelica Sertori, Angela Caterina's former confidante, was the lone Clarisse who still suffered, but Barberini was sure that even her "obstinacy" would soon come to an end.[51] His prediction was correct–Cardinal Barberini had not yet received a letter from Tinti, written six days earlier, that announced the definitive liberation of the spiritual woes of Sertori, for which the inquisitor gave credit to the new confessor.[52] Sertori was still suffering from a "natural illness," but by late June Tinti predicted that it, too, would pass shortly. Cardinal Barberini nevertheless encouraged the inquisitor and bishop of Modena to be ever vigilant lest the convent's troubles return.[53]

By this time even the Inquisitor Tinti had been won over. Tinti–whose first reaction upon witnessing the attack on Dealta on St. Luke's Day was to call an exorcist–concluded in May 1639 that the miseries of the Clarisses had been greatly aggravated by the intervention of the exorcists. The exorcisms themselves, he now believed, were the cause of many nuns either actually becoming possessed or thinking they were possessed. Still unwilling to conclude that none of the nuns had suffered from demon possession, Tinti now believed that if possessions did occur, exorcism was the cause, not the cure. Consequently, he not only renewed the edict banning exorcisms without permission from the *ordinario* but also recommended publicizing this more broadly, suggesting the ban be read in each parish church once a month.[54] It would have been quite impolitic for Tinti to defend exorcisms in his letters to Barberini, but he surely had good reason to believe that the exorcists had in fact done much more harm than good in Santa Chiara. No exorcisms had taken place in the convent since Mantica's "experiments" in December 1638, and the ten nuns had one by one been cured of their ills during the intervening months.

In October 1639 Barberini expressed his satisfaction of the return to normality at Santa Chiara. He had been told that at a certain point the nuns of Carpi had besought St. Dominic of Sora to intercede for the restoration of the spiritual health of the afflicted sisters. In honor of the end of their woes, Cardinal Barberini decided to send the convent a gift of a painting by an "excellent" Roman artist depicting the saint. Barberini obviously had much more faith in the utility of prayers to saints than in exorcisms.[55]

Conclusion

As calm eventually returned to Santa Chiara in Carpi, one is left wondering what actually took place there in the later 1630s. We cannot know for certain, but the Congregation of the Inquisition had no doubts that the Clarisses of Carpi were not the victims of witchcraft. The cardinal-inquisitors believed that the Clarisses had suffered from melancholic humors or, worse yet, may have even feigned their spiritual woes. The Congregation wrote a letter in 1643 to Cardinal Grimaldi, the papal nuncio in Paris, who had earlier written about some nuns in Louviers, Normandy, who were reportedly bewitched and diabolically possessed. In this letter, the cardinal-inquisitors discussed at length the tribulations in Carpi in order to urge a strong degree of skepticism concerning the alleged possessions:

> This Holy Congregation is not led to believe so easily that the signs described in the account and the upheavals that the nuns have generated are caused by supernatural factors and by the actions of the devil, because we have always found that for the most part, [all such things] are born from the melancholic humors of nuns [who are] unhappy and have been sent to the cloister against their will. Still worse, [some are] shams [who hope] to be able to leave the monastery under the pretext of a cure or to be able to spend time and converse with exorcists, from whom they quite often learn how to project as real effects of the devil [their own] melancholy and pretenses. It was less than four years ago that in the land of Carpi in a monastery of nuns of the order of Santa Chiara, one of them was suspected of having been bewitched by a lay sister. They started to use exorcists. Much time went by and, either because of the malice of nuns or of exorcists, as many as fourteen [of the nuns] were discovered possessed. Quite extravagant were the physical disorders that they exhibited, the blasphemies that they uttered. . . . And the suspicion grew more and more, so it was necessary that the Holy Congregation send there the bishop of Adria with the most talented physicians and exorcists of Bologna in order to uncover the truth of this supposed possession. The nuns knew how to act so well that they fooled the bishop, the physicians, and the exorcists. But these most eminent [members of the Holy Congregation] were not satisfied and, convinced that this was all pretense and melancholy, they decided to send to Carpi a minister of this Supreme and Venerable Inquisition, with prudent instructions, [who was] quite experienced in these matters . . . of the Holy Tribunal. And I can tell Your Excellency in all sincerity that as soon as he

> arrived there and put into action the guidelines given to him, the truth was discovered, and in four days ten were cured and slowly the others [were cured as well]. All of this was born in part of suspicion and in part of fabrication. Among the guidelines that were given to him, the first . . . was prohibiting them to be exorcized; then keeping the nuns who were believed possessed separated from each other; imposing upon them fasts of bread and water; letting them scream alone; prohibiting them to talk with anyone other than their overseers or to [write] letters; forbidding all other nuns to speak with [the so-called possessed nuns] and to speak about [demon] possessions among themselves; providing them with a wise and experienced confessor, in whom we valued the work of his services. With such diligences, it pleased Blessed God to discover the fraud and to quiet that very tumultuous cycle and to introduce into the monastery the peace that reigns there today with great edification. I wanted to point all this out to Your Excellency so that you may know from this example that for very good reason we must proceed here with caution before believing in the [demon] possessions of nuns.[1]

The author of this missive, the extant copy of which is unsigned, echoed some of the concerns found in Scaglia's inquisitorial guidelines for witchcraft cases, which had been circulating since the 1620s, and expressed considerable skepticism toward the possession of nuns. Another concern, articulated in the "Instructions for Witchcraft Cases" but not in this letter, was that nuns who feigned possession or truly believed they were bewitched might accuse, out of genuine fear or vicious spite, personal enemies of witchcraft.[2]

Were these concerns well founded? On the issue of dissembling, there is good reason to doubt that any of the nuns of Carpi feigned bewitchment. No one indicated that any of the afflicted nuns expressed a desire to leave the monastic life, and the only ailing women who left Santa Chiara were the young laywomen Paolina Forni and Leonora Galli, who served Angela Caterina's nieces. Forni and Galli were the first women afflicted, and far from faking their ills, they died from them. Otherwise the only residents of Santa Chiara who reportedly left the convent in the wake of these tribulations were Princess Angela Caterina and her two nieces, both of whom were merely *educande,* and the Martinelli sisters. Even though virtually all the Clarisses, like Angela Caterina, had taken the veil as teenagers under strong pressure from their families, the only member of Santa Chiara who was said to abhor the religious life was Dealta. And one must remember that the most negative comments about her came from sisters who strongly disliked her and suspected her of being a witch. In any event, the odds of a nun being released from her vows, even if taken under pressure, were quite slim.[3]

Feigning possession in order to get revenge also seems unlikely in this case. Bellacappa was no longer associated in any way with Santa Chiara. True, victims of his sexual overtures might justifiably be dismayed to see him go unpunished, but there was no need to invent accusations of witchcraft against him to get the attention of the Inquisition. Soliciting during or around confession was a very serious offense, and the Congregation of the Inquisition was far more likely to allow torture in solicitation than in witchcraft cases. Dealta had few friends in the convent, but it stretches the imagination to believe that ten nuns would endure a year and a half or so of turmoil in order to take vengeance on her.

The evidence from the investigation shows that the Clarisses of Santa Chiara had fully assimilated the prevailing ideas about demons and witchcraft. The nuns were most strongly concerned with *maleficia,* but several also feared that Dealta was a devil-worshiping witch who attended sabbats. When they were tormented by the alleged demons, the energumens behaved very much as the experts on witchcraft and exorcism expected. By seventeenth-century standards, the Clarisses had a very high educational level, which, combined with their frequent encounters with exorcists, can help explain why the nuns' understanding of witchcraft and possession differed little from the opinions of learned demonologists. But rather than simulating possession or maliciously fabricating accusations, the nuns of Carpi more likely had a knowledge and understanding of witchcraft that, to a degree, conditioned their behavior.[4] More broadly, by the 1630s the similarities between popular and elite understandings of witchcraft and possession were far greater than their differences. Robin Briggs notes that many witchcraft confessions in Lorraine were elicited with just the "minimum suggestion" from judges but contained all the features of the stereotypical witch. The stories found in these confessions, like those revealed by the Clarisses of Carpi, were "the common currency of witchcraft as it was actually experienced and punished. They were stories anyone could tell, drawing on a great reservoir of shared beliefs and fantasies, endlessly recycled as part of everyday experience."[5] Referring to the *benandanti* of Friuli who claimed to go out in spirit at night to fight witches and defend the crops, Norman Cohn asserts that this shows that "not only the waking thoughts but the trance experiences of individuals can be deeply conditioned by the generally accepted beliefs of the society in which they live."[6] By the same token, the shared values of seventeenth-century Emilian society shaped how the Clarisses, including the demoniacs, understood and experienced bewitchment.

Although conscious simulation seems highly unlikely, when a community was split into factions, a misfortune suffered could more easily be attributed to the machinations of the victims' known enemies. The Clarisses of Carpi were not beleaguered by the same turmoil that vexed the Ursulines in Loudun, a predominantly Calvinist city that suffered a terrible bout of the plague that killed off a fourth of the population just months before the outbreak of demon possessions in 1632.[7] Apart from a few Jews, everyone in Carpi was Catholic.[8] And although, as we have seen, the city was hit by the plague in

1630, several years lapsed before *Carpigiani* first expressed their fears about the intrigues of demons and witches.

Santa Chiara was, however, most definitely divided internally. An obvious source of division in the convent was Princess Angela Caterina d'Este. On the one hand, many Clarisses were certainly grateful for all the wealth she brought to the convent and for the impressive improvements to its physical structure that Este money made possible. She probably had a greater impact on Santa Chiara than any other member in its history other than its founder. Like many members of the Este dynasty, Angela Caterina was a true patron of the arts and clearly elevated the monastery's level of culture, most obviously in the area of music.[9] On the other hand, other nuns resented the inordinate power she wielded and the extraordinary privileges she received. Virtually all sisters at Santa Chiara were from well-to-do families, and many were of noble status, but only Angela Caterina had a retinue of *dame di compagnia* and personal servants. The other sisters took their turns doing the laundry and other menial tasks, whereas the princess was exempt from even the least burdensome chores. The order's rule mandated that all sisters, including the abbess, sleep in the large single-room dormitory, but the princess, both during and after her tenure as abbess, had her own apartments where she slept and had her meals, which were prepared by her personal cook. Even though group devotions were usually at the core of convent life, the princess quite often worshiped in her own private chapel, and she and her attendants ordinarily confessed their sins to the priest of her choice rather than the convent's official confessor. The office of abbess was usually held by an older nun who served for only three years, but Angela Caterina was elected abbess at twenty-seven and served almost ten years. True, each time her tenure was supposed to come to an end, the community of nuns petitioned to appoint her for another term. But even if the majority of Clarisses favored retaining her as abbess—either because of the wealth she brought to the convent or because of her leadership ability—a significant minority surely resented the undue influence she wielded, the immunity she enjoyed to a host of rules, and the superiority complex that she manifested in her interactions with others. The repeated meddling in the affairs of Santa Chiara by her brother, Fra Giovan Battista, surely did not enhance her popularity among her fellow Clarisses, even though the two siblings seemed at times to be working at cross purposes. The fact that the two principal suspects of witchcraft, Dealta and Bellacappa, both had the reputation of being hostile to the princess-abbess bore testimony to the fact that Angela Caterina definitely had some detractors.

To be sure, Angela Caterina still had some supporters at Santa Chiara. As the last of the nuns were being cured, several sisters at Santa Chiara voiced the opinion in early May 1639 that they wanted to vote for the princess as abbess again, notwithstanding the fact that she had transferred to another convent weeks before. After speaking with many Clarisses, however, Inquisitor Tinti concluded that very few wanted to reinstate Angela Caterina as abbess. Far more expressed to him the hope that she would never return to their convent, saying, as he quoted them, "Oh, Father Inquisitor, we are now, by the grace of God, enjoying peace and such great harmony that it seems to us to be in paradise. But if the sister princess returned, we would suffer again the same rancor, divisions, and factions as before."[10] Predictably, the Congregation of the Holy Office ruled that she was ineligible to be abbess since she was no longer a member of the convent.[11]

Demon Possession and Female Religious

The Inquisition records reveal that the ecstatic behavior of the demoniacs was less eroticized than that found in many other contemporary mass possessions in convents. The only explicit references to illicit sexual activity are found in the testimony of witnesses who confessed to their own sins but were not among the possessed. By contrast, examples can be found of European nuns who, forced to take the veil as youths against their will, developed a fantasy world in which, as willing and avid mistresses of the devil, they enjoyed the sex, love, and power they could not experience in the real world.[12]

Although erotic elements were not pronounced in the possessed behavior itself in Carpi, one cannot avoid the conclusion that sexual repression played a very significant part in Santa Chiara's travails. Arriving at this conclusion does not require delving into speculative psychoanalysis. Clearly, religious vows, sexual temptations, and the fear of Satan could make a volatile combination. Many Church authorities believed that nuns' sexual urges themselves might be a sign of increased spirituality, as the Evil One might be trying to reverse their spiritual progress by tormenting them with sexual temptations.[13] Having been pushed by their families to take vows of chastity in their teens, the Clarisses of Carpi were confronted with a charming confessor who flattered them, joked with them, and listened to them confess their most personal sinful thoughts. When Bellacappa, the only male whom they regularly saw and spoke with, began to show a sexual interest in these younger nuns, some may well have had very conflicted feelings. Although his responsibilities at the convent ended a year before the principal outbreak in the fall of 1637, thoughts of sexually charged conversations or illicit touching–even in the unlikely event that they had taken place only in their imaginations–could have plagued the consciences of those who feared the power of Satan and damnation and had sworn to remain celibate and to spend their lives in a religious community. One must certainly not dismiss the struggles many female religious endured between, on the one hand, their vows of chastity and the obligation of leading a religious life and, on the other, their self-doubts and mundane desires.[14] Unlike Dealta Martinelli, most nuns resigned themselves to life in the cloister and probably accepted the belief that what was best for their families was best for them. The group possession, however, may well have been an unconscious rebellion on the part of these fourteen women against being compelled to enter a convent.

Learned and popular opinion agreed that demonic possession was on the rise since the second half of the sixteenth century and that many forms of mental derangement or madness were caused by demons inhabiting a person's body. Unanimously agreeing that the afflicted nuns were caused by demons in their bodies, the Clarisses of Carpi fully shared the views of exorcists, demonologists, and theologians concerning the great dangers that demons posed. A few of the residents of Santa Chiara also expressed their fears of and belief in devil-worshiping sabbats, but they all agreed that the devils had entered the nuns' bodies as a result of a maleficent spell cast by a witch.

The findings from Santa Chiara hardly lend themselves, however, to the hypothesis that group possessions in seventeenth-century convents resulted from the rigors of Counter-Reformation religiosity.[15] By the standards of seventeenth-century female religious houses, Santa Chiara was remarkably lax in its discipline until after the troubles of the late 1630s. Although for decades, because of *clausura,* nuns had not been permitted to come and go as they pleased, Princess Angela Caterina had allowed and even promoted a very worldly atmosphere in the convent. Significantly, Santa Chiara's alleged possessions first appeared early in 1636, several months before the princess's tenure as abbess finally came to an end. Both during and immediately after her abbacy, the Clarisses of Carpi regularly sang secular songs, kept many personal belongings, masqueraded at Carnival, and received a steady stream of male and female visitors in the parlors. Greater discipline was imposed only after the outbreak of these possessions. True, the convent was removed from the control of the Observant Franciscans in July 1637, ostensibly because of lax governance, and most of the nuns did not show symptoms of possession until the following fall. Clearly, however, Archpriest Niccolini's principal motive in taking control of the convent was simply to increase his own power. Rather than being concerned about imposing strict moral discipline on the Clarisses, the ambitious Niccolini aimed to gain authority over Carpi's most prestigious ecclesiastical institution. That life at Santa Chiara did not dramatically change after the departure of the Observant Franciscans was evident in the complaints, described above, of Bishop Germanico Mantica, who still bemoaned the lax discipline in January 1639 and issued a number of directives that closely regulated behavior in the convent.[16]

The only medium through which strict reforms could possibly have been felt in the fall of 1637 was the confessional. As noted briefly in chapter 5,

Giovan Battista Bignardi, Bellacappa's successor as confessor, revealed to Tinti that he feared he may have been a bit severe toward Bellacappa—he refused to grant absolution to the nuns who confessed to illicit words and actions with Bellacappa unless they denounced the former confessor to the Inquisition. There is no way of knowing how Bignardi discussed these sins with the women in question, but he could have warned them of the fires of hell and attributed all lust to Satan, provoking great angst and outbursts that were perceived as the work of demons. This, however, would beg the question as to why the ire of the demoniacs was directed principally against Dealta rather than the man who reputedly seduced them with words and actions.

As subsequent events demonstrated, there were definite limits to how much discipline the Clarisses of Carpi were willing to tolerate and that even the Holy Office deemed appropriate. In 1640, just months after the demonic woes had subsided, Santa Chiara experienced some conflicts with the new confessor, the Jesuit Giacinto Manara. The Clarisses found Manara unduly harsh, as he aggressively pressured them to confess and take communion more often than their rule required. More shocking was his imposing "Jesuit" names—such as Ignatia and Xaviera—on the young women who were now taking vows. In May Cardinal Barberini advised Inquisitor Tinti to encourage Manara to be gentler in dealing with the Clarisses, but by September Manara had already been relieved of his charge at Santa Chiara. In the aftermath, Barberini opined that in dealing with nuns, a confessor is usually more effective employing gentle rather than harsh methods.[17]

Although some scholars have pointed out the common origins of the beliefs in divine and diabolical possession,[18] the evidence from Carpi shows that everyone, including all the nuns of Santa Chiara, was much more prone to see demonic rather than divine forces behind unusual events. At no time did anyone in Carpi suggest that the dozen afflicted nuns were divinely rather than diabolically possessed. Unlike Jeanne des Anges, the prioress of Loudun, Angela Caterina was not transformed by her ills into a saintly mystic. Moreover, when the first nuns took ill, the physician Abbati treated them for hysteria, indicating that he and the Clarisses initially suspected natural ills, not divine revelations. As we have seen, the only person involved who allegedly claimed to have divine visions was the incarcerated Dealta, who was suspected of being a maleficent witch rather than a demoniac. This, combined with the strong evidence of rather lax discipline at Santa Chiara, militates against a simple correlation between the strict discipline of Catholic reformers and the demonic possession of nuns. Counter-Reformation discipline arrived at Santa Chiara only in reaction to the witchcraft scare and was achieved only as the possessions were winding down.[19]

Similarly, though the possessed nuns of Carpi definitely demonstrated agency and were not merely being manipulated by exorcists and other priests, it is difficult to argue that they were expressing much of a religious message through their possessions. In early modern France, the possessions of some laywomen and nuns (clearly seen in the Loudun case) occurred in periods and in regions that experienced intense religious conflicts between Catholics and Protestants. Through their alleged possessions, these women, consciously or unconsciously, had a forum to express their concerns about contemporary moral transgressions, giving them a voice—more often than not in strong support of the Roman Catholic Church—that they otherwise would not have had.[20] Although some Protestants did indeed proselytize in and around Modena in the sixteenth century, the Inquisition had effectively eliminated this movement decades before any of the beleaguered Clarisses had even been born. As we have seen, the administration of Santa Chiara was the source of conflict between the Observant Franciscans and secular priests, especially the archpriest of Carpi, but this power struggle among Catholic clerics did not produce dramatic changes in life inside the cloister. If the possessions were a reaction to any specific change in mores, this was not articulated by any Clarisses. The only coherent message to emerge from the energumens' frenetic scenes was that Dealta and Bellacappa were evil witches.

Another question still cries out to be answered: why were group possessions of this nature rather common in convents but virtually nonexistent in monasteries that housed male religious? Male monastic orders, like their female counterparts, were being reformed in the post-Tridentine era. Monks and friars, like nuns, took vows of chastity, sought to lead a saintly life, and struggled to suppress their sexual impulses. Like many female religious, many men were obliged by their families to embrace the monastic life.[21] Why, then, was there not a flurry of demonic possessions in male orders to complement those found in female convents? A rare case of a "group" possession in an early modern monastery did occur in a Capuchin monastery in Sicily in 1671. This involved only two young men, a seventeen-year-old novice and a twenty-seven-year-old lay brother. Both were reputedly possessed by numerous demons, which claimed they had been sent by God at the request of the Virgin Mary and St. Francis of Assisi to preach against various sins, including pride, avarice, usury, and lust, which were supposedly rife in Sicily. The demons explained that they were obliged to possess the bodies of these Capuchins for twelve days, during which time the men exhibited supernatural strength and the ability to speak languages they had not studied, convincing signs that they were possessed and not suffering from melancholic humors, as some skeptical laymen initially believed. After preaching through the mouths of these Capuchins for twelve days, the demons left their bodies, leaving the weakened men with no memory of the preceding dozen days.[22]

Sluhovsky claims that monks were generally deemed impervious to demon possession, which necessarily involved losing control over one's body.

Although, as we have seen, the behavior of the afflicted Clarisses was not very sexually explicit, Sluhovsky stresses that possessed nuns were typically depicted and even described themselves as being *penetrated* by male spirits. Such heterosexual metaphors, he argues, could not be applied to male religious, and the theologians and exorcists who wrote about possession, many of whom belonged to religious orders, refused to allow that male religious could ever completely lose sexual control of themselves. Thus, although the Sicilian novice and lay brother showed unusual physical strength and were subject to seizures, shouting, and screaming, he rightly points out that chroniclers did not report that they utterly lost control over their bodies, especially over their sexual behavior and fantasies. For Sluhovsky, this gendering of sexual imagery was an important factor behind the different experiences between male and female religious.[23] Unfortunately Sluhovsky's analysis of the Sicilian monastery is based on his flawed claim that demons tormented the Capuchins' bodies from outside without penetrating and taking possession of them. The memoir describing this case indicates in no uncertain terms that the demons possessed the bodies of these two men.[24]

That said, it is undoubtedly true that exorcists, demonologists, and other clerics were more wont to see demon possession in women in general and nuns in particular than in men and priests. Similarly, as we have seen, the leading authorities of the Holy Office, including Scaglia and Barberini, believed that women, especially nuns, were prone to mistake their own fears or melancholic humors for possession or even to feign demon possession to get attention or bring about change in their lives. The evidence from Santa Chiara suggests that these contrasting beliefs concerning nuns' propensity for possession did not merely reflect sexist beliefs in female inferiority. Female religious in fact no doubt were more prone to possession, whether imagined or real, but the alleged sexual imagery of penetrating demons described by Sluhovsky was not likely a decisive factor.

Far more important were various features that were unique to the lives of Counter-Reformation nuns. As the life of Bellacappa demonstrated, members of male religious orders were not held in seclusion in their monasteries. Nuns normally joined one monastic community for life, whereas many friars, like Bellacappa, moved from one priory or monastery to another. More important, members of male religious orders had infinitely more freedom of movement outside monasteries than their female counterparts. Upon joining a convent as a girl, a seventeenth-century nun generally did not leave the cloister for the rest of her life. Far from being an innovation, however, claustration had been an essential part of Santa Chiara since its foundation. Even during Angela Caterina's tenure as abbess, when the nunnery was highly permeable to the outside world, the professed Clarisses generally could not leave the convent and conversed with visitors only on opposite sides of a grille or *ruota*. Although the afflicted nuns did not articulate that they were chafing under the rules of enclosure, the restricted space that they permanently shared with the same group of women was fertile breeding ground for spiritual or psychological ills. When the unprecedented fears of the powers of Satan, demons, and witches—endemic in sixteenth- and seventeenth-century Europe and part and parcel of the great hunts—penetrated the walls of a convent, the anxieties of a few nuns could easily spread and fester in the minds of others. Moreover, the Clarisses of Carpi and nuns elsewhere surely accepted the notion, reinforced by priests in sermons and confessions, that women were more vulnerable to diabolical temptation and possession. When exorcists examined the ailing nuns after medical treatment proved ineffective, the warnings of demonic possession that they and other clerics had long stressed proved self-fulfilling. The Clarisses of Carpi had so assimilated the dangers that Satan posed to them and the manner in which demons tormented people that they were all convinced that devils possessed the bodies of the miserable nuns. Thus the fear of Satan and demons, increasing in Europe since the fifteenth century and exacerbated in Carpi by the ministrations of the exorcists, and the close quarters in which over sixty nuns lived were vitally important factors behind Santa Chiara's witchcraft scare of the 1630s.[25]

If we cannot know exactly what afflicted the Clarisses of Carpi, their suffering was most definitely real. After all, three of the ailing residents of Santa Chiara supposedly died from their ills. Fears and psychosomatic forces can strongly influence one's physical well-being, and, as mentioned briefly in chapter 4, evidence suggests that in early modern Europe some people who were deemed bewitched may literally have been frightened to death. As Erik Midelfort has pointed out in his provocative book on early modern madness, various psychosomatic and neurotic ills have come and gone. Wisely eschewing the application of modern medical and psychological terms to premodern ills, Midelfort observes, for example, that St. Vitus' dance—a form of group mania in which people were subjected, often for days on end, to uncontrollable and exhausting dancing and jumping—was a malady that existed almost exclusively in the fifteenth and sixteenth centuries.[26]

In many early modern settings, some people, usually women, suffered convulsions, temporary paralysis, trances, and other physical effects of alleged demon possession similar to those of the Clarisses. The fear of witches and demons might be able to provoke such responses, but anthropologists have found women suffering similar ills in virtually all cultures, some of which do not even have a concept of witchcraft. Scholars have suggested that the possessed are in effect removing themselves temporarily from the "socially constructed world of everyday life" and allowing free expression to anger, bitterness, and other feelings ordinarily considered unacceptable. In doing so, the possessed are entering involuntarily an altered state of consciousness as a reaction to strong internal emotional conflict, which stems from the simultaneous desire both to conform to prevailing social mores and to rebel against them. Lacking direct means to express this conflict openly, the powerful intrapsychic tensions are expressed physically in the women's bodies in a variety of ways. This amounts to an indirect rebellion that does not provoke the reprisals or opprobrium that would follow the open rejection of prescribed female behavior. For the early modern era, it has also been averred that those living in the most religious environments experienced the strongest pressure to internalize social mores concerning female roles, which they were taught were divinely ordained. If the anthropologists are correct, then possession in early modern Europe was an interpretation imposed on the emotional and physical reactions to entrenched social conditions that had no direct connection to witches or Satan. The actions of the possessed were culturally sanctioned and gave these women the opportunity to have all attention temporarily focused on them and their unhappy lot. Their bodies revealed what they dared not express in words: that the pressure to conform to the male-dominated, religiously inspired social order was more than they could bear.[27]

Considering the Ursulines at Loudun, Michel de Certeau persuasively suggests that the possessions were, among other things, a "rebellion of women." Like the female subjects studied by anthropologists, the Ursulines, well-educated women from good families, could, through their "demons," express desires, make demands, and commit actions that they would not dare do under other circumstances. During exorcisms, the sisters of Loudun were wont to express openly their feelings, acknowledging the lust that Grandier incited in them, and to insult and even assault the priests and magistrates who examined and ministered to them, actions they would not have dared to take in any other circumstances.[28]

In a similar manner, the Clarisses of Carpi were no doubt taking part, though almost surely not consciously, in a form of rebellion. Confined to the space within the convent's walls, these young women, whose religious vocation in most cases had been chosen for them before puberty, probably experienced a wide range of ambivalent feelings. They might view the convent as either restricting or expanding their opportunities. Forbidden to marry and form families, they also might wield far more political and economic power within the religious community than they could possibly have had in secular society. Many Clarisses undoubtedly endured conflicting sentiments and inclinations: the wish to fulfill their religious vows and a yearning to be free of them, curiosity about the outside world and the obligation to renounce it, sexual urges and the need to suppress them, the aspirations of the individual and the demands of the community, the duty to conform and the longing to dissent. Notwithstanding the vow of obedience they had all taken, female religious could rebel and be assured of a sympathetic audience, provided the rebellion took the form of demonic possession. Far from feigning possession, the dozen Clarisses were certain they had demons in their bodies. Their possession both reflected their assimilation of prevailing ideas concerning witchcraft and diabolism and served as a means of expressing profound feelings of angst directed against no one thing in particular. In a different way, even if she was not a devil-worshiping witch casting maleficent spells, Dealta Martinelli was at the very least a rebel who refused to conform to the prescribed lifestyle of seventeenth-century female religious. All told, there is ample evidence from Santa Chiara to give credence to both the "agency" model and the older "oppression" model, which have together had a profound impact on historical studies of women.

The Holy Office and Witchcraft

Unlike so many other witchcraft stories from the early modern era, the Santa Chiara case had a reasonably happy ending. Despite the overwhelming belief in Carpi that the nuns were the victims of witchcraft, no one was executed. Evidence shows that, already in the late sixteenth century, most local inquisitors throughout Italy were fairly circumspect in weighing the proofs of witchcraft.[29] Italy's very low execution rate for witchcraft, however, was largely thanks to the Congregation of the Inquisition, which definitely served as an important brake on certain zealous local authorities. It prevented, for lack of proof, Carlo Borromeo from executing witches in his archdiocese of Milan in the 1570s and took aggressive actions in 1582 against a local official for his harsh treatment of suspected witches.[30] In a similar manner, the cardinal-inquisitors were most responsible for the bloodless conclusion to the tumultuous story of Santa Chiara. Like other studies, this case shows unequivocally that the Inquisition's harsh reputation is unwarranted, at least insofar as witchcraft is concerned. True, Fiscal Giudici and, to a lesser extent, Inquisitor Tinti were quick to believe that the beleaguered nuns were bewitched and aggressively sought to identify the authors of the *maleficia*. Nonetheless, at no point was Dealta, Bellacappa, or any other suspect subjected to judicial torture. The Congregation of the Inquisition in Rome insisted that no one suspected of witchcraft could be subjected to torture without its consent,[31] and neither Tinti nor anyone else in Modena and Carpi made any effort to obtain this permission.[32] Although the afflicted Clarisses came close to lynching Dealta, no one was put to death in this case, a dramatic contrast to so many witchcraft cases in central and northern Europe.[33]

Although fully believing in the reality of demonic power and possession, the cardinal-inquisitors recognized the difficulties in establishing the proof of witchcraft and diabolical pacts. They were most concerned about the *corpus delicti*, the facts that indicated that a crime had actually been committed, desiring to identify specifically what witches were guilty of before condemning them of witchcraft.[34] Aware of the dangers of mistaking natural maladies for the work of the devil, the cardinals insisted that inquisitors take witchcraft accusations with a grain of salt. Although the Carpi case did not raise the issue, the Congregation of the Holy Office even advocated skepticism when people freely admitted without torture to worshiping the devil and attending sabbats. Over a decade before the Santa Chiara case, Scaglia's instructions for inquisitors warned that such a confession might stem from the encouragement of another person, the "tedium" of prison, or the hope for a more lenient sentence. For some, it could be a mere illusion.[35] In the latter 1600s, the Congregation in Rome still had to put a brake on some local inquisitors who, without this restraint, might have been zealous witch-hunters.[36]

Scholars have persuasively argued that the decline in witch-hunts, apparent already in the early seventeenth century in certain regions, was rooted primarily in legal proceedings rather than in changes in the history of ideas. In Italy, France, and elsewhere, strict standards concerning proofs could result in the decline in the judicial persecution of witches even while belief in witchcraft remained very strong.[37] The Inquisition was clearly in the vanguard in this regard, evident in the fact that the Holy Office in Italy virtually never condemned to death anyone for magic or witchcraft. The denouement of the Santa Chiara case reinforces the impression that by and large the Roman Inquisition did not take magic and witchcraft very seriously, be it perpetrated by female witches or male magicians. It basically lumped such deviant behavior under the general rubric of superstitions that needed to be eradicated but, unlike various forms of heresy, did not pose a serious threat to Roman Catholicism.[38]

Brian Levack sees four key changes in judicial proceedings that led to the decline of witch-hunts: the closer supervision of local trials by centralized courts, the restriction or outright ban on torture of witchcraft defendants, the requirement of higher standards of proof, and the increased participation of defense attorneys in the trials.[39] In the case of Santa Chiara and in many other venues, the most decisive change was surely the first, out of which flowed the latter three. Throughout Europe higher courts, be they secular or ecclesiastical, consistently showed greater caution in considering witchcraft cases than did local tribunals. Although pressure to investigate witches virtually always came from the local community—as was the case in Santa Chiara—appellate courts, such as the Parlement of Paris or, as we have seen, the Congregation of the Holy Office in Rome, tended to restrain the aggressive actions of local officials who perhaps knew the accused personally and were convinced of their guilt even if the proof of witchcraft was rather murky. The absence of centralized judicial machinery in the Holy Roman Empire was a major factor behind the huge numbers of trials and executions there.[40]

The Carpi case also shows that the "black legend" of the Inquisition is a myth that is entirely unwarranted. As John Tedeschi has shown, the Holy

Office was not "a drumhead court, a chamber of horrors, or a judicial labyrinth from which there was no escape."[41] The Roman Inquisition probably provided the best criminal justice, from a defendant's perspective, in early modern Europe. Like other Holy Office tribunals, the Inquisition of Modena kept verbatim transcripts of investigations, respected defendants' right to counsel, followed detailed legal procedures that were laid out by the Congregation, and kept the cardinals fully informed of all proceedings. Closely scrutinized by the cardinals in Rome, by the 1630s inquisitors throughout Italy knew all too well that torture could be applied only with the Congregation of the Inquisition's permission (and only under very limited circumstances) and that they must be quite circumspect when weighing hearsay evidence.[42]

The judicial skepticism that was apparent in the Congregation's consideration of the Carpi case did not necessarily reflect a mentality that was strongly shaped by the rationalism of the Scientific Revolution. Rather, it stemmed from a realization that many Europeans had been convicted and executed for crimes they had not committed, even though most religious leaders and judicial authorities continued to believe in the reality of demon possessions and maleficent witches. It was this judicial skepticism, more than fundamental changes in beliefs about witches and witchcraft, that marks "the starting point for any investigation of the decline of witch-hunting."[43]

Some scholars view the Inquisition's mild treatment of witchcraft as a mixed blessing for women. It has been suggested that the Holy Office espoused a form of paternalistic sexism and that the low number of females it executed for witchcraft came at the price of a decline in status for women in general. Excluded from power and vulnerable to the whims of men, women supposedly might have recourse to magic in order to redress this imbalance in power. Regardless of their objectives–to win the love of another, to avenge misdeeds and violence, to protect themselves and others from a wide range of misadventures–women who reportedly had the knowledge and power to cast spells could inspire fear or respect in others. But when confronted with "witches" who confessed to having given themselves freely in body and soul to the devil, authorities of the Spanish Inquisition, for example, eventually dismissed such confessions, which they attributed to demonic illusions or to the imagination, dementia, or naiveté of these women, all of which pointed to their irrationality or even "stupidity." Inquisitors were thus supposedly depriving women of a traditional source of power and leaving them "voiceless."[44]

Was the Inquisition engaging in a condescending, sexist attack that, in effect, undermined one of the few means by which women could supposedly attain power: magic? The evidence from the Inquisition in Italy certainly does not reveal a deliberate attempt to remove a source of power for women. More important, the Holy Office's actions against magic, superstitions, and witchcraft did not weigh exclusively or even inordinately upon women. Records from the Inquisition in Friuli show, for example, that though the large majority of those accused specifically of *maleficia* from the 1590s through 1670 were indeed female, men comprised a little over 40 percent of those investigated for all types of the "magical arts," including divination, therapeutic magic, love magic, and other forms of dabbling in the occult. Still more striking was the fact that for the period 1670–1785, women were still in the majority (59 percent) of those investigated for casting maleficent spells, but males represented the overwhelming majority (78 percent) of those accused of all forms of magic.[45] These statistics imply that though authorities of the Holy Office, like virtually all writers on witchcraft and demonology, assumed that women were more prone to make pacts with the devil and cast maleficent spells, they certainly did not view magic as exclusively the domain of women and investigated male suspects—including many clerics who sought love or wealth through magical means—just as assiduously as females. More broadly, the evidence throughout early modern Europe indicates that though some women did engage in therapeutic and love magic, the overwhelming majority of those accused of maleficent witchcraft were no doubt innocent of even attempting to make pacts with the devil or to attend sabbats. Contrary to certain interpretations, the Inquisition's lenient treatment of witchcraft therefore did not appear to be a means of leaving women "voiceless." Though sharing the widespread belief that women were more prone to being witches, the Holy Office's high standard of proofs of witchcraft ultimately spared the lives of countless people, mostly females, who, like Dealta Martinelli, almost surely were entirely innocent of the charges made against them.

Had the "possessions" of Santa Chiara occurred a century earlier, before the creation of the Roman Inquisition in 1542, Carpi's diabolical woes almost certainly would have resulted in the executions of Dealta and Bellacappa at the very least. Had the investigation taken place at the same time but in another region, the suspects may also not have been so fortunate. A century after Santa Chiara's woes, the "possessions" themselves were much less likely to occur, as demons and Satan seemed less menacing even to those who continued to believe in them. The hunts and group possessions of the seventeenth century flamed the fears of demons and witches, but in the long run such incidents raised more doubts than they allayed.[46] By the early eighteenth century, the Holy Office itself was much less likely to pursue an investigation of witchcraft. Throughout the eighteenth century, the Inquisition of Modena continued to investigate cases of people who allegedly indulged in magic, including some women who admitted to conjuring demons for various ends. Unlike Inquisitor Tinti, however, his eighteenth-century successors were much more intent on disabusing people of such "superstitions" than in discovering maleficent spells or devil-worshipers.[47]

After the Possessions

By midsummer 1639 all eleven surviving demoniacs had been cured of their ills and thereafter dedicated themselves or at least resigned themselves to the religious life they had vowed to follow. If the possessions had in any way been a rebellion against the cloistered life, they all apparently either overcame or suppressed those feelings. Some went on to lead long lives and became key players in the monastery, whereas others did not live much beyond the turbulent episode, their names appearing in the *Memoriale* only when their deaths were announced. Anna Maria Martinelli, though the youngest demoniac, was the first to die, passing away on 6 April 1641 at the tender age of twenty. When receiving extreme unction, she expressed the desire to renew her monastic vows.[48] When Cinzia Ciarlatina died at forty-four in 1651, the confessor reported that she had been in poor health for almost all her monastic life but, as confessors were accustomed to eulogize, always bore her afflictions without complaint, much to the edification of herself and everyone around her.[49] By contrast, four of the "bewitched" choir nuns eventually served at least briefly as abbess: Paola Francesca Federici (1655–58, 1667–70), Degnamerita Solieri (1658–61), Clara Maria Amoldoni (1673–76 and 1681), and Caterina Margherita Ronchi (1679–81). Ronchi died in January 1681 while serving as abbess and was succeeded as interim abbess (*commissaria*) by Amoldoni, who passed away on 6 March of the same year, marking the disappearance of the last "demoniac."[50]

Missing among these leaders of Santa Chiara were the former protégés of Angela Caterina. Did this amount to a backlash against those who enjoyed privileges under the most powerful abbess in the history of the convent? There was almost certainly a degree of resentment toward those privileged few, particularly in the immediate aftermath of the spiritual woes. There were, however, a number of mundane reasons why none of the six "possessed" women in her service had risen to the highest ranks in the monastery. One must recall that two of them were laywomen serving the abbess's nieces and both died way back in 1636 after leaving the convent. Two of the choir nuns in her inner circle, Colevati and Castagnini, were rather humble servants who had no realistic chance of becoming leaders in this nunnery. Giulia Angelica Sertori, the former vicaress and confidante of Angela Caterina, was forty-four when she died in 1646, just seven years after the conclusion of the tumult, following a "great infirmity" that she bore with "great patience."[51] Both her ill health and her youth—even at the time of her death she would have been far younger than any abbess other than the princess—made Sertori an unlikely candidate for high office. That leaves only Barbara Leonora Forni, originally a *dama di compagnia* to the Este nieces, who passed away at the age of fifty-five in 1673. In the years that followed the possessions, Forni did hold several lesser but important offices in the community.

In 1664 she was a *ruotare,* one of the nuns who surveyed the turntable and the adjacent window, and served as bookkeeper (*contista*) in 1667, sacristan in 1669, and bookkeeper again in 1670, when she had to step down due to ill health. Three years later, the obituary eulogized her "exemplary patience" when confronted with this "long and almost continuous illness."[52] Far from being marginalized for her past service to the Este princesses, Forni assumed important responsibilities in the convent and might have held even more powerful positions were it not for her deteriorating health. Although many were surely glad to see Angela Caterina leave in 1639, the lengthy eulogy in the *Memoriale* announcing her death in 1661 was so effusive in its praise that it almost seemed like a first step in a campaign for her canonization.[53] As for her brother, Fra Giovan Battista continued to be a very active in both religious and, much to his son's dismay, political affairs for the remainder of his life.[54] With the departures of his sister and daughters, he no longer had a motive to be intimately involved in the affairs of the convent of Carpi and died in 1644, just five years after the end of the demonic woes. The wounds had healed in Santa Chiara.

Similarly, though silenced in 1638, the exorcists who had ministered to the beleaguered nuns of Santa Chiara did not suffer a permanent loss of prestige. The convent remained under the supervision of the bishop of Modena or the archpriest of Carpi rather than the Observant Franciscans. Although the Congregation in Rome had banned them from even approaching the monastery during the possessions, two of the exorcists eventually served as confessors to the nuns of Santa Chiara: Agostino Bertesi, the first native of Carpi to serve as the convent's confessor (1649–55); and Domenico Verrini, who was the Clarisses' confessor from 1655 until his death in 1657.[55] Starting in 1662, Bertesi was the *provicario* of the convent, whereby he served as deputy to the archpriest, who was again governor of the convent. When he died at eighty-eight in 1690, the obituary extolled him as a "fine exorcist."[56] Similarly, although Barberini and the other cardinals had been most disappointed with his handling of the Carpi case, Fiscal Orazio Giudici would not be forever estranged from the Inquisition. In 1659, twenty years after the Santa Chiara affair, the inquisitor of Modena asked the Congregation in Rome to affirm Giudici's appointment as legal adviser (*consultor legista*).[57]

As for the suspects, the Martinelli sisters disappeared from the historical record as Santa Chiara's demonic tribulations cooled. In all likelihood, they spent the rest of their lives quietly at Santa Maria Maddalena in Modena. Residing several miles from her native Carpi and chastened by the witchcraft accusations, Dealta almost certainly never again received a steady flow of visitors or expressed so openly a strong distaste for monastic life. Notwithstanding the suspicions of love magic and solicitation, Bellacappa resumed his impressive career. In 1644, just five years after the conclusion of the Holy Office's investigation, he was again elected *Definitore,* one of four advisers to the provincial minister. Even more impressive was the fact that in 1644 his fellow Observant Franciscans also named him *Lettore Giubilato,* an honorific title, roughly equivalent to "Distinguished Professor," that was bestowed upon only the most erudite scholars.[58] He also continued to write, including most notably some memoirs about the experiences of the *Zoccolanti* of his province from 1610, when he embraced the religious life, until 1650.[59] In 1651 he again served as guardian of the monastery in his native Parma, one of the most important centers of studies for Observant Franciscans in the province of Bologna.[60] The extant acts of this province reveal nothing about appointments of confessors to convents, but Bellacappa surely never again was assigned to a convent or, most likely, even heard women's confessions. The *Zoccolanti* of his province almost certainly believed that Bellacappa's talents were best utilized outside the confessional. At any rate, his reputation among his fellow Observant Franciscans was not tarnished by the Santa Chiara affair, and he enjoyed a brilliant career as a clergyman for the rest of his life.[61]

The convent of Santa Chiara survived this most difficult chapter in its history. Like many other convents, it experienced a decline in the number of nuns in the eighteenth century and was temporarily closed when the region was subjected to Napoleonic rule. But the convent has survived to the present, with seven Clarisses living in the same community and in the same building, though greatly remodeled, in which Angela Caterina organized concerts, Bellacappa heard confessions, Dealta received visitors, and Cabassi conducted exorcisms. Never again were the Clarisses of Carpi plagued by demons and witchcraft. Santa Chiara's diabolical woes and their denouement were profoundly shaped by the unique confluence of religious, cultural, judicial, and intellectual trends that flourished in the 1630s.

Appendix A

Chronological List of the Possessions of Santa Chiara

1) 26 January 1636: Paolina Forni, a "young" laywoman and lady-in-waiting; died from her ills on 23 May 1636.

2) February (?) 1636: Leonora Galli a "young" lay servant; died from her ills on 13 December 1636.

3) ca. 12 April 1637: Ottavia Bendidio; died from her ills on 23 January 1638 at age thirty-three.

4) 28 October 1637: Giulia Angelica Sertori, age thirty-nine.

5) 28 October 1637: Barbara Leonora Forni, age twenty.

6) 4 November 1637: Flerida (also known as Paola Francesca) Federici (also known as Cimadori), age thirty-five.

7) 4 November 1637: Degnamerita Solieri, age thirty-two.

8) 4 November 1637: Margherita Felice Castagnini, about thirty-nine, cured of her ills before the Holy Office's investigation began.

9) 8 November 1637: Clara Maria Amoldoni, age twenty-four.

10) December 1637–January 1638: Maria Maddalena Colevati, age fifty.

11) December 1637–January 1638: Cinzia Ciarlatina, age twenty-nine.

12) December 1637–January 1638: Veronica Maria Coccapani, age twenty-four.

13) 24 February 1638: Caterina Margherita Ronchi, age twenty-one.

14) 24 February 1638: Anna Maria Martinelli, age seventeen.

NB: The above ages of the Clarisses, other than that of Ottavia Bendidio, refer to the time at which the Holy Office's investigation began (19 April 1638).
Sources: ASM, Inq., b. 108; AMSCC, Memoriale secondo.

APPENDIX B

Time Line of the Holy Office's Investigation of the Santa Chiara Case

Interrogation of witnesses by Fiscal Orazio Giudici for the Inquisition of Modena in 1638 (all are Clarisses unless otherwise noted at their first appearance):

19 April: Claudia Cabassi
20 April: Claudia Cabassi, Maria Calefi
21 April: Maria Calefi
27 April: Alsuinda Malaspina
28 April: Alsuinda Malaspina
1 May: Giovan Battista Bignardi (confessor), Angelica Rocchi; perquisition of personal effects of Dealta Martinelli (incarcerated since 25 April)
5 May: Orsina Cipolla (lay sister), Dorotea Serafini Cabassi
6 May: Caterina Maria Poggi, Cassandra Felice Poggi, Clara Vittoria Massi
7 May: Clara Vittoria Massi
8 May: Geltruda Francesca Contessini, Margherita Felice Castagnini, Maria Calefi, Anna Caterina Zuccari
10 May: Claudia Cabassi, Grazia Lupagnini
12 May: Grazia Lupagnini, Ludovica Speroni, Beatrice Bendidio
14 May: Beatrice Bendidio
15 May: Silvia Montalti, Lucidaria Bellentani, Obizza Foschieri
16 May: Bradamante Puzzuoli, Leonora Brusati, Portia Muzzi
18 May: Giacinta Alessandrini, Portia Muzzi
19 May: Giacinta Alessandrini, Silveria Chechi, Gregorio Montaguti (exorcist)
20 May: Silveria Chechi, Caterina Maria Poggi, Olimpia Corradi
21 May: Silveria Chechi
22 May: Clarice Coccapani, Marcella Alessandrini
23 May: Paola Coccapani, Dianira Bergamaschi
24 May: Faustina Comì, Colomba Ciarlini
25 May: Chiara Grillenzoni, Leonora Fontana, Feliciana Grillenzoni, Alessandra Corradi, Florida Grillenzoni, Angelica Rocchi, Arcangela Donelli, Prudenzia Federici
27 May: Emerenziana Duosi

28 May: Prudenzia Federici, Emerenziana Duosi
29 May: Clelia Coccapani
30 May: Flavia Coccapani
31 May: Teodora Pattoni
1 June: Aurelia Bendidio, Angelica Rocchi, Beatrice Bendidio
4 June: Cherubina Giudici, Doralice Giudici, Fulvia Codebò
19 June: Orsina Cipolla
22 June: Margherita Felice Castagnini
23 June: Caterina Poletti (a laywoman who oversees the exterior side of the turntables)
25 June: Alfonso Cabassi (a young man studying for the priesthood who assists in the Mass at Santa Chiara)
26 June: Anna Caterina Zuccari

Continuation of the Investigation by Inquisitor Giacomo Tinti:

1 July: Florida Grillenzoni, Emilia Bellentani (abbess), Aurelia Bendidio (vicaress), Angelica Rocchi, Ippolita Martinelli (suspect)
13 July: Giovan Battista Zaretti (exorcist), Girolamo Cabassi (provost and exorcist)
14 July: Girolamo Cabassi
15 July: Agostino Bertesi (exorcist)
16 July: Agostino Bertesi, Domenico Verrini (exorcist)
17 July: Domenico Verrini, Giovan Battista Abbati (physician)
18 July: Francesco Donelli (barber-surgeon)
19 July: Emilia Bellentani, Camilla Violante Pio, Giacinta Alessandrini, Grazia Lupagnini
20 July: Alsuinda Malaspina, Anna Caterina Zuccari, Dorotea Serafini Cabassi, Cassandra Felice Poggi, Penelope Leonori, Ludovica Speroni
21 July: Anna Coccapani, Clelia Coccapani, Orsina Cipolla, Anna Caterina Zuccari, Maria Calefi, Clara Vittoria Massi
23 July: Colomba Ciarlini, Alsuinda Malaspina, Clarice Coccapani, Portia Muzzi, Silvia Montalti, Claudia Cabassi, Alessandra Corradi, Olimpia Corradi
24 July: Teodora Pattoni, Prudenzia Federici, Clelia Coccapani, Dianira Bergamaschi, Cristoforo Marchi (employee of Santa Chiara who works outside the cloister), Girolamo Cabassi
27 July: Antea Bellentani, Leonora Brusati, Clara Vittoria Massi
28 July: Princess Angela Caterina d'Este
29 July: Princess Angela Caterina d'Este, Aurelia Bendidio
30 July: Ippolita Martinelli
31 July: Clelia Coccapani, Alsuinda Malaspina, Doralice Giudici, Claudia Cabassi, Aurelia Bendidio, Ippolita Martinelli
2 August: Ippolita Martinelli
9 August: Angelo Bellacappa (suspect)

11 August: Angelo Bellacappa

12 August: Angelo Bellacappa, Claudia Cabassi, Florida Grillenzoni (the latter two are interrogated by Fra Andrea Marchetti, Inquisitor Tinti's vicar in Carpi)

27 August: Leonora Brusati (interrogated by Fra Andrea Marchetti)

4 September: Angelo Bellacappa

16 September: Angelo Bellacappa

19 September: Angelo Bellacappa requests release from prison

21 September: Angelo Bellacappa released to house arrest

24 September: Angelo Bellacappa

16 October: Girolamo Cabassi, Agostino Bertesi, Domenico Verrini (all promise to stay away from Santa Chiara)

19 October: Girolamo Cabassi, Alessandro Pezzoli (notary), Luigi Foresti (archdeacon), Martino Barbieri (priest), Giovan Francesco Bosio (priest)

1 November: attorney Francesco Barozzi submits "chapters" for the defense of Angelo Bellacappa

9 November: inspection of convent's confessionals and communion window for Bellacappa's defense

10 November: Emilia Bellentani

10–11 November: Giovanni dal Chierico, Tommaso Fabrizi, Francesco Quarantini, Fra Angelo of Bologna, Timoteo Gabrielli, Salvatore Valotti (Observant Franciscans who testify as character witnesses for Bellacappa before Pietro Giacinto, vicar of the inquisitor of Bologna)

11 November: Emerenziana Duosi, Paola Grillenzoni

12 November: Chiara Grillenzoni, Penelope Leonori, Obizza Foschieri

28 December: another inspection of the convent's lower confessional

29 December: Alsuinda Malaspina, Clelia Coccapani

8 January 1639: Dealta Martinelli (suspect) recounts her tribulations to Giovanni Lupi, commissioner for the Congregation of the Holy Office

Final decisions made by the Congregation of the Holy Office in Rome:

15 January 1639: Angelo Bellacappa is released from house arrest, though his case will remain open

12 February 1639: approval of transfer of Dealta and Ippolita Martinelli to Santa Maria Maddalena in Modena

Sources: ASM, Inq., bb. 108, 255, 295.

ABBREVIATIONS

ACDF	Archivio della Congregazione per la Dottrina della Fede
AMSCC	Archivio Monastero di Santa Chiara di Carpi
ASM	Archivio di Stato di Modena
b./bb.	busta/buste
f.	filza
fasc.	fascicolo
Inq.	Inquisizione di Modena
Memoriale secondo	Memoriale continente successi che giornalmente occorrono per questo Sacro Monasterio di S. Chiara di Carpi

NOTES

Introduction

1. Anna Maria Ori, "La vita della comunità (secc. XVI–XVII)," in *Clarisse in Carpi: Cinque secoli di storia (XVI–XX)*, vol. 1, *Saggi*, ed. Gabriella Zarri (Reggio Emilia: Diabasis, 2003), 198–99. See also Gigliola Fragnito, "Gli ordini religiosi tra Riforma e Contoriforma," in *Clero e società nell'Italia moderna*, ed. Mario Rosa (Rome and Bari: Laterza, 1997), 145; Hans Semper, *Carpi: Una sede principesca del Rinascimento*, trans. A. D'Amelio and Anna Elisabeth Werdehausen, ed. Luisa Giordano (Pisa: Edizioni ETS, 1999).

2. Clara Gennaro, "Clare, Agnes, and Their Earliest Followers: From the Poor Ladies of San Damiano to the Poor Clares," in *Women and Religion in Medieval and Renaissance Italy*, ed. Daniel Bornstein and Roberto Rusconi, trans. Margery J. Schneider (Chicago: University of Chicago Press, 1996), 39–55; Chiara Frugoni, *Una solitudine abitata: Chiara d'Assisi* (Rome and Bari: Laterza, 2006); Joan Mueller, *The Privilege of Poverty: Clare of Assisi, Agnes of Prague, and the Struggle for a Franciscan Rule for Women* (University Park: Pennsylvania State University Press, 2006). While in English a member of the Second Order of St. Francis is commonly referred to as a "Poor Clare," in Italian she is known as a "Clarissa," with no adjective referring to her poverty. In keeping with the Italian documents studied here, I have preferred the term "Clarisse" when referring to the nuns of Carpi. On Clare see also Maria Pia Alberzoni, *Clare of Assisi and the Poor Sisters in the Thirteenth Century* (St. Bonaventure: Franciscan Institute, St. Bonaventure University, 2004); and *Chiara d'Assisi e la memoria di Francesco: Atti del Convegno per l'VIII centenario della nascita di S. Chiara, Fara Sabina, 19–20 maggio 1994*, ed. Alfonso Marini and Maria Beatrice Mistretta (Città del Castello: Petruzzi, 1995).

3. AMSCC, Memoriale secondo, 3v–7v. On the foundation of Santa Chiara see various essays in *Clarisse in Carpi*, ed. Zarri.

4. Having already enjoyed suzerainty over these lands for centuries, the Este family acquired the title of Duke of Modena and Ferrara from the Holy Roman Emperor in 1452 and that of Duke of Ferrara from the pope in 1471. The Este court was centered in Ferrara and was one of the most brilliant cultural centers of Renaissance Italy. In 1597, however, Duke Alfonso II died without children, and the pope refused to legitimate Cesare d'Este, Alfonso's nephew who was born out of wedlock. Cesare was thus denied succession to the duchy of Ferrara, and its lands accordingly reverted to the papacy. The emperor, however, did allow Cesare to become duke of Modena, which remained the capital of Estense lands until the end of the dynasty in the nineteenth century. For a very brief narrative on the Este dynasty, see Giuseppe Panini, *La famiglia Estense da Ferrara a Modena* (Modena: Edizioni Archivi Riuniti Modena, 1996).

5. See especially Norman Cohn, *Europe's Inner Demons: The Demonization of Christians in Medieval Christendom,* revised ed. (Chicago: University of Chicago Press, 1993), 25–34; Jean Delumeau, *Sin and Fear: The Emergence of a Western Guilt Culture 13th–18th Centuries,* trans. Eric Nicholson (New York: St. Martin's Press, 1990), 168–85, 523–54; Jeffrey Burton Russell, *Lucifer: The Devil in the Middle Ages* (Ithaca: Cornell University Press, 1984), 275–95.

6. H. C. Erik Midelfort, *A History of Madness in Sixteenth-Century Germany* (Stanford: Stanford University Press, 1999), 19.

7. E. William Monter, *Witchcraft in France and Switzerland: The Borderlands during the Reformation* (Ithaca: Cornell University Press, 1976), 60.

8. H. C. Erik Midelfort, *Exorcism and Enlightenment: Johann Joseph Gassner and the Demons of Eighteenth-Century Germany* (New Haven: Yale University Press, 2005), 9; Nancy Caciola, *Discerning Spirits: Divine and Demonic Possession in the Middle Ages* (Ithaca: Cornell University Press, 2003), 315–19.

9. Robert Muchembled, *Le roi et la sorcière: L'Europe des bûchers (XVe–XVIIIe siècle)* (Paris: Desclée, 1993) 76–80.

10. For an introduction to the witch-hunts of the sixteenth and seventeenth centuries, see especially *Witchcraft and Magic in Europe: The Period of the Witch Trials,* ed. Bengt Ankarloo and Stuart Clark (Philadelphia: University of Pennsylvania Press, 2002); and Brian P. Levack, *The Witch-Hunt in Early Modern Europe,* 2d ed. (London: Longman, 1995). Still useful is Joseph Klaits, *Servants of Satan: The Age of the Witch Hunts* (Bloomington: Indiana University Press, 1985). For a broader examination see *Encyclopedia of Witchcraft: The Western Tradition,* 4 vols., ed. Richard Golden (Santa Barbara: ABC-Clio, 2006). Moshe Sluhovsky insists that early modern Europeans did not necessarily associate possession with *maleficium*; *Believe Not Every Spirit: Possession, Mysticism, and Discernment in Early Modern Catholicism* (Chicago: University of Chicago Press, 2007).

11. Richard Kieckhefer, *Magic in the Middle Ages* (Cambridge: Cambridge University Press, 1990), 1–14; Giuseppe Bonomo, *Caccia alle streghe: La credenza nelle streghe dal secolo XIII al XIX con particolare riferimento all'Italia* (Palermo: Palumbo, 1959).

12. See Cohn, *Europe's Inner Demons,* 102–17; H. C. Erik Midelfort, *Witch Hunting in Southwestern Germany, 1562–1684: The Social and Intellectual Foundations* (Stanford: Stanford University Press, 1972), 15–17; Adriano Prosperi, *Tribunali della coscienza: Inquisitori, confessori, missionari* (Turin: Giulio Einaudi, 1996), 396–97. See also D. P. Walker, *Spiritual and Demonic Magic from Ficino to Campanella* (London: Warburg Institute, University of London, 1958; reprint, University Park: Pennsylvania State University Press, 2000); and Stuart Clark, *Thinking with Demons: The Idea of Witchcraft in Early Modern Europe* (Oxford: Oxford University Press, 1997), 214–32.

13. Giovanni Romeo, *Inquisitori, esorcisti e streghe nell'Italia della Controriforma* (Florence: Sansoni, 1990), 67–108; John Tedeschi, "Preliminary Observations on Writing a History of the Roman Inquisition," in *The Prosecution of Heresy: Collected Studies on the Inquisition in Early Modern Italy* (Binghamton: Medieval and Renaissance Texts and Studies, 1991), 10.

14. Heinrich Kramer and James Sprenger, *The Malleus Maleficarum,* trans. and ed. Montague Summers (New York: Dover, 1971). There is general agreement today among scholars that Kramer was the sole author of this treatise, but Jacob Sprenger, another Dominican inquisitor, has traditionally been credited with assisting in its

composition. On this tract see Hans Peter Broedel, *The "Malleus Maleficarum" and the Construction of Witchcraft: Theology and Popular Belief* (Manchester: Manchester University Press, 2003); and *Der Hexenhammer: Malleus Maleficarum,* ed. Günter Jerouschek and Wolfgang Behringer (Munich: Deutcher Taschenbuch Verlag, 2000).

15. For a good overview of the development of ideas on witchcraft, see Levack, *Witch-Hunt,* 1–49. On medieval magic see Cohn, *Europe's Inner Demons;* and Edward Peters, *The Magician, the Witch, and the Law* (Philadelphia: University of Pennsylvania Press, 1978). Both disagree with Jeffrey Burton Russell, who avows that the idea of the early modern witch derived more from that of the medieval heretic than of the magician; *A History of Witchcraft: Sorcerers, Heretics, and Pagans* (New York: Thames and Hudson, 1995).

16. Robert Mandrou, *Magistrats et sorciers en France au XVIIe siècle: Une analyse de psychologie historique* (Paris: Plon, 1968), 137–52.

17. Midelfort, *History of Madness,* 67.

18. Prosperi, *Tribunali della coscienza,* 404–6.

19. Michel de Certeau, *The Possession at Loudun,* trans. Michael B. Smith (Chicago: University of Chicago Press, 1996). Other significant works on Loudun include Michel Carmona, *Les Diables de Loudun: Sorcellerie et politique sous Richelieu* (Paris: Fayard, 1988); Mandrou, *Magistrats et sorciers,* 197–261; and Aldous Huxley, *The Devils of Loudun* (New York: Carrol and Graf, 1986). For a narrative of the trial, see Robert Rapley, *A Case of Witchcraft: The Trial of Urbain Grandier* (Montreal: McGill-Queen's University Press, 1998). For a somewhat fictionalized account of a similar outbreak in an Ursuline convent a few years after the Loudun case, see Benoît Garnot, *Le diable au couvent: Les possédées d'Auxonne (1658–1663)* (Paris: Imago, 1995).

20. Giuliana Zanelli, *Streghe e società nell'Emilia e Romagna del Cinque-Seicento* (Ravenna: Longo A. Editore, 1992), 144–46. For an edition of fascinating documents concerning the possession, bewitchment, and exorcism of two nuns in the Spanish Netherlands, see Nicky Hallett, *Witchcraft, Exorcism and the Politics of Possession in a Seventeenth-Century Convent: "How Sister Ursula was once Bewitched and Sister Margaret Twice"* (Aldershot: Ashgate, 2007).

21. Kramer and Sprenger, *Malleus Maleficarum,* trans. and ed. Montague Summers, 97.

22. Jeffrey Burton Russell, *The Prince of Darkness: Radical Evil and the Power of Good in History* (Ithaca: Cornell University Press, 1988), 175–76.

23. Erik Midelfort, "The Devil and the German People: Reflections on the Popularity of Demon Possession in Sixteenth-Century Germany," in *Religion and Culture in the Renaissance and Reformation,* ed. Steven Ozment (Kirksville, MO: Sixteenth Century Journal Publishers, 1987), 109.

24. Klaits, *Servants of Satan,* 78, 113–19; Keith Thomas, *Religion and the Decline of Magic: Studies in Popular Beliefs in Sixteenth and Seventeenth Century England* (Oxford: Oxford University Press, 1971), 480–81.

25. Russell, *Prince of Darkness,* 176.

26. Caciola, *Discerning Spirits.*

27. Stephen Haliczer, *Between Exaltation and Infamy: Female Mystics in the Golden Age of Spain* (Oxford: Oxford University Press, 2002).

28. Moshe Sluhovsky, "The Devil in the Convent," *American Historical Review* 107 (2002): 1379–411; Sluhovsky, *Believe Not Every Spirit,* esp. 233–64.

29. Inquisitors concluded that the nuns were not possessed but were just suffering from illusions; Carlos Puyol Buil, *Inquisición y política en el reinado de Felipe IV: Los Procesos de Jerónimo de Villanueva y las monjas de San Plácido 1628–1660* (Madrid: Consejo Superior de Investigaciones Científicas, 1993), 118–64.

30. Writing in 1651, Candido Brognolo stressed the penchant of devout female religious almost to seek possession; *Manuale Exorcistarum ac Parochorum, hoc est Tractatus de curatione, ac Protectione Divina* (Venice: Nicolò Pezzana, 1720), 286. On Brognolo (Brugnoli, Brognolus), see *Dizionario biografico degli Italiani* (Rome: Istituto della Enciclopedia Italiana, 1972), s.v. "Brugnoli, Candido" by Antonio Rotondò; Anne Jacobson Schutte, *Aspiring Saints: Pretense of Holiness, Inquisition, and Gender in the Republic of Venice, 1618–1750* (Baltimore: Johns Hopkins University Press, 2001), 116–20.

31. Romano Canosa, "I diavoli di Carpi," in *Storia dell'Inquisizione in Italia dalla metà del cinquecento alla fine del settecento,* vol. 1, *Modena* (Rome: Sapere 2000, 1986), 68–86.

32. In a review of the book in which the Lavenia piece appeared, Anne Jacobson Schutte, a noted expert on female religious and the Roman Inquisition, wrote, "Vincenzo Lavenia's subject, an epidemic of diabolic possession in the convent of Santa Chiara in Carpi, had considerable potential. It might have yielded a fascinating microhistorical treatment comparable to that oft-told contemporaneous tale, 'the devils of Loudun.' In this inexpert narrator's hands, 'I diavoli di Carpi e il Sant'Uffizio (1636–1639)' is an excruciatingly detailed, tedious account of political infighting. This reader had great difficulty keeping the numerous male players straight, inferring the motives (let alone the experiences) of Lavenia's shadowy nun-protagonists, and remaining awake"; *Sixteenth Century Journal* 30 (2000): 55.

33. Vincenzo Lavenia, "I Diavoli di Carpi e il Sant'Uffizio (1636–1639)," in *Eretici, esuli e indemoniati nell'età moderna,* ed. Mario Rosa (Florence: Leo S. Olschki, 1998), 77–139. See also good brief summaries by Grazia Biondi, "Principesse, demoni ed esorcisti in convento: Il monastero di Santa Chiara di Carpi (1636–1639)," in *Il Principato di Carpi in epoca estense: Istituzioni, economia, società e cultura,* ed. Gilberto Zacchè (Rome: Bulzoni, 2002), 273–83; and by Maria Teresa Fattori, "Istituzioni, pastorale, giurisdizione (1530–1779)," in *La Storia della Chiesa di Carpi,* vol. 1, *Profilo cronologico,* ed. Andrea Beltrami and Anna Maria Ori (Carpi: Fondazione Cassa di Risparmio di Carpi, 2006), 76–83. A brief description of these demonic woes also appears in Anna Maria Ori, "Una principessa in monastero," in *Clarisse in Carpi,* ed. Zarri, 1:280–83.

34. Sluhovsky, "Devil in Convent," 1380–81. In a citation in his book, Sluhovsky indicates that he did consult the manuscript of this case in Modena's Archivio di Stato and read at least the first ten of its more than five hundred folios; *Believe Not Every Spirit,* 246n33.

35. On the Holy Office's struggles to secure jurisdiction over witchcraft cases, see Vincenzo Lavenia, "'Anticamente di misto foro': Inquisizione, stati e delitti di stregoneria nella prima età moderna," in *Inquisizioni: Percorsi di ricerca,* ed. Giovanna Paolin (Trieste: Università di Trieste, 2001), 35–80.

36. Levack, *Witch-Hunt,* 71–74; Kieckhefer, *Magic in the Middle Ages,* 199.

37. The best one-volume survey of the history of the Inquisition in its various forms is Edward Peters, *Inquisition* (New York: Free Press, 1988). See also Francisco Bethencourt, *L'Inquisition à l'époque moderne: Espagne, Italie, Portugal XVe–XIXe siècle* (Paris: Fayard, 1995). For good introductions to the history of the Spanish Inquisition, see

Henry Kamen, *The Spanish Inquisition: A Historical Revision* (New Haven: Yale University Press, 1997); *Inquisición española: Poder politíco y control social,* ed. Bartolomé Bennassar (Barcelona: Editorial Crítica, 1981); Helen Rawlings, *The Spanish Inquisition* (Oxford: Blackwell, 2006); John Edwards, *The Spanish Inquisition* (Stroud: Tempus, 1999). Still quite valuable is Henry Charles Lea's magisterial *History of the Inquisition of Spain,* 4 vols. (London: Macmillan, 1906–7).

38. Adriano Prosperi, "L'Inquisizione in Italia," in *Clero e società nell'Italia moderna,* ed. Rosa, 281.

39. Tedeschi, "Preliminary Observations" and "The Organization and Procedures of the Roman Inquisition," both in *Prosecution of Heresy,* 6, 128; *New Catholic Encyclopedia,* 2003 ed., s.v. "Inquisition"; Peters, *Inquisition,* 108–9. Local inquisitions also investigated and prosecuted cases involving forbidden publications, and a separate congregation in Rome (that of the Index) had jurisdiction over prohibited books.

40. On the Roman Inquisition see esp. the various essays in Tedeschi, *Prosecution of Heresy;* Prosperi, *Tribunali della coscienza;* Prosperi, "Inquisizione in Italia," in *Clero e società nell'Italia moderna,* ed. Rosa, 275–320; Prosperi, "Per la storia dell'Inquisizione romana," in *L'Inquisizione Romana in Italia nell'età moderna: Archivi, problemi di metodo e nuove ricerche: Atti del seminario internazionale, Trieste, 18–20 maggio 1988* (Rome: Ministero per i beni culturali e ambientali; Ufficio centrale per i beni archivistici, 1991), 27–64.

41. Prosperi, *Tribunali della coscienza,* xiv. On the organization and centralization of the various inquisitions, see Bethencourt, *Inquisition à l'époque moderne,* 35–83.

42. Umberto Locati, *Opus quod Iudiciale Inquisitorum* (Rome: apud Haeredes Antonii Bladii, 1568), 197, 200; Prosperi, *Tribunali della coscienza,* 234n30.

43. E. William Monter and John Tedeschi, "Toward a Statistical Profile of the Italian Inquisitions, Sixteenth to Eighteenth Centuries," in *The Inquisition in Early Modern Europe: Studies on Sources and Methods,* ed. Gustav Henningsen and John Tedeschi (DeKalb: Northern Illinois University Press, 1986), 130–57; John Tedeschi, "Inquisitorial Law and the Witch," in *Early Modern European Witchcraft: Centres and Peripheries,* Bengt Ankarloo and Gustav Henningsen (Oxford: Clarendon Press, 1990), 85; Peters, *Inquisition,* 112; Romeo, *Inquisitori,* 176–77, 201–46; Guido Ruggiero, "Introduction: Carne Vale and Carnival," in *Binding Passions: Tales of Magic, Marriage, and Power at the End of the Renaissance* (Oxford: Oxford University Press, 1993), 9; Schutte, *Aspiring Saints,* 28–29; E. William Monter, *Ritual, Myth and Magic in Early Modern Europe* (Athens: Ohio University Press, 1983), 64–66. For the Inquisition of Modena see Maria Carolina Capucci, "Una società di delatori? Appunti da processi modenesi del Santo Uffizio (1590–1630)," in *Il piacere del testo: Saggi e studi per Albano Biondi,* ed. Adriano Prosperi (Rome: Bulzoni, 2001), esp. 49–52.

44. Maria Pia Fantini, "Per un inventario analitico dell'Archivio modenese del Sant'Uffizio (1568–1602)," in *Stregoneria e streghe nell'Europa moderna: Convegno internazionale di studi (Pisa, 24–26 marzo 1994),* ed. Giovanna Bosco and Patrizia Castelli (Rome: Ministero per i beni culturali e ambientali; and Pisa: Biblioteca universitaria di Pisa, 1996), 447–71.

45. See, for example, Anne Jacobson Schutte, "La storia al femminile nelle fonti inquisitoriali veneziane: Una fattuchiera, una finta santa e numerose putte pericolanti," in *L'Inquisizione romana: Metodologia delle fonti e storia istituzionale: Atti del Seminario internazionale, Montereale Valcellini, 23 e 24 settembre 1999,* ed. Andrea Del Col and Giovanna Paolin (Trieste: Università di Trieste; and Montereale Valcellina:

Circolo Culturale Menocchio, 2000), 91–102. For an examination of Counter-Reformation attitudes toward female healers, see Marilena Lombardi, "Gli strumenti del mestiere," in *Gostanza, la strega di San Miniato: Processo a una guaritrice nella Toscana medicea,* ed. Franco Cardini (Rome and Bari: Laterza, 1989), 73–85.

46. Adriano Prosperi, "Riforma Cattolica, Controriforma, disciplinamento sociale," in *Storia dell'Italia Religiosa,* ed. Gabriele De Rosa, Tullio Gregory, and André Vauchez, vol. 2, *L'età moderna,* ed. De Rosa and Gregory (Rome and Bari: Laterza, 1994), 3–48.

47. Albano Biondi, "Streghe ed eretici nei domini estensi all'epoca dell'Ariosto," in *Il Rinascimento nelle corti padane: Società e cultura,* ed. Paolo Rossi (Bari: De Donato, 1977), 170.

48. See Matteo Duni, *Tra religione e magia: Storia del prete modenese Guiglielmo Campana (1460?–1541)* (Florence: Leo S. Olschki, 1999).

49. Prosperi, *Tribunali della coscienza,* 36–37.

50. On Protestantism in Modena see Massimo Firpo, *Riforma protestante ed eresia nell'Italia del Cinquecento* (Rome and Bari: Laterza, 1993), 53–69; Susanna Peyronel Rambaldi, *Speranze e crisi nel Cinquecento modenese: Tensioni religiose e vita cittadina ai tempi di Giovanni Morone* (Milan: Franco Angeli, 1979). On Bishop Egidio Foscarari's attempts of the mid-sixteenth century to reinvigorate Modenese Catholicism at the expense of Protestantism, see Michelle M. Fontaine, "Making Heresy Marginal in Modena," in *Heresy, Culture, and Religion in Early Modern Italy: Contexts and Contestations,* ed. Ronald K. Delph, Michelle M. Fontaine, and John Jeffries Martin (Kirksville, MO: Truman State University Press, 2006), 37–51.

51. In 1608 the inquisitor of Modena, Fra Michelangelo Lerri, published some important instructions for vicars on how to pursue cases of the Holy Office. This was largely reproduced in Eliseo Masini's very influential inquisitorial manual, the *Sacro Arsenale,* published in 1621; Prosperi, *Tribunali della coscienza,* 326–27. See also Susanna Peyronel Rambaldi, "Podestà e inquisitori nella montagna modenese: Riorganizzazione inquisitoriale e resistenze locali (1570–1590)," in *Inquisizione Romana in Italia nell'età moderna,* 203–31.

52. Prosperi, *Tribunali della coscienza,* 184; Carla Righi, "L'Inquisizione ecclesiastica a Modena nel '700," in *Formazione e controllo dell'opinione pubblica a Modena nel '700,* ed. Albano Biondi (Modena: Mucchi, 1986), 55.

53. Gianfranco Guaitoli, "L'Inquisizione a Carpi: Apparato inquisitorio, luoghi, personaggi, processi e sentenze (secoli XIV–XVI)," in *Principato di Carpi,* ed. Zacchè, 285–97.

54. Cases involving Jews were relatively numerous in Modena. The *Causae hebreorum* numbered seven volumes for the years 1599–1670, reflecting the significant number of Jews residing in the city and duchy. Confined to a ghetto in the city of Modena beginning in 1638, Jews could be convoked before the Holy Office for, among other things, possessing (usually through their pawnshops) Christian holy objects, intermarrying with Christians, employing Christians in their pawnshops, and having sexual relations or merely having too much familiarity with Christians. See Albano Biondi, "Gli ebrei e l'Inquisizione negli stati Estensi," in *L'Inquisizione e gli ebrei in Italia,* ed. Michele Luzzati (Rome and Bari: Laterza, 1994), 265–85; and in the same volume, Mauro Perani, "Confisca e censura di libri ebraici a Modena fra cinque e seicento," 287–320.

55. Giuseppe Trenti, *I processi del tribunale dell'Inquisizione di Modena: Inventario generale analitico 1489-1874* (Modena: Aedes Muratoriana, 2003). On the Inquisition of Modena's sources, see also Albano Biondi, "Lunga durata e microarticolazione nel territorio di un Ufficio dell'Inquisizione: Il 'Sacro Tribunale' a Modena (1292-1785)," *Annali dell'Istituto storico italo-germanico in Trento* 7 (1982): 73-90; Biondi, "La 'Nuova Inquisizione' a Modena: Tre inquisitori (1589-1609)," in *Città italiane del'500: Tra Riforma e Controriforma* (Lucca: M. Pacini Fazzi, 1988), 61-76.

56. John Tedeschi, "The Dispersed Archives of the Roman Inquisition," in *Inquisition in Early Modern Europe,* ed. Henningsen and Tedeschi, 13-32; Tedeschi, "Osservazioni preliminari sull'apertura dell'Archivio," in *L'apertura degli archivi del Sant'Uffizio romano* (Rome: Accademia nazionale dei Lincei, 1998), 131-39.

57. On this correspondence, see Grazia Biondi, "Le lettere della Sacra Congregazione romana del Santo Ufficio all'Inquisizione di Modena: Note in margine a un regesto," *Schifanoia* 4 (1987): 93-108. See also Tedeschi, "Inquisitorial Sources and Their Uses," in *Prosecuting Heresy,* 57-58.

58. AMSCC, Memoriale secondo; Ori, "Vita della communità," in *Clarisse in Carpi,* ed. Zarri, 1:213-42.

59. For an excellent discussion of the pluses and minuses of the registers of the Inquisition as historical sources, see Schutte, *Aspiring Saints,* 22-25.

60. Carlo Ginzburg, *The Night Battles: Witchcraft and Agrarian Cults in the Sixteenth and Seventeenth Centuries,* trans. John Tedeschi and Anne Tedeschi (Baltimore: Johns Hopkins University Press, 1983); Ginzburg, *The Cheese and the Worms: The Cosmos of a Sixteenth-Century Miller,* trans. John Tedeschi and Anne Tedeschi (Baltimore: Johns Hopkins University Press, 1980). In a revisionist work, Franco Nardon finds that the *benandanti* survived well into the eighteenth century and that their night battles were only tangential to their principal role as healers; *Benandanti e inquisitori nel Friuli del Seicento,* foreword by Andrea Del Col (Trieste: Edizioni Università di Trieste, 1999).

61. Carlo Ginzburg, "Les origines du sabbat," in *Le sabbat des sorciers en Europe (XVe-XVIIIe siècles),* ed. Nicole Jacques-Chaquin and Maxime Préaud (Grenoble: Jérôme Millon, 1993), 18-19.

62. Carlo Ginzburg, "L'inquisitore come antropologo," in *Studi in onore di Armando Saitta dei suoi allievi pisani,* ed. Regina Pozzi and Adriano Prosperi (Pisa: Giardini, 1989), 23-33.

63. Andrea Del Col, "Alcune osservazioni sui processi inquisitoriali come fonti storiche," *Metodi e ricerche* 13 (1994): 85-105; Del Col, "I criteri dello storico nell'uso delle fonti inquisitoriali moderne," in *Inquisizione romana,* ed. Del Col and Paolin, 51-72; Del Col, *L'Inquisizione nel patriarcato e diocesi di Aquileia, 1557-1559* (Trieste: Edizioni Università di Trieste; and Montereale Valcellina: Centro Studi Storici Menocchio, 1998), clxxvii-clxxviii, ccxviii-ccxxii; Del Col, "I processi dell'Inquisizione come fonte: Considerazioni diplomatiche e storiche," *Annuario dell'Istituto storico italiano per l'età moderna e contemporanea* 35-36 (1983-1984): 33-49.

64. Tedeschi, "Inquisitorial Sources" and "Organization and Procedures," both in *Prosecuting Heresy,* 47-88, 127-203; Tedeschi, "Inquisitorial Law and Witch," in *Early Modern European Witchcraft,* ed. Ankarloo and Henningsen, 83-118; Kamen, *Spanish Inquisition,* 191.

65. Zarri, introduction to *Clarisse in Carpi,* ed. Zarri, 1:34.

66. Lyndal Roper, introduction to *Oedipus and the Devil: Witchcraft, Sexuality and Religion in Early Modern Europe* (London: Routledge, 1994), 19–20. Carlo Ginzburg makes a similar argument, based on evidence from a Modenese witchcraft case from the early sixteenth century; Carlo Ginzburg, "Witchcraft and Popular Piety: Notes on a Modenese Trial of 1519," in Ginzburg, *Clues, Myths, and the Historical Method*, trans. John Tedeschi and Anne C. Tedeschi (Baltimore: Johns Hopkins University Press, 1989), 1–16.

67. Jonathan B. Durrant, *Witchcraft, Gender and Society in Early Modern Germany* (Leiden: Brill, 2007).

68. See E. William Monter, *Frontiers of Heresy: The Spanish Inquisition from the Basque Lands to Sicily* (Cambridge: Cambridge University Press, 1990), 260–61; Romeo, *Inquisitori*, 3–24; *The Spanish Inquisition, 1478–1614: An Anthology of Sources*, ed. Lu Ann Homza (Indianapolis: Hackett, 2006), 159–60.

69. In an important inquisitors' manual, people who invoked the devil were labeled heretics rather than magicians, witches, or diviners; Nicolau Eymerich and Francisco Peña, *Il manuale dell'Inquisitore*, trans. and ed. Louis Sala-Molins (Rome: Fanucci, 2000), 80. See Ruth Martin, *Witchcraft and the Inquisition in Venice 1550–1650* (Oxford: Basil Blackwell, 1989); Francisco Bethencourt, *O imaginário da magia: Feiticeiras, adivinhos e curandeiros em Portugal no século XVI*, rev. ed. (São Paulo: Companhia das Letras, 2004), 244–45. In the early seventeenth century, the Spanish Inquisition undertook an intense series of hunts in the Basque region that involved almost two thousand alleged witches, but these hunts resulted ultimately in the executions of only six people; Gustav Henningsen, *The Witches' Advocate: Basque Witchcraft and the Spanish Inquisition, 1609–1614* (Reno: University of Nevada Press, 1980). These cases, however, helped incite a witch scare in Catalonia in 1610–20, over which secular courts claimed and exercised jurisdiction, resulting in the executions of nearly a hundred purported witches; Monter, *Frontiers of Heresy*, 255–75.

70. On changing trends in scholarship on witchcraft, see Robin Briggs, "'Many Reasons Why': Witchcraft and the Problem of Multiple Explanations," in *Witchcraft in Early Modern Europe: Studies in Culture and Belief*, ed. Jonathan Barry, Marianne Hester, and Gareth Roberts (Cambridge: Cambridge University Press, 1996), 49–63; Bengt Ankarloo and Stuart Clark, introduction to *Witchcraft and Magic in Europe: Period of Witch Trials*, ed. Ankarloo and Clark, vii–xiv; and Stuart Clark, introduction to *Languages of Witchcraft: Narrative, Ideology and Meaning in Early Modern Culture*, ed. Stuart Clark (New York: St. Martin's Press, 2001), 1–18; *Witchcraft in Early Modern Europe*, ed. Merry E. Wiesner (New York: Houghton Mifflin, 2007); *The Witchcraft Reader*, ed. Darren Oldridge (London: Routledge, 2002).

71. Respectively, Montague Summers, *The History of Witchcraft and Demonology* (New York: Alfred A. Knopf, 1926); Russell, *History of Witchcraft;* Margaret Murray, *The Witch-Cult in Western Europe* (Oxford: Clarendon Press, 1962); Jules Michelet, *Satanism and Witchcraft: A Study in Medieval Superstition*, trans. A. R. Allinson (New York: Citadel Press, 1939).

72. Most obviously, Hugh R. Trevor-Roper, "The European Witch-Craze of the Sixteenth and Seventeenth Centuries," in *The European Witch-Craze of the Sixteenth and Seventeenth Centuries and Other Essays* (New York: Harper and Row, 1969), 90–192.

73. See, for example, Jean Delumeau, *Catholicism between Luther and Voltaire: A New View of the Counter-Reformation*, trans. Jeremy Moiser (London: Burns and Oates;

and Philadelphia: Westminster Press, 1977), esp. 161-74. See also various works by Robert Muchembled: *Popular Culture and Elite Culture in France 1400-1750,* trans. Lydia Cochrane (Baton Rouge: Louisiana State University Press, 1985), 235-78; *Sorcières, justice et société aux XVIe et XVIIe siècles* (Paris: Imago, 1987); and *Roi et sorcière.*

74. See, for example, Alan Macfarlane, *Witchcraft in Tudor and Stuart England: A Regional and Comparative Study* (London: Routledge and Kegan Paul, 1970), 139, 205, 246-49; Wolfgang Behringer, *Witchcraft Persecutions in Bavaria: Popular Magic, Religious Zealotry and Reason of State in Early Modern Europe,* trans. J. C. Grayson and David Lederer (Cambridge: Cambridge UniversityPress, 1997); Luciano Parinetto, *Streghe e politica: Dal Rinascimento italiano a Montaigne, da Bodin a Naudé* (Milan: Istituto Propaganda Libraria, 1983).

75. Kramer and Sprenger, *Malleus Maleficarum,* trans. and ed. Montague Summers, 41-48. See also Brian P. Levack, "La strega," trans. Giovanna Antongini, in *L'uomo barocco,* ed. Rosario Villari (Rome and Bari: Laterza, 1991), 280.

76. Friedrich von Langenfeld Spee, *Cautio Criminalis, or a Book on Witch Trials,* trans. Marcus Hellyer (Charlottesville: University of Virginia Press, 2003), 24.

77. *Witches, Devils, and Doctors in the Renaissance: Johann Weyer, "De praestigiis daemonum,"* ed. George Mora and Benjamin Kohl (Binghamton: Medieval and Renaissance Texts and Studies, 1991), 181-83, 189, 498-99; Clark, *Thinking with Demons,* 106-33, 198-203.

78. Anne Llewellyn Barstow, *Witchcraze: A New History of the European Witch Hunts* (San Francisco: Pandora, 1994); Barstow, "On Studying Witchcraft as Women's History: A Historiography of the European Witch Persecutions," in *New Perspectives on Witchcraft,* ed. Levack, vol. 4, *Gender and Witchcraft,* 1-13; Elspeth Whitney, "The Witch 'She'/the Historian 'He': Gender and the Historiography of the Europeans," in ibid., 15-39.

79. Marianne Hester, "Patriarchal Reconstruction and Witch Hunting," in *Witchcraft in Europe,* ed. Barry, Hester, and Roberts, 288-306. Employing a "revolutionary feminist approach," Hester develops these ideas fully in *Lewd Women and Wicked Witches: A Study of the Dynamics of Male Domination* (London: Routledge, 1992). For criticism of this book, see the review by Ralph A. Houlbrooke in *Reviewing Sociology* 9, no. 2 (1996) at http://www.rdg.ac.uk/RevSoc/archive/volume9/number2/9-2i.htm. Carol F. Karlsen argues that women most likely to be accused of witchcraft in New England were those who held property and had no male heirs; such women supposedly hindered the orderly transmission of property from one generation of males to the next; *The Devil in the Shape of a Woman: Witchcraft in Colonial New England* (New York: W. W. Norton, 1987). This explanation cannot readily be applied to European hunts since female witches were overwhelmingly poor; Robin Briggs, "Women as Victims? Witches, Judges, and the Community," *French History* 5 (1991): 441. On female accusers and witnesses against alleged witches, see also Clive Holmes, "Women: Witnesses and Witches," *Past and Present* 140 (1993): 45-78; Christina Larner, *Witchcraft and Religion: The Politics of Popular Belief* (New York: Blackwell, 1984), 62, 86.

80. Bengt Ankarloo, "Witch Trials in Northern Europe," in *Witchcraft in Early Modern Europe: Period of Witch Trials,* ed. Ankarloo and Clark, 71, 74-75, 90-93; Lara Apps and Andrew Gow, *Male Witches in Early Modern Europe* (Manchester: Manchester University Press, 2003); Antero Heikkinen and Timo Kervinen, "Finland: The

Male Domination," in *Early Modern European Witchcraft*, ed. Ankarloo and Henningsen, 319–38; William Monter, "Toads and Eucharists: The Male Witches of Normandy," *French Historical Studies* 20 (1997): 563–95. See also Eva Labouvie, "Men in Witchcraft Trials: Towards a Social Anthropology of 'Male' Understandings of Magic and Witchcraft," in *Gender in Early Modern German History*, ed. Ulinka Rublack (Cambridge: Cambridge University Press, 2002), 49–68.

81. Brian P. Levack, introduction to *New Perspectives on Witchcraft*, ed. Levack, vol. 4, *Gender and Witchcraft*, vii.

82. For a case study from early modern England, see Malcolm Gaskill, "Witchcraft and Power in Early Modern England: The Case of Margaret Moore," in *New Perspectives on Witchcraft*, ed. Levack, vol. 3, *Witchcraft in British Isles*, 301–23.

83. Monter, *Witchcraft in France and Switzerland*, 119–24.

84. James L. Brain, "An Anthropological Perspective on the Witchcraze," in *The Politics of Gender in Early Modern Europe*, ed. Jean R. Brink, Allison P. Coudert, and Maryanne C. Horowitz (Kirksville, MO: Sixteenth Century Journal Publishers 1989), 16–17.

85. Lyndal Roper asserts that some feminist historians have become too obsessed with the idea of gender as a social construct, that is, that the sexual differences between males and females are largely products of "cultural and linguistic practice." She now believes that differences between the sexes have their own "physiological and psychological reality" and is convinced that the outbreak of witch-hunting was not just an issue of asserting patriarchy or of misogyny run amok. Roper observes that the most common accusers in Augsburg were women who had just given birth, while those accused of witchcraft were generally poor postmenopausal women, who often served as lying-in maids for the new mothers. Roper believes that the phases of the lives of women, determined more by physiology (birth and menopause) than culture, played a key role in these trials; *Oedipus and the Devil*, esp. "Witchcraft and Fantasy in Early Modern Germany," 199–225. Roper again stresses the themes of motherhood, fertility, and birth in *Witch Craze: Terror and Fantasy in Baroque Germany* (New Haven: Yale University Press, 2004).

86. Robin Briggs, *Witches and Neighbors: The Social and Cultural Context of European Witchcraft* (New York: Penguin, 1996), 8, 260; William Monter, "Witch Trials in Continental Europe 1560–1660," in *Witchcraft and Magic in Europe: Period of Witch Trials*, ed. Ankarloo and Clark, 12–16; Richard M. Golden, "The Geography of Witch Hunts," in *New Perspectives on Witchcraft*, ed. Levack, vol. 2, *Witchcraft in Continental Europe*, 2–33. These figures are considerably lower than earlier estimates.

Chapter 1

1. Elizabeth Makowski, *Canon Law and Cloistered Women: "Periculoso" and Its Commentators, 1298-1545* (Washington, DC: Catholic University of America Press, 1997); Jane Tibbets Schulenburg, "Strict Active Enclosure and Its Effects on the Female Monastic Experience (ca. 500–1100)," in *Distant Echoes: Medieval Religious Women*, ed. John A. Nichols and Lilian T. Shank (Kalamazoo, MI: Cistercian Publications, 1984), 52–79.

2. *Canons and Decrees of the Council of Trent,* trans. H. J. Schroeder (St. Louis: B. Herder, 1941), Twentieth-fifth Session, chap. 5: 220–21. See also Barbara B. Diefendorf, *From Penitence to Charity: Pious Women and the Catholic Reformation in Paris* (Oxford: Oxford University Press, 2004), 145; Gabriella Zarri, "Monasteri femminili e città (secoli XV–XVIII)," in *La Chiesa e il potere politico dal Medioevo all'età contemporanea,* ed. Giorgio Chittolini and Giovanni Miccoli (Turin: Giulio Einaudi, 1986), 412–13.

3. Silvia Evangelisti, "'We do not have it, and we do not want it': Women, Power, and Convent Reform in Florence," *Sixteenth Century Journal* 34 (2003): 681. For a good examination of the third orders, see Gabriella Zarri, "The Third Status," in *Time, Space, and Women's Lives in Early Modern Europe,* ed. Anne Jacobson Schutte, Thomas Kuehn, and Silvana Seidel Menchi (Kirksville, MO: Truman State University Press, 2001), 181–99. Greater hostility and closer scrutiny of women's religious expression in the sixteenth and seventeenth centuries, compared with the previous two centuries, are themes in several essays in *Creative Women in Medieval and Early Modern Italy: A Religious and Artistic Renaissance,* ed. E. Ann Matter and John Coakley (Philadelphia: University of Pennsylvania Press, 1994). Interestingly, the Catholic Reformation apparently did not restrict the avenues of religious expression for French women. Lay confraternities offered a "semireligious" life and were among the most important vehicles for expressing female piety in seventeenth-century France. Groups such as the Daughters of Charity, whose members did not take formal vows, were very active in conducting charitable work, providing catechetical instruction, and ministering to the poor, sick, and orphaned. Diefendorf, *Penitence to Charity;* Elizabeth Rapley, *The Dévotes: Women and Church in Seventeenth-Century France* (Montreal: McGill-Queen's University Press, 1990); Susan E. Dinan, *Women and Poor Relief in Seventeenth-Century France: The Early History of the Daughters of Charity* (Aldershot: Ashgate, 2006).

4. Giovan Battista de Luca, *Il vescovo pratico, sopra le cose spettanti al buon governo delle chiese et all'offiti e degli altri prelati ecclesiastici* (Rome, 1675); cited in Francesca Medioli, "The Dimensions of the Cloister: Enclosure, Constraint, and Protection in Seventeenth-Century Italy," in *Time, Space, and Women's Lives,* ed. Schutte, Kuehn, and Menchi, 165.

5. Francesca Medioli maintains that the post-Tridentine Church was not as rigid on *clausura* as is often believed and that even in the mid-seventeenth century, physical *clausura* did not exist in all Italian nunneries; "La clausura delle monache nell'amministrazione della Congregazione romana sopra i regolari," in *Il monachesimo femminile in Italia dall'alto medioevo al secolo XVII, a confronto con l'oggi: Atti del VI Convegno del "Centro di studi farfensi": Santa Vittoria in Matenano 21–24 settembre 1995,* ed. Gabriella Zarri (San Pietro in Cariano: Il Segno dei Gabrielli, 1997), 264–66. See also Elizabeth A. Lehfeldt, "Discipline, Vocation, and Patronage: Spanish Religious Women in a Tridentine Microclimate," *Sixteenth Century Journal* 30 (1999): 1009–30.

6. Daniel Bornstein, introduction to Bartolomea Riccoboni, *Life and Death in a Venetian Convent: The Chronicle and Necrology of Corpus Domini, 1395–1436,* ed. Daniel Bornstein (Chicago: University of Chicago Press, 2000), 11; Craig Harline, *The Burdens of Sister Margaret: Inside a Seventeenth-Century Convent,* abridged ed. (New Haven: Yale University Press, 2000), 151, 153.

7. See Mariló Vigil, "Conformismo y rebeldía en los conventos femeninos de los siglos XVI y XVII," in *Religiosidad femenina: Expectativas y realidades (ss. VIII–XVII),*

ed. Angela Muñoz and María del Mar Graña (Madrid: Al-mudayna, 1991), 170. For a good overview of the historiography of early modern female monasticism in Italy, see Gianna Pomata and Gabriella Zarri's introduction to *I monasteri femminili come centri di cultura fra Rinascimento e Barocco: Atti del convegno storico internazionale, Bologna, 8-10 dicembre 2000,* ed. Gianna Pomata and Gabriella Zarri (Rome: Edizioni di Storia e Letteratura, 2005), ix–xliv.

8. For good examples of Italian women of the sixteenth and seventeenth centuries who sought a religious life in spite of parental resistance, see Cecilia Ferrazzi, *Autobiography of an Aspiring Saint,* trans. and ed. Anne Jacobson Schutte (Chicago: University of Chicago Press, 1996); and Anna Scattigno, "Maria Maddalena de' Pazzi: Tra esperienza e modello," in *Donna, disciplina, creanza cristiana dal XV al XVII secolo: Studi e testi a stampa,* ed. Gabriella Zarri (Rome: Edizioni di Storia e Letteratura, 1996), 85–101.

9. In 1661 Santa Chiara rejected an applicant, even though she enjoyed the support of Cardinal Rinaldo d'Este, in part because, at twenty-eight, she was deemed too old to learn the customs of religious life; Ori, "Vita della comunità," in *Clarisse in Carpi,* ed. Zarri, 1:221.

10. This is a central theme in Jutta Gisela Sperling, *Convents and the Body Politic in Late Renaissance Venice* (Chicago: University of Chicago Press, 1999).

11. Romolo Dodi, "Famiglie Pio a Carpi nei secoli XVI–XVIII," in *Principato di Carpi,* ed. Zacchè, 87–119; Alfonso Garuti and Dante Colli, *Il Monastero di Santa Chiara di Carpi* (Carpi: Il Portico, 1993), 56; Anna Maria Ori, "La famiglia Pio di Savoia e il monastero di Santa Chiara," in *Clarisse in Carpi,* ed. Zarri, 1:87–93.

12. In 1654 there were four supernumerary nuns, the minimum dowry for whom was 600 and 800 *scudi* for Carpi residents and foreigners, respectively, plus goods worth 300 *scudi;* Ori, "Vita della communità," in *Clarisse in Carpi,* ed. Zarri, 1:204–5.

13. AMSCC, Memoriale secondo, 49r. Ori, "Vita della communità," in *Clarisse in Carpi,* ed. Zarri, 1:199, 205, 220–21. Upon taking the veil, Amoldoni took the name of Clara Maria. As we shall see, she was one of the nuns who were believed demonically possessed.

14. Evangelisti, "'We do not have it,'" 679. Mary Laven finds that for Venetian noblewomen, a nun's dowry was perhaps only a twentieth of the value of a marriage dowry in the seventeenth century; *Virgins of Venice: Broken Vows and Cloistered Lives in the Renaissance Convent* (New York: Viking, 2003), 41.

15. Zarri, "Monasteri femminili e città," in *Chiesa e potere politico,* ed. Chittolini and Miccoli, 364–66, 420–21.

16. Ori estimates that male and female religious made up about 11 percent of Carpi's population in 1654. If Carpi's 3,587 residents were split evenly between the sexes, then the 156 nuns represented 8.7 percent of the female population; "Vita della communità," in *Clarisse in Carpi,* ed. Zarri, 1:198–99.

17. Dante E. Zanetti, *La demografia del patriziato Milanese nei secoli XVII, XVIII, XIX* (Pavia: Università di Pavia, 1972), 83; Evangelisti, "'We do not have it,'" 679.

18. Harline, *Burdens of Sister Margaret,* 15–16; Ori, "Vita della communità," in *Clarisse in Carpi,* ed. Zarri, 1:241.

19. *Canons and Decrees of Trent,* trans. Schroeder, Twenty-fifth Session, chap. 15: 226; Ori, "Vita della communità," in *Clarisse in Carpi,* ed. Zarri, 1:223. Only once in the sixteenth and seventeenth centuries did a novice not go on to take vows at

Santa Chiara. As if anticipating the convent's subsequent demonic woes, the confessor recorded in 1591 that a certain Suor Angelica of Modena was returned home because she was possessed (*spiritata*); ibid., 1:224.

20. AMSCC, Memoriale secondo, 53r, 69r, 70v; Ori, "Vita della communità," in *Clarisse in Carpi,* ed. Zarri, 1:204, 240–41.

21. Zarri, "Monasteri femminili e città," in *Chiesa e potere politico,* ed. Chittolini and Miccoli, 420–23; Zarri, introduction to *Clarisse in Carpi,* ed. Zarri, 1:35. In France the social gap between choir nuns and lay sisters must have been greater than in Italy as lay sisters ordinarily joined communities without dowries; Elizabeth Rapley, *A Social History of the Cloister: Daily Life in the Teaching Monasteries of the Old Regime* (Montreal: McGill-Queen's University Press, 2001), 182–97. In 1632 Orsina Cipolla was admitted as a *conversa* with a dowry of 150 *scudi,* a fourth of that for a choir nun from Carpi, and took vows a year later, in January 1633; AMSCC, Memoriale secondo, 53r, 54r, 70v.

22. *Canons and Decrees of Trent,* trans. Schroeder, Twenty-fifth Session, chap. 15: 226, chap. 18: 229.

23. Harline, *Burdens of Sister Margaret,* 17. See also Gabriella Zarri, "Gender, Religious Institutions and Social Discipline: The Reform of Regulars," in *Gender and Society in Renaissance Italy,* ed. Judith C. Brown and Robert C. Davis (London: Longman, 1998), 193–212.

24. Arcangela Tarabotti, *L'"Inferno monacale" di Arcangela Tarabotti,* ed. Francesca Medioli (Turin: Rosenberg and Sellier, 1990). On forced monachization see Romano Canosa, *Il velo e il cappuccio: Monacazioni forzate e sessualità nei conventi femminili in Italia tra Quattrocento e Settecento* (Rome: Sapere 2000, 1991), 147–61; Francesca Medioli, "Monacazioni forzate: Donne ribelli al proprio destino," *Clio* 30 (1994): 431–54; Enrico Cattaneo, "Le monacazioni forzate fra Cinque e Seicento," in *Vita e processo di suor Virginia Maria de Leyva, monaca di Monza,* ed. Giuseppe Farinelli and Ermanno Paccagnini (Milan: Garzanti, 1989), 145–95.

25. Rudolph M. Bell, *Holy Anorexia* (Chicago: University of Chicago Press, 1985), 54–56; Zanelli, *Streghe e società,* 142; Laven, *Virgins of Venice,* 53–66.

26. Elizabeth A. Lehfeldt, *Religious Women in Golden Age Spain: The Permeable Cloister* (Aldershot: Ashgate, 2005).

27. Gabriella Zarri, introduction to *Monachesimo femminile in Italia,* ed. Zarri, xi. See also her many other publications on the history of female monasticism and her synthetic work on women's history, *La memoria di lei: Storia delle donne, storia di genere* (Turin: Società Editrice Internazionale, 1996). In her very broad, provocative study, Jo Ann Kay McNamara depicts nuns as for centuries battling with spiritual evils and struggling with a male ecclesiastical hierarchy that sought strict separation of female from male religious; *Sisters in Arms: Catholic Nuns through Two Millennia* (Cambridge: Harvard University Press, 1996).

28. AMSCC, Memoriale secondo, 20v.

29. AMSCC, Memoriale secondo, 22v–23r, 36r. ASM, Casa e Stato, b. 358, fasc. 31/1984, undated document. See also Ori, "Principessa in monastero," in *Clarisse in Carpi,* ed. Zarri, 1:260. In a letter to her father, it is clear that the young Angela Caterina would have been happy to wait until she was actually sixteen to take vows: "ho sentito gusto di udire la licenza che Sua Santità mi concede per far la professione se ben non me ne servirò che potrò così aspettare il tempo fornisca li sedici anni

quando però VA non mi comandi in contrario"; ASM, Casa e Stato, b. 200, letter from Angela Caterina d'Este to Cesare d'Este, 21 February 1611.

30. Confessors to nuns were exhorted, "Procurerà di levar lor parenti, che non si glorino della loro nobiltà, grandezza, e ricchezze, ma che nè anche s'attristino per le cose a queste contrarie"; *Instruttione per li confessori di monache. Publicata di commissione dell'Illustriss. e Reverendiss. Sign. Card. Ludovisi Arcivescovo di Bologna* (Bologna: Vittorio Benacci, 1627), 16.

31. Ori, "Principessa in monastero," in *Clarisse in Carpi*, ed. Zarri, 1:266.

32. ASM, Casa e Stato, b. 200, letter from Angela Caterina d'Este to Cesare d'Este, 20 March 1620.

33. ASM, Casa e Stato, b. 358; this document is undated, but it almost surely was written at the time she took vows. In 1563 representatives at Trent decreed, "Private ownership is absolutely forbidden to regulars. To no regular, therefore, whether man or woman, shall it be lawful to possess or to hold as his own or even in the name of the convent any movable or immovable property, of whatever nature it may be or in whatever manner acquired; but the same shall be handed over immediately to the superior and be incorporated in the convent"; *Canons and Decrees of Trent,* trans. Schroeder, Twenty-fifth Session, chap. 2: 218. Angela Caterina complained in a letter that the three nun-servants were insufficient, in part because they were not very strong physically. She suggested that she be sent a sturdy peasant lay sister; ASM, Casa e Stato, b. 200, letter from Angela Caterina d'Este to Cesare d'Este, n.d. July 1615.

34. ASM, Mappario Estense, Fabbriche, 17 and 18; *Le Clarisse in Carpi: Cinque secoli di storia (XVI–XX),* vol. 2, *Fonti,* ed. Anna Maria Ori (Reggio Emilia: Diabasis, 2003), 163–67. Floor plans reveal that the princess's apartments took up approximately 1,180 square meters (12,700 sq ft), compared to about 5,500 square meters (59,200 sq ft) for the rest of the convent, not counting courtyards. The measurements were originally in *piedi ferraresi* (1 *piede ferrarese* = 40.4 cm). See also Garuti and Colli, *Monastero di Santa Chiara,* 55; Alfonso Garuti, "Lo sviluppo architettonico e le vicende artistiche del monastero," in *Clarisse di Carpi,* ed. Zarri, 1:120–21. These are the only extant floor plans of Santa Chiara for the seventeenth century.

35. AMSCC, Memoriale secondo, 41r–42v. The description was written by Angelo Lazzarino, the princess's confessor and big supporter. Archivio Storico di Carpi, Archivio Guaitoli, b. 9, fasc. 6, I Memoriale, 12–13. Documents concerning her first election are reproduced in Ori, "Principessa in monastero," in *Clarisse in Carpi,* ed. Zarri, 1:287–90. The Tridentine guidelines declared that abbesses should be at least forty and must have "lived commendably during the eight years after having made her profession." If no member of the convent met these qualifications—which almost surely was not the case at Santa Chiara—then a sister of another community of the same order could be appointed. If, however, "the superior who presides over the election [of abbess] should judge this inconvenient, with the consent of the bishop or other superior one of those in the same monastery who is beyond her thirtieth year and has lived commendably at least five years since her profession may be chosen"; *Canons and Decrees of Trent,* trans. Schroeder, Twenty-fifth Session, chap. 7: 222. At the time of her first election, Angela Caterina did not meet even this minimum age requirement.

36. AMSCC, Memoriale secondo, 43r–v.

37. Roberto Rusconi, "Gli Ordini religiosi maschili dalla Controriforma alle soppressioni settecentesche: Cultura, predicazione, missioni," in *Clero e società nell'Italia*

moderna, ed. Rosa, 211; Medioli, "Clausura delle monache," in *Monachesimo femminile in Italia,* ed. Zarri 262–63; *Dictionnaire de Théologie Catholique* (Paris: Letouzay et Ane, 1899–1950), s.v. "congrégations romaines."

38. Archivio Segreto Vaticano, Congregazione dei Vescovi e dei Regolari, Registra Regularium, b. 37: 24r, 28 May 1627; Lavenia, "Diavoli di Carpi," 81n24; AMSCC, Memoriale secondo, 46v–47r.

39. AMSCC, Memoriale secondo, 46v–47r.

40. Ibid., 47v.

41. Anna Coccapani was elected abbess in June 1630; ibid., 50v, 54r, 56r, 58r–v; Archivio Storico di Carpi, Archivio Guaitoli, b. 9, fasc. 6, I Memoriale,14, 17, 24 and a loose folio found between folios 32 and 33.

42. Ori, "Vita della communità," in *Clarisse in Carpi,* ed. Zarri, 1:232. On the powers of the office of abbess, see Maria Teresa Guerra Medici, "Sulla giurisdizione temporale e spirituale della abbadessa," in *Monachesimo femminile in Italia,* ed. Zarri, 75–86. The strong influence of nuns' families in the affairs of convents is a theme that is repeated throughout Laven, *Virgins of Venice.* For similar findings for the pre-Tridentine era, see Zarri, "Monasteri femminili e città," in *Chiesa e potere politico,* ed. Chittolini and Miccoli, 386–98.

43. AMSCC, Memoriale secondo, 45r.

44. Ibid., 45r–v; Archivio Storico di Carpi, Archivio Guaitoli, b. 9, fasc. 6, I Memoriale, 14–15; Garuti and Colli, *Monastero di Santa Chiara,* 55; Garuti, "Sviluppo architettonico," in *Clarisse di Carpi,* ed. Zarri, 1:120–21; Lavenia, "Diavoli di Carpi," 81n22; Alessandro Giuseppe Spinelli, *Notizie spettanti alla storia della musica in Carpi,* vol. 5 of *Memorie storiche e documenti sulla città e sull'antico principato di Carpi* (Carpi: Rossi, 1900), 45, 47; ASM, Soppressioni Napoleoniche, Regolari, Carpi, Santa Chiara, b. 2112, Rogiti dal 1601 al 1699, "Revd. Monialium Sanctae Clarae Carpi. Creditum scutorii 300 cum D. Ludivico Barzellio vigore depositi."

45. See Gabriella Zarri, "Le istituzioni dell'educazione femminile," in *Recinti: Donne, clausura e matrimonio nella prima età moderna* (Bologna: Il Mulino, 2000), 156–78.

46. On Alfonso III see Ferruccio Bravi, *Il principe frate: Alfonso III d'Este, Padre Giovan Battista da Modena* (Bolzano: Centro di documentazione storica per l'Alto Adige, 1972).

47. AMSCC, Memoriale secondo, 48v; Archivio Storico di Carpi, Archivio Guaitoli, b. 9, fasc. 6, I Memoriale, 19; Lavenia, "Diavoli di Carpi," 86n49.

48. AMSCC, Memoriale secondo, 48v; Archivio Storico di Carpi, Archivio Guaitoli, b. 9, fasc. 6, I Memoriale, 19–20.

49. Garuti and Colli, *Monastero di Santa Chiara,* 54–55. Unlike some other nunneries, Santa Chiara did not have a convent school per se, but it was not uncommon for young girls to be placed there under the guardianship of professed nuns who oversaw their education; Zarri, introduction to *Clarisse in Carpi,* ed. Zarri, 1:34.

50. Ori, "Vita della communità," in *Clarisse in Carpi,* ed. Zarri, 1:225.

51. *Gli Estensi,* ed. Mauro Bini, vol. 2, *La Corte di Modena* (Modena: Bulino, 1999), 25.

52. Medioli, "Dimensions of Cloister," in *Time, Space, and Women's Lives,* ed. Schutte, Kuehn, and Menchi, 165.

53. Laven, *Virgins of Venice,* 120–22.

54. AMSCC, Memoriale secondo, 49v, 51r–v, 54v, 56r, 57v.

55. Ibid., 46r, 47r, 54v, 57v. Ori, "Principessa in monastero," in *Clarisse in Carpi*, ed. Zarri, 1:272–75. In April 1655 records show that Santa Chiara had sixty-four professed nuns and nine lay sisters. Counted separately were two "Serve Professe, serve dell'Altezza Ser.ma Suor Angela Catterina d'Este, et una serva conversa loro"; Memoriale secondo, 69r; quoted in ibid., 269. Consequently, nine lay sisters served the other sixty-four professed nuns, whereas these two "professed servants" had a *conversa* all to themselves.

56. Silvia Evangelisti, "'Farne quello che pare e piace . . . ': L'uso e la trasmissione delle celle nel monastero di Santa Giulia di Brescia (1597–1688)," *Quaderni storici* 88 (1995): 85–109.

57. Ori, "Vita della communità" and "Principessa in monastero," in *Clarisse in Carpi*, ed. Zarri, 1:215, 265, 268. Garuti and Colli, *Monastero di Santa Chiara*, 55; Garuti, "Sviluppo architettonico," in *Clarisse di Carpi*, ed. Zarri, 1:119–22; Spinelli, *Musica in Carpi*, 42–44. In a marginalium added to the chapter on how one became a Clarisse, the Council of Trent mandated that before entering the convent, the novice was to give all her belongings to the poor; *Prima Regola delle Monache di Santa Chiara* . . . (Naples: Lazaro Scoriggio, 1629), chap. 2. Angela Caterina's confessor was first Francesco da Fugnano (1611–21) followed by Angelo Lazzarino from Venice (1621–36); Ori, "Vita della communità" in *Clarisse in Carpi*, ed. Zarri, 215; AMSCC, Memoriale secondo, 39r.

58. On early modern convents as centers of musical, theatrical, and literary culture, see essays in *Monasteri femminili come centri di cultura*, ed. Pomata and Zarri; Craig A. Monson, *Disembodied Voices: Music and Culture in an Early Modern Italian Convent* (Berkeley: University of California Press, 1995); Elissa B. Weaver, *Convent Theatre in Early Modern Italy: Spiritual Fun and Learning for Women* (Cambridge: Cambridge University Press, 2002). On the Este family as patrons of the arts, see *Sovrane passioni: Studi sul collezionismo estense*, ed. Jadranka Bentini (Milan: Federico Motta, 1998).

59. Zarri, introduction to *Clarisse in Carpi*, ed. Zarri, 1:32. In 1622 Angela Caterina wrote to her uncle the cardinal expressing her desire to improve the singing of the nuns of Santa Chiara. Being herself quite musically talented, the young abbess was searching for a nun with a perfect voice who could instruct the others in singing. So eager was she to include such a nun among the ranks of the Clarisses, Angela Caterina said that she would accept her without a dowry. She added, however, that the musical nun must not be so ignoble that she could not fit in with the other members of the community; Spinelli, *Musica in Carpi*, 45–46. See also Mario Bizzoccoli, "Musica, teatro e istituzioni pubbliche a Carpi nel secolo XVII," in *Principato di Carpi*, ed. Zacchè, 437–66.

60. *Regola delle Monache di S. Chiara di Carpi* (Carpi: Antonio Guidotti, 1637), chap. 4. A copy of this publication is preserved in Archivio Storico di Carpi, Archivio Guaitoli, b. 824. Anna Maria Ori has suggested that Angela Caterina had this translation printed in 1637 as a means of showing that "her" convent would be able to overcome the demonic woes it was suffering; "Vita della communità," in *Clarisse in Carpi*, ed. Zarri, 1:207–8.

61. *Prima Regola delle Monache di Santa Chiara*, chap. 2.

62. The Observant Franciscans were officially recognized as a separate order in 1517 by a bull issued by Pope Leo X, effectively acknowledging the failure of this

movement for stricter observance to attract all Franciscans; Fragnito, "Ordini religiosi," in *Clero e società nell'Italia moderna,* ed. Rosa, 116. The other two orders of Franciscans were the Conventuals and the Capuchins, the latter founded in 1525 and officially recognized in 1619 as an independent Franciscan order.

63. Zarri, "Monasteri femminili e città," in *Chiesa e potere politico,* ed. Chittolini and Miccoli, 408-10.

64. Lavenia, "Diavoli di Carpi," 83.

65. Ori, "Vita della communità," in *Clarisse in Carpi,* ed. Zarri, 1:207.

66. Archivio Storico di Carpi, Archivio Guaitoli, b. 9, fasc. 6, I Memoriale, 15-16. See, for example, ASM, Casa e Stato, b. 202, letters from Angela Caterina d'Este to Alfonso III, 30 May and 29 June 1629.

67. ASM, Cancelleria Ducale, Ambasciatori, Roma, b. 224, 5 March 1629; Lavenia, "Diavoli di Carpi," 85n39.

68. Archivio Storico di Carpi, Archivio Guaitoli, b. 246/2, Padre L. Tornini, "Della Storia della Città di Carpi," tome 2:51; Lavenia, "Diavoli di Carpi," 83n33.

69. Archivio Storico di Carpi, Archivio Guaitoli, b. 9, fasc. 6, I Memoriale, loose folio between folios 32 and 33. Angela Caterina also lobbied her nephew, Francesco I, not to implement the change mandated by a papal brief; ASM, Casa e Stato, b. 203, letters from Angela Caterina d'Este to Francesco I, 30 June and 4 July 1629. Francesco I temporarily acceded to this request; ibid., letter from Francesco I to Angela Caterina d'Este, 19 July 1629; AMSCC, Memoriale secondo, 47r-48v.

70. Archivio Storico di Carpi, Archivio Guaitoli, b. 246/2, Tornini, "Storia della Città di Carpi," tome 2:53; Lavenia, "Diavoli di Carpi," 99n99.

Chapter 2

1. The city of Modena lost about 40 percent of its preplague population of 10,000. Carpi and the surrounding rural districts had a population of over 14,000 in 1591 but less than 10,000 in 1641, largely because of the dramatic mortality caused by the plague in 1630; Simonetta Caliumi, "Carpi 1630: Il Governatore, i provvisori e i conservatori della Sanità di fronte alla peste," in *Principato di Carpi,* ed. Zacchè, 261-71.

2. Judith C. Brown, "Everyday Life, Longevity, and Nuns in Early Modern Florence," in *Renaissance Culture and the Everyday,* ed. Patricia Fumerton and Simon Hunt (Philadelphia: University of Pennsylvania Press, 1999), 115-38.

3. AMSCC, Memoriale secondo, 50r. Sisters Virginia Magnani, forty-seven, and Margherita Contessini, sixty, who died 15 June and 27 July, respectively, were both said to have been sick for "eight days," which suggests they may indeed have been plague victims. Magnani, however, was also reported to have been in poor health for quite some time.

4. Monter, *Witchcraft in France and Switzerland,* 207.

5. ASM, Inq., b. 102, f. 1A.

6. Ibid., b. 295, fasc. 2, letter from Inquisitor Giacomo Tinti to Cardinal Francesco Barberini, 14 May 1636.

7. Ibid., b. 108, f. 1A, 2r, 8v, 187v.

8. ASM, Casa e Stato, b.202, letter from Angela Caterina d'Este to Francesco I, 12 March 1636.

9. Ibid., b. 93, letter from Giovan Battista d'Este to Francesco I, 12 April 1636.

10. ASM Ibid., letter from Giovan Battista d'Este to Francesco I, 6 April 1636. See also Lavenia, "Diavoli di Carpi," 89–97.

11. See Valerio Polidori, *Practica Exorcistarum: Ad Daemones, et Maleficias de Christifidelibus eiiciendum*, pt. 2, *Dispersio Daemonum Quae Secunda Pars est Practice Exorcistarum* (Padua: Paulo Meieto, 1587), 6r.

12. ASM, Inq., b. 295, fasc. 2, letter from Tinti to Barberini, 14 May 1636. On vicars of the Inquisition, see Adriano Prosperi, "Vicari dell'Inquisizione fiorentina alla metà del seicento: Note d'archivio," in *L'Inquisizione romana: Letture e ricerche* (Rome: Edizioni di Storia e Letteratura, 2003), 153–81.

13. ASM, Inq., b. 295, fasc. 2, letter from Tinti to Barberini, 14 May 1636; Casa e Stato, b. 93, letter from Giovan Battista d'Este to Francesco I, 6 April 1636.

14. ASM, Inq., b. 295, fasc. 2, letter from Tinti to Barberini, 14 May 1636.

15. Ibid.

16. Ibid., letter from Tinti to Barberini, 17 May 1636.

17. Ibid., b. 254, 51r–v, letter from Barberini to Tinti, 31 May 1636. Barberini continued this theme in another letter when he rejected Giovan Battista's request to allow secular tribunals to "publish" an edict against these *maleficia;* ibid., 52r–v, letter from Barberini to Tinti, 7 June 1636.

18. Inq., b. 295, fasc. 2, letter from Tinti to Barberini, 18 June 1636.

19. ASM, Inq., b. 102, f. 1A, 94r. See also letters from Cardinal Barberini to Inquisitor Tinti, Inq., b. 254, 57r, 25 October 1636; 60r, 29 November 1636.

20. ASM, Inq., b. 108, f. 1A, 2r.

21. On Scaglia see Albano Biondi, "'L'inordinata devozione' nella *Prattica* del Cardinale Scaglia (ca. 1635)," in *Finzione e santità tra medioevo ed età moderna*, ed. Gabriella Zarri (Turin: Rosenberg and Sellier, 1991), 306–25; Schutte, *Aspiring Saints*, 67–71; John Tedeschi, "The Question of Magic and Witchcraft in Two Inquisitorial Manuals of the Seventeenth Century," in *Prosecution of Heresy*, 229–58; Angelo Turchini, "Il modello ideale dell'inquisitore: La *Prattica* del Cardinale Desiderio Scaglia," in *Inquisizione romana*, ed. Del Col and Paolin, 187–98.

22. ASM, Manoscritti biblioteca, no. 166, "Prattica per procedere nelle cause di S. Officio fatta dal Sr. Cardinale Scaglia," 200–202.

23. ASM, Casa e Stato, b. 93, letter from Giovan Battista d'Este to Francesco I, 6 April 1636; Inq., b. 102, f. 1A (10r–14r for Giovan Battista's testimony about his exorcism).

24. ASM, Inq., b. 108, f. 1A, 8v. Sluhovsky obviously errs in saying that all the nuns affected in the various group possessions were eventually cured of their ills; "Devil in Convent," 1385.

25. ASM, Inq., b. 108, f. 1A, 2r–v, 8v, 29v, 187v; AMSCC, Memoriale secondo, 33r, 59r.

26. ASM, Inq., b. 108, f. 1A, 145v.

27. On the structure of the Inquisition of Modena, see Prosperi, *Tribunali della coscienza*, 184–86.

28. ASM, Inq., b. 108, f. 1A, 1r; f. 1C, first document (unnumbered).

29. ASM, Inq., b. 108, f. 1C, filza 10, 1r–v. See also Tommaso Menghini, *Regole del Tribunale del Sant'Ofizio, Praticate in alcuni Casi immaginari* (Modena: Bartolomeo Soliani, 1722), 1.

30. Menghini, *Regole del Sant'Ofizio,* 5–6.
31. ASM, Inq., b. 108, f. 1A, 1r–v.
32. Ibid., 2r–v, 8v, 29v, 187v. Unless there is evidence to the contrary, I have assumed that these nuns took vows when they were sixteen, providing a basis for calculating their ages in the spring of 1638.
33. AMSCC, Memoriale secondo, 24r–v.
34. Ibid., 57v.
35. Ibid., 22r, 104r.
36. Ibid., 26r.
37. Ibid., 39v, 43r.
38. Ibid., 50v.
39. Ibid., 38v, 39v.
40. Ibid., 50v, 53r.
41. Ibid., 53r, 54v.
42. Ibid., 57v.
43. ASM, Inq., b. 108, f. 1A, 2r–v, 8v; AMSCC, Memoriale secondo, 49v.
44. ASM, Inq., b. 108, f. 1A, 1v–2r, 8v; f. 1B, fasc. 3, 73v–74r.
45. Garnot, *Diable au couvent,* 21. The seventeen afflicted nuns in Loudun ranged in age from seventeen or eighteen to thirty-five; Certeau, *Possession at Loudun,* 90–92.
46. Philip C. Almond, *Demonic Possession and Exorcism in Early Modern England: Contemporary Texts and their Cultural Contexts* (Cambridge: Cambridge University Press, 2004), 22–26. In New England for the years 1688–93, 44 percent of possessed females were aged sixteen to twenty; Karlsen, *Devil in Shape of Woman,* 39. It has also been suggested that those most likely to show symptoms of possession were women who had just started menstruating or had just married or lost their virginity. For sundry reasons, this explanation cannot explain the woes of the sisters of Carpi. Although menarche was late in early modern Europe, typically beginning in the midteens, with the possible exception of the two laywomen who died, only one of the demoniacs, Anna Maria Martinelli, was, at seventeen, even close to the age at which menstruation began and five of them were past thirty. Marriage was obviously not in the plans for any of them, and as residents of a cloistered community of female religious, they almost certainly were all still virgins. In short, anxieties associated with changes in the life cycle, centered upon menstruation, marriage, and pregnancy, cannot go far in explaining the possessions in Carpi. See Moshe Sluhovsky, "A Divine Apparition or Demonic Possession? Female Agency and Church Authority in Demonic Possession in Sixteenth-Century France," *Sixteenth Century Journal* 27 (1996): 1049–52; Peter Laslett, "Age at Menarche in Europe since the Eighteenth Century," in *Marriage and Fertility: Studies in Interdisciplinary History,* ed. Robert R. Rotberg and Theodore K. Rabb (Princeton: Princeton University Press, 1980), 285–300. Some early modern medical theory held that postmenopausal women were more at risk of demon possession because of their "excessive dryness"; H. C. Erik Midelfort, *History of Madness,* 69.
47. ASM, Inq., b. 108, f. 1A, 13r, 24r.
48. For a useful discussion of the distinction between possession and bewitchment, see David Harley, "Explaining Salem: Calvinist Psychology and the Diagnosis of Possession," *American Historical Review* 101 (1996): 307–30.
49. ASM, Inq., b. 108, f. 1A, 2v.

50. Ibid.

51. AMSCC, Memoriale secondo, 21r; Archivio Storico di Carpi, Archivio Guaitoli, b. 9, II Memoriale, 11. She professed "nelle mani della badessa Suor Catherina Bertacci"; Ori, "Vita della communità," in *Clarisse in Carpi,* ed. Zarri, 1:223–24. The vows that she would have taken were the following: "'Io Sore N. faccio voto, e prometto a Dio onnipotente, et alla Beata Maria sempre Vergine, et al Beato Francesco, et alla Beata Chiara, et a tutti li Santi, et a te Madre, tutto il tempo della vita mia osservare la Regola, e forma di vita delle povere Sorelle di Santa Chiara, per lo medesimo B. Francesco, alla medesima S. Chiara data, e dal Signor Papa Innocentio Quarto approbata, vivendo in obedienza, senza proprio, et in castità, servando la debita clausura per le Constitutioni dell'Ordine ordinata.' Et all'hora l'Abbadessa che la riceve, prometta a quella, e dica, 'Io da parte di Dio, e della sua ferma ordinatione' (se queste cose osservarai) 'ti prometto vita eterna.' E le circonstanti rispondano, 'Amen'"; *Prima Regola delle Monache di Santa Chiara,* 14.

52. ASM, Inq., b. 108, f. 1A, 5r–v.

53. Ibid., 90v. Ippolita took vows in October 1594; AMSCC, Memoriale secondo, 16v, 32r–v.

54. AMSCC, Memoriale secondo, 35v.

55. ASM, Inq., b. 108, f. 1A, 43v.

56. Ibid., 5v.

57. Ibid., 17r.

58. *Instruttione per confessori di monache,* 15–16.

59. See Laven, *Virgins of Venice,* 102–17; Harline, *Burdens of Sister Margaret,* 114.

60. Laven, *Virgins of Venice,* 91–92.

61. ASM, Inq., b. 108, f. 1A, 2v–3r,12r, 59r.

62. Ibid., 9r.

63. Ibid., 19r, 22r, 29r.

64. ASM, Inq., b. 106, f. 19; b. 295, fasc. 2, letters from Tinti to Barberini, 20 January and 24 February 1638.

65. ASM, Inq., b. 108, f. 1A, 24r. For his trial, see Inq., b. 100, f. 3; b. 254, letters from Barberini to Tinti, 82r, 7 February 1637; 92r, 18 April 1637.

66. ASM, Inq., b. 108, f. 1A, 9r, 29r, 42r–v, 162v–163r. For Fra Valerio's trial see Inq., b. 86, f. 2.

67. ASM, Inq., b. 108, f. 1A, 55v.

68. *Prima Regola delle Monache di Santa Chiara,* chap. 5.

69. *Le Constitutioni delle monache della prima regola di Santa Chiara* (Naples: Lazaro Scoriggio, 1624), chap. 9.

70. Ironically, Clare of Assisi and the original community of Clarisses did not lead a strictly enclosed life. Clare wrote the Rule with considerable help from a bishop and the pope while on her deathbed. The Rule ultimately transformed the Clarisses from missionaries, who actively tried to convert people in the world, to cloistered nuns; E. Ann Matter, "The Commentary on the Rule of Clare of Assisi by Maria Domitilla Galluzzi," in *Creative Women in Medieval and Early Modern Italy,* ed. Matter and Coakley, 2. See also Elizabeth Alvilda Petroff, "A Medieval Woman's Utopian Vision: The Rule of St. Clare of Assisi," in *Body and Soul: Essays on Medieval Women and Mysticism* (Oxford: Oxford University Press, 1994), 66–79.

71. ASM, Inq., b. 108, f. 1A, 9r, 14v, 31r, 72r–v.

72. Ibid., b. 52, f. 1, 25r, 54v, 126r–127r; b. 286, f. 3, loose letter, 29 April 1638. On the definition of sorcery, see Levack, *Witch-Hunt,* 6–7.

73. See Mandrou, *Magistrats et sorciers,* 115–17.

74. ASM, Inq., b. 108, f. 1A, 43v.

75. Ibid., 26r.

76. The precise words were "tu darai ben ancora nella rette"; ibid., 67v. *Dar rèta* is an Emilian regionalism that means 'to pay attention'; *Vocabolario Bolognese Italiano,* ed. Carolina Coronedi Berti (Bologna: G. Monti, 1869–1874; repr. Milan: Aldo Martello, 1969), s.v. "rèta." This testimony came from Clelia Coccapani, but when she reappeared a month later (31 July 1638), Sister Clelia reported that she no longer remembered hearing Ippolita say such words; ibid., 150v–151r.

77. Ibid., 150v.

78. Ibid., 36r.

79. Ibid., 25v–26r.

80. Ibid., 6v.

81. For a famous case of seventeenth-century lesbian nuns, see Judith C. Brown, *Immodest Acts: The Life of a Lesbian Nun in Renaissance Italy* (Oxford: Oxford University Press, 1986).

82. See Luisa Accati, "Lo spirito della fornicazione: Virtù dell'anima e virtù del corpo," *Quaderni storici* 41 (1979): 644–72. Already in the 1430s, an anonymous treatise declared that one of the principal motives to become a witch, the other two being the desire for revenge or riches, was to "wallow lewdly in the carnal act"; *Errores gazariorum, seu illorum qui scopam vel baculum equitare probantur,* in *L'imaginaire du sabbat: Edition critique des texts les plus anciens (1430 c.–1440 c.),* ed. Martine Ostorero, Agostino Paravicini Bagliani, and Kathrin Utz Tremp (Lausanne: Université de Lausanne, 1999), 294–97.

83. Cf. Brown, "Everyday Life," 126.

84. ASM, Inq., b. 295, letters from Tinti to Barberini, 15 July, 6 and 14 November 1638.

85. Ibid., b. 108, f. 1A, 3v.

86. Ibid., 63v. Maria Calefi reported that Cabassi told her about this conversation with Dealta about the sabbat shortly after it took place; ibid., 6v. Three witnesses also indicated that Dealta joked about going to a sabbat; ibid., 19v, 119v–120r.

87. See Stuart Clark, "Inversion, Misrule and the Meaning of Witchcraft," *Past and Present* 87 (1980): 98–127.

88. For an excellent edition of these earliest works that describe elements of the sabbat, see *Imaginaire du sabbat,* ed. Ostorero, Bagliani, and Tremp. See also Andreas Blauert, *Frühe Hexenverfolgungen: Ketzer-, Zauberei- und Hexenprozesse des 15. Jahrhunderts* (Hamburg: Junius, 1989); Martine Ostorero, *Folâtrer avec les démons: Sabbat et chasse aux sorciers à Vevey (1448)* (Lausanne: Université de Lausanne, 1999); and *Sabbat des sorciers,* ed. Jacques-Chaquin and Préaud. In his pioneering work on witchcraft, Julio Carlo Baroja asserts that the sabbat first appeared in inquisitorial trials in Toulouse and Carcassonne in southwestern France already in the 1330s; *The World of the Witches,* trans. O. N. V. Glendinning (Chicago: University of Chicago Press, 1971), 84–87. See also Richard Kieckhefer, *European Witch Trials: Their Foundations in Popular and Learned Culture 1300–1500* (Berkeley: University of California Press, 1976), 10–26.

89. Midelfort, *Witch Hunting in Southwestern Germany*, 19.

90. Girolamo Menghi, *Compendio dell'arte essorcistica, et possibilità delle mirabili, et stupende operationi delli Demoni, et de i Malefici con li rimedii opportuni alle infermità Maleficiali* (Venice: Paolo Ugolino, 1601), 277. See also Silvia Mantini, "'... Et chi vi andava una volta vi sarebbe tornata sempre': Una storia di strega," in *Gostanza*, ed. Cardini, 7. In an erudite study of demonological literature, Walter Stephens argues that the interest in sex between witches and demons, described by Kramer and many other authors, was not merely a function of deep-seated misogyny. Their interest in demonic sex was more metaphysical than pornographic, serving as a means of addressing the alleged growth in skepticism concerning the very existence of the spirit. According to Stephens, by arguing that humans and demons interacted in this most intimate way, demonologists hoped to convince people, including themselves, of the reality of spirits and the truth of Christian doctrine; *Demon Lovers: Witchcraft, Sex, and the Crisis of Belief* (Chicago: University of Chicago Press, 2002). For a probing critique of this work, see the review by Wolfgang Behringer in *American Historical Review* 108 (2003): 1207–8.

91. Candido Brognolo, *Alexicacon, Hoc est Opus de Maleficiis ac Morbis Maleficiis*, 2 vols. (Venice: Giovan Battista Catanei, 1668), 1:178–79, 184–85. See also Jean Bodin, *De la Démonomanie des sorciers* (Paris: Jacques du Puys, 1580), 85r–89r. For learned opinions on the sabbat, see Clark, *Thinking with Demons*, 11–30.

92. Bread supposedly was also not served at witches' feasts, because of bread's essential role in the Eucharist; Francesco Maria Guazzo, *Compendium Maleficarum*, ed. Montague Summers, trans. E. A. Ashwin (New York: Dover, 1988), 23, 37. See also Oscar Di Simplicio, *Autunno della stregoneria: Maleficio e magia nell'Italia moderna* (Bologna: Il Mulino, 2005), 328; Robert Muchembled, *Les derniers bûchers: Un village de Flandre et ses sorciers sous Louis XIV* (Paris: Editions Ramsay, 1981), 25; Roper, *Witch Craze*, 115.

93. Menghi, *Compendio*, 408–9. This anecdote is repeated in many standard early modern works on witchcraft, e.g., Guazzo, *Compendium Maleficarum*, ed. Summers, trans. Ashwin, 42–43; Bodin, *Démonomanie*, 62v, 82v–85r.

94. For examples, see Kramer and Sprenger, *Malleus Maleficarum*, trans. and ed. Summers, 97; Mantini, "'Et chi vi andava una volta,'" in *Gostanza*, ed. Cardini, 6; Thomas, *Religion and Decline of Magic*, 494; Briggs, *Witches and Neighbors*, 44–45. For theories concerning the origins of the sabbat, see Carlo Ginzburg, *Ecstasies: Deciphering the Witches' Sabbath*, trans. Raymond Rosenthal (New York: Penguin, 1991); Ginzburg, "The Witches' Sabbat: Popular Cult or Inquisitorial Stereotype?" in *Understanding Popular Culture: Europe from the Middle Ages to the Nineteenth Century*, ed. Steven L. Kaplan (Berlin: Mouton, 1984), 39–51; Mircea Eliade, "Some Observations on European Witchcraft," in *Occultism, Witchcraft, and Cultural Fashions: Essays in Comparative Religions* (Chicago: University of Chicago Press, 1976), 89–92; Laura de Mello e Souza, *Inferno Atlântico: Demonologia e colonizacão, séculos XVI–XVIII* (São Paulo: Companhia das Letras, 1993), 160–79.

95. Robert Muchembled, "Satanic Myths and Cultural Reality," in *Early Modern European Witchcraft*, ed. Ankarloo and Henningsen, 139; Muchembled, *La sorcière au village XVe–XVIIIe siècle* (Paris: Gallimard, 1991), 192–93.

96. See Jim Sharpe, "The Devil in East Anglia: The Matthew Hopkins Trials Reconsidered," in *Witchcraft in Early Modern Europe*, ed. Barry, Hester, and Roberts, 252. Cf. Martin, *Witchcraft and Inquisition*.

97. Zanelli, *Streghe e società nell'Emilia*, 35–46; Bethencourt, *Imaginário da magia*, 14; Briggs, *Witches and Neighbors*, 32; Bethencourt, "Le sabbat des sorciers en Lorraine," in *Sabbat des sorciers*, ed. Jacques-Chaquin and Préaud, 156, 164–81. In the same volume, see also Elisabeth Biesel, "Les descriptions du sabbat dans les confessions des inculpés lorrains et trévirois," 183–97.

98. ASM, Inq., b. 108, f. 1A, 16r, 28r.

99. Ibid., 12v. For her age, see AMSCC, Memoriale secondo, 53v.

100. ASM, Inq., b. 108, f. 1A, 4v.

101. Ibid., 14v.

102. Ibid., 25r, 43v. Born in 1590, Laura married Prince Alessandro I Pico, later duke of Mirandola, in 1603. Alessandro commissioned a painting in honor of her being cured of demonic possession, Santo Peranda's *L'Immacolata e i Santi Geminiano e Ubaldo con Laura d'Este Pico*, housed today in the parish church of San Possidonio in the province of Modena. Laura passed away in 1630; *L'arte degli Estensi: La pittura del Seicento e del Settecento a Modena e Reggio* (Modena: Panini, 1986), 235–37; Jadranka Bentini, ed., *Galleria Estense: Un percorso alternativo fra arredo e parato nel Palazzo Ducale di Modena* (Modena: Artestampa, 1993), 15; Lavenia, "Diavoli di Carpi," 90n61.

103. ASM, Inq., b. 108, f. 1A, 99v.

104. Ibid., 31r.

105. Mary R. O'Neil, "Missing Footprints: Maleficium in Modena," *Acta Ethnographica Hungarica* 37 (1991/1992): 123–42. See also Mantini, "'Et chi vi andava una volta,'" in *Gostanza*, ed. Cardini, 5–25; Ornella Lazzaro, *Le amare erbe: Un processo di stregoneria nel Friuli del Seicento: Il caso di Angioletta e Giustina delle Rive* (Pordenone: Edizioni Biblioteca dell'Immagine, 1992); and various references to "wise women" in David Gentilcore, *Healers and Healing in Early Modern Italy* (Manchester: Manchester University Press, 1998).

106. Guido Ruggiero found that the Venetian Holy Office was far more concerned with the misuse of sacred powers than in uncovering devil-worshiping witches; introduction to *Binding Passions*, 17.

107. Eymerich and Peña, *Manuale dell'Inquisitore*, trans. and ed. Sala-Molins, 77–78n21; Robert W. Scribner, "Ritual and Popular Belief in Catholic Germany at the Time of the Reformation," in *Popular Culture and Popular Movements in Reformation Germany* (London: Hambledon Press, 1987), 36, 39–40; Scribner, "Sorcery, Superstition and Society: The Witch of Urach," in ibid., 260–61.

108. ASM, Inq., b. 108, f. 1A, 68r.

109. Ibid., 16v, 113r. For Zuccari's age, see AMSCC, Memoriale secondo, 44r.

110. ASM, Inq., b. 108, f. 1A, 16v, 31r.

111. Menghi, *Compendio*, 493–94. For evidence on instruments in *maleficia* in early modern Emilia and Romagna, see Zanelli, *Streghe e società*, 63–67.

112. On the process of becoming a nun, see Laven, *Virgins of Venice*, 23–44.

113. Thomas, *Religion and Decline of Magic*, 437–38.

114. ASM, Inq., b. 108, f. 1A, 15v.

115. Ibid., 62r.

116. Ibid., 7r–v, 11v, 62r, 101r.

117. Ibid., 98r–v.

118. Brognolo, *Alexicacon*, 1:264. Lay folk in the Middle Ages often viewed the consecrated host as a type of amulet that could protect them from harm; Kieckhefer,

Magic in the Middle Ages, 79–80. See also Kramer and Sprenger, *Malleus Maleficarum,* trans. and ed. Summers, 116–17; Mantini, "'Et chi vi andava una volta,'" in *Gostanza,* ed. Cardini, 7; Stephens, *Demon Lovers,* 207–40.

119. ASM, Inq., b. 108, f. 1A, 15v–16r, 42v, 61r–v.

120. Menghi, *Compendio,* 279.

121. ASM, Inq., b. 108, f. 1A, 61r.

122. For reports of similar falls, see Guazzo, *Compendium Maleficarum,* ed. Summers, trans. Ashwin, 103; Briggs, *Witches and Neighbors,* 90; Garnot, *Diable au couvent,* 33.

123. ASM, Inq., b. 108, f. 1A, 42v, 77v–78r.

124. Ibid., 11v.

125. Ibid., 6r.

126. This painting, which is still housed in the convent today, has been the object of much veneration over the past four centuries, and Angela Caterina d'Este did much to promote reverence for the image; AMSCC, Libro della *Madonna di San Luca.* I am most grateful to the sisters of Santa Chiara and to Professor Anna Maria Ori for generously sharing with me the transcription of this document.

127. ASM, Inq., b. 108, f. 1A, 6r. Another nun claimed that of the possessed, only Amoldoni, Ronchi, and Forni were present; ibid., 61v.

128. Kramer and Sprenger, *Malleus Maleficarum,* trans. and ed. Summers, 18; Briggs, *Witches and Neighbors,* 167.

129. Menghi, *Compendio,* 429–35. See also Thomas, *Religion and Decline of Magic,* 437.

130. ASM, Inq., b. 108, f. 1A, 6v–7r.

131. Ibid., 17r, 140r. See Briggs, *Witches and Neighbors,* 63; Gentilcore, *Healers and Healing,* 163–64.

132. ASM, Inq., b. 108, f. 1A, 20r–v, 61v–62r. For a similar reputed incident several years earlier near Modena, see Menghi, *Compendio,* 426–27.

133. ASM, Inq., b. 108, f. 1A, 120v–121r, 154r–v.

134. Ibid., 10v.

135. Ibid., 10v, 25v.

136. Ibid., 43r.

137. Ibid., 38v. Clelia Coccapanni gave virtually identical testimony; ibid., 67r.

138. Ibid., 121v.

139. Ibid., 12v, 25v, 38v, 54v, 57r, 66v.

140. Menghi, *Compendio,* 551–52. See also Bodin, *Démonomanie,* 141r. An inquisitor and jurist, Cesare Carena, by contrast, advised inquisitors that they should place little faith in the notion that not weeping (in this case, under torture) was a sign of being guilty of witchcraft; Carena, *Tractatus de Officio Sanctissimae Inquisitionis et modo procedendi in causis fidei* (Bologna: Jacobus Montius, 1668), pt. 2, titulus 9, "De Sortilegii," ß24, "De nonnullis animadvertendis circa carcerationem, examen, & torturam Maleficarum," n. 215.

141. See Michael MacDonald, introduction to *Witchcraft and Hysteria in Elizabethan London: Edward Jorden and the Mary Glover Case,* ed. Michael MacDonald (London and New York: Tavistock/Routledge, 1991), xxxvi–xl.

142. ASM, Inq., b. 108, f. 1A, 18v.

143. Briggs, *Witches and Neighbors.* For an example in which an alleged witch may have used her bad reputation to her advantage, see Ginzburg, "Witchcraft and Popular Piety," in *Clues, Myths, and the Historical Method,* 1–16. For similar cases in which

neighbors had harbored suspicions for many years, see Di Simplicio, *Autunno della stregoneria,* 123; Holmes, "Women: Witnesses and Witches," 52–57; Larner, *Enemies of God,* 100; John Putnam Demos, *Entertaining Satan: Witchcraft and the Culture of Early New England* (Oxford: Oxford University Press, 1982), 86–94, 246–74.

144. For a case of an eighteenth-century woman who, having most likely been forced to become a nun, nurtured her reputation of being a witch, see Anne Jacobson Schutte, "Asmodea: A Nun-Witch in Eighteenth-Century Tuscany," in *Werewolves, Witches, and Wandering Spirits: Traditional Belief and Folklore in Early Modern Europe,* ed. Kathryn A. Edwards (Kirksville, MO: Truman State University Press, 2002), 119–35.

145. ASM, Inq., b. 108, f. 1A, 66r.

146. Guidelines for witchcraft cases, written in the 1620s, insisted that a person's reputation should be of very minor importance in weighing evidence against suspects and warned inquisitors that they must be wary of accusations against people who were generally disliked; *Instructio pro formandis processibus in causis strigum et maleficorum,* reproduced in Giovanni Tommaso Castaldi, *De Potestate Angelica sive de Potentia Motrice ac Mirandis Operibus Angelorum atque Daemonum* (Rome: Francesco Caballi, 1651), 2:244.

147. ASM, Inq., b. 108, f. 1A, 63v; f. 1B, fasc. 1, 1r–2r.

148. ASM, Inq., b. 108, 1B, fasc. 1, 1r–2r.

149. See, for example, *Prima Regola delle Monache di Santa Chiara,* chap. 6: "Qualmente le Sore non ricevano alcuna possessione, o proprietà per se, o per persone interposte." This prohibition of personal possessions was violated many times over at the convent in Carpi. But the "Constitutions" of the Clarisses appeared more lenient on this matter, allowing nuns to retain the use of goods so long as they did not conflict with their vow of poverty: Sisters may "godere l'uso di quelle cose, che a loro liberamente sono offerte, e mandate, overo cercate per amor di Dio. E di quelle ancora, che si haveranno guadagnate lavorando; Pur che le cose offerte, mendicate, o guadagnate, non ripugnino, ne siano discordi dallo stato della loro povertà promessa"; *Constitutioni delle monache,* chap. 10.

150. The post-Tridentine Church took aggressive actions, especially after the rigid Index issued by Pope Clement VIII in 1596, to eliminate Bibles in the vernacular in Italy. Consequently, it would have been most surprising if Dealta, who most likely had not studied Latin, had owned a copy of the scriptures. See Gigliola Fragnito, *La Bibbia al rogo: La censura ecclesiastica e i volgarizzamenti della Scrittura (1471–1605)* (Bologna: Il Mulino, 1997).

151. ASM, Inq., b. 108, 1B, fasc. 1, 1r–3v.

152. Cesare Carena, *Tractatus de Officio Sanctissimae Inquisitionis,* pt. 2, titulus 9, "De Sortilegii," ß23, "De nonnullis aliis Inditiis in hoc Crimine," n. 200.

153. Medieval medical texts recommended wearing the *Agnus Dei,* for example, as protection against evil, and suggested that keeping handwritten prayers on one's person could protect against sudden death, harmful spirits, and other woes; Kieckhefer, *Magic in the Middle Ages,* 78.

154. ASM, Inq., b. 108, 1B, fasc. 1, 3v–5r, 10v.

155. *Instructio,* in Castaldi, *De Potestate Angelica,* 2:243. See also Tedeschi, "Organization and Procedures," in *Prosecuting Heresy,* 134; Tedeschi, "Inquisitorial Law and Witch," in *Early Modern European Witchcraft,* ed. Ankarloo and Henningsen, 92.

156. ASM, Inq., b. 108, 1B, fasc. 1, 5v–10r.

157. Ibid., b. 295, fasc. 2, letters from Tinti to Barberini, 7 May and 15 December 1638.

158. Ibid., b. 108, 1B, fasc. 1, 6r.

159. Ibid.

160. Ibid., 8r–v.

161. Ibid., 8v.

162. Ibid., 9r. See also b. 295, fasc. 2, letter from Tinti to Barberini, 7 May 1638, which said that, other than these letters and the host, the search did not reveal anything particularly incriminating against Dealta or her sister.

163. Laven, *Virgins of Venice*, 167–85.

164. ASM, Inq., b. 108, f. 1C, f. 7, 2r.

165. Ibid., 2v–3v.

166. Ibid., b. 254, letter from Barberini to Tinti, 21 August 1636. Although the alleged demoniacs were not actually interrogated at the infamous Salem witch trials, they nonetheless wielded the de facto power of determining guilt. In Salem judicial authorities brought the suspects individually before the afflicted girls, who were instructed to look at the suspect and were asked if this person had caused them harm. Invariably, the girls were then immediately grievously tormented, which provided "evidence" of the witch's guilt; Mary Beth Norton, *In the Devil's Snare: The Salem Witchcraft Crisis of 1692* (New York: Alfred A. Knopf, 2002), 26. Such procedures would not have passed muster with the Inquisition.

167. ASM, Inq., b. 295, fasc. 2, letter from Tinti to Barberini, 7 May 1638.

168. Carmona, *Diables de Loudun*, 233.

169. ASM, Inq., b. 295, fasc. 2, letter from Tinti to Barberini, 14 August 1638.

170. Eymerich and Peña, *Manuale dell'Inquisitore*, trans. and ed. Sala-Molins, 135–36.

171. Menghini, *Regole del Sant'Ofizio*, 2–3.

172. ASM, Inq., b. 108, f. 1A, 18r.

173. Peter Rushton, "Texts of Authority: Witchcraft Accusations and the Demonstration of Truth in Early Modern England," in *Languages of Witchcraft*, ed. Clark, 30.

174. ASM, Inq., b. 108, f. 1A, 24v.

175. Ibid., b. 286, f. 3, loose letter, 9 May 1638; loose letter, 14 June 1638.

176. Ibid., b. 108, f. 1A, 26r, 44v–45r, 68v.

177. Ibid., 31r.

178. Ibid., 51v.

179. Ibid., b. 254, 116r–v, letter from Barberini to Tinti, 29 May 1638. Tinti apologized but claimed that he needed to rely on Giudici since he was currently without a vicar in Carpi; ibid., b. 295, fasc. 2, letter from Tinti to Barberini, 15 May 1638.

180. Ibid., b. 254, 120r–v, letter from Barberini to Tinti, 3 July 1638.

181. Carena, *Tractatus de Officio Sanctissimae Inquisitionis*, pt. 1, titulus 9, "De Advocato Fiscali S. Officii." In Spain the *fiscal* served as a public prosecutor who assisted the inquisitors and drew up charges; Lea, *History of Inquisition of Spain*, 2:241–43; Joseph Pérez, *The Spanish Inquisition: A History*, trans. Janet Lloyd (New Haven: Yale University Press, 2005), 112, 117.

182. ASM, Inq., b. 295, fasc. 2, letter from Tinti to Barberini, 15 July 1638.

183. Ibid., letter from Tinti to Barberini, 22 July 1638.

184. See Di Simplicio, *Autunno della stregoneria*, 273–74.

185. The Congregation of Bishops and Regulars granted this permission in a letter to the archpriest of Carpi; ASV, Congregazione dei Vescovi e dei Regolari, Registra Regularium, b. 46: 122v, 23 April 1638; Lavenia, "Diavoli di Carpi," 103n107.

186. ASM, Inq., b. 108, f. 1A, 147v.

187. The only hint of skepticism came from a most surprising source. In a letter to his son the duke, Giovan Battista d'Este reported that his "little daughter" was enjoying perfect health and was doing better than her aunt, Angela Caterina, with respect to the turmoil in the convent. Although he did not identify which daughter this was, the use of the diminutive (*la mia figliuolina*) would suggest it was Margherita, who was only about twelve at the time (her big sister, Anna Beatrice, was twenty-one). Whichever daughter this was, she believed the nuns were not possessed but were victims of their own fantasies: "non crede che siano spiritate et che siano fantasie che si sono poste in testa"; ASM, Casa e Stato, b. 93, letter from Giovan Battista d'Este to Francesco I, 5 March 1638.

Chapter 3

1. *Instruttione per confessori di monache*, 6–7. These same instructions had been printed in Milan in 1607 by Giovan Pietro Barchi, "vicar of the nuns in Milan"; cited in Prosperi, *Tribunali della coscienza*, 525n14.

2. Giacinto da Cantalupo, *Cenni biografici sugli uomini illustri della Francescana Osservante Provincia di Bologna* (Parma: SS. Nunziata, 1894), 76–78.

3. He wrote *Tre questioni lagali [sic] sopra il testamento di certo Cerati* and *Una Scrittura legale contro in Canonici Reolari Lateranesi di Parma*, the latter of which, Giacinto da Cantalupo suggests, was probably published; *Cenni biografici*, 79.

4. *Atti ufficiali della Provincia Osservante Francescana di Bologna*, vol. 1, *1460–1753*, ed. Diego Guidarini, Bruno Monfardini, and Giambattista Montorsi (Bologna: Edizioni francescane, 2002), 163, 165, 171; Roberto Zavalloni, *Provincia di "Cristo Re": Frati Minori dell'Emilia-Romagna nel 50° anno di vita* (Assisi: Edizioni Porziuncola, 1996), 12–19. I am most grateful to Father Bruno Monfardini for bringing to my attention this valuable published source and for patiently explaining the meanings of these various titles.

5. Bellacappa is never listed in the records of the Observant Franciscan province of Bologna as having the charge of confessor. Appointments of Franciscan confessors were regularly recorded except–for reasons unknown–when they were assigned to female monasteries; *Atti ufficiali*, vol. 1, *1460–1753*, ed. Guidarini, Monfardini, and Montorsi.

6. Archivio Storico di Carpi, Archivio Guaitoli, b. 9, fasc. 6, I Memoriale, 23. Bellacappa made his first entry in the *Memoriale* 20 February 1634; AMSCC, Memoriale secondo, 55r; Ori, "Vita della communità," in *Clarisse in Carpi*, ed. Zarri, 1:214, 217–18n64. Misreading Lavenia, Sluhovsky asserts, "The possession [at Santa Chiara] started as soon as a reforming priest was appointed as archbishop [sic] of Carpi, removed Bellacappa, and decided to establish his authority over the convent"; *Believe Not Every Spirit*, 246. Archpriest Niccolini did not assume authority over Santa

Chiara until July 1637 and therefore could not have been responsible for replacing Bellacappa eight months earlier. Bellacappa's departure was nothing more than a routine change in pastoral charges.

7. Ori, "Vita della communità," in *Clarisse in Carpi*, ed. Zarri, 1:214. Bellacappa actually served longer than most of his predecessors. He was the forty-ninth confessor appointed since 1546, and only one priest had served more than three years.

8. ASM, Inq., b. 108, f. 1A, 11r–v, 13r, 14v, 20v.

9. See, for example, John Bossy, "The Social History of Confession in the Age of the Reformation," *Transactions of the Royal Historical Society* 25 (1975): 21–38.

10. Prosperi, *Tribunali della coscienza*, 513–14. On confessionals in northern Italy, see Wietse de Boer, *The Conquest of the Soul: Confession, Discipline, and Public Order in Counter-Reformation Milan* (Leiden: Brill, 2001), 84–124. For an analysis of normative sources on confession, see Jean Delumeau, *L'aveu et le pardon: Les difficultés de la confession, XIIIe–XVIIIe siècle* (Paris: Fayard, 1990).

11. AMSCC, Memoriale secondo, 53r.

12. Ibid., 37v.

13. The demons even said that Contessini was also bewitched, even though she did not show the symptoms of the demoniacs; ASM, Inq., b. 108, f. 1A, 25r.

14. *Instruttione per confessori di monache*, 9–10, 23.

15. Ibid., 8.

16. ASM, Inq., b. 108, f. 1A, 23r, 29v, 32v, 53r.

17. Ibid., 46v.

18. Biondi, "Streghe ed eretici nei domini estensi," in *Rinascimento nelle corti padane*, ed. Rossi, 171–72, 177; Zanelli, *Streghe e società*, 125.

19. ASM, Inq., b. 108, f. 1A, 148v–149v.

20. Ibid., 21r, 22v, 29v, 56v.

21. Ibid., 11v, 13r, 14v, 19r, 69r.

22. Ibid., 105v. In February 1661 the Holy Office met with seven *qualificatori*, or consultants, experts in theology or canon law, in order to hear their opinions on a host of issues pertaining to solicitation. The seven all agreed that a confessor's praising a woman for her beauty while she confessed did not amount to solicitation; ACDF, Sant'Officio, Stanza Storica UV 23, 14v.

23. Jodi Bilinkoff, *Related Lives: Confessors and Their Female Penitents, 1450–1750* (Ithaca: Cornell University Press, 2005), 22; de Boer, *Conquest of Soul*, 92–93.

24. ASM, Inq., b. 108, f. 1A, 23r.

25. Ibid., 26v.

26. Ibid., 30r.

27. Ibid., 49v–50r. Clelia Coccapani defended Bellacappa by saying that there really was no other convenient place where the priest could meet and chat with nuns; ibid., 69r.

28. Ibid., 21r; emphasis in original.

29. Ibid., 23r.

30. Ibid., 26v.

31. Ibid., 26v.

32. Ibid., 27r.

33. This description is reminiscent of Lucien Febvre's astute observation that sixteenth-century Europeans emphasized "experienced time" over "measured time";

The Problem of Unbelief in the Sixteenth Century: The Religion of Rabelais, trans. Beatrice Gottlieb (Cambridge: Harvard University Press, 1982), 397.

34. ASM, Inq., b. 108, f. 1C, loose document, 2r–3r. Since the words she used were "le [sic] ho voluto bene ancor'io," Brusati was perhaps speaking of a platonic rather than romantic or sensual love.

35. Ibid., f. 1A, 22v. Zuccari was also the only witness who alleged a sexual liaison between Dealta and Bellacappa, ibid., 23r.

36. Ibid., 60v.

37. Ibid., 23r.

38. Brown, *Immodest Acts*, 8; and Laven, *Virgins of Venice*, 192–93; *Instruttione per confessori di monache*, 16–17.

39. Brown, *Immodest Acts*.

40. Garnot, *Diable au couvent*, 21–27, 136–38, 142. For a similar case a century later, see Romano Canosa and Isabella Colonnello, *Gli ultimi roghi: La fine della caccia alle streghe in Italia* (Rome: Sapere 2000, 1983), 96–100.

41. The text of the bull *Universi Dominici Gregis* was reproduced in Eliseo Masini, *Sacro arsenale overo Prattica dell'Officio della Santa Inquizitione* . . . (Rome: Reu. Cam. Apost., 1693), 396–400. See also Carena, *Tractatus de Officio Sanctissimae Inquisitionis*, pt. 2, titulus 6, "De Confessariis sollicitantibus," ß15, "De Abiuratione Confessario sollicitanti indicenda," nos. 75–76; Prosperi, "Inquisizione in Italia," in *Clero e società nell'Italia moderna*, ed. Rosa, 316–17; Juan Antonio Alejandre Garcia, *El veneno de Dios: La Inquisición de Sevilla ante el delito de solicitación en confesión* (Madrid: Siglo XXI de España, 1994), 15–24.

42. *Universi Dominici Gregis*, in Masini, *Sacro arsenale*, 399; Carena, *Tractatus de Officio Sanctissimae Inquisitionis*, pt. 2, titulus 6, "De Confessariis sollicitantibus," ß17, "De poenis salutaribus Poenitentiis istis Confessariis sollicitantibus imponendis," n. 89.

43. *Universi Dominici Gregis*, in Masini, *Sacro arsenale*, 398; "sive extra occasionem confessionis in Confessionario, *aut in loco* quocunque ubi confessiones sacramentales audiantur" [emphasis in original]. Stephen Haliczer notes that this Gregorian bull was likely intended to legitimize actions against solicitation that the Spanish Inquisition had already started taking: *Sexuality in the Confessional: A Sacrament Profaned* (Oxford: Oxford University Press, 1995), 56–57. See also Prosperi, *Tribunali della coscienza*, 508–19.

44. Carena, *Tractatus de Officio Sanctissimae Inquisitionis*, pt. 2, titulus 6, "De Confessariis sollicitantibus," ß15, "De Abiuratione Confessario sollicianti indicenda," no. 76.

45. ASM, Inq., b. 108, f. 1A, 23r–v.

46. ASM, Ibid., 21r.

47. Ibid., 21r–v.

48. Ibid., 27r.

49. Ibid., 48r.

50. Ibid., 32r.

51. Ibid., 113r.

52. In 1661, in the presence of the Holy Office, the seven experts in canon law who served as consultants considered the case of a priest who suggested to a woman that she put off confession until the next day and, once she concurred, immediately

propositioned her. Interestingly, the jurists unanimously agreed that in such a case the priest need not be denounced for solicitation; ACDF, Sant'Officio, Stanza Storica UV 23, 14r.

53. ASM, Inq., b. 108, f. 1A, 109v–110r.

54. Thomas N. Tentler, *Sin and Confession on the Eve of the Reformation* (Princeton: Princeton University Press, 1977). Cf. Lawrence G. Duggan, "Fear and Confession on the Eve of the Reformation," *Archiv für Reformationsgeschichte* 84 (1984): 153–75.

55. De Boer, *Conquest of Soul.* For a good analysis of changes in confession in Counter-Reformation Germany, see W. David Myers, *"Poor, Sinning Folk": Confession and Conscience in Counter-Reformation Germany* (Ithaca: Cornell University Press, 1996).

56. The connection between the two is aptly seen in the work of Henry Charles Lea, who wrote pioneering histories of the Inquisition and of auricular confession. In addition to his multivolume works on the medieval and Spanish Inquisitions, see his *History of Auricular Confession and Indulgences in the Latin Church*, 3 vols. (Philadelphia: Lea Brothers, 1896).

57. Bossy, "Social History of Confession."

58. Giovanni Romeo finds that by the late sixteenth century, parishioners in Italy confessed much more willingly and even found consolation in the frank confession of their sins; *Ricerche su confessione dei peccati e Inquisizione nell'Italia del Cinquecento* (Naples: La Città del Sole, 1997), 122–23; Romeo, *Esorcisti, confessori e sessualità nell'Italia della Controriforma: A proposito di due casi modenesi del primo Seicento* (Florence: Le Lettere, 1998), 127–61.

59. Eymerich and Peña, *Manuale dell'Inquisitore*, trans. and ed. Sala-Molins, 72–73.

60. Prosperi, *Tribunali della coscienza.* By the same author, see also "L'inquisitore come confessore," in *Disciplina dell'anima, disciplina del corpo e disciplina della società tra medioevo ed età moderna*, ed. Paolo Prodi (Bologna: Il Mulino, 1994), 187–224; "Il sigillo infranto: Confessione e Inquisizione in Portogallo nel '700," in Prosperi, *Inquisizione romana*, 413–34; and "Credere alle streghe: Inquisitori e confessori davanti alla 'superstizione,'" in *Bibliotheca Lamiarum: Documenti e immagini della stregoneria dal Medioevo all'Età Moderna* (Ospedaletto [Pisa], Italy: Pacini, 1991), 17–33. Romeo finds that the confessor was ultimately much more important than the inquisitor in overseeing behavior, especially for women and for sins of a sexual nature; *Ricerche su confessione*, 115–41. The evidence from Prosperi causes one to question whether the post-Tridentine confessor really came to resemble more a judge meting out punishments than a physician prescribing cures; cf. Bossy, "Social History of Confession."

61. Prosperi, "Inquisizione in Italia," in *Clero e società nell'Italia moderna*, ed. Rosa, 315. See also Eymerich and Peña, *Manuale dell'Inquisitore*, trans. and ed. Sala-Molins, 127. The Holy Office did not accept evidence from a priest that originated in a confession, as this would violate the secrecy surrounding the sacrament of penance, which also explains why inquisitors were forbidden to hear confessions; Tedeschi, "Organization and Procedures," in *Prosecuting Heresy*, 133. In an impressive though dense study, Vicenzo Lavenia traces, through the works of theologians, canon lawyers, and other writers, the emergence in the fifteenth to the seventeenth centuries of the separation between sin and crime and between penance and earthly penalties; *L'infamia e il perdono: Tributi, pene e confessione nella teologia morale della prima età moderna* (Bologna: Il Mulino, 2004).

62. In the 1560s the priest Giovanni Pedrazza wrote a manual for confessors in which he advised clerics to avoid scandal by never hearing the confession of women in a "secret place." He surely would not have approved of the setup at Santa Chiara that provided more privacy for the confessor and the penitent than he thought advisable; *Somma, over Breve Instruttione per Confessori, Per saper bene amministrare il Sacramento della Penitenza*, trans. Camillo Camilli (Venice: Giorgio Angelieri, 1584), 5v–7r. Stephen Haliczer has written an interesting and useful study of cases of sexual solicitation by confessors that were heard by the Spanish Inquisition; *Sexuality in Confessional*. See also Adelina Sarrión Mora, *Sexualidad y confesión: La solicitación ante el Tribunal del Santo Oficio (siglos XVI–XIX)* (Madrid: Alianza Editorial, 1994); Alejandre García, *Veneno de Dios*; Michèle Escamilla-Colin, *Crimes et châtiments dans l'Espagne inquisitoriale* (Paris: Berg International, 1992), 2:167–214.

63. Kramer and Sprenger, *Malleus Maleficarum*, trans. and ed. Summers, 170.

64. Romano Canosa, *Sessualità e Inquisizione in Italia tra Cinquecento e Seicento* (Rome: Sapere 2000, 1994), 223.

65. On love magic in early modern Italy, see Jeffrey R. Watt, "Love Magic and the Inquisition: A Case from Seventeenth-Century Italy," *Sixteenth Century Journal* (forthcoming); Mary O'Neil, "Magical Healing, Love Magic and the Inquisition in Late Sixteenth-Century Modena," in *Inquisition and Society in Early Modern Europe*, ed. Stephen Haliczer (London: Croom Helm, 1987), 88–114; Ruggiero, "That Old Black Magic Called Love," in *Binding Passions*, 88–129; Ruggiero, "Love Bound: Andriana Savorgnan, Common Whore, Courtesan, and Noble Wife," in ibid., 24–56; David Gentilcore, *From Bishop to Witch: The System of the Sacred in Early Modern Terra d'Otranto* (Manchester: Manchester University Press, 1992), 211–14.

66. ASM, Inq., b. 108, f. 1A, 42r–45v.

67. Ibid., 48r.

68. For an examination of close and nonrepressive relationships between female penitents and their confessors, see Jodi Bilinkoff, *Related Lives*; Bilinkoff, "Confessors, Penitents, and the Construction of Identities in Early Modern Avila," in *Culture and Identity in Early Modern Europe (1500–1800): Essays in Honor of Natalie Zemon Davis*, ed. Barbara B. Diefendorf and Carla Hesse (Ann Arbor: University of Michigan Press, 1993), 83–100.

69. Haliczer, *Sexuality in Confessional*, 148; Prosperi, *Tribunali della coscienza*, 452; Sarrión Mora, *Sexualidad y confesión*, 17, 138–40.

70. See Haliczer, *Sexuality in Confessional*, 157. Haliczer also finds that sexual frustration among "false" mystics resulted in vivid descriptions of sexual fantasies; *Between Exaltation and Infamy*, 200–202.

71. Menghi, *Compendio*, 322; Menghi, *Fuga Daemonum, Adiurationes potentissimas, et Exorcismos formidabiles, atque efficaces in malignos spiritus propulsandos, et maleficia ab energumenis pellenda* (Venice: apud Haeredes Iohannis Varisci, 1596), 83r–89r. For virtually identical conclusions, see Brognolo, *Alexicacon*, 1:86–87.

72. ASM, Manoscritti biblioteca, no. 166, "Prattica per procedere nelle cause di S. Officio," 58–60.

73. Many magical spells, be they for love or something else, included reciting or writing down the Lord's Prayer or the Hail Mary, based on the belief that these words had intrinsic supernatural power; Stuart Clark, "Witchcraft and Magic in Early

Modern Culture," in *Witchcraft and Magic in Europe: Period of Witch Trials*, ed. Ankarloo and Clark, 108–9.

74. Eymerich and Peña, *Manuale dell'Inquisitore*, trans. and ed. Sala-Molins, 76, 78.

75. ASM, Manoscritti biblioteca, no. 166, "Prattica per procedere nelle cause di S. Officio," 63–64.

76. The close ties between *maleficia* and love magic were also evident in a case in Agen in southwestern France in 1618 that resulted in the execution of a Franciscan who allegedly cast a spell on a young woman who regularly confessed to him and whom he wished to seduce; Gregory Hanlon and Geoffrey Snow, "Exorcisme et cosmologie tridentine: Trois cas agenais en 1619," *Revue de la Bibliothèque nationale* 28 (1988): 12–27.

77. ASM, Inq., b. 108, f. 1A, 63r.

78. Clark, "Witchcraft and Magic in Early Modern Culture," in *Witchcraft and Magic in Europe: Period of Witch Trials*, ed. Ankarloo and Clark, 153.

79. ASM, Inq., b. 108, f. 1A, 17v–18r, 30r, 46v.

80. Ibid., 11r–v.

81. Menghi, *Compendio*, 316.

82. ASM, Inq., b. 108, f. 1A, 79v–80r, 100v.

83. Ibid., 158v–161v.

84. Ibid., 112v, 149v–150r, 155v–156r. Ruggiero describes an interesting case of a priest who used the candles of Holy Saturday to counter a love spell that had been cast against him; "'More Dear to Me Than Life Itself,'" in *Binding Passions*, 83–84.

85. ASM, Inq., b. 108, f. 1A, 13r, 30r.

86. Ibid., 40r.

87. Spinelli, *Musica in Carpi*, 47.

88. ASM, Inq., b. 108, f. 1A, 36v, 40r.

89. See, for example, Adriano Prosperi, *Dare l'anima: Storia di un infanticidio* (Turin: Giulio Einaudi, 2005), 91.

90. Bravi, *Principe frate*, 90.

91. *Instruttione per confessori di monache*, 9, 17–18.

92. ASM, Inq., b. 108, f. 1A, 13r, 32r.

93. Ibid., 116v.

94. Ibid., 115v–116r. For Ciarlini's age see AMSCC, Memoriale secondo, 68r.

95. ASM, Inq., b. 108, f. 1A, 116r.

96. ASM, Casa e Stato, b. 358, fasc. 31/1984, letter, 30 July 1638.

97. Garuti and Colli, *Monastero di Santa Chiara di Carpi*, 56; Ori, "Principessa in monastero," in *Clarisse in Carpi*, ed. Zarri, 1:260, 282. At San Gemignano, Angela Caterina again received papal permission to lead a privileged lifestyle, including the right to have three women in her service in that convent; ASM, Casa e Stato, b. 358, fasc. 31/1984, brief from Pope Innocent X, 6 February 1645. Contrary to Lavenia's claim ("Diavoli di Carpi," 135–36), nothing in the record suggests that Angela Caterina was compelled to leave Santa Chiara.

98. ASM, Inq., b. 108, f. 1A, 33r, 118r.

99. Ibid., 123r–v.

100. Harley, "Explaining Salem," 307–30.

101. ASM, Inq., b. 108, f. 1A, 131v–132r. After the conclusion of Angela Caterina's testimony on 29 July, Tinti and colleagues went to the infirmary to interrogate

there the monastery's vicaress, Aurelia Bendidio. Her ailments were apparently entirely natural; ibid., 139v.

102. Ibid., 136r.
103. Ibid., 132r–133r.
104. Ibid., 133r.
105. Ibid., 133r–134v.
106. Ibid., 134v–135r, 136r.
107. Ibid., 135r–136r. In light of the extremely confident way in which Bellacappa later tried to dismiss all accusations against him, involving both *maleficia* and solicitation, this abject expression of *mea culpa* seems quite out of character.
108. Ibid., 136v–138r.
109. Ibid., 139r.
110. At no point did Angela Caterina or anyone else suggest that her travails were a means of God's testing her saintliness. By contrast, the prioress Jeanne des Anges, the most famous of the possessed Ursulines of Loudun, was revered by many as a saintly mystic; Carmona, *Diables de Loudun*, 299–313; Certeau, *Possession at Loudun*, 213–26; Mandrou, *Magistrats et sorciers*, 216–17.
111. Lavenia, "Diavoli di Carpi," 90n61.
112. Romeo, *Esorcisti, confessori e sessualità*, 49–86; Grazia Biondi, "Donne di casa d'Este tra realtà e maniera devota," in *Sovrane passioni*, ed. Bentini, 188–91.
113. See Ori, "Principessa in monastero," in *Clarisse in Carpi*, ed. Zarri, 1:281.
114. Rather striking are the similarities between Angela Caterina and the character Gertrude, better known as "La monaca di Monza," in Alessandro Manzoni's classic novel *I promessi sposi*, set in northern Italy in the 1630s. This was based on an actual historical "monaca di Monza," Virginia Maria de Leyva from near Milan. Born in 1565 to a wealthy noble family, de Leyva was obliged to take the veil at the age of twelve. She later had an affair with a layman that produced two children, the first of whom was stillborn. Some fellow nuns helped conceal these indiscretions, but her lover eventually committed or arranged some murders, including that of a *conversa* who had intended to divulge de Leyva's sexual liaison. Brought to trial, de Leyva defended herself by saying that her monastic vows were null because she had been forced to take the veil and that she had been the victim of diabolical love magic. Convicted, she was sentenced in 1608 to incarceration in a tiny isolated cell in a convent but was liberated in 1622. Resuming monastic life, de Leyva met with Archbishop Federico Borromeo, who eventually became convinced that the "monaca di Monza" was truly repentant for her many sins. See *Vita e processe di Suor Virginia Maria de Leyva, monaca di Monza*, ed. Giuseppe Farinelli and Ermanno Paccagnini (Milan: Garzanti, 1989).
115. Zanelli, *Streghe e società nell'Emilia*, 144–46.
116. ASM, Inq., b. 108, f. 1A, 19v–20r.
117. Ibid., 32v, 35r.
118. Ibid., 63r, 64r–65r. Guidelines discouraged confessors from corresponding with any of their female religious confessants and mandated that nuns were not to learn to write from anyone other than their own fathers, brothers, "or other pious persons"; *Instruttione per confessori di monache*, 24, 30.
119. Spinelli, *Musica in Carpi*, 43.
120. ASM, Inq., b. 108, f. 1A, 32v. Bellacappa supposedly showed strong devotion to the Eucharist, requesting a baldachin of white damask with a gold fringe to

celebrate this sacrament; AMSCC, Memoriale secondo, 57r; Anna Maria Ori, "Le devozioni del monastero nel Seicento," in *Clarisse in Carpi*, ed. Zarri, 1:307.

121. ASM, Inq., b. 108, f. 1A, 51r.
122. Ibid., 50v–51r.
123. Ibid., 53v–54r.
124. Ibid., 40v.
125. See, for example, Menghi, *Compendio*, 127–45.
126. Ibid., 423–25.
127. The Salem witch trials relied heavily on spectral evidence, as demoniacs reported being tormented by specters of the suspects. According to Cotton Mather, unless God provided evidence to the contrary, a specter was an indication that the person whose form the demon assumed had made a pact with the devil; Norton, *Devil's Snare*, 203.
128. ASM, Inq., b. 108, f. 1A, 155r–v.
129. See AMSCC, Memoriale secondo, 55r–58v; Ori, "Vita della communità," in *Clarisse in Carpi*, ed. Zarri, 1:218.
130. *Possession et sorcellerie au XVIIe siècle: Textes inédits*, ed. Robert Mandrou (Paris: Fayard, 1979), 121–33. It is quite likely that the king never even saw the letter. If he did, Richelieu surely dissuaded him from showing any mercy to the priest.
131. See Carmona, *Diables de Loudun*, 72, 96–97, 188, 233; Certeau, *Possession at Loudun*, 52–64, 72–73, 104–5, 165–66; Rapley, *Case of Witchcraft*, 22–40, 67–69.

Chapter 4

1. ASM, Inq., b. 108, f. 1A, 100v; b. 295, fasc. 2, letter from Tinti to Barberini, 3 February 1639.
2. Menghi, *Compendio*, 478–84.
3. Ibid., 489–93.
4. See Caciola, *Discerning Spirits*, 238–39, 241.
5. Sluhovsky, *Believe Not Every Spirit*, esp. 13–93.
6. Clark, *Thinking with Demons*, 389–422. See also Sarah Ferber, *Demonic Possession and Exorcism in Early Modern France* (London: Routledge, 2004); Kathleen R. Sands, *Demon Possession in Elizabethan England* (Westport, CT: Praeger, 2004); Bodo Nischan, "The Exorcism Controversy and Baptism in the Late Reformation," *Sixteenth Century Journal* 18 (1987): 31–52.
7. MacDonald, introduction to *Witchcraft and Hysteria*, ed. MacDonald, xxxvi.
8. See Clark, *Thinking with Demons*, 398–402.
9. For a good analysis of his work, see Mary R. O'Neil, "Discerning Superstition: Popular Errors and Orthodox Response in Late Sixteenth Century Italy" (PhD diss., Stanford University, 1981), 292–381. See also O'Neil, "*Sacerdote ovvvero strione*: Ecclesiastical and Superstitious Remedies in 16th Century Italy," in *Understanding Popular Culture*, ed. Kaplan, 53–83; Ottavio Franceschini, "L'esorcista," in *Medicina, erbe e magia: Cultura popolare nell'Emilia Romagna*, ed. Giuseppe Adani and Gastone Tamagnini (Milan: Silvana, 1981), 99–115; Sluhovsky, *Believe Not Every Spirit*, 61–93.
10. Zavalloni, *Provincia*, 18.

11. At least one book by Menghi could be found in one in five monastic libraries and one in ten libraries of individual priests in Lombardy, Veneto, and Emilia, and exorcist manuals were far more numerous than works on witchcraft; Romeo, *Inquisitori*, 123.

12. See Sluhovsky, "Devil in Convent," 1386.

13. Menghi, *Compendio*, 74, 256–69.

14. Brognolo, *Alexicacon*, 1:175–77.

15. Menghi, *Compendio*, 280–88.

16. Kramer and Sprenger, *Malleus Maleficarum*, trans. and ed. Summers, 122; Broedel, *"Malleus Maleficarum,"* 44, 60, 84–85.

17. Menghi, *Compendio*, 308–9.

18. Guazzo, *Compendium Maleficarum*, ed. Summers, trans. Ashwin, 111.

19. Menghi, *Compendio*, 366.

20. Girolamo Menghi, *Flagellum daemonum* . . . (Venice: Petrus Milocus, 1626), 6.

21. Menghi, *Compendio*, 519–26; see also O'Neil, "Discerning Superstition," 354. Although Menghi initially defended the right of exorcists to apply herbs and other medicinal cures, the Congregation of the Inquisition censured him for doing so, causing him to retreat from this position in the early seventeenth century; Romeo, *Inquisitori*, 141–43.

22. Menghi, *Compendio*, 73–74.

23. Menghi, *Fuga*, 89v–94r.

24. Menghi, *Compendio*, 538–39.

25. On arguments among early modern Italian clerics for and against exorcism, see Vicenzo Lavenia, "'Tenere i malefici per cosa vera': Esorcismi e censura nell'Italia moderna," in *Dal torchio alle fiamme: Inquisizione e censura: Nuovi contributi dall più antica biblioteca provinciale d'Italia. Atti del Convegno di Studi Salerno, 5–6 novembre 2004*, ed. Vittoria Bonani (Salerno: Biblioteca Provinciale di Salerno, 2005), 129–72.

26. Menghi, *Fuga*, 10r–v.

27. Menghi, *Compendio*, 545.

28. Menghi, *Fuga*, 20r–v, 25r; O'Neil, "Discerning Superstition," 357.

29. Ferber, *Demon Possession and Exorcism*, 20–21.

30. Scribner, "Ritual and Popular Belief," in *Popular Culture*, 40.

31. Ferber, *Demonic Possession and Exorcism*, 65–66, 79.

32. Brognolo, *Alexicacon*, 2:153; Albano Biondi, "Tra corpo ed anima: Medicina ed esorcistica nel Seicento (L'*Alexicacon* di Candido Brugnoli)," in *Disciplina dell'anima*, ed. Prodi, 408.

33. In the *Rituale Romanum*, passed by Pope Paul V in 1614, exorcists were specifically forbidden to prescribe any medicines; *Rituale Romanum Pauli Quinti Pontificis Maximi iussu editum* (Venice: Nicolaus Pezzana, 1725), 204; Giovanni Romeo, "I processi di stregoneria," in *Storia dell'Italia religiosa*, ed. De Rosa, Gregory, and Vauchez, vol. 2, *Età moderna*, ed. Rosa and Gregory, 202–3.

34. Menghi, *Fuga*, 47r–50v.

35. Menghi, *Compendio*, 542–45; Menghi, *Eversio daemonum* . . . (Bologna: Giovanni Rossi, 1588), 7–8.

36. Menghi, *Eversio*, 1–2; Menghi, *Flagellum*, chap. 15.

37. Menghi, *Flagellum*, chap. 18; Menghi, *Fuga*, 22r–v.

38. Silvestro Mazzolini, *Aureus Tractatus Exorcismique Pulcherrimi et efficaces in malignos spiritus effugandos de obsessis corporibus* (Bologna: Giovanni Rossi, 1573), 25.

Mazzolini was also known as Silvestro da Prierio, after his birthplace. For a literary analysis of a Mazzolini treatise, see Armando Maggi, *Satan's Rhetoric: A Study of Renaissance Demonology* (Chicago: University of Chicago Press, 2001), 21–53.

39. Menghi, *Compendio*, 542; Menghi, *Eversio*, 1–2.

40. Menghi, *Eversio*, 53. He assumed the demoniac would be a female, telling the demons to exit "from her" (*ab ea*).

41. Ibid., 54–55.

42. The formulas for different exorcisms varied enormously in length. In one of his publications, Menghi included seventeen different exorcisms. The prayers, incantations, and readings ranged from just 3 pages to 135 pages; the longest was written by Mazzolini; Menghi, *Eversio*, 370–72, 406–540; Mazzolini, *Aureus Tractatus*.

43. Menghi, *Compendio*, 546; Menghi, *Eversio*, 12–13; Menghi, *Flagellum*, chap. 6. See also Mazzolini, *Aureus Tractatus*, 44–45.

44. Menghi, *Compendio*, 548.

45. Ibid., 532–33; Menghi, *Flagellum*, chaps. 8, 11. For a literary examination of the power of the words in the exorcisms of Menghi and Valerio Polidori, see Maggi, *Satan's Rhetoric*, 96–136.

46. Menghi, *Compendio*, 545.

47. Mazzolini, *Aureus Tractatus*, 10. Experts disagreed over the utility of striking the body of the possessed to upset the demons. Some dismissed such tactics, arguing that corporal pains do nothing to expel demons, who are entirely spiritual. For both sides see Carlo de Baucio, *Modus Interrogandi Daemonum ab Exorcista* (Venice: Turrinum, 1643), 8–9.

48. Menghi, *Fuga*, 29r–46v. See also Mazzolini, *Aureus Tractatus*, 14–22, 30. These standards concerning what the exorcist should ask demons were reinforced in the chapter on exorcism in Pope Paul V's *Rituale Romanum*, 204.

49. Menghi, *Fuga*, esp. 30r, 94v–100v; Romeo, *Inquisitori*, 161. See also Sluhovsky, "Devil in Convent," 1386; Guido Dall'Olio, "Alle origini della nuova esorcistica: I maestri bolognesi di Girolamo Menghi," in *Inquisizioni*, ed. Paolin, 81–129.

50. ASM, Inq., b. 108, 1B, fasc. 2, 6r–v, 10v, 25r–v, 33r.

51. Ibid., 1r–2r.

52. Ibid., 6r–v.

53. Ibid., 7r.

54. Ibid., 2v, 27v.

55. Menghi, *Eversio*, 5–6; Zacharia Visconti, *Complementum Artis Exorcisticae: Cum Litaniis, Benedictionibus, et Doctrinis novis, Exorcismis efficacissimis, ac remediis copiosis in Maleficiatis expertis* (Venice: Turrinum, 1643), 16.

56. ASM, Inq., b. 108, 1B, fasc. 2, 7r.

57. Ibid., 7r–v.

58. Ibid., 2v, 8v.

59. E.g., ASM, Inq., b. 254, 116r, letter from Barberini to Tinti, 29 May 1638.

60. ASM, Inq., b. 108, 1B, fasc. 2, 8r–v.

61. Clark, *Thinking with Demons*, 413.

62. Anita M. Walker and Edmund H. Dickerman, "'A Woman under the Influence': A Case of Alleged Possession in Sixteenth-Century France," *Sixteenth Century Journal* 22 (1991): 549; Lyndal Roper, "Exorcism and the Theology of the Body," in *Oedipus and the Devil*, 176; Karlsen, *Devil in Shape of Woman*, 232–33; Puyol Buil,

Inquisición y política, 142; Thomas, *Religion and Decline of Magic*, 478. In Auxonne some of the demoniac Ursulines could supposedly bend all the way backward and lick the floor; Garnot, *Diable au couvent*, 35.

63. ASM, Inq., b. 108, 1B, fasc. 2, 2v–3r, 8v, 12r.
64. See Sluhovsky, "Devil in Convent," 1397–99; Certeau, *Possession at Loudun*, 44–46, 87, 114, 139.
65. ASM, Inq., b. 108, 1B, fasc. 2, 11v.
66. Roper, "Exorcism," in *Oedipus and the Devil*, 176.
67. Almond, *Demonic Possession*, 20.
68. ASM, Inq., b. 108, 1B, fasc. 2, 3r, 26r–v; Mazzolini, *Aureus Tractatus*, 38; Polidori, *Practica Exorcistarum*, pt. 2, *Dispersio Daemonum*, 6v; Visconti, *Complementum Artis Exorcisticae*, 17; Guazzo, *Compendium Maleficarum*, ed. Summers, trans. Ashwin, 170.
69. ASM, Inq., b. 108, 1B, fasc. 2, 3r–v, 28v–29v.
70. Ibid., 28v–29r.
71. For example, ibid., 26v–27r.
72. Ibid., 12v, 27r.
73. Ibid., 12v, 34r–v.
74. Domingo Soto, *De Iustitia et Iure* (Venice: Floravantem a Prato, 1584), bk. 8, q. 3, 797; quoted in Henry Charles Lea, *Materials toward a History of Witchcraft*, ed. Arthur C. Howland (New York: T. Yoseloff, 1957), 3:1052.
75. *Rituale Romanum*, 203. According to Menghi, other sure signs of demon possession were the ability of an unlettered and "idiotic" person to speak eloquently or to sing beautifully; *Eversio*, 5–6. See also Brognolo, *Manuale Exorcistarum*, 62–72; Kramer and Sprenger, *Malleus Maleficarum*, trans. and ed. Summers, 57; Menghi, *Compendio*, 352–53. Attacking the skeptics of witchcraft, Bodin derisively said that melancholy could not have taught Greek, Hebrew, or Latin to a group of possessed, who spoke all three even though they had not learned them; *Démonomanie*, 76v.
76. Carmona, *Diables de Loudun*, 180; Certeau, *Possession at Loudun*, 41–43. In the letter in which he begged for mercy from Louis XIII in 1634, Grandier referred to the same standards of proof to argue that the Ursulines were in fact not possessed. He claimed the nuns garbled the Latin language so badly that one could never mistake them for demons with supernatural knowledge; *Possession et sorcellerie*, ed. Mandrou, 126–28.
77. Garnot, *Diable au couvent*, 37–38. See also Puyol Buil, *Inquisición y política*, 166.
78. ASM, Inq., b. 108, 1B, fasc. 2, 29v.
79. Menghi, *Fuga*, 50v–51r.
80. Unlike exorcisms elsewhere, those of Santa Chiara did not seem to exhibit much eroticism. The nuns were said to contort their bodies and scream, but the flatulence, swollen tongues, and foaming mouths hardly sound likely to excite the libido of onlookers. By contrast, Roper describes exorcism scenes as often "titillating" and adds, "Exorcisms were often carried out on beds [never so in Carpi], where the possessed woman, rolling about and dress askew, sunk in the toils of complete bodily submission to the male Devil, recalled only too vividly the woman lost to the body and to lust"; "Exorcism," in *Oedipus and the Devil*, 190. See also Sluhovsky, *Believe Not Every Spirit*, 137–65. Though requiring that exorcisms be conducted in public places, Menghi would surely have disapproved of the theatrical way in which the Ursulines were exorcized in front of huge audiences in Loudun; Certeau, *Possession at Loudun*, 85–108.

81. John Tedeschi notes that an Italian abridged version of Scaglia's *Instructio* actually did appear in print already in 1625; "The Roman Inquisition and Witchcraft: An Early Seventeenth-Century 'Instruction' on Correct Trial Procedure," in *Prosecution of Heresy*, 208.

82. ASM, Manoscritti biblioteca, no. 166, "Prattica per procedere nelle cause di S. Officio," 200–202. See also Biondi, "'Inordinata devozione'" in *Finzione e santità*, ed. Zarri, 306–25; Tedeschi, "Question of Magic and Witchcraft," in *Prosecution of Heresy*, 229–58; Turchini, "Modello ideale," in *Inquisizione romana*, ed. Del Col and Paolin, 187–98. On the various manuals that inquisitors regularly consulted, see Adriano Prosperi, "L'arsenale degli inquisitori," in *Inquisizione romana*, 311–24.

83. *Instructio*, in Castaldi, *De Potestate Angelica*, 2:243. Tedeschi, "Roman Inquisition and Witchcraft," in *Prosecution of Heresy*, 205–27.

84. Mandrou, *Magistrats et sorciers*, 264–84.

85. Giovanni Levi, *Inheriting Power: The Story of an Exorcist*, trans. Lydia G. Cochrane (Chicago: University of Chicago Press, 1988), 24–26.

86. ASM, Inq., b. 108, 1B, fasc. 2, 26r.

87. On melancholic humors as both cause and effect of demon possession, see Visconti, *Complementum Artis Exorcisticae*, 13, 17.

88. ASM, Inq., b. 108, 1B, fasc. 2, 39v. Expert exorcists acknowledged that physicians could conclude authoritatively that a person was possessed after seeing that there was no natural cause of the illness; Brognolo, *Manuale Exorcistarum*, 46.

89. ASM, Inq., b. 108, 1B, fasc. 2, 38v–40r.

90. See H. C. Erik Midelfort, *Mad Princes of Renaissance Germany* (Charlottesville: University Press of Virginia, 1994), 46, 149. On the opinions of medical experts at Loudun, see Certeau, *Possession at Loudun*, 109–38.

91. ASM, Inq., b. 108, 1B, fasc. 2, 40r–v. In a letter written 24 August 1638, Abbati reiterated these explanations; Archivio Storico di Carpi, Archivio Guaitoli, b. 246/2, Tornini, "Storia della Città di Carpi," tome 2, 54–56.

92. ASM, Inq., b. 108, 1B, fasc. 2, 40v–41v.

93. Ibid., 7v–8r, 26v.

94. Romeo, *Esorcisti, confessori e sessualità*, 123.

95. Midelfort, *History of Madness*.

96. ASM, Inq., b. 108, 1B, fasc. 2, 4r–v, 6v, 11r–v.

97. Ibid., 4v–5v.

98. Ibid., 27r.

99. Ibid., 13r–v, 27r–v.

100. Ibid., 13r–v, 42r.

101. Ibid., 13v–14r, 15v.

102. Ibid., 14v.

103. Menghi, *Compendio*, 214.

104. ASM, Inq., b. 108, 1B, fasc. 2, 21r–v.

105. Ibid., 21v.

106. Ibid.

107. Ibid., 17r–v.

108. Ibid., 17v, 29v–30r.

109. Ibid., 17v–18r, 29v–31r.

110. Ibid., 35r–v, 37r–38r.

111. Ibid., f. 1A, 23v–24r.
112. Ibid., 1B, fasc. 2, 14v–15r.
113. Ibid., 15r–v.
114. Ibid., 15v–17r.
115. Ibid., 20r–v, 24r.
116. Ibid., b. 286, f. 3, loose letter, Giudici to Tinti, 1 May 1638.

117. Ibid., loose letter, Giudici to Tinti, 21 May 1638. Menghi and other experts on demonic power insisted that demons under no circumstances had the power to free criminals from prison. God did not allow such actions and impeded devils from doing so through good angels; Menghi, *Compendio*, 417.

118. ASM, Inq., b. 108, 1B, fasc. 2, 19r–v.
119. Ibid., 8v–9r.
120. Ibid., 10r–v.

121. Ibid., 38r–v. Zaretti could have added that the possessed Ottavia Bendidio died in January 1638.

122. Ibid., 22v, 38r–v.
123. Menghi, *Compendio*, 356.

124. Brognolo, *Manuale Exorcistarum*, 35. In the early seventeenth century, the English physician Edward Jorden also maintained that many mistook hysteria or "the suffocation of the mother" or the womb for demon possession; Almond, *Demonic Possession*, 3.

125. ASM, Inq., b. 108, 1B, fasc. 2, 22v–23v.
126. Ibid., f. 1A, 127v–128r.
127. Ibid., 16r, 17r, 114v.
128. Ibid., 15v.
129. Ibid., 116r–v, 117v.

130. Elaine G. Breslaw, *Tituba, Reluctant Witch of Salem: Devilish Indians and Puritan Fantasies* (New York: New York University Press, 1996); Karlsen, *Devil in Shape of Woman*; Norton, *Devil's Snare*.

131. Midelfort, *Exorcism and Enlightenment*, 26.
132. ASM, Inq., b. 254, 57r, letter from Barberini to Tinti, 25 October 1636.
133. Ibid., b. 295, fasc. 2, letter from Tinti to Barberini, 20 December 1636.
134. Ibid., b. 254, letters from Barberini to Tinti, 62r, 27 December 1636; 81r, 10 January 1637.

135. Archivio Segreto Vaticano, Congregazione dei Vescovi e dei Regolari, Registra Regularium, b. 46: 164v, 21 May 1638; Lavenia, "Diavoli di Carpi," 112n145. There is no trace of this permission in the Congregation's records for 1638, and the Congregation of Bishops and Regulars has no surviving records for 1636 and only a handful for 1637.

136. ASM, Inq., b. 254, 116r, letter from Barberini to Tinti, 29 May 1638.
137. Ibid., 123r–v, letter from Barberini to Tinti, 31 July 1638.
138. Ibid., b. 295, letter from Tinti to Barberini, 7 August 1638.

139. In several letters spread out over many months, Tinti also informed Cardinal Barberini that the convent did not have the facilities to keep the ten nuns separated from each other and from everybody else. As noted above, the cells or oratories were too small to accommodate a bed. The best that could be done was to keep some of the most severely afflicted nuns largely separated from the rest of the community,

but assisted by some of the healthy sisters; ibid., letters from Tinti to Barberini, 15 July, 6 and 14 November 1638.

140. Ibid., b. 108, f. 1C, f. 4, 11r–v.

141. Ibid., loose folio.

142. Ibid., loose document, 1r.

143. Ibid., f. 4, 14r. In a letter he wrote to another cleric on 3 September, Inquisitor Tinti expressed his anger at the rumor that the ban on exorcisms was his idea, a clear sign of his disagreement with the policy of the Congregation in Rome concerning the exorcists; f. 1C, loose document.

144. Ibid., b. 254, 127r, letter from Barberini to Tinti, 4 September 1638.

145. Ibid., b. 108, f. 1C, a loose folio dated October 16, 1638; b. 254, 129r, letter from Barberini to Tinti, 2 October 1638; b. 295, fasc. 2, letter from Tinti to Barberini, 23 October 1638.

146. ASM, Inq., b. 108, f. 1A, 203r–v. The letter is found in f. 1C, f. 4, unnumbered folio. We do not know who actually wrote the letter, as it is signed vaguely, "Aff[ezionatissi]me. figlie et serve, Le Vessate."

147. Romeo, *Inquisitori*, 145–68.

148. Menghi, *Fuga*, 53r–59r; see also O'Neil, "Discerning Superstition," 312–17, 378nn62, 63.

149. Romeo, *Esorcisti, confessori e sessualità*, 13–48 and esp. 98n27. See also Ottavia Niccoli, "L'esorcista prudente: Il *Manuale Exorcistarum ac Parochorum* di Fra Candido Brugnoli da Sarnico," in *Piacere del testo*, ed. Prosperi, 208–12. For the period 1580–1600, twelve of the sixty-four people who were tried for "superstition" by the Inquisition of Modena were clerics, four of whom were exorcists; O'Neil, "*Sacerdote ovvero strione*," in *Understanding Popular Culture*, ed. Kaplan, 56, 65. A dozen years before the outbreak of Santa Chiara's woes, some clerics in Modena attracted the attention of the Inquisition for using some very unorthodox methods in exorcisms, namely the manipulation of the genitals of female demoniacs, based on the conviction that demons first took hold and possessed the private parts; Romeo, *Esorcisti, confessori e sessualità*, 13–48, and for the trial transcript itself, 201–62. Citing, among other things, Candido Brognolo's concerns about such practices, Ottavia Niccoli argues that the manipulation of genitalia in exorcisms, though surely not widespread, was probably not terribly rare in sixteenth- and seventeenth-century Italy; Niccoli, "Esorcista prudente," in *Piacere del testo*, ed. Prosperi, 208–12.

150. *Instructio*, in Castaldi, *De Potestate Angelica*, 2:244.

151. ASM, Manoscritti biblioteca, no. 166, Scaglia, "Prattica per procedere nelle cause di S. Officio," 66–67. Tedeschi, "Question of Magic and Witchcraft," in *Prosecution of Heresy*, 229–58; Schutte, *Aspiring Saints*, 67–72.

152. Tedeschi, "Roman Inquisition and Witchcraft" and "Question of Magic and Witchcraft," both in *Prosecution of Heresy*, 205–27, 229–58.

153. Prosperi, *Tribunali della coscienza*, 463–64. A seventeenth-century confessor was also critical of exorcizing female religious, fearing that *donnicciole* were mendacious and might manipulate gullible clerics to attain a reputation of saintliness; Anne Jacobson Schutte, "Tra scilla e cariddi: Giorgio Polacco, donne e disciplina nella Venezia del Seicento," in *Donna, disciplina, creanza cristiana*, ed. Zarri, 215–36. On authorities' growing distrust of exorcisms in seventeenth-century Bavaria, see David

Lederer, *Madness, Religion and the State in Early Modern Europe: A Bavarian Beacon* (Cambridge: Cambridge Universiy Press, 2006), 197-241.

154. Mario Rosa, "La religiosa," in *Uomo barocco*, ed. Villari, 228.

155. Brognolo, *Manuale Exorcistarum*, 121.

156. Ibid., 121-32. Exorcism enjoyed greater support among Catholic leaders in France than in Italy. Rejected by Huguenots, exorcism could in effect serve as a form of pro-Catholic propaganda—expelling demons from the bodies of the possessed might show that God was on the side of the Catholics and serve as a means of converting people back to Catholicism; D. P. Walker, *Unclean Sprits: Possession and Exorcism in France and England in the Late Sixteenth and Early Seventeenth Centuries* (Philadelphia: University of Pennsylvania Press, 1981), 5, 19-42; Hanlon and Snow, "Exorcisme et cosmologie tridentine," 12-27; Ferber, *Demon Possession and Exorcism*, 4-6, 23-33; Denis Crouzet, "A Woman and the Devil: Possession and Exorcism in Sixteenth-Century France," in *Changing Identities in Early Modern France*, ed. Michael Wolfe (Durham: Duke University Press, 1997), 191-215; Jonathan L. Pearl, *The Crime of Crimes: Demonology and Politics in France, 1560-1620* (Waterloo: Wilfrid Laurier University Press, 1999). For a similar take on a German writer, see William Bradford Smith, "Friedrich Förner, the Catholic Reformation, and Witch-Hunting in Bamberg," *Sixteenth Century Journal* 36 (2005): 115-28.

157. Brognolo himself had run-ins with the Holy Office because his exorcisms did not conform entirely with the *Rituale Romanum*, and the Congregazione dell'Indice eventually banned his *Manuale Exorcistarum* in 1727; *Dizionario biografico degli Italiani*, s.v. "Brugnoli, Candido" by Rotondò; Schutte, *Aspiring Saints*, 116-20. For more on Brognolo see Niccoli, "Esorcista prudente," in *Piacere del testo*, ed. Prosperi, 193-215.

158. *Possession et sorcellerie*, ed. Mandrou, 130-31.

159. Righi, "Inquisizione ecclesiastica a Modena nel '700," in *Formazione e controllo dell'opinione pubblica*, ed. Biondi, 72-74.

160. Thomas, *Religion and the Decline of Magic*, 493-501.

161. See, for example, O'Neil, "*Sacerdote ovvero strione*," in *Understanding Popular Culture*, ed. Kaplan, 81n42.

162. Prosperi, *Tribunali della coscienza*, 422. See also Di Simplicio, *Autunno della stregoneria*, 275-77; Romeo, *Inquisitori*, 143, 244.

163. Roper, "Exorcism," in *Oedipus and the Devil*, 192.

164. MacDonald, introduction to *Witchcraft and Hysteria*, ed. MacDonald, xxxvi.

165. Ibid., xxxvi-xl. See also Holmes, "Women: Witnesses and Witches," 64-65.

166. Briggs, *Witches and Neighbors*, 168; Karlsen, *Devil in Shape of Woman*, 133.

Chapter 5

1. Prosperi, *Tribunali della coscienza*, 197; Tedeschi, "Organization and Procedures," in *Prosecution of Heresy*, 149; Carena, *Tractatus de Officio Sanctissimae Inquisitionis*, pt. 2, titulus 9, "De Sortilegii," ß24, "De nonnullis animadvertendis circa carcerationem, examen, & torturam Maleficarum," n. 210. To be sure, the logistics of keeping suspects isolated in monasteries were often challenging.

2. ASM, Inq., b. 108, f. 1A, 74r, 81r-v.

3. Ibid., 74r–76v.
4. Ibid., 74v.
5. Ibid., 81v.
6. Ibid., 81v–82r.
7. Ibid., 90v–93v.
8. Ibid., 94r–95r.
9. Ibid., 164r.
10. Ibid., 164v–165r.
11. Ibid., 165r–167v.

12. Michael D. Bailey, *Battling Demons: Witchcraft, Heresy, and Reform in the Late Middle Ages* (University Park: Pennsylvania State University Press, 2003), 111–16; Gabriella Zarri, "'Vera' santità, 'simulata' santità: Ipotesi e riscontri," in *Finzione e santità*, ed. Zarri, 9–36.

13. ASM, Manoscritti biblioteca, no. 166, "Prattica per procedere nelle cause di S. Officio," 207–25.

14. Guazzo, *Compendium Maleficarum*, ed. Summers, trans. Ashwin, 137.

15. Russell, *Prince of Darkness*, 175.

16. Anne Jacobson Schutte, "'Saints' and 'Witches' in Early Modern Italy: Stepsisters or Strangers?" in *Time, Space, and Women's Lives*, ed. Schutte, Kuehn, and Menchi, 153–64. See also David Gentilcore, "The Church, the Devil and the Healing Activities of Living Saints in the Kingdom of Naples after the Council of Trent," in *New Perspectives on Witchcraft*, ed. Levack, vol. 5, *Witchcraft, Healing, and Popular Diseases*, 200–21; and, for the late Middle Ages, Peter Dinzelbacher, "Sante o streghe: Alcuni casi del tardo medioevo," in *Finzione e santità*, ed. Zarri, 52–87.

17. For cases of pretense of sanctity heard by the Roman Inquisition, see Schutte, *Aspiring Saints*; Prosperi, *Tribunali della coscienza*, 431–64; Adelisa Malena, *L'Eresia dei perfetti: Inquisizione romana ed esperienze mistiche nel seicento italiano* (Rome: Edizioni di Storia e Letteratura, 2003); Ottavia Niccoli, "The End of Prophecy," *Journal of Modern History* 61 (1989): 667–82; and various essays in *Finzione e santità*, ed. Zarri. Among the large number of publications on female mystics in Spain, be they "true" or "false," see Gillian T. W. Ahlgren, *Teresa of Avila and the Politics of Sanctity* (Ithaca: Cornell University Press, 1996); Jodi Bilinkoff, *Avila of Saint Teresa: Religious Reform in a Sixteenth-Century City* (Ithaca: Cornell University Press, 1989); Alastair Hamilton, *Heresy and Mysticism in Sixteenth-Century Spain: The Alumbrados* (Toronto: University of Toronto Press, 1992); Stephen Haliczer, *Inquisition and Society in the Kingdom of Valencia, 1478–1834* (Berkeley: University of California Press, 1990), 273–94; Richard Kagan, *Lucrecia's Dreams: Politics and Prophecy in Sixteenth-Century Spain* (Berkeley: University of California Press, 1990); Stefania Pastore, *Un'eresia spagnola: Spiritualità conversa, alumbradismo e Inquisizione (1449–1559)* (Florence: Leo S. Olschki, 2004); Mary Elizabeth Perry, *Gender and Disorder in Early Modern Seville* (Princeton: Princeton University Press, 1990); Ronald E. Surtz, *The Guitar of God: Gender, Power, and Authority in the Visionary World of Mother Juana de la Cruz (1481–1534)* (Philadelphia: University of Pennsylvania Press, 1990); several essays in *Women in the Inquisition: Spain and the New World*, ed. Mary E. Giles (Baltimore: Johns Hopkins University Press, 1999); Alison Weber, *Teresa of Avila and the Rhetoric of Femininity* (Princeton: Princeton University Press, 1990); and Francisca de los Apóstoles, *The Inquisition of Francisca: A Sixteenth-Century Visionary on Trial*, ed. and trans. Gillian T. W. Ahlgren

(Chicago: University of Chicago Press, 2005). Among the last cases heard by the Inquisition of Modena was that of Lucia Roveri, who claimed to be not merely a saint but even the second incarnation. Attracting a number of followers, Roveri asserted that God had previously come in the form of a man, Jesus, to redress the evil caused by the first man. To complete the redemption of humanity, God now came in the form of a woman, Roveri herself, to make amends for the sins of the first woman. See Grazia Biondi's fine study, *E Iddio si fece donna: La storia di Lucia Roveri della Mirandola (1728–1788)* (Modena: Unione Donne Italiae, Centro documentazione donna, 1996).

18. See esp. Haliczer, *Between Exaltation and Infamy*.

19. Ulrike Strasser, *State of Virginity: Gender, Religion, and Politics in an Early Modern Catholic State* (Ann Arbor: University of Michigan Press, 2004).

20. Gabriella Zarri, "From Prophecy to Discipline, 1450–1650," trans. Keith Botsford, in *Women and Faith: Catholic Religious Life in Italy from Late Antiquity to the Present*, ed. Lucetta Scaraffia and Gabriella Zarri (Cambridge: Harvard University Press, 1999), 83–112. On the shift from mystical ecstasy to prayer and contemplation as the foundation for female sanctity, see Zarri, "Living Saints: A Typology of Female Sanctity in the Early Sixteenth Century," in *Women and Religion in Medieval and Renaissance Italy*, ed. Bornstein and Rusconi, 219–303.

21. *Enciclopedia Cattolica* (Vatican City: Ente per l'Enciclopedia Cattolica e per il Libro Cattolico, 1948), s.v. "Antonio di Padova, santo."

22. ASM, Inq., b. 108, f. 1A, 103v–104r.

23. For the testimony of the vicaress, Aurelia Bendidio, see ibid., 140r–v.

24. See, for example, Menghi, *Compendio*, 230–40.

25. ASM, Inq., b. 108, 1B, fasc. 2, 20v–21r. According to the witchcraft expert Candido Brognolo, writing about three decades after this trial, demons could appear in almost any form they wished, unless God prevented them from doing so. Interestingly, one form in which a demon could never appear, Brognolo avowed, was that of Christ hanging on the cross, because God would not allow such irreverence; *Alexicacon*, 1:136.

26. ASM, Inq., b. 108, f. 1A, 67r.

27. See Giambattista Montorsi, "Storia della causa di canonizzazione di Camilla Pio," in *Clarisse in Carpi*, ed. Zarri, 1:163–92.

28. Ori, "Devozioni del monastero," in *Clarisse in Carpi*, ed. Zarri, 1:297–340; for the accounts of the miraculous cures of illnesses, see "'Libro delle Grazie della Beata Camilla Pio' (ms. 1632–1702)," ed. Paolo Trionfini, in ibid., 2:93–127.

29. ASM, Inq., b. 108, f. 1A, 163r. In his guidebook for inquisitors, Cesare Carena spoke of false visions as if only women experienced them; *Tractatus de Officio Sanctissimae Inquisitionis*, pt. 2, titulus 17, "De variis delictis spectantibus ad S. Officio," n. 19. Confessors were also to be on the lookout for such false visions among nuns; *Instruttione per confessori di monache*, 20.

30. ASM, Inq., b. 108, f. 1A, 101v; b. 295, fasc. 2, letter from Tinti to Barberini, 28 August 1638.

31. Guazzo, *Compendium Maleficarum*, ed. Summers, trans. Ashwin, 129–132.

32. ASM, Inq., b. 108, f. 1A, 101v–102v.

33. Ibid., 102v–103r.

34. See, for example, Brognolo, *Manuale Exorcistarum*, 63, 67. For fuller discussions of suicide and diabolism, see Michael MacDonald and Terence R. Murphy, *Sleepless*

Souls: Suicide in Early Modern England (Oxford: Clarendon Press, 1990); Georges Minois, *History of Suicide: Voluntary Death in Western Culture*, trans. Lydia G. Cochrane (Baltimore: Johns Hopkins University Press, 1999); Jeffrey R. Watt, *Choosing Death: Suicide and Calvinism in Early Modern Geneva* (Kirksville, MO: Truman University Press, 2001); and *From Sin to Insanity: Suicide in Early Modern Europe*, ed. Jeffrey R. Watt (Ithaca: Cornell University Press, 2004).

35. ASM, Inq., b. 108, f. 1A, 104r.

36. ASM, Inq., b. 295, fasc. 2, letter from Tinti to Barberini, 25 September 1638.

37. ASM, Inq., b. 254, 130r–v, letter from Barberini to Tinti, 9 October 1636; quotations from 130v. The experience with Giudici was probably a factor behind the Congregation's decision in January 1640 to forbid inquisitors to appoint vicars. If an inquisitor really needed the assistance of a parish priest or another clergyman, he could not delegate authority to anyone without the express consent of the Congregation of the Inquisition; b. 255, letter from Barberini to Tinti, 28 January 1640.

38. ASM, Inq., b. 108, f. 1A, 202r–v.

39. Ibid., 207r–v*. After folio 204, the remaining eleven folios in this *filza* (1A) are not actually numbered. Since they represent the continuation of this interrogation, I have assigned the appropriate numbers, adding an asterisk to indicate that the numeral does not actually appear on the folios themselves.

40. Ibid., 204r–208r*.

41. This incident bore a striking resemblance to an attack that occurred several years later in Auxonne in eastern France, where an Ursuline convent suffered travails that were similar to those of Santa Chiara. Several nuns were deemed possessed and bewitched, and in 1660 the "demoniac" Ursulines resorted to a similar form of rough justice by violently attacking Barbe Buvée, the mother superior and principal suspect of witchcraft; Garnot, *Diable au couvent*, 59.

42. ASM, Inq., b. 108, f. 1A, 206v*–207r*, 211v*–212v*.

43. Ibid., 205v*–206r*.

44. Tinti did not convoke Villani, who could not reveal to anyone what was said to him in confession; ibid., 215r*.

45. Ibid., 206r–v*.

46. Ibid., 206v*.

47. Ibid., 208r*.

48. Ibid., 208v*–209r*.

49. Ibid., 205r*.

50. Ibid., 209r–v*.

51. Cf. Puyol Buil, *Inquisición y política*, 166.

52. ASM, Inq., b. 108, f. 1A, 205v*, 210v*, 211v*.

53. Ibid., 210v*.

54. Ibid., 205v*.

55. Kramer and Sprenger, *Malleus Maleficarum*, trans. and ed. Summers, 227.

56. For criticism of this belief, see Spee, *Cautio Criminalis*, trans. Hellyer, 101–4.

57. ASM, Inq., b. 108, f. 1A, 205v*, 210v*–211r*.

58. Ibid., 209v*.

59. Ibid., 209v*–210v*.

60. Ibid., 213r*.

61. Ibid., 212v*–214v*; b. 295, fasc. 2, letter from Tinti to Barberini, 23 October 1638.

62. Ibid., b. 108, f. 1A, 211r*.
63. Ibid., 211r–v*.
64. Ibid., 214v*.
65. Ibid., 210r–v*.
66. Ibid., b. 295, fasc. 2, letter from Tinti to Barberini, 23 October 1638.

Chapter 6

1. There is no record of the precise date on which Bellacappa was arrested, but it is safe to assume that it took place just days before his first appearance before Tinti on 9 August. Before the interrogation began on that day, the scribe noted that Tinti had ordered the arrest and the transfer to Modena of the Observant Franciscan; ASM, Inq., b. 108, f. 1A, 169v.
2. Ibid., 169v–170v. Coincidentally, a few decades earlier Girolamo Menghi, the influential exorcist, had lived for many years in the Annunziata; Franceschini, "Esorcista," in *Medicina, erbe e magia*, ed. Adani and Tamagnini, 107. On the questioning of defendants, see Eymerich and Peña, *Manuale dell'Inquisitore*, trans. and ed. Sala-Molins, 137–39.
3. ASM, Inq., b. 108, f. 1A, 170r–v.
4. Ibid., 170v–171r, 175r–176v, 177v, 194r–v.
5. Ibid., 174r–175r.
6. Ibid., 177r–v. A total of six members of the extended Coccapani family were Clarisses at Santa Chiara, including the bewitched Veroncia Maria. As we have seen, Alsuinda's suspicions were directed mainly against Dealta.
7. Ibid., 178v.
8. Ibid., 179r–180r, 185v–186r.
9. Ibid., 180r–183r, 184v–185r.
10. Ibid., 182v.
11. Ibid., 183r–184r.
12. Ibid., 184v.
13. Ibid., 187v–188r.
14. Paolina Forni and Leonora Galli, both deceased, also probably confessed to Lazzarino.
15. Ibid., 188v–189r.
16. Ibid., 189v.
17. Ibid., 190r.
18. Ibid., 190r–191r.
19. Ibid., 191r.
20. Ibid., 189v.
21. Ibid., 191v–192r.
22. Ibid., 192r–v.
23. Ibid., 192v–193r.
24. Ibid., 193v.
25. See Prosperi, *Tribunali della conscienza*, esp. 202.
26. ASM, Inq., b. 108, f. 1A, 193v–194r.

27. Ibid., 195v–196r.
28. Ibid., 200r–v.
29. Ibid., 195v–196v.
30. Ibid., 196v–198v.
31. Ibid., 198v–199r.
32. Ibid., 199r–v. On the investigation of Trionfanti, see Inq., b. 86, fasc. 2; Watt, "Love Magic and Inquisition."
33. ASM, Inq., b. 108, f. 1A, 200r–v.
34. Ibid., 201r–v; b. 295, fasc. 2, letter from Tinti to Barberini, 24 November 1638. In a document dated 19 September 1638, Bellacappa was initially told that he would have to post bond of one thousand silver ducats in order to be released to house arrest. There is no indication that he actually posted such a large bond; b. 108, f. 1C, loose document, 1r–2v.
35. Massimo Firpo, "La fase [difensiva] del processo inquisitoriale del cardinal Morone: Documenti e problemi," *Critica storia* 23 (1986): 123.
36. Eymerich and Peña, *Manuale dell'Inquisitore*, trans. and ed. Sala-Molins, 159, 163; Prosperi, *Tribunali della coscienza*, 196. On concealing the identify of accusers in Spain, see Escamilla-Colin, *Crimes et châtiments*, 1:189–96.
37. Schutte, *Aspiring Saints*, 38–39. Kramer described similar procedures for the defense of the accused; *Malleus Maleficarum*, trans. and ed. Summers, 222. Attorneys who were appointed for the accused by the Spanish Inquisition–rarely could defendants choose their own lawyers–viewed their principal task as getting their clients to confess rather than mounting a defense for them. At no time were these attorneys allowed to be alone with the accused; an inquisitor was always supposed to be present; Pérez, *Spanish Inquisition*, 146; Henningsen, *Witches' Advocate*, 42; Rawlings, *Spanish Inquisition*, 32.
38. ASM, Inq., b. 108, f. 1A, 201v–202r. Tinti was disinclined to oblige the nuns to repeat their testimony, which they had made earlier before Giudici, about illicit sexual acts, in part because he did not want to make these female religious "blush" by having these obscene acts read in front of them in the presence of the inquisitor and perhaps the archpriest, whom they all feared somewhat; b. 295, fasc. 2, letter from Tinti to Barberini, 11 September 1638. On the Roman Inquisition's procedures concerning the defense of the accused, see Tedeschi, "Organization and Procedures," in *Prosecuting Heresy*, 135–40; Tedeschi, "Inquisitorial Law and Witch," in *Early Modern European Witchcraft*, ed. Ankarloo and Henningsen, 94–97.
39. After his departure from Carpi, Bellacappa reportedly stayed for some time at a monastery in his native Parma. There is no record, however, of any interrogation of Observant Franciscans in Parma; ASM, Inq., b. 295, fasc. 2, letter from Tinti to Barberini, 15 May 1638.
40. Firpo, "Fase [difensiva]," 123.
41. ASM, Inq., b. 108, f. 1C, filza 11, 11r–v.
42. Ibid., 1r.
43. Ibid., 1r–3v.
44. Ibid., filza 2, 1r*–3v*, 5v* (I have assigned numbers to these unnumbered folios). The window, as described here, conformed to the requirements spelled out in the Rule of Santa Chiara; *Regola delle Monache di S. Chiara di Carpi*, chap. 16.
45. AMSCC, Memoriale secondo, 58r–v; Ori, "Vita della communità," in *Clarisse in Carpi*, ed. Zarri, 1:232.

46. ASM, Inq., b. 108, f. 1C, filza 2, 7v*.
47. Ibid., 4r*–19r*.
48. Ibid., filza 3, 18r–v.
49. *Instruttione per confessori di monache*, 7–8.
50. Ibid., 8.
51. ASM, Inq., b. 108, f. 1C, filza 3, 16r.
52. Ibid., filza 5, 1r–v, 5v.
53. Ibid., 1r–2v, 5v.
54. Ibid., 5r–6v.
55. Ibid., 8r.
56. Ibid., 7v–8v.
57. Tedeschi, "Inquisitorial Law and Witch," in *Early Modern European Witchcraft*, ed. Ankarloo and Henningsen, 95–96.
58. ASM, Inq., b. 108, f. 1C, filza 8, 1r–v.
59. Ibid., 1v–2r.
60. Ibid., 2r.
61. The Gregorian bull read, "ob probationum defectum impunitum cum difficilis sit probationis, *testibus etiam singularitibus concurrentibus praesumptionibus, indiciis, et aliis adminiculis delictum probatum esse arbitrio suo iudicandi*" (emphasis in original; "About proving an unpunished fault: When it is difficult to prove, and when individual witnesses, indications and other supporting evidence are in agreement, the fault ought to be decided by their judgment"); *Universi Dominici Gregis*, in Masini, *Sacro arsenale*, 399. See also Carena, *Tractatus de Officio Sanctissimae Inquisitionis*, pt. 2, titulus 6, "De Confessariis sollicitantibus," ß7, An hoc delictum sufficienter probetur testibus singularibus, n. 52.
62. It was at the discretion of the inquisitor to determine how many accusers, alleging separate cases of solicitation, were needed to convict a priest; Carena, *Tractatus de Officio Sanctissimae Inquisitionis*, pt. 2, titulus 6, "De Confessariis sollicitantibus," ß8–9, 11. The denunciation of just one person against a priest was not enough even to begin an inquiry against him for solicitation; ibid., ß13.
63. ASM, Inq., b. 108, f. 1C, filza 8, 9v.
64. Ibid., 2r–v.
65. Ibid., 3r–4r; Prospero Farinacci, *Tractatus de Testibus* (Venice: Georgium Variscum, 1609 [first published in 1596]), q. 65, n. 144. Farinacci gave as examples of unlikely actions a man killing his son, a teacher killing his pupil, or a male lying with "a girl without pollution"! Giuseppe Mascardi, *De Probationibus* . . . 3 vols., 3rd ed. (Frankfurt am Main: Ioannem Saurium, 1607). In his abbreviated citation, Barozzi referred to Mascardi's conclusion 1370, but he surely meant 1371: "Testi non verisimilia deponenti, credendum non esse" (Witnesses who testify of things that seem unlikely are not to be believed).
66. ASM, Inq., b. 108, f. 1C, filza 8, 7r–v.
67. Mascardi, *De Probationibus*, conclusion 743, no. 4.
68. Ibid., no. 5: "Si plura sunt Capitula in aliquo instrumento ad invicem separata, falsitas commissa in uno non reddit falsa alia capitula."
69. ASM, Inq., b. 108, f. 1C, filza 8, 10v.
70. Ibid., b. 295, fasc. 2, letter from Tinti to Barberini, 24 November 1638.
71. Ibid., b. 108, f. 1C, filza 8, 10v.

72. Ibid., 4v–5r. His abbreviated citation of Carena was incorrect (or he was citing another edition), but the passage in question can be found at *Tractatus de Officio Sanctissimae Inquisitionis*, pt. 2, titulus 6, "De Confessariis sollicitantibus," ß5, n. 30: "Sive extra ocasionem confessionis, in Confessionario, aut in loco quocumque, ubi confessiones Sacramentales audiuntur, seu ad confessionem audiendam electo, simulantes ibidem confessiones audire" ("About Confessors' Propositioning [Penitents]," ß5, n. 30: "Whether outside the occasion of confession, in the confessional, or in any other place where sacramental confessions are heard or chosen for hearing a confession, there simulated confessions can be heard").

73. ASM, Inq., b. 108, f. 1C, filza 8, 5r–v.

74. Ibid., 6r–v.

75. Ibid., 8r–v.

76. Ibid., 11r–12r.

77. Ibid., 13v.

78. Carena, *Tractatus de Officio Sanctissimae Inquisitionis*, pt. 2, titulus 6, "De Confessariis sollicitantibus," ß10, An mulieres, quae sollicitanti confessario, consenserunt sint sufficientes testes in hoc crimine. See also Prosperi, *Tribunali della coscienza*, 536.

79. ASM, Inq., b. 108, f. 1C, filza 8, 8v.

80. Ibid., 12r–14r.

81. Ibid., 12v–13r; Farinacci, *Tractatus de Testibus*, q. 69, no. 2, "Testis de auditu alieno regulariter non probat."

82. Farinacci, *Tractatus de Testibus*, q. 69, no. 24, "Probat tamen si concurrant alia adminicula" ("Then [hearsay] is a proof if the other supporting evidence should agree"); no. 25, "Etiam sine adminiculis iuncta fama inducit violentam praesumptionem" ("Even without supporting evidence, a common report leads to the violent presumption [of guilt]").

83. Farinacci, *Tractatus de Testibus*, q. 65, no. 107, "Testibus pluribus, magis creditur, quam paucioribus." Farinacci added that one should give more credence to richer witnesses than poorer ones. Although Bellacappa came from a fairly comfortable background, most of the Clarisses who testified against him almost surely came from even more affluent families; ibid., no. 117, "Testibus ditioribus magis creditur, quam pauperiorius."

84. ASM, Inq., b. 108, f. 1C, filza 8, 13v.

85. Ibid., b. 295, fasc. 2, letter from Tinti to Barberini, 28 August 1638.

86. Ibid., b. 108, f. 1C, filza 8, 4v.

87. Ibid., b. 295, fasc. 2, letter from Tinti to Barberini, 11 September 1638. It must be noted that Barozzi's statement for the defense, which is neither dated nor signed, may not have survived in its entirety. On the bottom of folio 14v, the last extant folio, is written "2e ubi." This would seem to refer to the first words of the next folio. So it is possible, though not likely, that Barozzi did address the witchcraft/magic allegations on folios that have not survived. Be that as it may, the fact that he filled fourteen folios, front and back, with arguments to discredit the accusations of solicitation shows the importance he gave to them.

88. See Firpo, "Fase [difensiva]."

89. Tedeschi also observes that the Inquisition was the first tribunal to impose prison sentences as a form of punishment. Secular courts traditionally incarcerated defendants only for the duration of their trial and could basically impose only the fol-

lowing sentences: banishment, the galleys, mutilation, and execution; introduction to *Prosecution of Heresy*, xii–xiii, 8–9. Although the Roman Inquisition required a defense attorney if the defendant requested one even if he or she admitted committing the crime, the Spanish Inquisition withheld counsel for the defense in such cases; Tedeschi, "Inquisitorial Sources," in ibid., 53. On the Holy Office's procedures governing the application of torture, see Tedeschi, "Inquisitorial Law and Witch," in *Early Modern European Witchcraft*, ed. Ankarloo and Henningsen, 97–104.

Chapter 7

1. ASM, Inq., b. 254, 136r-v, copy of letter from Barberini to archpriest of Carpi, 30 October 1638.

2. ASM, Inq., b. 295, fasc. 2, letter from Tinti to Barberini, 14 November 1638.

3. ASM, Inq., b. 254, 136r-v, copy of letter from Barberini to archpriest of Carpi, 30 October 1638. Associated with the Holy Office in the mid-seventeenth century, Francesco Albizzi was convinced that most nuns who were supposedly possessed actually suffered from melancholy or some other natural malady. He warned against attributing ills that physicians could not cure to *maleficia*, stating that at times God, upon whose will all remedies depend, does not want the medical cures to work; *De Inconstantia in jure Admittenda, vel non* (Amsterdam: Ioannis Antonii Huguetan, 1683), 344–45; Romeo, "Processi di stregoneria," in *Storia dell'Italia religiosa*, ed. De Rosa, Gregory, and Vauchez, vol. 2, *Età moderna*, ed. De Rosa and Gregory, 205n22.

4. ASM, Inq., b. 254, 135r, letter from Barberini to Tinti, 30 October 1636.

5. ASM, Inq., b. 295, fasc. 2, letters from Tinti to Barberini, 2 and 15 December 1638; b. 111, fasc. 2, "Narrative et precetti," 2 folios (unnumbered).

6. Ibid., b. 111, fasc. 2, "Narrativa dell'esperienze," 1r–2r, 2v–3r. The six folios of this undated narrative are not numbered, but I have assigned numbers to them.

7. Ibid., 2v.

8. Ibid., 3r-v.

9. Ibid., 4r–5v.

10. Ibid., 6r.

11. Ibid., 5v–6r.

12. Ibid., 6r-v.

13. Brognolo, *Manuale Exorcistarum*, 141–42.

14. ASM, Inq., b. 108, f. 1C, filza 3, 3r.

15. Ibid., b. 111, fasc. 2, orders by Mantica, 5, 7, 10, 18, 20, 24 January and 7 February 1639.

16. Ibid., b. 108, f. 1C, filza 3, 3v.

17. Albizzi, *De Inconstantia in jure Admittenda*, 356–57; Lucien Ceyssens, "Le cardinal François Albizzi (1593–1684): Son autobiographie et son testament," *Bulletin de l'Institut historique belge de Rome* 45 (1979): 343–70; Ceyssens, *Le cardinal François Albizzi (1593–1684): Un cas important dans l'histoire du jansénisme* (Rome: Pontificium Athenaeum Antonianum, 1977). Romeo, "Processi di stregoneria," in *Storia dell'Italia religiosa*, ed. De Rosa, Gregory, and Vauchez, vol. 2, *Età moderna*, ed. De Rosa and Gregory, 202.

18. ASM, Inq., b. 108, f. 1C, filza 3, 4r-v.

19. Ibid., 5r–v.
20. Ibid., 5v.
21. Ibid. Mantica did not live to see his reforms fully implemented, as he died in Carpi after a four-day illness on 3 February 1639; ibid., b. 295, fasc. 2, letter from Tinti to Barberini, 3 February 1639.
22. ASM, Manoscritti biblioteca, no. 166, "Prattica per procedere nelle cause di S. Officio," 202–5.
23. ASM, Inq., b. 295, fasc. 2, letter from Tinti to Barberini, 11 January 1639.
24. Ibid., b. 255, letter from Barberini to Tinti, 1 January 1639.
25. Ibid., b. 108, f. 1C, filza 3, 9v–10r.
26. Ibid., b. 295, fasc. 2, letters from Tinti to Barberini, 11 and 13 January 1639.
27. Earlier Tinti had intended to interrogate Dealta but had said, back in August 1638, that he wanted to question Bellacappa first, believing that the ex-confessor's testimony could shed light on accusations against Dealta; ibid., letter from Tinti to Barberini, 14 August 1638.
28. Ibid., letter from Tinti to Barberini, 5 December 1638.
29. Ibid., b. 108, f. 1C, filza 3, 19r. Although the Inquisition of Modena's lengthy Santa Chiara case was technically an investigation and not a trial, Sluhovsky, as mentioned in the introduction, is misleading in labeling this merely a case of possession and not witchcraft. Even though there was no formal trial for witchcraft, as we have seen, everyone in Carpi was convinced that witchcraft was behind the alleged possessions. The primary concern of all residents was the apparent *maleficia*, and the Martinellis and Bellacappa were incarcerated for months during the investigation. Only the Congregation in Rome prevented the Inquisition of Modena from formally pressing charges against them; "Devil in Convent," 1380–81.
30. ASM, Inq., b. 108, f. 1C, filza 3, 19r–20r.
31. Ibid., 20r.
32. Ibid., 20v.
33. Ibid., b. 255, letter from Barberini to Tinti, 15 January 1639; b. 295, letter from Tinti to Barberini, 26 January 1639.
34. ASM, Manoscritti biblioteca, no. 166, "Prattica per procedere nelle cause di S. Officio," 46–47.
35. Prosperi, *Tribunali della coscienza*, 538; Carena, *Tractatus de Officio Sanctissimae Inquisitionis*, pt. 2, titulus 6, "De Confessariis sollicitantibus," ß18, "De speciali poena suspensionis a confessionibus imponenda Confessario sollicitanti, vel de sollicitatione suspecto," n. 90; ASM, Manoscritti biblioteca, no. 166, "Prattica per procedere nelle cause di S. Officio," 49.
36. He had been released at least by 24 January; ASM, Inq., b. 255, letter from Barberini to Tinti, 12 February 1639.
37. Ibid., letter from Barberini to Tinti, 22 January 1639.
38. Ibid., b. 286, f. 3, loose letter, 29 January 1639.
39. Ibid.
40. Ibid.
41. Bodin, *Démonomanie*, 175v.
42. Romeo, *Inquisitori*, vii–ix, 3–108, 247–74; Romeo, "Processi di stregoneria," in *Storia dell'Italia Religiosa*, ed. De Rosa, Gregory, and Vauchez, vol. 2, *Età moderna*, ed. De Rosa and Gregory, 189–209; Schutte, *Aspiring Saints*, 61–63.

43. *Instructio*, in Castaldi, *De Potestate Angelica*, 2:244; Propseri, *Tribunali della coscienza*, 403–4.

44. ASM, Inq., b. 108, f. 1C, loose folio. Barberini asked the bishop of Modena to assuage the fears of relatives of the nuns at Santa Maria Maddalena, assuring them that Dealta and Ippolita were absolutely innocent of any wrongdoing and were being moved only because of the stubbornness of so many Clarisses; b. 286, f 3, loose letter, 19 March 1639. Barberini became incensed in April 1641 when the Clarisses of Carpi complained about the amount of money they had to pay the convent of Maria Maddalena to compensate for the expenses of the Martinellis. Pointing out that this was all of their making and that it had not been easy to find a convent that would take Dealta and Ippolita, the cardinal warned the nuns not to say another word about this ever again; b. 255, letter from Barberini to Tinti, 6 April 1641.

45. Ibid., letters from Barberini to Tinti, 26 February 1639, 9 April 1639; Cancelleria Ducale, Ambasciatori, Roma, b. 237, 11 and 18 July 1637, 2, 6, and 13 April 1639; Lavenia, "Diavoli di Carpi," 100n101, 134–35n228.

46. Ibid., b. 295, fasc. 2, letters from Tinti to Barberini, 12 and 19 March 1639; b. 286, f. 3, loose letter, 23 April 1639. The abbess of Santa Chiara was also upset with this ruling and preferred to be under the direction of the archpriest; b. 111, fasc. 2, letter from Tinti to the Abbess of Santa Chiara, 24 March 1639. When a new bishop assumed power in Modena in 1640, following the death of Alessandro Rangoni in late April of that year, the vicaress of Santa Chiara petitioned to be placed again under the Observant Franciscans. Cardinal Barberini said that he was "scandalized" by this request in light of the troubles that members of that order, including Bellacappa, had caused at Santa Chiara. He declared that he would never accede to that request; b. 255, letter from Barberini to Tinti, 13 October 1640. When Obizzo d'Este, a member of Modena's reigning dynasty, became the new bishop of Modena, the Congregation ruled that it, rather than Modena's bishop, would now serve as governor of Santa Chiara, unconvincingly claiming that the convent had been assigned only to the late Rangoni, not to the office of bishop he had held. Barberini and colleagues then clarified that, though Obizzo might prove fit to govern the convent, they wanted to reserve judgment until a later date; b. 255, letters from Barberini to Tinti, 2, 9, and 23 March 1641. Although at this time Rome seemed to want to limit the influence of the Este family, in October 1654 Santa Chiara was placed under the control of Cardinal Rinaldo d'Este, nephew of Angela Caterina; AMSCC, Memoriale secondo, 68r.

47. Though not dated or signed, this document was almost surely written by Giovanni Lupi, the Holy Office's special commissioner to Santa Chiara. He arrived in January, and all but one nun had been healed by late March; ASM, Inq., b. 286, f. 3, two loose folios.

48. Ibid., b. 295, fasc. 2, letter from Tinti to Barberini, 30 March 1639.

49. Ibid., b. 255, letter from Barberini to Tinti, 16 April 1639.

50. Ibid., b. 286, f. 3, loose letter, 21 May 1639.

51. Ibid., b. 255, letter from Barberini to Tinti, 21 May 1639.

52. Ibid., b. 295, fasc. 2, letter from Tinti to Barberini, 15 May 1639.

53. Ibid., letter from Tinti to Barberini, 27 June 1639; b. 255, letter from Barberini to Tinti, 2 July 1639.

54. Ibid., b. 295, fasc. 2, letter from Tinti to Barberini, 11 May 1639.

55. The only entry in the *Memoriale* that in any way refers to the "demonic" woes of Santa Chiara is the following announcement of the prayers to the saint and Barberini's gift: "1639 Adi 24 8bre. Essendo stato questo Mon.^{rio} appreso da certa infermità stimata da molte persone malia, o spiritam.°, si votarono le Monache all'intercess.^{e} di S. Domenico da Soriano, per la quale guarirono; da qui pres'occ.^{ne} l'Emin.^{mo} Sig.^{r} Cardinal Franc.° Barberini di mandare alle d.^{e} Monach'un quadro sopra il quale stà dipinta l'imag.^{e} del d.° Santo fatto di mano d'un eccellente pittore in Roma"; AMSCC, Memoriale secondo, 59v.

Conclusion

1. Biblioteca Apostolica Vaticana, Borgiano Latino, vol. 558: 518r–519v. Actually there was never any suggestion that a lay sister (*una monaca conversa*) had anything to do with Santa Chiara's tribulations. As we have seen, the cures also took considerably longer than this letter indicated. See also Lavenia, "Diavoli di Carpi," 138.

2. *Instructio*, in Castaldi, *De Potestate Angelica*, 2:244.

3. Francesca Medioli did find that out of a sample of thirty requests for annulment of monastic vows, the Congregation of Bishops and Regulars granted about half of them. Those most likely to succeed, however, were novices who had not taken formal vows; "Dimensions of Cloister," in *Time, Space, and Women's Lives*, ed. Schutte, Kuehn, and Menchi, 171–78.

4. See Harline, *Burdens of Sister Margaret*, 56.

5. Briggs, *Witches and Neighbors*, 19.

6. Cohn, *Europe's Inner Demons*, 179.

7. Carmona, *Diables de Loudun*, 165; Certeau, *Possession at Loudun*, 11, 24–25; Rapley, *Case of Witchcraft*, 69, 77. Paul Boyer and Stephen Nissenbaum argue that deep divisions–centered on kinship rivalries, farmers' resistance to commercial capitalism, and a polarizing pastor–served as a catalyst to witchcraft accusations in Salem; *Salem Possessed: The Social Origins of Witchcraft* (Cambridge: Harvard University Press, 1974).

8. See Gabriele Fabbrici, "Osservazioni sulla storia degli ebrei carpigiani nel Cinquecento: Le testimonianze dei partiti della comunità," in *Principato di Carpi*, ed. Zacchè, 299–314.

9. Ori, "Principessa in monastero," in *Clarisse in Carpi*, ed. Zarri, 1:283. In the same volume, see Andrea Beltrami, "Feste e musica in convento nei secoli XVII e XVIII," 341–54.

10. ASM, Inq., b. 295, fasc. 2, letter from Tinti to Barberini, 15 May 1639; ibid., letter from Tinti to Barberini, 6 June 1640.

11. Ibid., b. 255, letter from Barberini to Tinti, 23 June 1640.

12. Schutte, "Asmodea," in *Werewolves*, ed. Edwards, 119–35.

13. Sluhovsky, *Believe Not Every Spirit*, 252–54.

14. See Sluhovsky, "Devil in Convent," 1399–402. Nicky Hallett finds that sexual fantasies and temptations were prominent in the torments that demons allegedly inflicted on two nuns they possessed; *Witchcraft, Exorcism and the Politics of Possession*, 33. In his study of possession in a seventeenth-century French convent, Albrecht Burkardt

suggests that some young women who had been obliged to take the veil by their parents perceived their temptations to commit carnal sins as diabolical; "Les déboires d'une vocation: Un cas d'obsession démoniaque chez les Visitandines parisiennes au début des années 1620," in *Visitation et Visitandines aux XVIIe et XVIIIe siècles*, ed. Bernard Dompnier (Saint-Etienne, France: Publications Université de Saint-Etienne, 2001), 417–39. Certain anthropological studies also see a connection between possession behavior and sexuality. Melford E. Spiro maintains that one can look at various forms of "possession states" and methods of healing from the perspectives of both Western psychoanalysis and of the culture of indigenous healers. He finds that the most common conflict associated with possession was sexual in nature, most notably fear of retaliation; *Burmese Supernaturalism: A Study in the Explanation and Reduction in Suffering* (Englewood Cliffs, NJ: Prentice-Hall, 1967).

15. See, for example, Klaits, *Servants of Satan*, 118; Sluhovsky, *Believe Not Every Spirit*; Sluhovsky, "Devil in Convent," 1379–411.

16. Sluhovsky most definitely errs when he says that the outbreak of Santa Chiara's possessions was caused by the "imposition of an extremely severe regimen"; *Believe Not Every Spirit*, 245.

17. ASM, Inq., b. 255, letter from Barberini to Tinti, 12 May 1640; b. 295, fasc. 2, letter from Tinti to Barberini, 6 June 1640; b. 255, letter from Barberini to Tinti, 15 September 1640.

18. See esp. Caciola, *Discerning Spirits*; Sluhovsky, "Devil in Convent," 1379–411.

19. On the basis of the article by Lavenia, Sluhovsky claims that the removal of Santa Chiara from the Observant Franciscans was a question of a reformation of morals. This action had far less to do with the morals of Santa Chiara than with the ongoing struggle for power, found throughout Italy and other parts of Catholic Europe, between regular and secular clergy; "Devil in Convent," 1392–93; Lavenia, "Diavoli di Carpi," 81–83.

20. Sluhovsky, "Divine Apparition," 1039–55.

21. See Anne Jacobson Schutte, "Legal Remedies for Forced Monachization in Early Modern Italy," in *Heresy, Culture, and Religion in Early Modern Italy*, ed. Delph, Fontaine, and Martin, 231–46.

22. The contemporary description of this case is reproduced as the appendix in Salvatore Mazzarella, *Diavoli a Caltanissetta: Il 'caso memorabile' del 1671* (Caltanissetta and Rome: Salvatore Sciascia, 1990), 143–64.

23. Sluhovsky, *Believe Not Every Spirit*, 262–63; Sluhovsky, "Devil in Convent," 1406–7. Sluhovsky also errs in saying that the two Capuchins themselves felt stained by the sins of usury and concupiscence. According to the record, the Capuchins claimed they were merely the instruments through which the demons (and therefore God) could exhort Sicilians to forswear their sinful ways.

24. Sluhovsky, "Devil in Convent," 1406–7. Although the men were described as obsessed (*ossessi*), passages such as the following clearly show that demons supposedly penetrated and possessed their bodies: one demon said, "ho entrato nel corpo di questa perra Creatura con altri centomila compagni con tutta facilità" (Mazzarella, *Diavoli*, 143); asked how many spirits were in the afflicted lay brother's body, a demon declared, "Millia millium, con facilità [*sic*] entrammo, e colla medesima facilità [*sic*] ne usciremo dopo duodeci giorni" (ibid., 149); a cleric asked a demon "il motivo per cui siete entrate [*sic*] in queste Creature" (ibid., 152).

25. In regard to the Ursulines of Loudun, the physician Claude Quillet allegedly reduced their ills to sexual frustration and isolation, identifying their malady as "hysteromania or erotomania," and impishly recommended sexual activity as a cure: "Those poor she-devil religious, finding themselves shut up between four walls, go crazy, fall into a melancholic delirium, tortured by the urges of the flesh, and in reality what they need is a carnal remedy in order to be perfectly cured"; quoted in Certeau, *Possession at Loudun*, 135.

26. Midelfort, *History of Madness*, 18–19, 32–49.

27. Karlsen, *Devil in Shape of Woman*, 248–51. Quotation from Vincent Crapanzano, introduction to *Case Studies in Spirit Possession*, ed. Vincent Crapanzano and Vivian Garrison (New York: John Wiley and Sons, 1977), 9. For similar views concerning possessed nuns in Madrid in the 1620s, see Puyol Buil, *Inquisición y politica*, 180. James Sharpe asserts that, though they did not reside in convents, young women who were most prone to demon possession in early modern England lived in "godly" households. Possession allowed them to express "forbidden impulses" with impunity, and their frequent blasphemy suggested they were rebelling against religion; *Instruments of Darkness: Witchcraft in Early Modern England* (Philadelphia: University of Pennsylvania Press, 1996), 202–3, 206.

28. Certeau, *Possession at Loudun*, 104–5. Similarly, possession in England, which was most common among children and youth, has been construed as a means of empowerment against overbearing adult authority; Almond, *Demonic Possession*, 22–26.

29. Romeo, *Inquisitori*, 25–65.

30. Prosperi, *Tribunali della coscienza*, 374–77; Romeo, *Inquisitori*, 28.

31. *Instructio*, in Castaldi, *De Potestate Angelica*, 2:245.

32. Over a century before the Carpi case, the Inquisition of Modena did use aggressive tactics against accused witches. Carlo Ginzburg found that the Inquisition used torture and tricky questioning in order to transform the "superstitious" practices and beliefs of defendants into a form of devil-worshiping witchcraft; "Witchcraft and Popular Piety," in *Clues, Myths, and Historical Method*, 1–16; Prosperi, *Tribunali della coscienza*, 385–86. Diametrically opposed were the actions of the Inquisition in Ferrara over a century later. For the years 1653–72, the Holy Office there did not have any witchcraft cases per se but did try some women for having accused others of witchcraft. During these two decades, inquisitors in Ferrara viewed denunciations of witchcraft as a form of defamation and sought to restore the honor of the woman thus maligned; Prosperi, *Tribunali della coscienza*, 191–92. It should be noted that even Cardinal Barberini was known to permit the torture of accused witches. He allowed torture in the case of Oriana da Pienza, but the evidence was overwhelming that Oriana, a well-educated woman, actually had many clients who sought, through her magic, cures for ills or the location of buried treasure; Di Simplicio, *Autunno della stregoneria*, 279–94.

33. In this era, the only person in Carpi accused of witchcraft who was subjected to torture was Marco Blesio. Tried by the Inquisition of Modena in 1618–20, Blesio was condemned of casting spells to find buried treasure, win the love of another, and endure torture; ASM, Inq., b. 52, f. 1, esp. 163v–170v; b. 252, letters from Congregation of the Holy Office to Inquisitor of Modena, 17 November 1619, 3 January and 8 February 1620; b. 253, letter from Congregation of the Holy Office to Inquisitor of Modena, 6 November 1621. Blesio was initially sentenced to five years in the galleys,

later commuted to five years in prison, which in turn was commuted to five years of house arrest. The most notable difference between Blesio's case and the convent's later woes is that he confessed to abusing sacraments and sacramentals by having a magnet baptized and procuring holy water for magical purposes. He also stole some prohibited books from the inquisitor's vicar; b. 252, letter from Congregation of the Holy Office to Inquisitor of Modena, 17 November 1619. Significantly, some Clarisses maintained that Blesio was a close friend of Dealta; b. 108, f. 1A, 17r, 29r, 39r.

34. Prosperi, *Tribunali della coscienza*, 375. It has been suggested that an important reason for the Holy Office's leniency in witchcraft is that the most popular manual was still Nicolau Eymerich's *Directorium Inquisitorum* (1376), edited in 1503 by Francisco Peña, which equated witchcraft with ritual magic and labeled it a form of heresy. Although Eymerich assumed a diabolical pact, he had no notion of the sabbat and put no emphasis on *maleficium*; Levack, *Witch-Hunt*, 225–26.

35. *Instructio*, in Castaldi, *De Potestate Angelica*, 2:245. John Tedeschi has quite plausibly suggested that the Congregation of the Holy Office waited several decades before publishing these instructions to avoid raising the ire of secular authorities, many of whom felt the Inquisition was too lenient toward witches; "Roman Inquisition and Witchcraft," in *Prosecution of Heresy*, 205–27.

36. Adriano Prosperi, "Inquisitori e streghe nel Seicento fiorentino," in *Gostanza*, ed. Cardini, 217–50; Rainer Decker, "Die Haltung der römischen Inquisition gegenüber Hexenglauben Exorzismus am Beispiel der Teufelsaustreibungen in Paderborn 1657," in *Das Ende der Hexenverfolgung*, ed. Sönke Lorenz and Dieter R. Bauer (Stuttgart: Franz Steiner, 1995), 97–115.

37. See especially works by Alfred Soman: "La décriminalisation de la sorcellerie en France," *Histoire, économie et société* 4 (1985): 179–203; and "Decriminalizing Witchcraft: Does the French Experience Furnish a European Model?" *Criminal Justice History* 10 (1989): 1–22; both reprinted in Soman, *Sorcellerie et Justice Criminelle: Le Parlement de Paris (16e–18e siècles)* (Hampshire, England: Variorum, 1992). There could also be a considerable gap between the cessation of executions and the decriminalization of witchcraft. In England, witchcraft was not officially decriminalized until 1736, a half century after the last execution in England. See also Ian Bostridge, *Witchcraft and Its Transformations, c. 1650–1750* (Oxford: Clarendon Press, 1997); Mandrou, *Magistrats et sorciers*, esp. 539–64.

38. William Monter, "Women and the Italian Inquisitions," in *Women in the Middle Ages and Renaissance: Literary and Historical Perspectives*, ed. Mary Beth Rose (Syracuse: Syracuse University Press, 1986), 82–83.

39. Brian Levack, "The Decline and End of Witchcraft Prosecutions," in *Witchcraft and Magic in Europe: The Eighteenth and Nineteenth Centuries*, ed. Bengt Ankarloo and Stuart Clark (Philadelphia: University of Pennsylvania Press, 1999), 13.

40. Monter, "Witch Trials in Continental Europe, 1560–1660," in *Witchcraft and Magic in Europe: Period of Witch Trials*, ed. Ankarloo and Clark, 9, 40–41. On the Parlement of Paris, see esp. works by Alfred Soman: "Décriminalization de sorcellerie," 179–203; "Le sabbat des sorciers: Preuve juridique," in *Sabbat des sorciers*, ed. Jacques-Chaquin and Préaud, 85–99; and other works reprinted in *Sorcellerie et Justice Criminelle*. Cf. Mandrou, *Magistrats et sorciers*, esp. 313–63.

41. Tedeschi, "Preliminary Observations," in *Prosecution of Heresy*, 8. See also articles in Adriano Prosperi, *Inquisizione romana*, esp. "L'Inquisizione: Verso una nuova

immagine?" 3–27; and "L'Inquisizione nella storia: I caratteri originali di una controversia secolare," 69–96.

42. It should also be noted that the introduction of judicial torture was initially part of a move away from appeals to the supernatural, reflecting a certain skepticism toward various forms of ordeals. The accused might be forced to plunge an arm into boiling water or to walk on burning coals, and serious burns were a sign of guilt, based on the assumption that God protected the innocent. Appealing to traditions of Roman Law, beginning in the twelfth century various jurists insisted on more "rational" forms of proof, the most important being the confession of guilt by the accused, commonly referred to as the "queen of proofs." Torture was viewed as a viable means of eliciting a confession, provided there were already significant grounds for supposing guilt and the torture was not excessive; Edward Peters, *Torture* (New York: Basil Blackwell, 1985), esp. 40–73.

43. Levack, "Decline and End of Witchcraft Prosecutions," in *Witchcraft and Magic in Europe: Eighteenth and Nineteenth Centuries*, ed. Ankarloo and Clark, 7. On judicial skepticism in England, see Sharpe, *Instruments of Darkness*, 213–34.

44. Claire Guilhem, "La Inquisición y la devaluación del verbo femenino," in *Inquisición española*, ed. Bennassar, 199–207.

45. Monter and Tedeschi, "Statistical Profile of Italian Inquisitions," in *Inquisition in Early Modern Europe*, ed. Henningsen and Tedeschi, 135–36; Monter, "Women and Italian Inquisitions," in *Women in Middle Ages and Renaissance*, ed. Rose, 73–87.

46. Cf. Gaskill, *Witchfinders*, 279.

47. To be sure, belief in demonic possession did not die in the seventeenth century. Erik Midelfort has conducted a very interesting study of the Catholic priest Johann Joseph Gassner (1727–79), a controversial exorcist, who into the 1770s purportedly healed hundreds of sick, blind, and crippled whose ills, Gassner determined, were of diabolical origin even though they appeared natural. Eventually he was forbidden to practice his cures, as Church leaders, including Pope Pius VI, condemned the public nature of his exorcisms, and political authorities were unnerved by the huge enthusiastic crowds, including Protestants as well as Catholics, he attracted. Evidence is quite strong that his ministrations did work in many cases and that his cures did not lend themselves to modern "scientific" explanations. The key distinction between his actions and those of the exorcists in Carpi was that Gassner generally did not associate demonic possessions with witchcraft and therefore did not try to identify witches; *Exorcism and Enlightenment.*

48. AMSCC, Memoriale secondo, 60r–v.

49. Ibid., 64v, 65r.

50. Ibid., 69v, 76v, 81r–v, 83r, 84r–v, 86r–87r, 101v, 107v, 108v–109r; Ori, "Vita della communità," in *Clarisse in Carpi*, ed. Zarri, 1:232. Ronchi had actually inspired others several years earlier when she supposedly received a miraculous cure of a crippled arm in 1666, thanks to a relic of the Virgin Mary; AMSCC, Memoriale secondo, 80r. We do not know when Veronica Maria Coccapani died. Her name last appears in the *Memoriale* 29 June 1661, when she assumed the responsibilities of *ruotare*; ibid., 77v.

51. Ibid., 61v.

52. Ibid., 78v, 81r–82r, 105r.

53. Ibid., 101v–103r.

54. See Bravi, *Principe frate*, 89–97.

55. AMSCC, Memoriale secondo, 62v, 69v, 71r.

56. Ori, "Vita della communità," in *Clarisse in Carpi*, ed. Zarri, 1:204n39; 214; in the same volume see Ori, "Devozioni del monastero," in 1:307.

57. Vatican City, Archivio della Congregazione per la Dottrina della Fede, Stanza Storica GG 4-e, Inquisizione di Modena (1656–1763).

58. *Atti ufficiali*, vol. 1, *1460–1753*, ed. Guidarini, Monfardini, and Montorsi, 180. There was also a certain gradation among the *Lettori Giubilati*. When they took part in a procession, the *Lettori Giubilati* walked in order based on seniority. In 1648, following the death of a distinguished professor, there was a dispute as to who should be the fourth *Lettore* in a procession, Bellacappa or Fra Pietro da Rimini. Ultimately it was decided that Fra Pietro should precede Bellacappa, who was assigned the fifth position in processions; ibid., 186.

59. To my great dismay, there is no extent copy of this manuscript. All that remains is the title of the treatise, copied by a friar in 1850: "Fuggio l'ozio overo de la Relazione di quello che è occorso dal 1610 che io ho ricevuto l'abito dal questa serafica religione de' Minori Osservanti del N.S.P. Francesco, ne la [sic] stessa religione e provincia di Bologna fino al 1650. Definitta [sic] da me P. Angelo Bellacappa da Parma, lettore della medesima provincia, e predicatore generale tra tanti il minimo e indegno servo di G.C.S. No." Bologna, Archivio Storico della Provincia di Cristo Re dei Frati Minori dell'Emilia-Romagna, R Stagni 147, Memorie degli Uomini illustri dell'Osservante Provincia di Bologna, f. 89. See also Cantalupo, *Cenni biografici*, 79–80.

60. Cantalupo, *Cenni biografici*, 78; Zavalloni, *Provincia*, 15, 18.

61. There is uncertainty as to when Bellacappa died. According to one source, he died 2 July 1651 while serving as guardian in Parma. Another source suggests that he was still alive and teaching and preaching in 1656; Cantalupo, *Cenni biografici*, 78–79.

SELECTED BIBLIOGRAPHY

Archival Sources

Bologna, Italy. Archivio Storico della Provincia di Cristo Re dei Frati Minori dell'Emilia-Romagna.
>R Stagni 147, Memorie degli Uomini illustri dell'Osservante Provincia di Bologna.

Carpi, Italy. Archivio Monastero di Santa Chiara di Carpi.
>Libro della *Madonna di San Luca*.
>Memoriale continente successi che giornalmente occorrono per questo Sacro Monasterio di S. Chiara di Carpi, e particolarmente della Recettione, et professione delle Monache di detto Monasterio, non per l'avvenire ancora, tanto quelle del Commune, quanto quelle del Servizio dell'Illustrissima et Eccellentissima Signora Suor Angela Caterina Principessa d'Este.

Carpi, Italy. Archivio Storico di Carpi.
>Archivio Guaitoli, b. 9, fasc. 6, I Memoriale; b. 246/2, Padre L. Tornini, "Della Storia della Città di Carpi," tome 2:51; b. 824.

Modena, Italy. Archivio di Stato di Modena.
>Cancelleria Ducale, Ambasciatori, Roma, b. 224.
>Casa e Stato, bb. 93, 202, 203, 358/1984.
>Inquisizione di Modena, bb. 52, 86, 101, 102, 106, 108, 111, 252, 253, 254, 255, 286, 295.
>Manoscritti biblioteca, no. 166, "Prattica per procedere nelle cause di S. Officio fatta dal Sr. Cardinale Scaglia."
>Mappario Estense, Fabbriche, 17, 18.
>Soppressioni Napoleoniche, Regolari, Carpi, Santa Chiara.

Vatican City. Archivio della Congregazione per la Dottrina della Fede.
>Sant'Officio, Stanza Storica E5-e; GG 4-e; M7-r,-s,-t; UV 23.

Vatican City. Archivio Segreto Vaticano.
>Congregazione dei Vescovi e dei Regolari, Registra Regularium, bb. 37, 46.

Vatican City. Biblioteca Apostolica Vaticana.
>Borgiano Latino, vol. 558.

Published Sources

Albizzi, Francesco. *De Inconstantia in jure Admittenda, vel non*. Amsterdam: Ioannis Antonii Huguetan, 1683.
Baucio, Carlo de. *Modus Interrogandi Daemonum ab Exorcista*. Venice: Turrinum, 1643.
Bodin, Jean. *De la Démonomanie des sorciers*. Paris: Jacques du Puys, 1580.

Brognolo, Candido. *Alexicacon, Hoc est Opus de Maleficiis ac Morbis Maleficiis.* 2 vols. Venice: Giovan Battista Catanei, 1668.

———. *Manuale Exorcistarum ac Parochorum, hoc est Tractatus de curatione, ac Protectione Divina.* Venice: Nicolò Pezzana, 1720 (first published in 1651).

Canons and Decrees of the Council of Trent. Translated by H. J. Schroeder. St. Louis: B. Herder, 1941.

Carena, Cesare. *Tractatus de Officio Sanctissimae Inquisitionis et modo procedendi in causis fidei.* Bologna: Jacobus Montius, 1668 (first published 1631).

Castaldi, Giovanni Tommaso. *De Potestate Angelica sive de Potentia Motrice ac Mirandis Operibus Angelorum atque Daemonum.* 3 vols. Rome: Francesco Caballi, 1650–1652.

Le Constitutioni delle monache della prima regola di Santa Chiara. Naples: Lazaro Scoriggio, 1624.

Eymerich, Nicolau. *Directorium Inquisitorum, Cum scholiis seu annotationibus eruditissimis D. Francisci Pegnae Hispani, S. Theologiae et Iuris Uriusque Doctoris.* Rome: in aedibus Populi Romani, 1578.

Eymerich, Nicolau, and Francisco Peña. *Il manuale dell'Inquisitore.* Translated and edited by Louis Sala-Molins. Rome: Fanucci, 2000.

Farinacci, Prospero. *Tractatus de Testibus.* Venice: Georgium Variscum, 1609.

Ferrazzi, Cecilia. *Autobiography of an Aspiring Saint.* Translated and edited by Anne Jacobson Schutte. Chicago: University of Chicago Press, 1996.

Guidarini, Diego, Bruno Monfardini, and Giambattista Montorsi, eds. *Atti ufficiali della Provincia Osservante Francescana di Bologna.* Vol. 1, *1460–1753.* Bologna: Edizioni francescane, 2002.

Instruttione per li confessori di monache. Publicata di commissione dell'Illustriss. e Reverendiss. Sign. Card. Ludovisi Arcivescovo di Bologna. Bologna: Vittorio Benacci, 1627.

Kramer, Heinrich, and James Sprenger. *The Malleus Maleficarum.* Translated and edited by Montague Summers. New York: Dover, 1971.

Licenza et avvertimenti per li confessori straordinarii delle monache. Publicata di commissione dell'Illustriss. e Reverendiss. Sign. Card. Ludovisi Arcivescovo di Bologna. Bologna: Herede del Benacci, 1630.

MacDonald, Michael, ed. *Witchcraft and Hysteria in Elizabethan London: Edward Jorden and the Mary Glover Case.* London and New York: Tavistock/Routledge, 1991.

Mascardi, Giuseppi. *De Probationibus. Conclusiones Probationum Omnium, quae in utroque Foro quotidie versantur, Iudicibus, Advocatis, Causidicis, omnibus denique Iuris Pontificii, Caesareique Professoribus utiles, practicabiles, ac necessariae.* 3 vols. 3rd ed. Frankfurt am Main: Ioannem Saurium, 1607.

Masini, Eliseo. *Sacro arsenale overo Prattica dell'Officio della Santa Inquizitione. Con l'inserzione d'alcune Regole fatte dal P. Inquisitore Tomaso Menghini Domenicano e di diverse annotationi del Dott. Giovanni Pasqualone, Fiscale della Suprema Generale Inquisizione di Roma.* Rome: Reu. Cam. Apost., 1693 (first published 1621).

Mazzolini, Silvestro (da Prierio). *Aureus Tractatus Exorcismique Pulcherrimi et efficaces in malignos spiritus effugandos de obsessis corporibus.* Bologna: Giovanni Rossi, 1573.

Menghi, Girolamo. *Compendio dell'arte essorcistica, et possibilità delle mirabili, et stupende operationi delli Demoni, et de i Malefici con li rimedii opportuni alle infermità Maleficiali.* Venice: Paolo Ugolino, 1601 (first published 1572).

———. *Eversio daemonum e corporibus oppressis cum divorum tum aliorum auctorum potentissimos & efficaces in malignos spiritus propulsandos & maleficia ab energumenis pellenda, continens exorcismos*. Bologna: Giovanni Rossi, 1588.

———. *Flagellum daemonum, Exorcismos terribiles, potentissimos, et efficaces. Remediaque probatissima, ac doctrinam singularem in malignos spiritus expellendos; facturasque et maleficia fuganda de obsessis corporibus complectens, cum suis benedictionibus, et omnibus requisitis ad eorum expulsionsem*. Venice: Petrus Milocus, 1626 (first published 1577).

———. *Fuga Daemonum, Adiurationes potentissimas, et Exorcismos formidabiles, atque efficaces in malignos spiritus propulsandos, et maleficia ab energumenis pellenda*. Venice: apud Haeredes Iohannis Varisci, 1596.

———. *Fustis Daemonum adiurationes formidabiles, potentissimas, et efficaces in malignos spiritus fugandos de oppressis corporibus humanis*. Venice: Petrus Milocus, 1626.

Menghini, Tommaso. *Regole del Tribunale del Sant'Ofizio, Praticate in alcuni Casi immaginari*. Modena: Bartolomeo Soliani, 1722.

Ori, Anna Maria, ed. *Le Clarisse in Carpi: Cinque secoli di storia (XVI–XX)*. Vol. 2, *Fonti*. Reggio Emilia: Diabasis, 2003.

Ostorero, Martine, Agostino Paravicini Bagliani, and Kathrin Utz Tremp, eds. With the collaboration of Catherine Chène. *L'imaginaire du sabbat: Edition critique des texts les plus anciens (1430 c.–1440 c.)*. Lausanne: Université de Lausanne, 1999.

Pedrazza, Giovanni. *Somma, over Breve Instruttione per Confessori, Per saper bene amministrare il Sacramento della Penitenza*. Translated by Camillo Camilli. Venice: Giorgio Angelieri, 1584.

Pico della Mirandola, Gianfrancesco. *Libro detto Strega, o, Delle illusioni del demonio*. Translated by Leandro Alberti. Edited by Albano Biondi. Venice: Marsilio, 1989.

Polidori, Valerio. *Practica Exorcistarum: Ad Daemones, et Maleficias de Christifidelibus eiiciendum*. Padua: Paulo Meieto, 1587.

Prima Regola delle Monache di Santa Chiara, datale dal Padre S. Francesco e confirmata da Papa Innocentio IIII. Con il modo di ricever le Novitie all'Ordine, et alla professione. Revista, corretta dal Rev. Padre Procuratore di Corte de'Frati Minori Capuccini, con l'aggiunta nel margine del Concilio Tridentino. Naples: Lazaro Scoriggio, 1629.

Regola delle Monache di S. Chiara di Carpi. Carpi: Antonio Guidotti, 1637.

Rituale Romanum Pauli Quinti Pontificis Maximi iussu editum. Venice: Nicolaus Pezzana, 1725.

Soto, Domingo. *De Iustitia et Iure*. Venice: Floravantem a Prato, 1584.

Tarabotti, Arcangela. *L'"inferno monacale" di Arcangela Tarabotti*. Edited by Francesca Medioli. Turin: Rosenberg and Sellier, 1990.

Visconti [Vicecomes], Zacharia. *Complementum Artis Exorcisticae: Cum Litaniis, Benedictionibus, et Doctrinis novis, Exorcismis efficacissimis, ac remediis copiosis in Maleficiatis expertis*. Venice: Turrinum, 1643.

Secondary Literature

Ahlgren, Gillian T.W. *Teresa of Avila and the Politics of Sanctity*. Ithaca: Cornell University Press, 1996.

Alberzoni, Maria Pia. *Chiara e il papato*. Milan: Edizioni biblioteca francescana, 1995.

Almond, Philip C. *Demonic Possession and Exorcism in Early Modern England: Contemporary Texts and their Cultural Contexts*. Cambridge: Cambridge University Press, 2004.

Ankarloo, Bengt, and Stuart Clark, eds. *Witchcraft and Magic in Europe: The Period of the Witch Trials*. Philadelphia: University of Pennsylvania Press, 2001.

Ankarloo, Bengt, and Gustav Henningsen, eds. *Early Modern European Witchcraft: Centres and Peripheries*. Oxford: Clarendon Press, 1990.

L'apertura degli archivi del Sant'Uffizio romano. [No ed.] Rome: Accademia nazionale dei Lincei, 1998.

L'arte degli Estensi: La pittura del Seicento e del Settecento a Modena e Reggio. [No ed.] Modena: Panini, 1986.

Bailey, Michael D. *Battling Demons: Witchcraft, Heresy, and Reform in the Late Middle Ages*. University Park: Pennsylvania State University Press, 2003.

———. "The Disenchantment of Magic: Spells, Charms, and Superstition in Early European Witchcraft Literature." *American Historical Review* 111 (2006): 383–404.

Baroja, Julio Carlo. *The World of the Witches*. Translated by O. N. V. Glendinning. Chicago: University of Chicago Press, 1971.

Barry, Jonathan, Marianne Hester, and Gareth Roberts, eds. *Witchcraft in Early Modern Europe: Studies in Culture and Belief*. Cambridge: Cambridge University Press, 1996.

Behringer, Wolfgang. *Witchcraft Persecutions in Bavaria: Popular Magic, Religious Zealotry and Reason of State in Early Modern Europe*. Translated by J. C. Grayson and David Lederer. Cambridge: Cambridge University Press, 1997.

Bell, Rudolph M. *Holy Anorexia*. Chicago: University of Chicago Press, 1985.

Beltrami, Andrea, and Anna Maria Ori, eds. *La Storia della Chiesa di Carpi*. Vol. 1, *Profilo cronologico*. Carpi: Fondazione Cassa di Risparmio di Carpi, 2006.

Bentini, Jadranka, ed. *Galleria Estense: Un percorso alternativo fra arredo e parato nel Palazzo Ducale di Modena*. Modena: Artestampa, 1993.

Bethencourt, Francisco. *O imaginário da magia: Feiticeiras, adivinhos e curandeiros em Portugal no século XVI*. Rev. ed. São Paulo: Companhia das Letras, 2004.

———. *L'Inquisition à l'époque moderne: Espagne, Italie, Portugal XVe–XIXe siècle*. Paris: Fayard, 1995.

Bilinkoff, Jodi. *Avila of Saint Teresa: Religious Reform in a Sixteenth-Century City*. Ithaca: Cornell University Press, 1989.

———. *Related Lives: Confessors and Their Female Penitents, 1450–1750*. Ithaca: Cornell University Press, 2005.

Biondi, Albano. "Lunga durata e microarticolazione nel territorio di un Ufficio dell'Inquisizione: Il 'Sacro Tribunale' a Modena (1292–1785)." *Annali dell'Istituto storico italo-germanico in Trento* 7 (1982): 73–90.

———. "La 'Nuova Inquisizione' a Modena: Tre inquisitori (1589–1609)." In *Città italiane del '500: Tra Riforma e Controriforma* [no ed.], 61–76. Lucca: M. Pacini Fazzi, 1988.

———. "Streghe ed eretici nei domini estensi all'epoca dell'Ariosto." In *Il Rinascimento nelle corti padane: Società e cultura*, edited by Paolo Rossi, 165–99. Bari: De Donato, 1977.

Biondi, Grazia. *Benvenuta e l'Inquisitore: Un destino di donna nella Modena del '300.* Modena: Unione Donne Italiae, Centro documentazione donna, 1993.

———. *E Iddio si fece donna: La storia di Lucia Roveri della Mirandola (1728-1788).* Modena: Unione Donne Italiae, Centro documentazione donna, 1996.

Bornstein, Daniel, and Roberto Rusconi, eds. *Women and Religion in Medieval and Renaissance Italy.* Translated by Margery J. Schneider. Chicago: University of Chicago Press, 1996.

Bossy, John. *Christianity in the West 1400-1700.* Oxford: Oxford University Press, 1985.

———. "The Social History of Confession in the Age of the Reformation." *Transactions of the Royal Historical Society* 25 (1975): 21-38.

Bravi, Ferruccio. *Il principe frate: Alfonso III d'Este, Padre Giovan Battista da Modena.* Bolzano: Centro di documentazione storica per l'Alto Adige, 1972.

Briggs, Robin. *Witches and Neighbors: The Social and Cultural Context of European Witchcraft.* New York: Penguin, 1996.

———. "Women as Victims? Witches, Judges, and the Community." *French History* 5 (1991): 438-50.

Broedel, Hans Peter. *The "Malleus Maleficarum" and the Construction of Witchcraft: Theology and Popular Belief.* Manchester: Manchester University Press, 2003.

Brown, Judith C. "Everyday Life, Longevity, and Nuns in Early Modern Florence." In *Renaissance Culture and the Everyday,* edited by Patricia Fumerton and Simon Hunt, 115-38. Philadelphia: University of Pennsylvania Press, 1999.

———. *Immodest Acts: The Life of a Lesbian Nun in Renaissance Italy.* Oxford: Oxford University Press, 1986.

Brucker, Gene A. "Sorcery in Early Renaissance Florence." *Studies in the Renaissance* 10 (1963): 7-24.

Caciola, Nancy. *Discerning Spirits: Divine and Demonic Possession in the Middle Ages.* Ithaca: Cornell University Press, 2003.

Canosa, Romano. *Sessualità e Inquisizione in Italia tra Cinquecento e Seicento.* Rome: Sapere 2000, 1994.

———. *Storia dell'Inquisizione in Italia dalla metà del cinquecento alla fine del settecento.* Vol. 1, *Modena.* Rome: Sapere 2000, 1986.

Cantalupo, Giacinto da. *Cenni biografici sugli uomini illustri della Francescana Osservante Provincia di Bologna.* Parma: SS. Nunziata, 1894.

Carmona, Michel. *Les Diables de Loudun: Sorcellerie et politique sous Richelieu.* Paris: Fayard, 1988.

Cattaneo, Enrico. "Le monacazioni forzate fra Cinque e Seicento." In *Vita e processo di suor Virginia Maria de Leyva, monaca di Monza,* edited by Giuseppe Farinelli and Ermanno Paccagnini, 145-95. Milan: Garzanti, 1989.

Certeau, Michel de. *The Possession at Loudun.* Translated by Michael B. Smith. With a foreword by Stephen Greenblatt. Chicago: University of Chicago Press, 1996.

Cervantes, Fernando. *The Devil in the New World: The Impact of Diabolism in New Spain.* New Haven: Yale University Press, 1994.

Ceyssens, Lucien. *Le cardinal François Albizzi (1593-1684): Un cas important dans l'histoire du jansénisme.* Rome: Pontificium Athenaeum Antonianum, 1977.

Clark, Stuart. "Inversion, Misrule and the Meaning of Witchcraft." *Past and Present* 87 (1980): 98-127.

———. *Thinking with Demons: The Idea of Witchcraft in Early Modern Europe.* Oxford: Oxford University Press, 1997.
Cohn, Norman. *Europe's Inner Demons: The Demonization of Christians in Medieval Christendom.* Rev. ed. Chicago: University of Chicago Press, 1993.
Crapanzano, Vincent, and Vivian Garrison, eds. *Case Studies in Spirit Possession.* New York: John Wiley and Sons, 1977.
Crouzet, Denis. "A Woman and the Devil: Possession and Exorcism in Sixteenth-Century France." In *Changing Identities in Early Modern France,* edited by Michael Wolfe, 191–215. Durham: Duke University Press, 1997.
de Boer, Wietse. *The Conquest of the Soul: Confession, Discipline, and Public Order in Counter-Reformation Milan.* Leiden: Brill, 2001.
Decker, Rainer. "Die Haltung der römischen Inquisition gegenüber Hexenglauben Exorzismus am Beispiel der Teufelsaustreibungen in Paderborn 1657." In *Das Ende der Hexenverfolgung,* edited by Sönke Lorenz and Dieter R. Bauer, 97–115. Stuttgart: Franz Steiner, 1995.
Del Col, Andrea. "Alcune osservazioni sui processi inquisitoriali come fonti storiche." *Metodi e ricerche* 13 (1994): 85–105.
———. *L'Inquisizione nel patriarcato e diocesi di Aquileia, 1557–1559.* Trieste: Edizioni Università di Trieste; and Montereale Valcellina: Centro Studi Storici Menocchio, 1998.
———. "Strumenti di ricerca per le fonti inquisitoriali in Italia in età moderna." *Società e storia* 75 (1997): 143–67, 417–24.
Del Col, Andrea, and Giovanna Paolin, eds. *L'Inquisizione romana: Metodologia delle fonti e storia istituzionale. Atti del Seminario internazionale, Montereale Valcellina, 23 e 24 settembre 1999.* Trieste: Università di Trieste; Montereale Valcellina: Circolo Culturale Menocchio, 2000.
Delumeau, Jean. *L'aveu et le pardon: Les difficultés de la confession XIIIe–XVIIIe siècle.* Paris: Fayard, 1990.
———. *Sin and Fear: The Emergence of a Western Guilt Culture 13th–18th Centuries.* Translated by Eric Nicholson. New York: St. Martin's Press, 1990.
De Rosa, Gabriele. *Chiesa e religione popolare nel Mezzogiorno.* Rome and Bari: Laterza, 1978.
———. *Vescovi, popolo e magia nel Sud: Ricerche di storia socio-religiosa dal XVII al XIX secolo.* Naples: Guida Editori, 1971.
De Rosa, Gabriele, and Tullio Gregory, eds. *Storia dell'Italia religiosa.* Vol. 2, *L'età moderna.* Gabriele De Rosa, Tullio Gregory, and André Vauchez, general eds. Rome and Bari: Laterza, 1994.
Diefendorf, Barbara B. *From Penitence to Charity: Pious Women and the Catholic Reformation in Paris.* Oxford: Oxford University Press, 2004.
Dinan, Susan E. *Women and Poor Relief in Seventeenth-Century France: The Early History of the Daughters of Charity.* Aldershot: Ashgate, 2006.
Di Simplicio, Oscar. *Autunno della stregoneria: Maleficio e magia nell'Italia moderna.* Bologna: Il Mulino, 2005.
Duggan, Lawrence G. "Fear and Confession on the Eve of the Reformation." *Archiv für Reformationsgeschichte* 84 (1984): 153–75.
Duni, Matteo. *Tra religione e magia: Storia del prete modenese Guiglielmo Campana (1460?–1541).* Florence: Leo S. Olschki, 1999.

Edwards, Kathryn A., ed. *Werewolves, Witches, and Wandering Spirits: Traditional Belief and Folklore in Early Modern Europe.* Kirksville, MO: Truman State University Press, 2002.
Eliade, Mircea. *Occultism, Witchcraft, and Cultural Fashions: Essays in Comparative Religions.* Chicago: University of Chicago Press, 1976.
Evangelisti, Silvia. "'Farne quello che pare e piace . . . ': L'uso e la trasmissione delle celle nel monastero di Santa Giulia di Brescia (1597–1688)." *Quaderni storici* 88 (1995): 85–109.
——. "'We do not have it, and we do not want it': Women, Power, and Convent Reform in Florence." *Sixteenth Century Journal* 34 (2003): 677–700.
Ferber, Sarah. *Demonic Possession and Exorcism in Early Modern France.* London: Routledge, 2004.
Ferraironi, Francesco. *Le streghe e l'Inquisizione: Superstizioni e realtà.* Rome: Sallustiana, 1955.
Ferri, Luigi, ed. *Vocabolario Ferrarese-Italiano.* Ferrara: Premiata Tipografia Sociale, 1889.
Firpo, Massimo. "La fase [difensiva] del processo inquisitoriale del cardinal Morone: Documenti e problemi." *Critica storia* 23 (1986): 121–48.
——. *Riforma protestante ed eresia nell'Italia del Cinquecento.* Rome and Bari: Laterza, 1993.
Fontaine, Michelle. "For the Good of the City: The Bishop and the Ruling Elite in Tridentine Modena." *Sixteenth Century Journal* 28 (1997): 29–43.
Franceschini, Ottavio. "L'esorcista." In *Medicina, erbe e magia: Cultura popolare nell'Emilia Romagna,* ed. Giuseppe Adani and Gastone Tamagnini, 99–115. Milan: Silvana, 1981.
Frugoni, Chiara. *Una solitudine abitata: Chiara d'Assisi.* Rome and Bari: Laterza, 2006.
Garnot, Benoît. *Le diable au couvent: Les possédées d'Auxonne (1658–1663).* Paris: Imago, 1995.
Garuti, Alfonso, and Dante Colli. *Il Monastero di Santa Chiara di Carpi.* Carpi: Il Portico, 1993.
Gentilcore, David. *Healers and Healing in Early Modern Italy.* Manchester: Manchester University Press, 1998.
Giles, Mary E., ed. *Women in the Inquisition: Spain and the New World.* Baltimore: Johns Hopkins University Press, 1999.
Ginzburg, Carlo. *The Cheese and the Worms: The Cosmos of a Sixteenth-Century Miller.* Translated by John Tedeschi and Anne Tedeschi. Baltimore: Johns Hopkins University Press, 1980.
——. *Ecstasies: Deciphering the Witches' Sabbath.* Translated by Raymond Rosenthal. New York: Penguin, 1991.
——. "L'inquisitore come antropologo." In *Studi in onore di Armando Saitta dei suoi allievi pisani,* edited by Regina Pozzi and Adriano Prosperi, 23–33. Pisa: Giardini, 1989.
——. *The Night Battles: Witchcraft and Agrarian Cults in the Sixteenth and Seventeenth Centuries.* Translated by John Tedeschi and Anne Tedeschi. Baltimore: Johns Hopkins University Press, 1983.
Golden, Richard, ed. *Encyclopedia of Witchcraft: The Western Tradition,* 4 vols. Santa Barbara: ABC-Clio, 2006.

Haliczer, Stephen. *Between Exaltation and Infamy: Female Mystics in the Golden Age of Spain.* Oxford: Oxford University Press, 2002.

———. *Sexuality in the Confessional: A Sacrament Profaned.* Oxford: Oxford University Press, 1995.

———, ed. *Inquisition and Society in Early Modern Europe.* London: Croom Helm, 1987.

Hallett, Nicky. *Witchcraft, Exorcism and the Politics of Possession in a Seventeenth-Century Convent: "How Sister Ursula was once Bewitched and Sister Margaret Twice."* Aldershot: Ashgate, 2007.

Hanlon, Gregory, and Geoffrey Snow. "Exorcisme et cosmologie tridentine: Trois cas agenais en 1619." *Revue de la Bibliothèque nationale* 28 (1988): 12–27.

Harley, David. "Explaining Salem: Calvinist Psychology and the Diagnosis of Possession." *American Historical Review* 101 (1996): 307–30.

———. "Historians as Demonologists: The Myth of the Midwife-Witch." *Social History of Medicine* 3 (1990): 1–26.

Harline, Craig. *The Burdens of Sister Margaret: Inside a Seventeenth-Century Convent.* Abridged ed. New Haven: Yale University Press, 2000.

Henningsen, Gustav. *The Witches' Advocate: Basque Witchcraft and the Spanish Inquisition, 1609–1614.* Reno: University of Nevada Press, 1980.

Henningsen, Gustav, and John Tedeschi, eds., with Charles Amiel. *The Inquisition in Early Modern Europe: Studies on Sources and Methods.* DeKalb: Northern Illinois University Press, 1986.

Hester, Marianne. *Lewd Women and Wicked Witches: A Study of the Dynamics of Male Domination.* London: Routledge, 1992.

Holmes, Clive. "Women: Witnesses and Witches." *Past and Present* 140 (1993): 45–78.

Houlbrooke, Ralph A. Review of *Lewd Women and Wicked Witches: A Study of the Dynamics of Male Domination,* by Marianne Hester. In *Reviewing Sociology* 9 (1996); http://www.rdg.ac.uk/RevSoc/archive/volume9/number2/9-2i.htm.

Huxley, Aldous. *The Devils of Loudun.* New York: Carrol and Graf, 1986.

L'Inquisizione Romana in Italia nell'età moderna: Archivi, problemi di metodo e nuove ricerche: Atti del seminario internazionale, Trieste, 18–20 maggio 1988. [No ed.] Rome: Ministero per i beni culturali e ambientali; Ufficio centrale per i beni archivistici, 1991.

Jacques-Chaquin, Nicole, and Maxime Préaud, eds. *Le sabbat des sorciers en Europe (XVe–XVIIIe siècles).* Grenoble: Jérôme Millon, 1993.

Jerouschek, Günter, and Wolfgang Behringer, eds. *Der Hexenhammer: Malleus Maleficarum.* Munich: Deutcher Taschenbuch Verlag, 2000.

Karlsen, Carol F. *The Devil in the Shape of a Woman: Witchcraft in Colonial New England.* New York: W. W. Norton, 1987.

Kieckhefer, Richard. *European Witch Trials: Their Foundations in Popular and Learned Culture 1300–1500.* Berkeley: University of California Press, 1976.

———. *Magic in the Middle Ages.* Cambridge: Cambridge University Press, 1990.

Larner, Christina. *Enemies of God: The Witch-Hunt in Scotland.* Baltimore: Johns Hopkins University Press, 1981.

Laven, Mary. *Virgins of Venice: Broken Vows and Cloistered Lives in the Renaissance Convent.* New York: Viking, 2003.

Lavenia, Vincenzo. "I diavoli di Carpi e il Sant'Uffizio (1636–1639)." In *Eretici, esuli e indemoniati nell'età moderna,* edited by Mario Rosa, 77–139. Florence: Leo S. Olschki, 1998.

———. *L'infamia e il perdono: Tributi, pene e confessione nella geologia morale della prima età moderna*. Bologna: Il Mulino, 2004.

———. "'Tenere i malefici per cosa vera': Esorcismi e censura nell'Italia moderna." In *Dal torchio alle fiamme: Inquisizione e censura: Nuovi contributi dall più antica biblioteca provinciale d'Italia. Atti del Convegno di Studi Salerno, 5–6 novembre 2004*, edited by Vittoria Bonani, 129–72. Salerno: Biblioteca Provinciale di Salerno, 2005.

Lea, Henry Charles. *A History of Auricular Confession and Indulgences in the Latin Church*. 3 vols. Philadelphia: Lea Brothers, 1896.

———. *Materials toward a History of Witchcraft*. Edited by Arthur C. Howland. 3 vols. New York: T. Yoseloff, 1957.

Lehfeldt, Elizabeth A. *Religious Women in Golden Age Spain: The Permeable Cloister*. Aldershot: Ashgate, 2005.

Levack, Brian P. *The Witch-Hunt in Early Modern Europe*. 2d ed. London: Longman, 1995.

———, ed. *New Perspectives on Witchcraft, Magic, and Demonology*. 6 vols. New York: Routledge, 2001.

Levi, Giovanni. *Inheriting Power: The Story of an Exorcist*. Translated by Lydia G. Cochrane. Chicago: University of Chicago Press, 1988.

Maggi, Armando. *Satan's Rhetoric: A Study of Renaissance Demonology*. Chicago: University of Chicago Press, 2001.

Malena, Adelisa. *L'Eresia dei perfetti: Inquisizione romana ed esperienze mistiche nel seicento italiano*. Rome: Edizioni di Storia e Letteratura, 2003.

Mandrou, Robert. *Magistrats et sorciers en France au XVIIe siècle: Une analyse de psychologie historique*. Paris: Plon, 1968.

Martin, Ruth. *Witchcraft and the Inquisition in Venice 1550–1650*. Oxford: Basil Blackwell, 1989.

McNamara, Jo Ann Kay. *Sisters in Arms: Catholic Nuns through Two Millennia*. Cambridge: Harvard University Press, 1996.

Medioli, Francesca. "Monacazioni forzate: Donne ribelli al proprio destino." *Clio* 30 (1994): 431–54.

Midelfort, H. C. Erik. *Exorcism and Enlightenment: Johann Joseph Gassner and the Demons of Eighteenth-Century Germany*. New Haven: Yale University Press, 2005.

———. *A History of Madness in Sixteenth-Century Germany*. Stanford: Stanford University Press, 1999.

———. *Witch Hunting in Southwestern Germany, 1562–1684: The Social and Intellectual Foundations*. Stanford: Stanford University Press, 1972.

Monter, E. William. *Frontiers of Heresy: The Spanish Inquisition from the Basque Lands to Sicily*. Cambridge: Cambridge University Press, 1990.

———. "Toads and Eucharists: The Male Witches of Normandy." *French Historical Studies* 20 (1997): 563–95.

———. *Witchcraft in France and Switzerland: The Borderlands during the Reformation*. Ithaca: Cornell University Press, 1976.

Muchembled, Robert. *A History of the Devil from the Middle Ages to the Present*. Translated by Jean Birrell. Cambridge: Polity Press, 2003.

———. *Le roi et la sorcière: L'Europe des bûchers (XVe–XVIIIe siècle)*. Paris: Desclée, 1993.

———. *La sorcière au village XVe–XVIIIe siècle*. Paris: Gallimard, 1991.

Murray, Margaret. *The Witch-Cult in Western Europe*. Oxford: Clarendon Press, 1962.

Myers, W. David. *"Poor, Sinning Folk: Confession and Conscience in Counter-Reformation Germany*. Ithaca: Cornell University Press, 1996.
Nischan, Bodo. "The Exorcism Controversy and Baptism in the Late Reformation." *Sixteenth Century Journal* 18 (1987): 31–52.
O'Neil, Mary Rose. "Discerning Superstition: Popular Errors and Orthodox Response in Late Sixteenth Century Italy." PhD diss., Stanford University, 1982.
———. "Missing Footprints: Maleficium in Modena." *Acta Ethnographica Hungarica* 37 (1991/1992): 123–42.
Panini, Giuseppe. *La famiglia Estense da Ferrara a Modena*. Modena: Edizioni Archivi Riuniti Modena, 1996.
Paolin, Giovanna, ed. *Inquisizioni: Percorsi di ricerca*. Trieste: Università di Trieste, 2001.
Peters, Edward. *Inquisition*. New York: Free Press, 1988.
———. *The Magician, the Witch, and the Law*. Philadelphia: University of Pennsylvania Press, 1978.
Pomata, Gianna, and Gabriella Zarri, eds. *I monasteri femminili come centri di cultura fra Rinascimento e Barocco: Atti del convegno storico internazionale, Bologna, 8–10 dicembre 2000*. Rome: Edizioni di Storia e Letteratura, 2005.
Prodi, Paolo, ed. *Disciplina dell'anima, disciplina del corpo e disciplina della società tra medioevo ed età moderna*. Bologna: Il Mulino, 1994.
Prosperi, Adriano. *L'Inquisizione romana: Letture e ricerche*. Rome: Edizioni di Storia e Letteratura, 2003.
———. "L'Inquisizione romana: Verso una nuova immagine?" *Critica storica* 25 (1988): 119–45.
———. *Tribunali della coscienza: Inquisitori, confessori, missionari*. Turin: Giulio Einaudi, 1996.
———, ed. *Il piacere del testo: Saggi e studi per Albano Biondi*. Rome: Bulzoni, 2001.
Puyol Buil, Carlos. *Inquisición y política en el reinado de Felipe IV: Los Procesos de Jerónimo de Villanueva y las monjas de San Plácido 1628–1660*. Madrid: Consejo Superior de Investigaciones Científicas, 1993.
Rapley, Elizabeth. *A Social History of the Cloister: Daily Life in the Teaching Monasteries of the Old Regime*. Montreal: McGill-Queen's University Press, 2001.
Rapley, Robert. *A Case of Witchcraft: The Trial of Urbain Grandier*. Montreal: McGill-Queen's University Press, 1998.
Romeo, Giovanni. *Esorcisti, confessori e sessualità nell'Italia della Controriforma: A proposito di due casi modenesi del primo Seicento*. Florence: Le Lettere, 1998.
———. *Inquisitori, esorcisti e streghe nell'Italia della Controriforma*. Florence: Sansoni, 1990.
———. *Ricerche su confessione dei peccati e Inquisizione nell'Italia delCinquecento*. Naples: La Città del Sole, 1997.
Roper, Lyndal. *Oedipus and the Devil: Witchcraft, Sexuality and Religion in Early Modern Europe*. London: Routledge, 1994.
———. *Witch Craze: Terror and Fantasy in Baroque Germany*. New Haven: Yale University Press, 2004.
Rosa, Mario, ed. *Clero e società nell'Italia moderna*. Rome and Bari: Laterza, 1997.
Ruggiero, Guido. *Binding Passions: Tales of Magic, Marriage, and Power at the End of the Renaissance*. Oxford: Oxford University Press, 1993.

Rusconi, Roberto. *L'ordine dei peccati: La confessione tra Medioevo ed età moderna*. Bologna: Il Mulino, 2002.
Russell, Jeffrey Burton. *A History of Witchcraft: Sorcerers, Heretics, and Pagans*. New York: Thames and Hudson, 1995.
———. *The Prince of Darkness: Radical Evil and the Power of Good in History*. Ithaca: Cornell University Press, 1988.
Sands, Kathleen R. *Demon Possession in Elizabethan England*. Westport, CT: Praeger, 2004.
Sarrión Mora, Adelina. *Sexualidad y confesión: La solicitación ante el Tribunal del Santo Oficio (siglos XVI–XIX)*. Madrid: Alianza Editorial, 1994.
Scaraffia, Lucetta, and Gabriella Zarri, eds. *Women and Faith: Catholic Religious Life in Italy from Late Antiquity to the Present*. Cambridge: Harvard University Press, 1999.
Schutte, Anne Jacobson. "Asmodea, A Nun-Witch in Eighteenth-Century Tuscany." In *Werewolves, Witches, and Wandering Spirits: Traditional Beliefs and Folklore in Early Modern Europe*, edited by Kathryn A. Edwards, 119–35. Kirksville, MO: Truman State University Press, 2002.
———. *Aspiring Saints: Pretense of Holiness, Inquisition, and Gender in the Republic of Venice, 1618–1750*. Baltimore: Johns Hopkins University Press, 2001.
Schutte, Anne Jacobson, Thomas Kuehn, and Silvana Seidel Menchi, eds. *Time, Space, and Women's Lives in Early Modern Europe*. Kirksville, MO: Truman State University Press, 2001.
Scribner, Robert W. *Popular Culture and Popular Movements in Reformation Germany*. London: Hambledon Press, 1987.
Seidel Menchi, Silvana, and Diego Quaglioni, eds. *Trasgressioni: Seduzione, oncubinato, adulterio, bigamia (XIV–XIII secolo)*. Bologna: Il Mulino, 2004.
Sharpe, James. *Instruments of Darkness: Witchcraft in Early Modern England*. Philadelphia: University of Pennsylvania Press, 1996.
Sluhovsky, Moshe. *Believe Not Every Spirit: Possession, Mysticism, and Discernment in Early Modern Catholicism*. Chicago: University of Chicago Press, 2007.
———. "The Devil in the Convent." *American Historical Review* 107 (2002): 1379–411.
———. "A Divine Apparition or Demonic Possession? Female Agency and Church Authority in Demonic Possession in Sixteenth-Century France." *Sixteenth Century Journal* 27 (1996): 1039–55.
Soman, Alfred. *Sorcellerie et Justice Criminelle: Le Parlement de Paris (16e–18e siècles)*. Hampshire, England, Variorum, 1992.
Souza, Laura de Mello e. *O diabo e a Terra de Santa Cruz: Feitiçaria e religiosidade popular no Brasil colonial*. São Paulo: Companhia das Letras, 1986.
Sperling, Jutta Gisela. *Convents and the Body Politic in Late Renaissance Venice*. Chicago: University of Chicago Press, 1999.
Spinelli, Alessandro Giuseppe. *Notizie spettanti alla storia della musica in Carpi*. Volume 5 of *Memorie storiche e documenti sulla città e sull'antico principato di Carpi*. Carpi: Rossi, 1900.
Strasser, Ulrike. *State of Virginity: Gender, Religion, and Politics in an Early Modern Catholic State*. Ann Arbor: University of Michigan Press, 2004.
Tedeschi, John. *The Prosecution of Heresy: Collected Studies on the Inquisition in Early Modern Italy*. Binghamton: Medieval and Renaissance Texts and Studies, 1991.
Tentler, Thomas N. *Sin and Confession on the Eve of the Reformation*. Princeton: Princeton University Press, 1977.

Thomas, Keith. *Religion and the Decline of Magic: Studies in Popular Beliefs in Sixteenth and Seventeenth Century England.* Oxford: Oxford University Press, 1971.

Trenti, Giuseppe. *I processi del tribunale dell'Inquisizione di Modena: Inventario generale analitico 1489–1874.* With a preface by Paolo Prodi and an introduction by Angelo Spaggiari. Modena: Aedes Muratoriana, 2003.

Waite, Gary K. *Heresy, Magic, and Witchcraft in Early Modern Europe.* Houndmills and New York: Palgrave Macmillan, 2003.

Walker, Anita M., and Edmund H. Dickerman. "'A Woman under the Influence': A Case of Alleged Possession in Sixteenth-Century France." *Sixteenth Century Journal* 22 (1991): 535–54.

Walker, D. P. *Spiritual and Demonic Magic from Ficino to Campanella.* London: Warburg Institute, University of London, 1958; reprint, University Park: Pennsylvania State University Press, 2000.

———. *Unclean Sprits: Possession and Exorcism in France and England in the Late Sixteenth and Early Seventeenth Centuries.* Philadelphia: University of Pennsylvania Press, 1981.

Watt, Jeffrey R. *Choosing Death: Suicide and Calvinism in Early Modern Geneva.* Kirksville, MO: Truman State University Press, 2001.

———. "The Demons of Carpi: Exorcism, Witchcraft, and the Inquisition in a Seventeenth-Century Convent." *Archive for Reformation History* 98 (2007): 107–33.

———. "Love Magic and the Inquisition: A Case from Seventeenth-Century Italy." *Sixteenth Century Journal* (forthcoming).

———, ed. *From Sin to Insanity: Suicide in Early Modern Europe.* Ithaca: Cornell University Press, 2004.

Weaver, Elissa B. *Convent Theatre in Early Modern Italy: Spiritual Fun and Learning for Women.* Cambridge: Cambridge University Press, 2002.

Wiesner, Merry E., ed. *Witchcraft in Early Modern Europe.* New York: Houghton Mifflin, 2007.

Zacchè, Gilberto, ed. *Il Principato di Carpi in epoca estense: Istituzioni, economia, società e cultura.* Rome: Bulzoni, 2002.

Zanelli, Giuliana. *Streghe e società nell'Emilia e Romagna del Cinque-Seicento.* Ravenna: Longo A. Editore, 1992.

Zarri, Gabriella. *La memoria di lei: Storia delle donne, storia di genere.* With the collaboration of Claudia Pancino and Fiorenza Tarozzi. Turin: Società Editrice Internazionale, 1996.

———. *Recinti: Donne, clausura e matrimonio nella prima età moderna.* Bologna: Il Mulino, 2000.

———, ed. *Le Clarisse in Carpi: Cinque secoli di storia (XVI–XX).* Vol. 1, *Saggi.* Reggio Emilia: Diabasis, 2003.

———, ed. *Donna, disciplina, creanza cristiana dal XV al XVII secolo: Studi e testi a stampa.* Rome: Edizioni di Storia e Letteratura, 1996.

———, ed. *Finzione e santità: Tra medioevo ed età moderna.* Turin: Rosenberg and Sellier, 1991.

———, ed. *Il monachesimo femminile in Italia dall'alto medioevo al secolo XVII, a confronto con l'oggi: Atti del VI Convegno del "Centro di studi farfensi": Santa Vittoria in Matenano 21–24 settembre 1995.* San Pietro in Cariano: Il Segno dei Gabrielli, 1997.

Zavalloni, Roberto. *Provincia di "Cristo Re": Frati Minori dell'Emilia-Romagna nel 50° anno di vita.* Assisi: Edizioni Porziuncola, 1996.

INDEX

Page numbers in *italics* indicate illustrations.

abbacucca, 100–101, 158, 160, 169, 170
Abbati, Giovan Battista, 120–22, 203
Aix-en-Provence convent, 8
Albizzi, Francesco, 185, 269n3
Alessandrini, Giancinta, 101
Alessandrini, Marcella, 78
Alessandro II, Duke of Mirandola, 33
Alfonso II, Duke of Ferrara, 221n4
Alfonso III, Duke of Modena, 32–33, 36. *See also* Este, Giovan Battista d'
Amoldoni, Clara Maria, 23, 58, 232n13; as abbess, 212; Bellacappa and, 75–76, 90; possession of, 45, 59, 60, 122, 147, 148
amulets, 66, 104. *See also* spells, magical
Anabaptism, 16
Anthony of Padua, Saint, 127, 145, 146, 163
Aquinas, Thomas, Saint, 73, 106
astrology, 49
Augustine of Hippo, Saint, 4, 106, 107
Auxonne convent, 46, 81, 118, 223n19, 257n62, 264n41

baptism, 49–50, 53, 56, 77, 89, 151–52
Barberini, Francesco, 40, 41, 68, 148, 181, 188–95; Giudici and, 70–71; Manara and, 203; Mantica and, 181, 184; Martinelli sisters and, 188–89, 271n44; skepticism of, 132–35, 148–49, 184, 191–94; use of torture by, 274n32
Barbieri, Martino, 154
Baroja, Julio Carlo, 241n88
Barozzi, Francesco, 167–80
Bartolomeo, Father, 68
Basque witch-hunts, 228n69

beatas, 145, 147
Bellacappa, Angelo, 47, 68, 73–83, 86–103, 140; career of, 73–74, 213–14, 247n5; Carnival and, 91–92; charges against, 75, 76, 125, 126, 198–99; death of, 277n61; defenders of, 99–103, 171–72, 248n27; Angela Caterina d'Este and, 74, 92–99, 159–61, 200; gifts from, 89–90; Urbain Grandier and, 102–3; imprisonment of, 128, 157, 166, 265n1; legal defense of, 157–80; love magic and, 86–91, 151, 152; Dealta Martinelli and, 77, 80–81, 90, 151–52, 165–66, 189–91; Ippolita Martinelli and, 77, 90; solicitation by, 77–80, 82, 161–80, 199; verdict on, 191, 192
Bellentani, Emilia, 141, 149, 150
benandanti of Friuli, 14, 199, 227n60
Bendidio, Aurelia, 101, 141
Bendidio, Beatrice, 78, 83, 100, 146
Bendidio, Ottavia, 41, 42, 45
Bergamaschi, Dianira, 69–72, 129
Bertesi, Agostino, 135; as confessor, 213; exorcisms by, 46, 113, 116–23, 126–27, 146
Bibles: demonic possession in, 7, 104, 108, 137–38; used for spells, 104, 123–24, 126; in vernacular, 245n150
Bignardi, Giovan Battista, 178, 203
Blesio, Marco, 274n33
Bodin, Jean, 193, 257n75
Boer, Wietse de, 84
Bonacorsi (physician), 181–82
Boniface VIII (pope), 21
Borromeo, Carlo, Saint, 75, 84, 91, 208

291

Borromeo family, 73
Borromeo, Federico, 253n114
Bosellino, Bernardino, 37, 39, 41, 133
Bosio, Giovan Francesco, 151, 154–55
Bossy, John, 85
Boyer, Paul, 272n7
Bridget of Sweden, Saint, 7, 144, 145
Briggs, Robin, 64, 199
Brognolo, Candido, 53, 58, 106, 110, 224n30; on demonic visions, 263n25; on exorcism, 137–38, 184, 261n157; on menstruation, 130
Brown, Judith, 81
Brusati, Claudio, 49
Brusati, Leonor, 79–80
Brusati, Riccialda, 47
Burkardt, Albrecht, 272n14
Buvée, Barbe, 81, 264n41

Cabassi, Claudia, 44, 176, 184; Dealta Martinelli and, 51–55, 61, 64, 146, 190; Ippolita Martinelli and, 69
Cabassi, Dorotea Serafini, 54, 163
Cabassi, Girolamo, 60, 61, 65, 135, 152; diagnoses of, 122, 130; exorcisms by, 46, 113, 117, 124–30; witch-hunting by, 123–24, 131
Calefi, Maria, 51, 56; Bellacappa and, 79, 82, 163, 176; testimony of, 59–60
Calvinism, 12–13, 16, 105. *See also* Protestantism
candles, 56, 104, 125; Easter, 56, 90–91, 159, 172; for labor pains, 91; for love magic, 86
Canosa, Romano, 8
Capuchins, 33, 172, 204–5
Carafa, Gian Pietro, 10
Carena, Cesare, 71, 176, 244n140, 263n29
Carlini, Benedetta, 81
Carmelites, 22, 145
Carnival, 91–92, 161–62, 202
Carpi, 1–3, 20, 23; archpriest of, 35–36, 43; exorcists of, 113–19; Inquisition of Modena and, 13; map of, 2; plague in, 37, 199–200; San Nicolò monastery in, 74; witch-hunt in, 39–40. *See also* Santa Chiara convent

Castagnini, Margherita Felice, 45, 75, 99, 161
Catherine of Siena, Saint, 7, 144, 145
Certeau, Michel de, 5, 207
chastity. *See* virginity
Chechi, Silveria, 83, 86–87, 176–77
Chierico, Giovanni dal, 171
Ciarlatina, Cinzia, 45, 59, 131, 212
Ciarlini, Colomba, 93, 158
Cimadori, Paola Francesca, 45, 61–62; as abbess, 212; Bellacappa and, 76, 83; bewitchment of, 122, 152–53
Cipolla, Orsina, 24, 59, 233n21
Clare of Assisi, Saint, 1, 240n70
Clarisses, 1, 35, 49, 200, 221n2
claustration, 8, 21–22, 33, 37, 88, 145, 185–87, 205–6, 231n5, 274n25
Clement VIII (pope), 245n150
Coccapani, Anna, 235n41
Coccapani, Clelia, 65, 146, 189, 248n27
Coccapani, Flavia, 185
Coccapani, Hercole, 158
Coccapani, Laura, 49, 127
Coccapani, Paola, 100–101
Coccapani, Veronica Maria, 45, 54, 55, 64; Bellacappa and, 75, 189; bewitchment of, 154, 265n6; exorcism of, 182
Codebo, Caterina, 31
Cohn, Norman, 199, 222n5, 223n15
Colevati, Maria Maddalena, 45, 75, 101
Comi, Faustina, 72
confession, 158; Counter-Reformation and, 75, 83–86; frequency of, 76, 84, 203; privacy of, 75, 84, 95–96, 178, 250n61; role of priest in, 83, 85, 174–75; Romeo on, 250n58, 250n60; solicitation during, 77–80, 82, 161–80, 199, 248n22, 249n52. *See also* penance
confessionals, 75, 78, 168–71
confessors, 32, 33; guidelines for, 73, 76; inquisitors and, 11, 85, 164, 250n60; as tutors, 100
confraternities, 231n3
Congregation of Bishops and Regulars, 31; Giovan Battista d'Este and, 133;

exorcism guidelines of, 137; music regulations of, 34–35
Congregation of the Doctrine of the Faith, 13
Congregation of the Inquisition, 13, 40–41, 70–72, 99, 103, 209–10; authorization of torture by, 15, 180, 199, 208, 210; skepticism of, 119–20, 132–40, 148–49, 184–85, 193–94, 197–98, 208–11; verdicts of, 85, 191–94, 268n89. *See also* Roman Inquisition
Consulta Teologica, 11
Contessini, Geltruda Francesca, 64, 76
Contessini, Margherita, 237n3
converse. See lay sisters
Corradi, Olimpia, 76
Counter-Reformation, 203–6; confession and, 75, 83–86; women saints and, 145. *See also* Tridentine reforms
Crapanzano, Vincent, 274n27

dal Chierico, Giovanni, 171
dancing, 92. *See also* music
Daughters of Charity, 231n3
de Boer, Wietse, 84
Definitori Provinciali, 74
Del Col, Andrea, 15, 16
de Leyva, Virginia Maria, 253n114
demonic possession, 94, 201–8; in Bible, 7, 104, 108, 137–38; convents and, 5–9; cross-cultural aspects of, 206–7; Freudian view of, 6, 272n14; gendered beliefs about, 5–9, 17–19, 110, 118–20, 129–30, 204–5, 224n30; herbs for, 108; historical trends of, 17–18; mental illness versus, 98, 114–17, 120, 136, 197, 202–6, 206, 269n3; skepticism about, 18, 118–20, 132–40, 148–49, 184–85, 191–94, 197–98, 208–11; suicide and, 129, 135, 148, 181; symptoms of, 1–3, 42–43, 46, 55, 96, 115–18, 130, 204–5, 257n75; terms for, 46; witchcraft and, 3–5, 9, 39, 94, 106, 113, 122, 137–38. *See also* exorcism
depression, postpartum, 98. *See also* melancholy

devil, 5–6, 147; pact with, 4, 18, 62–63, 94, 106–7, 113, 193; renouncement of, 155; worship of, 4–5, 16, 17. *See also* witches' sabbat
divination, 4, 59, 106, 112–13, 211
divine offices, 22, 25, 47
domestic abuse, 33
Dominic of Sora, Saint, 163
Donelli, Francesco, 121–22
dowries, 23–25, 47, 187, 232n14, 233n21. *See also* marriage
dozzina, 24, 33
Duosi, Emerenziana, 57, 60, 100, 159
Durrant, Jonathan, 16

educande, 32, 33, 35, 38, 198
epilepsy, 120, 205
Este, Angela Caterina d', 23, 147, 173, 200–201, 234n35; apartments of, 26, 27–30; Bellacappa and, 74, 92–99, 159–61, 200; Carnival and, 91; death of, 213; education of, 100; elections as abbess of, 31–32; entourage of, 26, 34, 44, 46, 92, 99, 200, 236n55; exorcism of, 46, 93–94; illnesses of, 46, 55, 92–99; on *maleficia*, 38–39; Martinelli sisters and, 50, 95–97, 143, 146, 200; possession of, 55, 93–94, 97, 98; testimony of, 94–97, 143
Este, Anna Beatrice d', 32, 40, 247n187; entourage of, 33, 34, 38, 44, 46; marriage of, 33; transfer of, 38, 71
Este, Cesare d', Duke of Modena, 26, 100, 221n4
Este, Eleonora d'. *See* Este, Angela Caterina d'
Este family, 1, 12–13, 55, 94, 146, 221n4; demonic possessions in, 46, 55, 97–99; Santa Chiara convent and, 23, 26, 31–33, 36, 113, 194
Este, Giovan Battista d', 33, 39–40, 164, 192, 194, 200; Angela Caterina's illness and, 93, 99; Bellacappa and, 172–73; Carnival and, 91–92; death of, 213; exorcisms and, 41, 113, 114, 133, 134. *See also* Alfonso III
Este, Leonora d', 143

Index

Este, Margherita d,' 32–34, 40, 247n187; bewitchment of, 55; entourage of, 33, 34, 44, 46; marriage of, 33

Eucharist, 55–56, 135–36, 187; for exorcisms, 109, 110, 130, 131; folk beliefs about, 104, 243n118; misuses of, 56–58, 62, 66, 77, 89, 90, 125; withholding of, 84, 85

exorcism, 55–56, 113–19, 122–32, 182, 196; eroticism and, 116, 257n80, 260n149; of Angela Caterina d'Este, 46, 93–94; Menghi on, 104–13, 118–19; physicians and, 110, 113, 120–22, 182; procedures for, 41, 63, 110–13, 119, 183; relics for, 45, 114, 135, 183, 185; Scaglia on, 41; Sluhovsky on, 104–5; Soto on, 118; superstitions and, 105–7, 110; testimony after, 68; witch-hunts and, 113, 122–32, 139. *See also* demonic possession; witchcraft

Eymerich, Nicolau, 228n69, 275n34

Fabrizi, Tommaso, 171–72
Farinacci, Prospero, 175, 178
Febvre, Lucien, 248n33
Federici, Flerida. *See* Cimadori, Paola Francesca
Federici, Prudenzia, 80
Ferdinand I, Duke of Tuscany, 97, 98
Ferrara, 1, 26, 221n4; Leonora d'Este and, 143; Inquisition in, 12, 274n32; witchcraft trials in, 274n32
fiscal, office of, 71
Fognano, Francesco, 100
Foresti, Luigi, 149–55
Forni, Barbara Leonora, 34; Bellacappa and, 75, 90, 92, 99–102; bewitchment of, 38, 122, 125–26; death of, 42, 212–13; exorcism of, 182; "hysteria" of, 121; possession of, 44, 45, 57, 59, 90, 131–32, 183
Forni, Camillo, 58–59
Forni, Paolina, 38, 41, 44, 101, 198
Forni, Paolo Francesco, 34
fortune-telling. *See* divination
Foscarari, Egidio, 226n50

Foschieri, Obizza, 76, 161
Francesco I, Duke of Modena, 33, 38, 40, 93
Franciscans, 13, 33, 172–73, 214; archpriest of Carpi and, 31–32; Clare of Assisi and, 1; oversight of Santa Chiara by, 31, 35–36, 202, 204
Francis of Assisi, Saint, 1, 35, 172, 204
Freud, Sigmund, 6, 201, 273n14
Friuli, 211; *benandanti* of, 14, 199, 227n60
Fuga Daemonum (Menghi), 108–13

galleys, as punishment, 41, 82, 85, 110, 135, 191, 269n89
Galli, Leonora, 38–39, 41–44, 101, 161, 198
Gassner, Johann Joseph, 276n47
gendered beliefs, 33, 34, 164, 239n46; demonic possession and, 5–9, 17–19, 110, 118–20, 129–30, 204–5, 224n30; mysticism and, 7; saints and, 144–45; witchcraft and, 17–19, 210–11, 229n79, 230n85
Geneva, 37
Gerson, Jean, 144
Ginzburg, Carlo, 14–15, 228n66, 274n32
Giudici, Cherubina, 58–59, 71
Giudici, Doralice, 189
Giudici, Orazio, 42–43, 64, 65; career of, 213; criticisms of, 70–71, 149; exorcists and, 113–14, 128, 134–35; questioning Angela Caterina d'Este by, 94–97; questioning Ippolita Martinelli by, 147; questioning witnesses by, 68–69
Gonzaga, Ferrante, Duke of Guastalla, 33
Grandier, Urbain, 5, 102–3, 118, 138, 207, 257n76. *See also* Loudun convent
Greek, possessed nuns speaking, 118, 257n75
Gregorian chants, 35
Gregory XV (pope), 82
Grillenzoni, Chiara, 101, 169
Grimaldi, Cardinal, 197–98
Guadagni, Giovan Battista, 195
Guazzo, Francesco Maria, 107, 144

hair, for magical spells, 57, 67, 89, 132
Haliczer, Stephen, 7, 249n43
Hallett, Nicky, 223n20, 272n14
Henningsen, Gustav, 228n69
herbal medicine, 89, 108, 255n21
heresy: Inquisition and, 10, 11, 17, 85; magic versus, 88, 209, 223n15; solicitation as, 82; superstition and, 4, 17; Waldensian, 52
hexes, 127. *See also* spells, magical
Holy Office. *See* Roman Inquisition
hysteria, 120, 121, 203, 259n124, 274n25. *See also* mental illness

Imola convent, 5
Innocent VII (pope), 1
Innocent IX (pope), 10
Inquisition. *See* Roman Inquisition
inspiritata, 46
Instructio (Scaglia), 119, 120, 137

Jeanne des Anges, 203, 253n110. *See also* Loudun convent
Jesuits, 33, 74, 102, 203
John XXII (pope), 10
Jorden, Edward, 259n124
Judaism, 10, 13, 199, 226n54

Karlsen, Carol F., 229n79
Kramer, Heinrich, 4, 7, 18, 107, 112. See also *Malleus Maleficarum*

Latin, 15, 44, 66, 100, 183; possessed nuns speaking, 117–19, 121, 257n75, 257n76
Lavenia, Vincenzo, 8–9, 224n32, 250n61
lay sisters, 22, 24–25, 33, 38, 233n21, 236n55
Lazzarino, Angelo, 32, 35, 161, 234n35
Lea, Henry Charles, 225n38, 250n56
Lehfeldt, Elizabeth, 25
Leonio, Cesare, 65
Leonori, Penelope, 169
Leo X (pope), 236n62
Lerri, Michelangelo, 226n51
Levack, Brian, 209

Leyva, Virginia Maria de, 253n114
literacy, 15–16, 25, 54, 100, 199, 253n118
Loia, Ginevra, 38, 39, 41, 133
Losi, Marsilio, 37–39, 41, 133
Loudun convent, 5, 8, 199, 203, 204; ages of afflicted at, 46, 239n45; Certeau on, 5, 207; Grandier and, 5, 102–3, 118, 138, 207; Jeanne des Anges and, 203, 253n110; medical opinions about, 120, 274n25; testimony of afflicted at, 68. *See also* Ursulines
Louis XIII, King of France, 102, 138, 257n76
Louviers convent, 197
love magic, 13, 49, 57–59, 86–92, 165, 211, 251n65; hexes and, 127; magnet for, 89, 151, 152; *maleficia* and, 37–38, 77, 89, 123; menstrual blood for, 86; sacramentals for, 56, 58, 77, 89; Song of Songs and, 126. *See also* spells, magical
Luca, Giovan Battista de, 22
Ludovisi, Cardinal, 73
Lupagnini, Grazia, 174; Bellacappa and, 79–80, 83; Dealta Martinelli and, 50, 61
Lupi, Giovanni, 184, 187–92, 194
lust, 18, 21, 48, 87–92, 203, 207. *See also* sexuality
Lutheranism, 16, 18, 85. *See also* Protestantism

MacDonald, Michael, 140
madness. *See* mental illness
magic. *See* spells, magical
Magnani, Virginia, 237n3
magnets, 89, 151, 152, 275n33
Malaspina, Alfonso, 23, 92
Malaspina, Alsuinda, 23, 48, 185; Bellacappa and, 158; Dealta Martinelli and, 61–62, 149, 189, 265n6
malefica (witch), 106
maleficia (spells), 123–24, 211; charms against, 104; exorcists for, 139; love magic and, 37–38, 77, 89, 123. *See also* spells, magical

maleficiata (bewitched), 38, 46
Malleus Maleficarum, 4, 5, 107, 112; authorship of, 222n14; evil gaze and, 60; love magic and, 86; Menghi on, 106, 109; misogyny in, 7, 18; torture and, 153–54
Manara, Giacinto, 203
Mantica, Germanico, 181–88, 192, 194, 202, 270n21
Manzoni, Alessandro, 37, 253n114
Marcellus II (pope), 10
marriage, 239n46; dowries for, 23–25, 47, 187, 232n14, 233n21; Urbain Grandier on, 102; religious life versus, 22–26, 33, 46, 207
Martinelli, Anna Maria, 45, 59, 239n46; Bellacappa and, 75–76; death of, 212; exorcism of, 182; possession of, 130
Martinelli, Arcangelo, 49–50
Martinelli, Dealta, 46–61, 198, 202, 208, 211, 213; assaults on, 61–63, 65, 72, 149–54, 190, 195; Bellacappa and, 77, 80–81, 90, 151–52, 165–66, 189–91; charges of witchcraft against, 127–28, 131, 179; confession of, 155–56; Angela Caterina d'Este and, 50–51, 95–97, 200; incarceration of, 128, 141, 147; love letters of, 67; misusing sacramentals by, 55–56; personal property of, 65–66; protective custody for, 65, 156, 157, 188–89; release from prison of, 148–49; sexual activities of, 80–81, 156, 191; social isolation of, 63–68, 102, 145; testimony of, 189–91; transfer of, 194, 271n44; verdict on, 191–92; visions of, 144–48, 203; witches' sabbat and, 51–52, 59
Martinelli, Gasparo, 49
Martinelli, Giuliano, 47
Martinelli, Ippolita, 47, 61, 62, 159, 213; Bellacappa and, 77, 90, 165; Angela Caterina d'Este and, 50, 95–97, 143; incarceration of, 141, 142; interrogation of, 72, 142–43; misusing sacramentals by, 55–56, 90–91; personal property of, 67–68; protective custody for, 188–89; release from prison of, 148–49; social isolation of, 156; suspicious behavior of, 57, 69, 141–43, 146, 151; transfer of, 194, 271n44; verdict on, 192; visions of, 146–47
Mascardi, Giuseppe, 175
Masini, Eliseo, 226n51
Massi, Clara Maria, 131–32
Massi, Clara Vittoria, 57, 68–69, 131
Mather, Cotton, 254n127
Mazzolini, Silvestro, 109, 110, 112, 256n42
Medici, Virginia de,' 26, 97–98, 122
Medioli, Francesca, 231n5, 272n3
melancholy, 122; herbs for, 108; insanity versus, 114; possession versus, 98, 114–15, 120, 197, 202–6, 269n3. *See also* mental illness
Memoriale of Santa Chiara, 14, 33, 38, 42, 44–45, 212–13, 272n55
menarche, 239n46
Menghi, Girolamo, 53, 101, 105–13, 130, 136; on casting spells, 57, 60; on exorcism, 104–13, 118–19; on love magic, 88; on proof of witchcraft, 63, 137
menopause, 230n85, 239n46
menstruation, 86, 129–30, 239n46
mental illness, 105, 122, 192, 206; hysteria and, 121, 203, 259n124, 274n25; physicians and, 110, 120–21; possession versus, 98, 114–17, 120, 136, 197, 202–6, 269n3; types of, 114. *See also* melancholy
Merici, Angela, 22
Midelfort, Erik, 122, 206, 276n47
Modena, 1, 26, 32–33; Inquisition of, xi, 11–13, 20, 40–41, 43–47, 86; Jews of, 226n54; love magic beliefs in, 86; plague in, 37, 237n1; Protestants in, 12–13, 226n50; Sant'Eufemia convent in, 5, 99
Montaguti, Gregorio, 113–14, 122–23, 133
Montalti, Silvia, 93
Morisi, Francesco Maria, 49, 77, 158, 165

Muratori, Ludovico Antonio, 132
music, 26, 34–35, 91, 92, 126, 200, 236n58, 236n59
Muzzi, Portia, 61, 62
mysticism: sexuality and, 81; visions and, 7–8, 144–45, 148, 203, 253n110

naming practices, 35, 47, 203
Nardon, Franco, 227n60
Niccolini, Ludovico, 43, 114, 126, 168, 247n6; Barberini's instructions to, 181; career of, 36; Angela Caterina d'Este and, 94–97; after inquiry of possessions, 194, 202, 204; Martinelli sisters and, 65, 149
Nider, Johannes, 52
Nissenbaum, Stephen, 272n7
novices, 186–87; dowry for, 24, 47; release from vows of, 272n3

Observant Franciscans. *See* Franciscans
oil, holy, 50, 56, 58, 77, 90, 159, 179
Ori, Anna Maria, 14

pact. *See* devil, pact with
Paris, Council of (1212), 81
Pattoni, Teodora, 93–94, 158
Paul III (pope), 10
Paul IV (pope), 10, 82
Paul V (pope), 10, 118, 255n33, 256n48
Pedrazza, Giovanni, 251n62
Peña, Francisco, 228n69
penance, 84–85, 153, 187; for solicitation, 82; for witchcraft, 41. *See also* confession
Peters, Edward, 223n15, 224n37
Pezzoli, Alessandro, 150–53
physicians, 18, 42, 96, 104; bleeding by, 121–22; exorcists and, 110, 113, 120–22, 182
Pico, Alessandro, Duke of Mirandola, 55, 243n102
Pico family, 33
Pico, Laura, Duchess of Mirandola, 55, 97–98, 243n102
Pienza, Oriana da, 274n32

Pio, Camilla Violante, 1, 23, 146–47, 185, 263n28
Pius V (pope), 10, 22
Pius VI (pope), 276n47
plague, 37, 199–200, 237n1
Poggi, Cassandra Felice, 77–78, 177
Poggi, Caterina Maria, 54–55
Poor Clares, 1, 221n2
possession. *See* demonic possession
Prattica (Scaglia), 119–20, 137
Predicatore, 74
Prosperi, Adriano, 11, 12, 85
Protestantism, 16, 18, 85, 204; exorcism and, 105; Inquisition and, 11–13; in Modena, 12–13, 226n50; visionaries and, 145; witch trials and, 139
psychoanalysis, 6, 201, 273n14. *See also* sexuality
Puyol Buil, Carlos, 224n29

Rangoni, Alessandro, 5, 36, 99, 194, 271n46
relics, 65–67; for exorcism, 45, 114, 135, 183, 185; miracle cure from, 276n50
Richelieu, Cardinal, 5, 102–3, 254n130
Rio, Martin del, 127–28
Rocchi, Angelica, 141
Roman Inquisition, 9–17, 99, 208–11; confession and, 11, 85, 164, 250n60; executions of witches and, 19, 107, 208; investigations by, 12, 39, 43–47, 260n149; judicial reform by, 180; legal procedures of, 64, 68, 119, 132, 157, 166–67, 173–74, 180, 208–10; organization of, 11; Protestants and, 11–13; records of, xi, 13–15, 44; solicitation cases and, 82, 248n22, 249n52; torture and, 15–16, 180, 199, 208, 210. *See also* Congregation of the Inquisition; Spanish Inquisition
Romeo, Giovanni, 193, 250n58, 250n60
Ronchi, Caterina Margherita: as abbess, 212; Bellacappa and, 75–77, 80, 90, 165–66, 189; exorcism of, 131, 146; miracle cure of, 276n50; possession of, 45, 60, 117, 122, 126, 135, 146, 148

Roper, Lyndal, 16, 228n66, 230n85, 257n80
Rouen, Council of (1214), 81
Roveri, Lucia, 263n17
Russell, Jeffrey Burton, 223n15

sabbat. *See* witches' sabbat
sacramentals: misuse of, 50, 55–58, 62, 66, 77, 90–91, 123, 125, 159, 173; selling of, 10
sacraments, 55–56. *See also* Eucharist; penance
Salem, Mass., witch trials, 132, 246n166, 254n127, 272n7
salt, 53, 56, 89, 104
San Gemignano convent, 93
San Giovanni, Madonna of, 132
San Nicolò monastery (Carpi), 74
San Plácido convent, 224n29
Santa Chiara convent, 1–5, 194–201, 206–8, 212–14; discipline at, 35, 36, 49, 184–88, 195, 202–3; *educande* of, 32, 33, 35, 38, 198; election of abbess of, 31–32; Este family and, 23, 26, 31–33, 36, 113, 194; fate of, 194–96; floor plans of, *27–30;* literacy at, 15–16, 25, 54, 100, 199, 253n118; map of Carpi and, *2; Memoriale* of, 14, 33, 38, 42, 44–45, 212–13, 272n55; music at, 34–35, 200; nuns' vows at, 240n51; oversight of, 35–36, 74, 194, 202, 204, 273n19; population of, 23, 236n55; Rule of, 35, 49, 200
Sant'Eufemia convent (Modena), 5, 99
Satan. *See* devil
Scaglia, Desiderio, 41, 137; on demonic possession, 119–20; on false visions, 144; *Instructio,* 119, 120, 137, 188, 193; on love magic, 88, 89; *Prattica,* 119–20, 137
Schutte, Anne Jacobson, 224n32, 227n59, 245n144
Sertori, Giulia Angelica, 34; Bellacappa and, 75, 76, 92, 99–100; cure of, 195; death of, 212; exorcisms of, 124, 125, 182; possession of, 44, 45, 58, 117, 122, 127–28
sexuality, 205, 272n14; claustration and, 8, 21–22, 88, 274n25; erotic friendships and, 48–52, 73, 80–81, 191, 241n81; exorcisms and, 116, 257n80, 260n149; lust and, 18, 21, 48, 87–92, 203, 207; mysticism and, 81; pain of love and, 88–92; repression of, 6, 87–88, 183, 201–2; virginity and, 5, 21, 145, 183, 239n46; witches and, 52–53, 80–81, 241n82, 242n90
Sicilian monastery, Capuchin, 204–5
Sixtus V (pope), 10, 11
Sluhovsky, Moshe, 7–9, 104–5, 204–5, 222n10
solicitation, during confession, 77–80, 82, 158, 161–80, 199, 248n22, 249n52
Solieri, Degnamerita, 45, 182, 212
sorcery, 50, 52, 106, 153–54. *See also* witchcraft
Soto, Domingo, 118
Spanish Inquisition, 10, 16–17, 145, 193–94, 210; defense attorneys and, 266n37; records of, 15; studies of, 224n37; Teresa of Avila and, 144. *See also* Roman Inquisition
spectral evidence, 132, 246n166, 254n127
Spee, Friedrich, 18
spells, magical, 4, 37–38, 50, 89, 210–11; amulets for, 66, 104; Bible for, 104, 123–24, 126; evil gaze and, 60; hair for, 57, 67, 89, 132; heresy and, 88, 209, 223n15; Menghi on, 57, 60; sacramentals for, 50, 56–58, 62, 66, 77, 90–91, 123, 159, 179; superstitions and, 13, 142, 209. *See also* love magic; *maleficia*
Spiro, Melford E., 273n14
Sprenger, Jacob, 222n14. See also *Malleus Maleficarum*
Stephens, Walter, 242n90
St. John's wort, 108
Strasser, Ulrike, 145

strigimaghe (witch-magicians), 106
St. Vitus' dance, 206
suicide: precautions against, 147, 181; threats by possessed of, 129, 135, 148
superstitions, 84, 85, 209–11; Augustine on, 4; exorcism and, 105–7, 110; Inquisition trials for, 12, 13, 260n149; witchcraft and, 17, 274n32. *See also* spells, magical

Tacitus, 183
Tarabotti, Arcangela, 25
Tedeschi, John, 15, 180, 209–10, 268n89
Tentler, Thomas, 84
Teresa of Avila, Saint, 5–6, 144, 145
Thomas Aquinas, Saint, 73, 106
Thomas, Keith, 139
Tinti, Giacomo, 38–43, 65, 68–72, 192, 195–96, 211; Francesco Barberini and, 41, 148, 181; Angelo Bellacappa and, 157–80; Angela Caterina d'Este and, 92–94, 97–99, 201; evidence procedures and, 132; exorcists and, 114, 129; Inquisition's instructions to, 133–35; Germanico Mantica and, 181–84; Dealta Martinelli and, 147–49, 151–52, 194; Ippolita Martinelli and, 142–43, 147–49, 194
torture, 16, 49, 176, 209, 274n32; authorization of, 15, 180, 199, 208, 210; charms against, 37, 153–54; trial by ordeal and, 276n42
Trenti, Giuseppe, xi, 13
Trevor-Roper, Hugh R., 228n72
trial by ordeal, 276n42
Tridentine reforms, 8, 9, 13, 24; abbess qualifications and, 234n35; Carnival and, 91–92; claustration and, 8, 21–22, 88, 186–87, 205–6, 231n5; confession and, 75, 84–86; monasticism and, 25, 34–35; mysticism and, 145, 203. *See also* Counter-Reformation
Trionfanti, Valerio, 49, 166

Urban VII (pope), 10

Urban VIII (pope), 8, 40, 194
Ursulines, 8, 22. *See also* Loudun convent

Vacchi, Antonio, 32
Valotti, Salvatore, 172
Verrini, Domenico, 129, 135; as confessor, 213; exorcisms by, 46, 113, 123
Villani, Marc'Antonio, 151, 154, 264n44
Villanueva, Jerónimo de, 224n29
virginity, 5, 21, 145, 183, 239n46. *See also* sexuality
visions, 101; Brognolo on, 263n25; Carena on, 263n29; of Dealta Martinelli, 144–48; of Ippolita Martinelli, 146–47; mysticism and, 7–8, 144–45, 148, 203, 253n110

Waldensians, 52
water, holy, 22, 65–66, 86, 104, 123, 125, 181
Weyer, Johann, 18
widows, 33, 34
witchcraft, 46, 50–54, 122–32; cross-cultural aspects of, 206–7; decriminalization of, 275n37; definitions of, 4, 39, 106; demonic possession and, 3–5, 9, 39, 94, 106, 113, 122, 137–38; ecclesiastical jurisdiction for, 9–10; executions for, 19, 107, 208; folk beliefs of, 14–16; gendered beliefs about, 17–19, 210–11, 229n79, 230n85; historical trends of, 17–20; Kramer on, 107; motives for, 122–23, 241n82; proof of, 63, 193–94, 276n42; Salem, Mass., trials for, 132, 246n166, 254n127, 272n7; sexuality and, 52–53, 80–81, 241n82, 242n90; sorcery, 50, 52, 106, 153–54; superstitions and, 274n32. *See also* demonic possession
witches' sabbat, 4, 18, 51–54, 149, 191, 193, 202, 209, 241n88
witch-hunts, 4, 16–17, 39–40, 206, 209; in Basque region, 228n69; demonic assistance with, 156; exorcism and, 113, 122–32, 139; judicial reforms and, 210; plague and, 37

women. *See* gendered beliefs

Zaretti, Giovan Battista, 114; diagnoses of, 122, 129; exorcisms by, 113–15, 190
Zarri, Gabriella, 25, 145

Zoccolanti, 35, 172–73, 192, 214. *See also* Franciscans
Zuccari, Anna Caterina, 56; Amoldoni and, 147; Bellacappa and, 76, 78, 79, 82, 83, 163, 177; Martinelli and, 81, 141, 145–46, 249n35; Ronchi and, 148

In 1636, residents at the convent of Santa Chiara in Carpi in northern Italy were struck by an extraordinary illness that provoked bizarre behavior. Eventually numbering fourteen, the afflicted nuns were subject to screaming fits, throwing themselves on the floor, and falling abruptly into a deep sleep. When medical experts' cures proved ineffective, exorcists ministered to the women and concluded that they were possessed by demons and the victims of witchcraft. Catering to women from elite families, the nunnery suffered much turmoil for three years and, remarkably, three of the victims died from their ills. A maverick nun and a former confessor were widely suspected to be responsible, through witchcraft, for these woes.

Based primarily on the exhaustive investigation by the Inquisition of Modena, *The Scourge of Demons* examines this fascinating case in its historical context. The travails of Santa Chiara occurred at a time when Europe witnessed peaks in both witch-hunting and in the numbers of people reputedly possessed by demons. Female religious figures appeared particularly prone to demonic attacks, and Counter-Reformation Church authorities were especially interested in imposing stricter discipline on convents. Watt carefully considers how the nuns of Santa Chiara understood and experienced alleged possession and witchcraft, concluding that Santa Chiara's diabolical troubles and their denouement—involving the actions of nuns, confessors, inquisitorial authorities, and exorcists—were profoundly shaped by the unique confluence of religious, cultural, judicial, and intellectual trends that flourished in the 1630s.

Jeffrey R. Watt is professor of history at the University of Mississippi.

www.ingramcontent.com/pod-product-compliance
Lightning Source LLC
Chambersburg PA
CBHW021651230426
43668CB00008B/587